Playing to the World's Biggest Audience

Playing to the World's Biggest Audience
Biggest Audience

The Globalization of Chinese Film and TV

MICHAEL CURTIN

University of California Press

BERKELEY   LOS ANGELES   LONDON

University of California Press, one of the most distinguished university presses in the United States, enriches lives around the world by advancing scholarship in the humanities, social sciences, and natural sciences. Its activities are supported by the UC Press Foundation and by philanthropic contributions from individuals and institutions. For more information, visit www.ucpress.edu.

University of California Press
Berkeley and Los Angeles, California

University of California Press, Ltd.
London, England

Library of Congress Cataloging-in-Publication Data

Curtin, Michael.
    Playing to the world's biggest audience : the globalization of Chinese film and TV / Michael Curtin.
        p.   cm.
    Includes bibliographical references and index.
    ISBN 978-0-520-25133-5 (cloth : alk. paper)—ISBN 978-0-520-25134-2 (pbk. : alk. paper)
        1. Motion pictures—China.   2. Motion picture industry—China.   3. Motion pictures—Taiwan.   4. Motion picture industry—Taiwan.   5. Television broadcasting—China.   6. Television broadcasting—Taiwan. I. Title.

PN1993.5.C4C87   2007
791.430951—dc22   2007004610

Manufactured in the United States of America

16   15   14   13   12   11   10   09   08   07
10   9   8   7   6   5   4   3   2   1

This book is printed on New Leaf EcoBook 50, a 100% recycled fiber of which 50% is de-inked post-consumer waste, processed chlorine-free. EcoBook 50 is acid-free and meets the minimum requirements of ANSI/ASTM D5634–01 (*Permanence of Paper*).

For Melissa

Contents

Acknowledgments

From its very inception this project was designed as an exercise in defamiliarization. That is, I hoped that shifting my attention from North America across the Pacific would encourage me to rethink my presumptions about the ways that media industries operate and the impact of globalization on them. Of course this meant that I was venturing into unfamiliar territory, and the extent to which I have succeeded depended substantially on the generosity of hundreds of media professionals, academics, and everyday acquaintances who patiently endured my endless queries about matters large and small. A major debt of gratitude is owed first to those professionals who took time from their busy schedules to sit for formal interviews, many more than once. They are listed individually in the appendix, each of them contributing significantly to my understanding of Chinese commercial film and TV.

During the course of my research I had the good fortune to work alongside supportive and engaging colleagues at Indiana University, the Chinese University of Hong Kong, Academia Sinica, and the University of Wisconsin–Madison. I'm grateful to all of them and to the wonderful office administrators who kept the wheels of department life spinning smoothly. Special thanks as well to Hong Kong colleagues and friends for lifting my spirits and offering encouragement throughout: Joseph Man Chan, Darrell Davis, Kathy Edwards, John Nguyet Erni, Steve Fore, Anthony Fung, Chin-Chuan Lee, Eric Kit-wai Ma, and Emilie Yueh-yu Yeh. David Bordwell and Kristin Thompson buoyed me along the way with sage advice and memorable evenings at the Spring Deer after Hong Kong film festival screenings. Likewise in Taipei, I relied on the generosity of Allen Chun, Pen-juin Chen, Lilly Yu-li Liu, Tain-dow Lee, and Wu Jin-jyi. I also wish to thank other colleagues who share my passion for the study of Chinese media and have generously offered insights and resources at various stages of my research; these include Joe Allen, Cindy Chan, Yvonne Chang, Pei-chi Chung, Siew Keng Chua, Fan Wei, Heidi Fung, Poshek Fu, Eddie Guo, Ho Tsai-ping, Michael Keane, Steve Lewis, Liu Fei-wen, Liu Kang, Gordon Matthews, Stanley Rosen, Joseph Straubhaar, Jing Wang, Shujen Wang, Mayfair Yang, and Yingjin Zhang.

I am furthermore grateful for the warm and steadfast encouragement of colleagues in the Media and Cultural Studies area of the Department of Communication Arts at UW–Madison: Julie D'Acci, Mary Beltran, and Michele Hilmes, and until recently Shanti Kumar and Lisa Nakamura. Our Thursday lunches sustained me in many ways, as did evenings at The City. I also benefited greatly from collaborative adventures with Pan Zhongdang and Hemant Shah and from the departmental leadership of J. J. Murphy and Vance Kepley. At the University of Wisconsin International Institute, Gilles Bousquet and Aili Tripp have been staunch supporters, as has the office crew at Global Studies, especially the unflappable Steve Smith. Thank you all.

I also wish to mention colleagues at Indiana University who encouraged me during the initial phases of this venture and remain close friends, among them Chris Anderson, Dick Bauman, Purnima Bose, Joan Hawkins, Bob Ivie, Barb Klinger, Jim Naremore, Radhika Parameswaran, Beverly Stoelje, Sue Tuohy, and Jeff Wasserstrom. Other longtime benefactors of my scholarship are Lynn Spigel and Tom Streeter, special colleagues in every way. Kudos also to the graduate and undergraduate students who challenged me along the way with spirited questions and observations. I should especially mention Lori Hitchcock, Caryn Murphy, Shawn Vancour, and Sean Tzu-hsuan Chen, who provided research assistance at various stages. At the University of California Press, Mary Francis, Mary Severance, and Robin Whitaker provided wise counsel and skillful assistance throughout the publishing process. Finally, heartfelt thanks to my family, especially Melissa, who nurtured this venture in more ways than I can enumerate and who, along with her sister, coined a working title that proved fitting for a project that lasted longer than I initially imagined: That Goddamn Book.

No doubt unaware of the working title, several institutions supported my research with significant grants and fellowships, including the U.S. Fulbright Commission, Taiwan's National Endowment for Culture and the Arts, the College of Arts and Sciences at Indiana University, the Hamel Faculty Fellowship Fund, the Wisconsin Alumni Research Foundation, and the University of Wisconsin Division of International Studies. My abiding thanks to these organizations for critical funding, without which this project never would have succeeded.

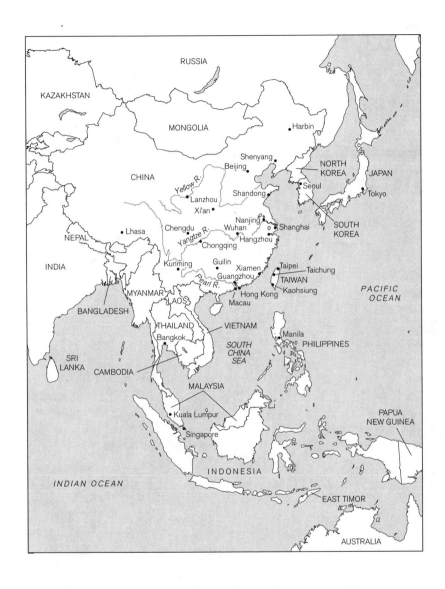

Introduction

*Media Capital in Chinese Film
and Television*

At the turn of the twenty-first century, feature films such as *Crouching Tiger, Kung Fu Hustle,* and *Hero*—each of them coproduced with major Hollywood studios—marched out of Asia to capture widespread acclaim from critics, audiences, and industry executives. Taken together they seemed to point to a new phase in Hollywood's ongoing exploitation of talent, labor, and locations around the globe, simply the latest turn in a strategy that has perpetuated American media dominance in global markets for almost a century and contributed to the homogenization of popular culture under the aegis of Western institutions.[1] These movies seem to represent the expanding ambitions of the world's largest movie studios as they begin to refashion Chinese narratives for a Westernized global audience. Yet behind these marquee attractions lies a more elaborate endgame as Hollywood moguls reconsider prior assumptions regarding the dynamics of transnational media institutions and reassess the cultural geographies of media consumption. For increasingly they find themselves playing not only to the Westernized global audience but also to the world's biggest audience: the Chinese audience.

With more than a billion television viewers and a moviegoing public estimated at more than two hundred million, the People's Republic of China (PRC) figures prominently in such calculations. Just as compelling, however, are the sixty million "overseas Chinese" living in such places as Taiwan, Malaysia, and Vancouver. Their aggregate numbers and relative prosperity make them, in the eyes of media executives, a highly desirable audience, one comparable in scale to the audience in France or Great Britain. Taken together, Chinese audiences around the globe are growing daily in numbers, wealth, and sophistication. If the twentieth century was—as *Time* magazine founder Henry Luce put it—the American century, then the twenty-first surely belongs to the people that Luce grew up with, the Chinese. Although dispersed across vast stretches of Asia and around the world, this audience is now connected for the very first time via the intricate matrix of digital and satellite media.

Rupert Murdoch, the most ambitious global media baron of the past twenty years, enthusiastically embraced the commercial potential of Chinese film and television when in 1994 he launched a stunning billion-dollar takeover of Star TV, Asia's first pancontinental telecaster, founded only three years earlier by Li Ka-shing, Hong Kong's richest tycoon. Yet if Western executives are sharpening their focus on Chinese audiences, Asian entrepreneurs have been equally active, expanding and refiguring their media services to meet burgeoning demand, so that today, in addition to Star, hundreds of satellite channels target Chinese audiences in Asia, Europe, Australia, and North America, delivering an elaborate buffet of news, music, sports, and entertainment programming. Among Star's leading competitors is TVB, a Hong Kong-based media conglomerate built on the foundations of a transnational movie studio and now the most commercially successful television station in southern China. Its modern state-of-the-art production facilities and its far-reaching satellite and video distribution platforms position it as a significant cultural force in Europe, Australia, and North America. Equally impressive, Taiwanese and Singaporean media enterprises are extending their operations abroad in hopes of attracting new audiences and shoring up profitability in the face of escalating competition, both at home and abroad. Finally, PRC film and TV institutions, though still controlled by the state and therefore constrained by ideological and infrastructural limitations, are globalizing their strategies, if not yet their operations, regularly taking account of commercial competitors from abroad and aiming to extend their reach as conditions allow.

Based on in-depth interviews with a diverse array of media executives, this book peeks behind the screen to examine the operations of commercial film and television companies as they position themselves to meet the burgeoning demands of Chinese audiences.[2] It includes stories of Hong Kong media moguls Run Run Shaw and Raymond Chow as well as their junior counterparts, Thomas Chung and Peter Chan; of Rupert Murdoch and his enigmatic mainland partner, Liu Changle; of Sony chair Nobuyuki Idei and his Connecticut whiz-kid, William Pfeiffer. It also includes tales of legendary Asian billionaires, such as Li Ka-shing, Koo Chen-fu, and Ananda Krishnan, lured by the scent of fresh new markets, as well as stories of aspiring billionaires Chiu Fu-sheng and Richard Li, each determined to find a seat at the table for what is becoming one of the most high-stakes media plays of the new millennium.

But this volume is more than a collection of colorful accounts of personal and corporate ambition; it is furthermore a reflection on the shifting dynamics of the film and television industries in an era of increasing global connectivity. For several centuries, the imperial powers of the West exercised sway over much of the world by virtue of their economic and military might. In time, cultural influence came to figure prominently in Western hegemony, as the production and distribution of silver screen fantasies helped to disseminate capitalist values, consumerist attitudes, and Anglo supremacy. Likewise, Western news agencies dominated the flow of information, setting the agenda for policy deliberations worldwide. Indeed, throughout the twentieth century, media industries were considered so strategically significant that the U.S. government consistently sought to protect and extend the interests of NBC, Disney, Paramount, and other media enterprises. All of which helps to explain why Hollywood feature films have dominated world markets for almost a century and U.S. television has prevailed since the 1950s. Besides profiting from government favoritism, U.S. media has benefited from access to a large and wealthy domestic market that serves as a springboard for their global operations. By comparison, for most of the twentieth century, the European market was splintered, and the Indian and Chinese markets suffered from government constraints and the relative poverty of their populations. Yet recent changes in trade, industry, politics, and media technologies have fueled the rapid expansion and transformation of media industries in Asia, so that Indian and Chinese centers of film and television production have increasingly emerged as significant competitors of Hollywood in the size and enthusiasm of their audiences, if not yet in gross revenues.

In particular, Chinese film and television industries have changed dramatically since the 1980s with the end of the Cold War, the rise of the World Trade Organization, the modernization policies of the PRC, the end of martial law in Taiwan, the transfer of Hong Kong to Chinese sovereignty, the high-tech liberalization of Singapore, the rise of consumer and youth cultures across the region, and the growing wealth and influence of overseas Chinese in such cities as Vancouver, London, and Kuala Lumpur. Consequently, media executives can, for the very first time, begin to contemplate the prospect of a global Chinese audience that includes more moviegoers and more television households than the United States and Europe combined. Many experts believe this vast and increasingly wealthy Global

China market will serve as a foundation for emerging media conglomerates that could shake the very foundations of Hollywood's century-long hegemony.[3]

Despite these changes, Hollywood today is nevertheless very much like Detroit forty years ago, a factory town that produces big, bloated vehicles with plenty of chrome. As production budgets mushroom, quality declines in large part as a result of institutional inertia and a lack of competition. Like Detroit, Hollywood has dominated for so long that many of its executives have difficulty envisioning the transformations now on the horizon. Because of this myopia, the global future is commonly imagined as a world brought together by homogeneous cultural products produced and circulated by American media, a process referred to by some as Disneyfication.[4] Other compelling scenarios must be considered, however. What if, for example, Chinese feature films and television programs began to rival the substantial budgets and lavish production values of their Western counterparts? What if Chinese media were to strengthen and extend their distribution networks, becoming truly global enterprises? That is, what if the future were to take an unexpected detour on the road to Disneyland, heading instead toward a more complicated global terrain characterized by overlapping and at times intersecting cultural spheres served by diverse media enterprises based in media capitals around the world? *Playing to the World's Biggest Audience* explains the histories and strategies of commercial enterprises that aim to become central players in the Global China market, and in so doing it provides an alternative perspective to recent debates about globalization.

Transcending the presumption that Hollywood hegemony is forever, this volume joins a growing literature that is beginning to offer alternative accounts of global media.[5] *Playing* describes the challenges and opportunities that confront Chinese commercial media, and it shows, unexpectedly, that these industries are nurturing a fertile breeze of democratization that is wafting across Asia today. The winds of change are gusty and unpredictable, nevertheless, and sometimes given to dramatic reversals. After more than a decade of torrid expansion, commercial media enterprises were hit hard by the Asian financial crisis of 1997, the dotcom meltdown of 2000, and a dramatic escalation of digital piracy. By the end of the last century, Chinese media enterprises were for the very first time thoroughly globalized in outlook but had slowed the pace of their expansion while seeking to consolidate their operations and reformulate their business plans. The focus of this book therefore is on the wave of globalization during the 1990s and early 2000s,

Stephen Chow stars in *Kung Fu Hustle,* a coproduction between China Film and Columbia Pictures. Courtesy Sony Pictures Classic.

providing a context for analyzing the current constraints and future opportunities of these industries. It focuses furthermore on commercial media enterprises, although some discussion of state media in the PRC is offered to present a more inclusive account of the market dynamics driving Chinese media. In all, my aim is to portray the ways in which successful Chinese media enterprises have adapted—at times grudgingly or haphazardly—to the shifting social and institutional dynamics of the global millennium.[6]

By venturing into the realm of transnational media, markets, and culture, this book traverses a terrain of critical research that has been strongly influenced by theories of media imperialism. Two of the early proponents of this approach, Thomas Guback and Herbert Schiller, published contemporaneous assessments of international film and television in the late 1960s, providing foundational explanations of the ways in which American media institutions extended their influence overseas during the twentieth century.[7] Both describe self-conscious collaboration between media executives and government officials seeking cultural, commercial, and strategic influence abroad. Ariel Dorfman and Armand Mattelart elaborated this approach by showing how national elites in South America were complicit with practices that promoted cultural hegemony of leading industrialized nations.[8] Karl Nordenstreng and Tapio Varis furthermore contributed potent empirical evidence of television programming exports from the West to the rest of the world, arguing that trade imbalances were part of larger structural patterns of dominance.[9] Throughout the 1970s and 1980s this body of scholarship flourished, asserting that the United States and its European allies control the international flow of images and information, imposing media texts and industrial practices on unwilling nations and susceptible audiences around the world. According to this view, Western media hegemony diminishes indigenous production capacity and undermines the expressive potential of national cultures, imposing foreign values and contributing to cultural homogenization worldwide.

The basic unit of analysis for researchers of media imperialism was the modern nation-state, which meant that domination was usually figured as a relationship between countries, with powerful states imposing their will on subordinate ones, especially in news reporting, cinematic entertainment, and television programming. On the basis of data gathered in the 1960s and 1970s, when American media had few international competitors, media imperialism's founding scholars initially anticipated enduring relations of domination, presuming that media exporters would be able to perpetuate their structural advantages. So influential was this critique that it helped to inspire an energetic reform movement among less developed nations, calling for the New World Information and Communication Order (NWICO), a campaign that crested in the 1980s with a set of United Nations reform proposals that would have sailed through the General Assembly if not for the fierce opposition of the Reagan and Thatcher governments, both champions of "free flow" over the reformers' demands for "fair and balanced flow."[10] This neoliberal, Anglo-American alliance thoroughly undermined the momentum behind NWICO and furthermore mounted a counteroffensive aimed at promoting the marketization of media institutions around the world.

When this concerted political assault on NWICO started to emerge from the political right, scholars on the left also began to critically reexamine some of the essential tenets of the media imperialism thesis. One of the first and most telling critiques was posed by Chin-Chuan Lee, a young scholar from Taiwan who interrogated the theoretical consistency and empirical validity of the media imperialism hypothesis by considering case studies of media in Canada, Taiwan, and the People's Republic of China.[11] Lee argued that foundational assumptions, such as a correspondence between economic domination and media domination, simply did not hold up under close scrutiny. Canada, a wealthy developed nation, was thoroughly saturated by

Hollywood media, while Taiwan, a thoroughly dependent and less developed nation, had established a relatively independent media system that nevertheless failed to nurture "authentic" local culture, preferring instead commercial hybrid forms of mass culture. The PRC, although least developed of the three, was even more removed from Hollywood domination but thoroughly authoritarian, making it the most elitist and least popular media system at the time. Supporting neither free flow doctrines nor the media imperialism critique, Lee argued for middle-range theories and regulatory policies that would be sensitive to the complexities of specific local circumstances.

Scholars in cultural studies and postcolonial studies also began to question media imperialism, especially the presumption that commercial media industries had clear and uniform effects on audiences. Might audiences read Hollywood's dominant texts "against the grain," they wondered? Might they be more strongly influenced by family, education, and peer groups than by foreign media? Critics also challenged the presumption that all foreign values have deleterious effects, noting that the emphasis on aspiration and agency found in many Hollywood narratives might actually have positive effects among audiences living in social systems burdened by oppressive forms of hierarchy or patriarchy or both.[12] Moreover, critics pointed to the media imperialism school's troubling assumption that *national* values were generally positive and relatively uncontested, arguing, for example, that in the case of India, national media tended to cater to Hindu elites at the expense of populations from diverse cultural and linguistic backgrounds, such as Tamil and Telegu.[13] Moreover, they pointed out that cultures are rarely pure, autonomous entities, since most societies throughout history have interacted with other societies, creating hybrid cultural forms that often reenergize a society by encouraging dynamic adaptations.[14] According to these critics, media imperialism's notion of a singular, enduring, and authentic national culture simply overlooks the many divisions within modern nation-states, especially in countries that emerged with borders imposed by their former colonial masters, such as Indonesia and Nigeria. Overall, cultural studies scholars pointed out that media imperialism's privileging of "indigenous culture" tends to obscure the complex dynamics of cultural interaction and exchange.

Empirical research data furthermore began to demonstrate that the dominance of Western media might be diminishing. As television industries around the world matured, audiences increasingly showed a preference for national and regional productions, especially in news, talk, and variety formats but also in drama and comedy. In Latin America, for example, Peruvian TV audiences tend to prefer Mexican or Venezuelan telenovelas to Hollywood soap operas.[15] Further complicating these scholarly debates was the growing impact of new media technologies, with VCRs and satellites beginning to expand the range and quantity of available films and television programming in the 1980s, a trend that was further amplified by digital media in the 1990s. Concurrently, the fall of the Berlin Wall, demonstrations at Tiananmen, and the demise of authoritarian regimes in countries such as Taiwan and South Korea led numerous critics to observe that a revolution in communication technologies seemed to be facilitating a wave of cultural and political transformations.[16] When these transformations were coupled with dramatic changes in shipping and transportation as well as the continuing march of neoliberal free trade policies, popular and scholarly critics began to contemplate a seismic shift from the existing state-based international system to a nascent global order, one that was more open, more hybrid, and more thoroughly interconnected than any previous communication system.

Since the 1980s, the number of media producers, distributors, and consumers has grown dramatically, first in Europe and then in Asia, with China and India adding almost two billion new viewers during this period. Although powerful global media conglomerates were active contributors to these trends, local, national, and regional media firms expanded rapidly as well. In India, Rupert Murdoch's Star TV challenged the state's television monopoly only to find itself beleaguered in turn by dozens of new indigenous competitors, many of them telecasting in subaltern languages, all of them commercially driven.[17] Such developments complicated media imperialism's structural notions of center and periphery, for it became increasingly difficult to argue that the United States was engaged in a centralized and coherent project to sustain its cultural dominance around the world. Instead, Western media companies such as Star TV were rapidly localizing their programming and institutional practices so as to adapt to competitive forces in places like India. Though Star's original intention was to penetrate and dominate subcontinental markets with Western technology and Hollywood programming, the organization nevertheless found itself pulled into lively competition with creative and competitive Indian media enterprises. As in many parts of the world, Star was pressed to localize its operations at the very same time that South Asian telecasters were becoming more globalized in their perspectives and practices. Rather than exhibiting concrete patterns of domination and subordination, Indian media institutions at a variety of levels seemed to be responding to the push-pull of globalization, since increasing connectivity inspired significant changes in textual and institutional practices. As we shall see, similar dynamics took place in Chinese media, auguring a growing fascination with globalization among Asian media executives and creative talent since the 1990s.

Globalization of media therefore should not be understood reductively as cultural homogenization or Western hegemony. Instead, it is part of a larger set of processes that operate translocally, interactively, and dynamically in a variety of spheres: economic, institutional, technological, and ideological.[18] As John Tomlinson observes, globalization "happens as the result of economic and cultural practices which do not, of themselves, aim at global integration, but which nonetheless produce it. More importantly, the effects of globalization are to weaken the cultural coherence of all nation-states, including the economically powerful ones—the 'imperialist powers' of a previous era."[19] In other words, unlike theories of media imperialism that emphasize the self-conscious extension of centralized power, globalization theories suggest that the world's increasingly interconnected media environment is the outcome of messy and complicated interactions across space. What globalization theorists have failed to produce, however, is a persuasive account of the most significant forces driving these processes and a clear explanation of why some places become centers of cultural production and therefore tend to be more influential in shaping the emerging global system.

This concern with *location* is perhaps the most significant and enduring continuity between the media imperialism and globalization schools of scholarship. Where and why do certain locations emerge as significant centers of media production? What is the extent of their geographical reach? How do spatial dynamics influence power valences among groups, institutions, and societies? Whether stated explicitly or implicitly, these are the central concerns that continue to stimulate most of the research on international media. Although Hollywood is perhaps no longer perceived as a singular cultural force worldwide, issues of power and influence are nevertheless matters of ongoing concern. Who has the power to produce, to distribute, and to prefer particular images and ideas? To what extent might we expect alternative centers of cultural production, such as Cairo, Mumbai, and Hong Kong, to flourish and prosper? In essence, how might we begin to map the complicated contours and practices of global media?

My approach to such questions in this book is both empirical and theoretical. On the one hand, I examine the history and operations of the major commercial Chinese film and television companies, portraying the dis-

course of media personnel as they reflect on past performance, current circumstances, and future prospects of their firms. And on the other hand, I
step back from industry discourse to ponder the tendencies and patterns
that seem to be at work in contemporary media. Central to my analysis
throughout are several hypotheses regarding the operations of *media capital,* directing attention to the dynamics of accumulation, agglomeration,
and circulation. In the section that follows I explain my use of the term, employing examples from familiar Western contexts in order to elucidate core
concepts. Western contexts are, of course, more familiar simply because
their media industries have received far more attention than commercial
media in Asia. This volume is one attempt to remedy that imbalance, but before proceeding I wish to explain the dynamics of media capital in the West,
both as a way to introduce the concept and as a way to provide a basis for
comparison with Chinese media. Furthermore, I begin with this assessment
because Hollywood, as we shall see, has been one of the most powerful and
enduring centers of media capital, consequently influencing Chinese media
as well as Arab, Indian, and Latin American media. It is nevertheless important to reiterate that Hollywood hegemony is far more tenuous than it
might appear, and the growing significance of Chinese commercial media is
but one significant example of the ways in which media production and circulation are changing worldwide.

When describing the terrain of contemporary culture, critics often invoke such adjectives as *fractal, disjunctive,* and *rhizomatic,* words that aim
to characterize a complex terrain of textual circulation, reception, and ap-
propriation in the "postmodern era."[20] Even though these adjectives may
aptly describe a rupture with prior cultural regimes, the industries that produce popular texts—in particular screen industries—have followed fairly
consistent patterns of operation for almost a century. The amount of textual
production may have increased dramatically, and the patterns of circulation
may have grown ever more complicated, but the spatial dynamics of media
capital have remained fairly consistent, playing a structuring role in the film
and broadcasting industries since the early twentieth century. Most prominently, media capital operates according to (1) a logic of accumulation, (2)
trajectories of creative migration, and (3) forces of sociocultural variation.

The logic of accumulation is not unique to media industries, since all capitalist enterprises exhibit innately dynamic and expansionist tendencies. As
David Harvey points out, most firms seek efficiencies through the concentration of productive resources and through the extension of markets so as
to utilize their productive capacity fully and realize the greatest possible return. These tendencies are most explicitly revealed during periodic down-

turns in the business cycle, when enterprises are compelled to intensify production or extensify distribution or both in order to survive. Such moments of crisis call for a "spatial fix," says Harvey, because on the one hand capital must concentrate and integrate sites of production to reduce the amount of time and resources expended in manufacture, and on the other hand it must increase the speed of distribution to reduce the time it takes to bring distant locales into the orbit of its operations.[21] These *centripetal* tendencies in the sphere of production and *centrifugal* tendencies in distribution were observed by Karl Marx more than a century ago when he trenchantly explained that capital must "annihilate space with time" if it is to overcome barriers to accumulation.[22] As applied to contemporary media, this insight suggests that even though a film or TV company may be founded with the aim of serving particular national cultures or local markets, it must over time redeploy its creative resources and reshape its terrain of operations if it is to survive competition and enhance profitability.[23] Implicit in this logic of accumulation is the contributing influence of the "managerial revolution" that accompanied the rise of industrial capitalism.[24] Indeed, it was the intersection of capitalist accumulation with the reflexive knowledge systems of the Enlightenment that engendered the transition from mercantile to industrial capitalism. Capitalism became more than a mode of accumulation; it also became a disposition toward surveillance and adaptation, since it continually refined and integrated manufacturing and marketing processes, achieving efficiencies through a concentration of productive resources and through the ongoing extension of delivery systems.

The history of the American cinema—the world's most commercial and most intensively studied media industry—provides an instructive example of these core tendencies.[25] During the first decade of the twentieth century, U.S. movie exhibitors depended on small collaborative filmmaking crews to service demand for filmed entertainment. Yet as theater chains emerged, as distribution grew more sophisticated, and as competition intensified, movie companies began to centralize creative labor in large factorylike studios with an eye toward improving quality, reducing costs, and increasing output. By refiguring the spatial relations of production, managers concentrated the creative labor force in a single location where it could be deployed among a diverse menu of projects under the guidance of each studio's central production office. Inspired by Taylorism, then in vogue among industrial manufacturers, the major film companies furthermore separated the domains of planning and execution, creating a blueprint for each film that guided the work of specialized craftspeople in lighting, makeup, and dozens of other departments deployed across the studio lot. As American cinema entered this factory phase during the 1910s, the intensification of production accelerated output and yielded cost efficiencies, providing theater operators around the country with a dependable flow of quality products.[26] It also increased fixed capital outlays dramatically, which meant that selecting a *location* for one's studio became a matter of significant strategic concern. Although today Hollywood's emergence as the moviemaking capital of the world seems almost preordained, one must nevertheless ask, why Hollywood?

In the early days of the American movie industry, filmmakers operated close to their major exhibition markets and close to related entertainment industries that might be tapped for creative talent. New York and Chicago were prominent centers of production initially, but both suffered from weather limitations during the winter months, making it difficult to shoot exterior scenes on low-light days. Companies therefore seasonally dispatched filmmaking crews to southern climates, such as Florida, Cuba, New Orleans, and, of course, California. So common were these pilgrimages that this sunshine circuit soon spawned the growth of resident creative communities, and by 1911 Southern California boasted more than fifteen thousand film-related jobs.[27] Consequently, filmmaking operations were initially dispersed across the country for a variety of reasons, but when managers began to consider investment in a single filmmaking factory, their attention shifted to the West Coast for a number of reasons.

Weather was no doubt a factor, since production schedules at studios in northern climates were interrupted on a seasonal basis. Conversely, some southern locales, such as Florida, Cuba, and Louisiana, presented problems during the summer months, when, lacking air conditioning, they suffered from oppressive heat and humidity. Southern California, on the other hand, remained temperate year-round and enjoyed the added benefit of diverse topography for location shooting. A sizable skilled-labor pool was already in place, and the West Coast provided a relatively remote location in which to sequester and discipline screen stars to the factory routines of the studio. Free from the temptations and distractions of other cultural venues, contract talent put in long workdays, focusing their energy primarily on the film business. California's remote location was also attractive in relation to legal pressures exerted during the early years of film production by patent holders who controlled key technologies used in cameras, projectors, and film stock. In the freewheeling culture of the West Coast, filmmakers could ply their trade with greater attention to narrative concerns than to legal niceties. Movie entrepreneurs were furthermore attracted by inexpensive real estate prices, which made it possible to buy up vast tracts of land where they could strategically deploy interrelated departments (e.g., wardrobe, makeup, scenery) on a single studio lot. Like the Ford Motor Company at River Rouge, the major studios methodically integrated productive operations so as to improve quality and intensify the tempo of output. For all of these reasons, Hollywood, despite its relative geographical isolation, proved to be an appealing locale for centralized filmmaking facilities.

Soon the capital-intensive factory model prevailed with all the major movie companies, but it is nevertheless important to note that filmmaking employees were creating distinctive *prototypes*, unlike the auto or steel industries' redundant batches of products with interchangeable parts. This is a significant distinction, since some critics mistakenly refer to mass production as the guiding principle of Hollywood's studio era, when instead, as Janet Staiger points out, it is more appropriate to say that the studios employed a detailed "division of labor with craftsmen collectively and serially producing a commodity," and each commodity was relatively unique, even if production routines grew increasingly standardized and even if the films were intended for mass audiences.[28]

Not only was film production fairly distinctive among forms of industrialized manufacturing, but so too was film distribution, since movies are what economists refer to as public goods.[29] That is, each feature film is a commodity that can be consumed without diminishing its availability to other prospective customers. And given the relatively low costs of reproducing and circulating a film print when compared with the costs of creating the prototype, it behooves the manufacturer to circulate each artifact as widely as possible, thereby encouraging the establishment of an expansive distribution infrastructure. Unlike other cultural industries that needed to be close to their live audiences and patrons (e.g., vaudeville) and unlike industrial manufacturers, who incurred substantial shipping costs for their finished products (e.g., automobiles), movie studios could dispatch their feature films expansively and economically. The key aim of Hollywood's distribution apparatus was therefore to stimulate audience demand and ensure access to theaters in far-flung locales. In the United States they achieved the latter by establishing theater chains and collaborating with other major exhibitors.[30] Overseas markets offered another attractive opportunity early on when "silent films" circulated across international borders with relative ease. Consequently, American movie distribution operations grew ever more expansive while their European competitors were suffering through World War I and the ensuing economic morass of the 1920s. Seizing the moment, American companies amplified their market power by establishing overseas sales offices, setting in place a circulation network so durable that even the arrival of sound technology in the late 1920s failed to undermine the profitability of Hollywood feature films in non-English-speaking markets.[31] During the 1910s and 1920s, these centripetal and centrifugal tendencies of media capital unfolded in relatively unmitigated form before local censorship boards in the United States and trade tariffs abroad began to challenge the spatial logic of accumulation. By the end of 1920s, Hollywood was such a dominant force that the only hope for fledgling competitors was to carve out parallel spheres of operation, ones that were often protected by government policies or by cultural impediments that kept Hollywood at bay.

The second principle of media capital emphasizes trajectories of creative migration, since audiovisual industries are especially reliant on creativity as a core resource. Recurring demand for new prototypes requires pools of labor that are self-consciously motivated by aesthetic innovation as well as market considerations. Yet the marriage of art and commerce is always an uneasy one, especially in large institutional settings, and therefore the media business involves placing substantial wagers on forms of labor that are difficult to manage. As Asu Aksoy and Kevin Robins observe, "Whether the output will be a hit or a miss cannot be prejudged. However, the golden rule in the film business is that if you do not have creative talent to start with, then there is no business to talk about at all, no hits or misses."[32] Indeed, attracting and managing talent is one of the most difficult challenges that screen producers confront. In the sphere of the firm, this involves offering attractive compensation and favorable working conditions, but in a broader sphere it also requires maintaining access to reservoirs of specialized labor that replenish themselves on a regular basis, which is why media companies tend to cluster in particular cities.[33]

Nevertheless, such centers of creativity rarely emerge strictly as a response to market forces; therefore, history suggests that we should look beyond the logic of accumulation to understand patterns of creative migration. During the premodern era, artists and craftspeople congregated at sites where sovereigns and clergy erected grand edifices or commissioned regular works of art. Patronage drew artists to specific locales and often kept them in place for much of their working lives, and they, in turn, passed their skills along to succeeding generations and to newly arrived migrants. Artistic labor in this context was no doubt devotional in certain respects, influencing an artist's training and career. One might imagine that spiritual inspiration and feudal relations of patronage, rather than market forces, significantly influenced trajectories of creative migration during this period, but also important is acknowledgment of the tendency of artists to seek out others of their kind. Artists are drawn to colocate with their peers because of the mutual learning effects engendered by such proximity.

As the bourgeoisie rose to prominence in the early modern era, commercial cities became new centers of artistic production and exhibition, even though preexisting centers retained residual prestige among the cognoscenti.[34] Industrialists built performance venues, established galleries, and subsidized educational institutions, all of which enhanced the cultural capital of the emergent entrepreneurial class and attracted fresh talent to cities such as Berlin, New York, and Shanghai. Popular culture was layered over this topography of the fine arts, further elaborating the trajectories of migration, since scarce resources and dispersed populations made it difficult for popular artists and performers to subsist in any one locale. Instead, they established circuits of recurring migration, playing to crowds in diverse towns and villages. These circuits were formalized in the nineteenth century by booking agents, who rationalized the scheduling of talent across a regional chain of performance venues. The apex of each circuit was located in a major city that provided exposure to the wealthiest and most discriminating audiences, as well as providing cross-fertilization with other domains of the creative arts.[35] This historical sketch suggests that the spatial circulation of performers and the rise of creative centers were shaped by diverse practices that were increasingly rationalized and commodified during the nineteenth century.

Interestingly, the rise of Hollywood confounded these historical patterns, for unlike preceding nodes of creativity, Los Angeles was neither a center of the fine arts nor the apex of a prominent performance circuit. Movie executives no doubt accepted Southern California's relative isolation from the leading cultural institutions of the United States because of other attractions and because cinema itself had become a powerful magnet for aspiring young talent, having captured the imagination of millions via fan magazines and the promotional machinery of the industry. The elixir of cinematic stardom drew tens of thousands to California, luring them with dreams that were no doubt as fantastic as those entertained by the gold rush generation only decades before. As feature film production facilities began to congregate in Southern California, the area became the undisputed apex of creative migrations in the movie business. This newfound cultural prominence was challenged, however, by a 1948 U.S. Supreme Court ruling that forced the major studios to relinquish ownership of their theater chains. Without assured outlets for their products and without regular cash flow to underwrite new movie projects, the future prospects of the industry seemed doubtful. When the studios began to sell off their theaters, they also began to cut back their production facilities and their contract laborers, leading some observers to wonder if the industry itself might collapse in the face of growing competition from television entertainment, then based at network headquarters in New York.[36] As land and labor costs in Southern California spiraled dramatically upward during the latter half of the twentieth century, industry observers periodically warned that "runaway productions" were threatening to undermine Hollywood's status as movie capital of the world.[37]

Why, then, does Hollywood continue to act as a magnet for cultural labor? One might suggest that, like prior transitions, the residual aura of the city helps to sustain its status as a center of creative endeavor. Although this may indeed have some effect, geographers Michael Storper and Susan Christopherson contend that more important is the disintegrated (or flexible) mode of production in the movie industry, which actually encourages and sustains the agglomeration of creative labor, because constant changes in product output require frequent transactions among contractors, subcontractors, and creative talent. They show that the number of interfirm transactions in the movie business has grown dramatically over the past fifty years at the very same time that the scale of transactions has diminished, indicating that many small subcontractors now provide the studios with crucial services, such as wardrobe, set construction, and lighting, as well as key talent, with many stars now incorporated as independent enterprises rather than as contract labor. Storper and Christopherson argue that this pattern of disintegration encourages studios to employ *local* subcontractors and talent, because proximity allows directors and managers to oversee outsourced creative labor and make changes more easily and more frequently as work progresses. As for the workers, they cluster around Hollywood, where studios and subcontracting firms are based, since it helps them "offset the instability of short-term contractual work by remaining close to the largest pool of employment opportunities."[38]

Geographer Allen J. Scott extends this principle of talent agglomeration to industries as diverse as jewelry, furniture, and fashion apparel, arguing that manufacturers of *cultural* goods tend to locate where subcontractors and skilled laborers form dense transactional networks. Besides apparent cost efficiencies, Scott points to the mutual learning effects that stem from a clustering of interrelated producers. Whether through informal learning (such as sharing ideas and techniques while collaborating on a particular project) or more formal transfers of knowledge (craft schools, trade associations, and awards ceremonies), clustering enhances product quality and fuels innovation. "Place-based communities such as these are not just foci of cultural labor in the narrow sense," observes Scott, "but also are active hubs of social reproduction in which crucial cultural competencies are maintained and circulated."[39]

This agglomeration of labor encourages path-dependent evolution, such that small chance events or innovations may spark the appearance of a culture industry in a particular location, and clustering then engenders a growth spiral, because creative labor's migration to the region in search of work further enhances its attraction to other talent. Locales that fail to make an early start in such industries are subject to "lock-out," since disrupting the dynamics of agglomeration is difficult, even with massive infusions of capital or government subsidies. Scott suggests that the only way a new cluster might arise is if its producers offer an appreciably distinctive product line.

Much of the scholarship regarding labor agglomeration and transaction networks was written in response to the dramatic success of fashion industries in the "Third Italy" during the 1980s and 1990s, when analysts sought to theorize distinctions between Fordist and post-Fordist modes of industrial organization.[40] Although this literature is enormously insightful, it is important to note that most of it tends to emphasize the *recent* behaviors of labor markets while obscuring the historical patterns of creative migration mentioned earlier. For example, Scott analyzes Paris as a center of cultural production but only vaguely refers to the historical factors ("the small chance events") that initiated the clustering of creative labor in the French capital, factors such as the absolutist monarchy and its successor, the equally centralized imperialist regime of the nineteenth century, both of which fostered systems of artistic patronage that attracted talent from far and wide. Likewise, the Third Italy arose on a foundation laid by craft traditions stretching back to the transcontinental merchant economy of the Middle Ages. In both instances, the initial agglomeration of labor preceded post-Fordism and even Fordism itself.

It therefore seems reasonable to suggest that the centripetal migrations of creative labor are not necessarily specific to post-Fordist regimes of flexible specialization or even to capitalism but have, in fact, existed under various regimes of production. In post-Fordist industrial settings mutual learning effects are no doubt an animating force behind the concentration of creative labor, but just as interesting is that many *Fordist* enterprises self-consciously sought to realize these effects as well. For example, Alfred Chandler observes that large corporations in the information industry internalized and compounded learning effects throughout the twentieth century.[41] Indeed, he contends that leading firms in the electronics and computer industries, such as AT&T and IBM, were distinguished by their ability to foster continuous paths of organizational learning. Moreover, firms that successfully manage ongoing innovation (i.e., the production of prototypes) tend to concentrate their creative workforce and to establish effective conduits for channeling information among production units and from consumers back to producers. For Chandler, learning effects may take place within a single integrated enterprise, or they may extend to a nexus of interconnected and complementary firms that support a core company. In either case, geographical clustering stimulates innovation.

Furthermore, Bordwell, Thompson, and Staiger demonstrate similar patterns in the early movie industry. Under the classical studio system, a set of creative norms emerged out of complex and extended interactions among employees within a given studio and among the local filmmaking community. The "Hollywood style" grew out of collective reflection and discussion regarding various experiments in cinematic representation. This ongoing negotiation improved the quality of studio films, enhanced the market dominance of Hollywood product, and acted as a powerful attraction to those around the world who aspired to make movies. Hollywood not only absorbed migrant actors and craftspeople; it also periodically tapped pools of renowned expertise from countries around the world, such as Russia (Sergei Eisenstein), Germany (Ernst Lubitsch), and the United Kingdom (Alfred Hitchcock). Thus, mutual learning effects prevailed in both the integrated studio era and, after 1948, in the disintegrated studio era. The industry's ability to adapt to shifting circumstances while maintaining its infrastructure for organizational learning suggests why Hollywood endures as a center of creativity and why creative labor continues to migrate to Southern California.

In general, we can conclude that cultural production is especially reliant on mutual learning effects and trajectories of creative migration and that, inevitably, particular locations emerge as centers of creativity. These principles have operated throughout history under various modes of production, but the modern era is distinctive because the centripetal logic of capitalist production has been married to the centripetal trajectories of creative migration, engendering the rise of Hollywood as an unparalleled center of media capital. Nevertheless, the significant symbolic content of media products attenuates the reach of Hollywood movies, despite the generative power of the industry. That is, the cultural distance between American filmmakers and Turkish or Indian audiences introduces the prospect that the meaningfulness and therefore the value of certain products may be undermined at the moment of consumption or use. Although the centripetal logic of accumulation and of creative migration helps us identify the concentrations of media capital, the centrifugal patterns of distribution are much more complicated, especially when products rub up against counterparts in distant cultural domains, which are often served, even if minimally, by competing media capitals that are centers of creative migration in their own right.

Cities such as Cairo, Mumbai, and Hong Kong lie across significant cultural divides from their Hollywood counterpart, which helps to explain why producers in these cities have been able to sustain distinctive product lines and survive the onslaught of a much more powerful competitor. These media capitals are further supported by intervening factors that modify and complicate the spatial tendencies outlined above. Consequently, the third principle of media capital focuses on forces of sociocultural variation, demonstrating that national and local institutions have remained significant actors despite the spatial tendencies of production and distribution. Indeed, the early years of cinema were exceptional in large part because the logic of media capital unfolded relatively unimpeded by national regulation, but as the popularity of Hollywood narratives increased, many countries established cultural policies to address the growing influence of this new commodity form. Indeed, motion pictures presented governments with a unique policy challenge, since they were distributed even more widely than newspapers, magazines, and books, the circulation of which was limited to literate consumers within shared linguistic spheres. By comparison, silent-era cinema challenged linguistic, class, and national boundaries, because films circulated widely within the United States and overseas, swelling the size of audiences dramatically and fueling the growth of large-scale enterprises. According to Kristin Thompson, U.S. movie companies became dominant exporters by the mid-1910s, a trend that contributed to a further concentration of resources and talent and encouraged the refinement of film styles and production values.[42] By the 1920s, however, opinion leaders and politicians abroad grew wary of Hollywood movies, and cultural critics began to clamor for regulation. Many countries imposed import quotas and content regulations on Hollywood films, and some set up national film boards to subsidize cinema productions with national themes and talent.[43] Similar measures were considered, if not adopted, by countries around the world.

Most important, however, was state-subsidized radio broadcasting, which in most every country outside the Western Hemisphere was established as a public service system and remained so until the 1980s. Britain, which would serve as a model to others, explicitly charged the British Broadcasting Corporation with responsibility to clear a space for the circulation of British values, culture, and information.[44] Radio seemed an especially appropriate medium for intervention, since many of its characteristics helped to insulate national systems from foreign competition. Technologically, radio signals traveled only thirty to sixty miles from any given transmitter. As in Britain, one could interconnect a chain of transmitters that would blanket the countryside, but the only way for foreign competitors to reach one's home audiences was via shortwave radio, a temperamental technology that was comparatively inaccessible to the masses. Such insulation was further ensured by an international regulatory regime that allocated radio frequencies on a national basis, thereby minimizing technical as well as cultural interference among countries. Language provided another bulwark, since radio relied on aural competence in the state's official language, thereby helping to distinguish national productions that played in domestic settings from Hollywood "talkies" that played at the cinema. Finally, public service radio systems were bolstered by indigenous cultural resources to which the state laid claim. Literary and theatrical works were commonly appropriated to the new medium, as were folk tales and music. State ceremonies and eventually sporting events also filled the airwaves as the medium participated in self-conscious efforts to foster a common national culture.

Radio also promoted a shared temporality among audiences. Its predecessor, the nineteenth-century newspaper, pioneered this transformation, for it not only directed readers to stories that the editors considered significant but also encouraged them to absorb these stories at a synchronous daily pace. Hegel's reference to the morning ritual of reading the newspaper suggests the ways in which readers partook of common narratives and furthermore did so at more or less the same time.[45] Radio extended such rituals to nonliterate groups, and it expanded the horizon of synchronization, such that programming schedules began to shape daily household routines and create a national calendar of social and cultural events. Radio insinuated itself into the household, interlacing public and private spheres and situating national culture in the everyday world of its listeners.[46] Even though radio systems were founded under the guiding hand of politicians, educators, and cultural bureaucrats, over time they would open themselves up to audience participation, employing yet another distinctive cultural resource as part of their programming repertoire: the voice of the people. In each of these ways public service radio accentuated national contours of difference in opposition to media capital's desire to operate on a smooth plane of market relations worldwide.[47] As we can see, the forces of sociocultural variation were often influenced by assertions of political will, which no doubt is one of the reasons that Hollywood film companies go to such great lengths to present themselves as apolitical institutions. By self-consciously presenting their products as "mere entertainment," they try to move them outside the realm of political deliberation, thereby destabilizing the core rationale for national cultural policies.

Although government regulation often focuses on ways to attenuate or refigure the centripetal and centrifugal tendencies of media capital, it can also act as an influential enabler by establishing institutions and policies that foster the growth of media industries. Intellectual property laws are an especially compelling example in this regard. In the United States, for example, court rulings during the 1910s provided movie studios with intellectual property rights so that they, rather than their employees, might claim protection for the films they "authored." Although copyright laws originally aimed to foster creative endeavor by *individuals*, the courts allowed movie factories to claim artistic inspiration as well. Interestingly, they further ruled that waged and salaried laborers at the major studios were neither creators nor authors but were rather "work for hire." In this way, the American legal system profoundly transformed copyright law, facilitating the industrialization of cinematic production and providing expansive legal protection for movie distributors.[48]

In addition, the U.S. courts handed down rulings during the 1920s that allowed the federal government to parcel out commercial broadcasting licenses, effectively turning a public resource—the airwaves—into a private commodity that could be owned and controlled by large corporations. Regulators then granted locally licensed stations the liberty to contract with national networks, a policy that effectively handed over large segments of the broadcast day to national programming and advertising. Rather than acting primarily as local trustees of a community resource, radio station executives soon focused most of their attention on managing the public airwaves as profit-generating enterprises. By "selling the air," in Thomas Streeter's felicitous phrase, the government created a market-driven system out of an intangible public resource, enabling a national program distribution system, stimulating the growth of national advertising, and concentrating creative resources in a handful of urban centers.[49] During the transition to television, the government again favored the very same corporations and set in place a system that was even less responsive to local markets, institutions,

and audiences. By the end of the 1950s, national program production—
which during the radio era had been dispersed in such cities as New York,
Chicago, Cincinnati, and Nashville—became concentrated in Hollywood,
churning out telefilm narratives that came to dominate larger and larger
shares of each local station's broadcasting schedule.[50] Manufactured on cel-
luloid like their theatrical counterparts, these TV series were then available
for export overseas, where they infiltrated emerging television systems in
such countries as Germany, Singapore, and Saudi Arabia. The U.S. government extended a helping hand to Hollywood distributors by providing dubbing services and most important by advocating a free flow doctrine in an
attempt to preclude the prospect that import quotas might undermine the
spatial reach of American TV shows. More recently, the U.S. government
has been a powerful advocate of international copyright enforcement, hoping to enforce uniform standards worldwide that would maximize the profits of film, television, music, and computer companies, many of them significant contributors to the major American political parties.

Although market forces have been primary engines of cultural production and circulation in the modern era, the boundaries and contours of markets are subject to political interventions that enable, shape, and attenuate
the dynamics of media capital. Accordingly, this volume reasserts the importance of policy, suggesting that concepts such as free flow and market
forces are in fact meaningless without self-conscious state interventions to
fashion a terrain for commercial operations. Markets are made, not given.
And the logic of accumulation must therefore be interrogated in relation to
specific and complex mixtures of sociocultural forces.

Finally, it should also be pointed out that self-conscious state policies are
not the only actors that organize and exploit the forces of sociocultural variation. Media industries in Bombay, Cairo, and Hong Kong have for decades
taken advantage of social and cultural differences in their production and
distribution practices. Operating across significant cultural divides from
Hollywood and from other powerful exporters, they have employed creative talent and cultural forms that distinctively resonate with their audiences. They have furthermore sought to fashion films and programs featuring protagonists who, in the words of audience members, "look just like
us." Although these media industries commonly manufacture fantastic
narratives, their heroes and stars offer audiences points of identification that
are more accessible than their American counterparts. In addition, these industries have made use of social networks and insider information to secure
market advantages, and they have invoked cultural and national pride in
their promotional campaigns. As we shall see in the chapter discussions,

forces of sociocultural variation provide opportunities for carving out market niches that are beyond the reach of Hollywood competitors.

Media capital is therefore a concept that at once acknowledges the *spatial* logics of capital, creativity, culture, and polity without privileging one among the four. Just as the logic of capital provides a fundamental structuring influence, so too do forces of sociocultural variation shape the diverse contexts in which media are made and consumed. The concept media capital encourages us to provide dynamic and historicized accounts that delineate the operations of capital and the migrations of talent and at the same time directs our attention to forces and contingencies that can engender alternative discourses, practices, and spatialities.[51] As we shift our attention to Chinese media, we will see, for example, that practices within Chinese enterprises often differ significantly from the their Western counterparts and that a cultural divide between East and West registers in the perceptions and tastes of Chinese audiences. Moreover, within the sphere of Global China itself, audiences in different locales express distinctively different attitudes toward fashion, music, and imagery. Initial fantasies of a sprawling but organically coherent Chinese culture—a "Greater China"—have faded as businesses have confronted the very difficult challenges of creating and promoting transnational products while also keeping an eye on niche markets within diverse Chinese societies around the world.[52]

My initial interest in Chinese media was sparked by the realization that they, too, are globalizing alongside and intersecting with Western media. The concept of media capital helps us to examine such developments without presuming that Hollywood acts as a singular globalizing force or that Chinese media are a singular countervailing force. Instead, media capital encourages us to consider alternative, overlapping, intersecting processes of cultural globalization, and it is in this context that careful examination of the commercial Chinese film and television industries provides a lens through which to assess the prospects of these industries and the processes of cultural globalization.[53] All of which returns our attention squarely to questions of location: Where and under what conditions have global Chinese media enterprises emerged? Where are their audiences and markets located? In what ways has the spatial configuration of these media enterprises been shaped by market forces, creative migrations, and sociocultural dynamics? And what might we expect in the future? That is, where will we find prominent creative centers, and what might we expect so far as the reach of their products?

The first two chapters provide historical background regarding the development of Chinese commercial cinema. Focusing first on the fortunes of

Shaw Brothers, in chapter 1 I show how civil war and world war disrupted the social environs of East Asia, encouraging Chinese movie companies to refigure the geography of their operations and to imagine themselves as transnational enterprises almost from the very beginning. Shaw Brothers became one of the most successful studios, relocating from Shanghai to Singapore to Hong Kong and developing a distribution and exhibition chain that has reached Chinese audiences across East Asia and around the world. By the late 1950s, Run Run Shaw would concentrate the company's production operations in Hong Kong, establishing one of the largest integrated film studios in the world. Yet by the end of the 1960s, Shaw would declare the movie business a sunset industry and turn his attention to local television, taking control of Hong Kong's first commercial broadcast service, TVB.

In chapter 2 I chronicle the unexpected revival of the film industry during the 1970s and 1980s, sparking a "new wave" cinema resolutely attentive to its local Hong Kong audiences but also dependent on overseas presales of distribution rights in order to fund its operations. Golden Harvest, the most prominent studio of the era, parlayed the success of Bruce Lee, Jackie Chan, and Michael Hui into a lucrative production and distribution empire that emphasized location shooting and partnerships with independent producers. Besides Golden Harvest, in chapter 2 I also analyze the operations of one of the leading independent production houses, Cinema City, a company that thrived on local hits such as *Aces Go Places*.[54] During the 1980s, Hong Kong emerged as one of the world's most vibrant cinemas, characterized by hybrid genres and exuberant experimentation that proved popular with local mass audiences. Yet as filmmakers concentrated their attention on local theater audiences, producing what critics now characterize as "authentic" or "golden age" Hong Kong cinema, they serendipitously created movies that proved popular with overseas audiences as well.

Chapter 3 turns our attention to Taiwan—one of the most important overseas markets for Hong Kong films during its heyday—and explains how the Chinese movie business paradoxically crumbled during a period of escalating demand. By the 1990s, presales to Taiwan provided 30 to 50 percent of the total financing for an average film, and as new media technologies proliferated, video and cable revenues magnified the attractiveness of Hong Kong movies even more, sparking feverish competition among Taiwanese distributors. Ironically, the very technologies that enhanced demand for Chinese films and extended their reach into private homes would prove to be the industry's undoing, for they triggered a period of hyperproduction, in which the quantity of films escalated while the quality plummeted. In this chapter I explain how the practices of producers and distributors failed to adapt to changing technological forces and audience tastes, leading to a period of decline and uncertainty.

As the fortunes of Chinese commercial cinema waned, Hollywood studios came to dominate in Taiwan, not so much because they crushed the local competition, but because they filled a void and exploited the promotional possibilities of a media sector that was growing rapidly due to the end of martial law in 1987. In chapter 3 I also discuss the attitudes of local audiences and argue that, although Hollywood now prevails in Taiwan, there remains a broad-ranging popular awareness of stars and entertainment products from Global China. Despite current uncertainties in the industry, demand for Chinese entertainment products remains strong, even if many them flow through pirate distribution channels. I conclude that the Chinese film industry is now passing through a process of structural adjustment and that past practices of the movie business are giving way to globalized multimedia strategies.

Most interesting perhaps is that, despite the collapse in attendance at Chinese cinemas, Hong Kong movies remained a very popular form of programming on cable and satellite TV during the 1990s. Chapters 5 through 8 chart the emergence of new local and transnational television services in Hong Kong, Singapore, and Taiwan, where political transformations, trade liberalization, media deregulation, and new technologies provided new opportunities for media enterprises. Chapter 5 details TVB's escalating international ventures, first in video retailing, then in satellite and cable TV. In part, the Hong Kong broadcaster was encouraged to look abroad because of the fragmentation of its local mass audience and the appearance of new competitors, such as Hong Kong property mogul Peter Woo, who landed the government franchise for the territory's first cable system, and the son of another mogul, Richard Li, who launched Star TV, a pan-Asian satellite platform with expansive ambitions. In this chapter I describe the complex maneuvering and intense rivalry among leading Hong Kong capitalists, each with an eye on the emerging Global China media market.

In Taiwan, where the government had long taken a proprietary interest in television, the end of martial law in the late 1980s sparked a wave of experimentation with cable TV, which in the following decade would flourish into one of the most robust cable markets in the world. In chapter 6 I describe the shift from a government-controlled oligopoly to a competitive market system, which forced the dominant terrestrial television stations to forge new coproduction partnerships with, surprisingly, TV stations in mainland China. At the very moment when the governments of Taiwan and the People's Republic of China were locked in a heated political standoff, television executives found ways to cooperate on the production of historical dramas that proved popular with audiences throughout Global China. In chapter 7 I follow up on these developments with profiles of important new cable competitors—TVBS, FTV, and SET—explaining how each entered the Taiwan market by focusing on a particular audience niche but was in time forced to pursue a more globalized perspective on future growth.

In chapter 8 our attention shifts to Singapore, where the government likewise had a direct and controlling interest in television. During the 1990s, however, new pressures emerged when the island's economy shifted from manufacturing and shipping to communication and service industries. Investing heavily in transoceanic cable and satellite technology, government planners tried to refashion the Lion City as an important node in the global communication grid. In order to do so, Singapore needed to deemphasize its reputation for censorship and government propaganda by encouraging privatization of the media industries and liberalization of media content. Accordingly, the government's broadcasting operations were transformed into MediaCorp, a multimedia firm that could achieve profitability only by globalizing its operations. As with Hong Kong and Taiwan, changing political circumstances in Singapore along with new technologies and trade liberalization stimulated a transformation of sociocultural forces and an amplification of the logic of accumulation. Whereas Singaporean television initially emerged in the 1960s as a self-conscious assertion of political will, it increasingly became subject to market forces that encouraged executives and producers to think transnationally and imagine the prospects of a Global Chinese audience.

Of course, Chinese television enterprises were changing their perspectives in part because foreign media conglomerates were showing increasing interest in Asia, especially as a result of political transformations in the PRC. In chapters 9 through 12 I detail the growing engagement between local media and global institutions in the realms of satellite, cable, Internet, and cinema. Although Western executives had been following developments in Asia closely since the 1980s, things took a dramatic turn in 1994, when Rupert Murdoch bought Star TV from Hong Kong tycoon Richard Li for almost $1 billion. Chapter 9 provides a comprehensive account of Murdoch's mercurial fortunes in the region, showing how his pan-Asian aspirations faltered, leaving him with a collection of niche TV channels rather than the continental broadcasting juggernaut he thought he was buying. Like others, Murdoch originally imagined satellite technologies as transcending frontiers and unleashing the centrifugal power of his media empire. Instead, he found himself mired in infrastructural, regulatory, competitive, and programming issues in diverse markets throughout the region. Paying particular attention to Star TV's development in the PRC, in chapter 9 I show how forces of sociocultural variation on the ground reshaped the distribution and production strategies of a major Western media conglomerate with global aspirations. Murdoch's experience was not unique, however, as chapter 10 makes clear. HBO, MTV, and ESPN all found that their strategies for expansion into Asia had to be dramatically refigured as they learned to balance panregional efficiencies with distinctive factors at play in the various national and local markets throughout Asia.

Richard Li, the founder of Star TV, would have to learn these lessons yet a second time, when he returned to the media scene in the late 1990s with a new transnational broadband venture known as Pacific Century Cyberworks. As I show in chapter 11, PCCW burst into the headlines in 1999, capturing the imagination of investors and the popular press much as Star TV had done only eight years earlier. Like Star, the venture was long on ambition and self-promotion and short on crucial infrastructure and compelling content. After briskly rising to a total worth of more than $18 billion—eclipsing the value of Amazon and Yahoo at the time—PCCW sank like a rock in the global dotcom meltdown of 2001. Just as important, however, the collapse of Li's company pointed to enduring challenges in the realm of content creation, issues that continue to trouble Chinese media enterprises today.

In chapter 12 I therefore return to an examination of the commercial movie industry, a core content creator and in its heyday the foundation of Chinese audiovisual entertainment. In the early 2000s, Golden Harvest tactically withdrew from filmmaking, concentrating instead on extending its cinema circuit. China Star has remained an active producer but likewise has sought to bolster its infrastructure by establishing an expansive video distribution network. Most successful, however, is Media Asia, a producer of high-profile blockbusters that are qualitatively competitive with Hollywood. Now a division of an expanding multimedia conglomerate, Media Asia provides foundational content that is leveraged through various divisions of the eSun corporation. Though still not fully realized, eSun's strategy is to create distinctive products for a broad array of markets and to establish a brand identity built around quality content that moves fluidly across media platforms and national borders. Although some movie moguls imagined a pan-Chinese cinema as early as the 1930s, the emergence of conglomerates such as eSun heralds a new era in media strategies and practices, one that specifically imagines the global Chinese media market as lucrative, expansive, and multidimensional.

Finally, in the conclusion, I summarize my findings and refocus attention on questions of cultural geography and public policy. Chinese media present an especially rich case study because their spatial configurations have varied dramatically over the past century. Now, in an era increasingly characterized by globalizing forces and flows, it is worthwhile to reflect on the prospects of Chinese screen industries as they look to the future and to consider which strategies and policy interventions might help to augment their current capacities. If indeed the twenty-first century is to be the Chinese century, then one must wonder which centers of media activity will play a prominent role and to what extent they will truly integrate and extend their operations transnationally. Those who succeed are destined to shape not only the future of Global China but other futures as well.

1   The Pan-Chinese Studio System and Capitalist Paternalism

In 1966, Run Run Shaw reached the peak of his movie career as the head of the biggest and most influential motion picture studio in Asia. A reporter for *Life* magazine, inquiring about the secret of Shaw's success, turned for explanation to the movie mogul's daily regimen, which began at 6 A.M. with a spare breakfast of noodles and tea followed by qigong exercises at his expansive ocean-front mansion situated in the rugged headlands above Clearwater Bay in Hong Kong. Invigorated, Shaw would then set to work reviewing movie scripts before leaving at eight o'clock for a five-minute ride in one of his prized Rolls Royces, heading down a winding road to the sprawling Shaw Brothers studio. After an hour spent touring the production sets, the boss would then retire to his second-floor corner office in Shaw House, perched on a rise above the main gate to Movie Town. There he would continue reading scripts, reviewing rushes from the previous day, and viewing recent releases from competitors. Just before lunch Shaw often met with Raymond Chow, head of production, to go over detailed recommendations for writers and directors, paying close attention to each of the forty or so films annually produced by the studio. A shrewd businessman who started his career managing a chain of movie theaters, Shaw also paid careful attention to every aspect of the creative process, and many believed that the studio's success was in large part due to his acute awareness of audience tastes and preferences. This was especially apparent whenever competing movie studios, and later television stations, challenged Shaw's dominant market position. In each instance, the boss provided hands-on leadership, guiding the work of production and programming staffs.

Yet if Shaw's mornings were devoted to the creative side of the business, his afternoons and evenings were set aside for the far-flung distribution and exhibition operations of Shaw Brothers' empire. Over the course of his ca-

Run Run Shaw ruled over the Movie Town studio lot during the early 1960s from a corner office in Shaw House. Author photo.

reer, Run Run managed hundreds of cinemas and the world's most commercially successful Chinese television station. He also built the largest library of Chinese feature films and television programs, and he distributed thousands of hours of Hollywood product throughout Asia. As one of the world's first multimedia enterprises, Shaw's company ventured into television, magazines, popular music, amusement parks, and the Internet. It furthermore diversified into a broad array of real estate ventures, which today exceed the asset value of Shaw's media holdings. Now in his nineties and chairman of the largest commercial Chinese television company in the world, Run Run Shaw alone has come closest to building a global empire in Chinese media.

Shaw's career brings into focus key principles of media capital within an Asian context. Like their counterparts in the U.S. movie industry during the early part of the twentieth century, the Shaw brothers focused their initial attention on exhibition, growing their business from a single theater to a small chain and then, in response to competition and rising demand, moving into film distribution and finally production. Unlike American movie companies, however, Shaw Brothers never enjoyed a large and stable domestic market, so its business became much more reliant on international operations, cobbling together theater circuits in various parts of East and Southeast Asia and shifting its operations with the winds of economic and political change. So successful were the Shaws that by the end of the 1950s they had built the largest integrated film studio outside Hollywood, concentrating productive resources in Hong Kong and distributing products throughout Asia and to overseas Chinese theaters in such cities as San Francisco and London. They also recruited and groomed talent, becoming a magnet for aspiring artistes and a renowned center of creativity among Chinese societies worldwide. Despite their success, the continuing uncertainties of the transnational Chinese market made Run Run Shaw receptive to the possibilities of television, a medium that took Hong Kong by storm in the late 1960s. He consequently shifted his considerable resources to broadcasting, favoring the expanding prosperity and stability of the local Hong Kong market over the far-flung cinema empire that had shaped his early career.

Siao Yi-fu—also known as Run Run Shaw—entered the film business along with his three brothers in 1920s Shanghai. The family had made its fortune in textile manufacturing, and no independent record exists indicating why or how the brothers initially became involved in movies, but a company history suggests that Runje, the oldest of the brothers and a lawyer by training, had an affinity for the arts and in his spare time wrote scripts for Chinese operas that were performed at local theaters. In 1923, Runje acquired his own theater, which proved to be such a success that he soon opened two more and encouraged his brothers to join the business. Yet this expanding investment in theaters came at the very moment when Shanghai audiences were beginning to shift their attention from live performances to motion pictures. As in many other parts of the world, short films began to maneuver their way onto theater marquees as part of an evening's ensemble of attractions, and before long feature films started to crowd out live entertainment, with some theaters beginning to specialize in motion picture exhibition. The Shaws' theaters followed this trend, but, like other operators, Runje soon became frustrated by the uncertain supply of quality titles, leading him and his brothers inexorably into the movie production business as the Tian Yi (First) studio.[1]

The Shaw brothers' enthusiasm for the new medium was matched by that of other entrepreneurs, and Shanghai soon became recognized as the movie capital of China. This was due in part to international character of the city, situated at the mouth of the Yangtze River, where European, American, and Japanese trading enterprises thrived during the nineteenth and early twentieth centuries. Just as goods and currencies from around the world commingled in this cosmopolitan center, so too did cultures and ideas. Everything from architecture to hairstyles to restaurant cuisine reflected international influences. Yet even though the introduction of motion pictures owed a great deal to the cosmopolitan character of Shanghai, their enduring success with Chinese audiences owed just as much to the vibrant ensemble of popular stars and genres of the period.

Talented people from all over the Chinese world made their way to the mouth of the Yangtze in hopes of signing with a studio, and, conversely, the popular films of Shanghai made their way to cities across China and to overseas Chinese communities. Tian Yi was doing a lively business in the local market, but trouble loomed when a distribution cartel of six leading Shanghai studios sought to dominate the market by pressuring theater owners to boycott the films of their competitors. Consequently, the brothers decided to dispatch the two youngest Shaws, Runme and Run Run, to Singapore as a hedge against the market maneuvers of the so-called Ming Xing cartel. At the time, Southeast Asia was becoming one of the most important export markets for Shanghai movie producers, as colonial tin, rubber, timber, and tea industries flourished in the region, creating jobs and new wealth for Chinese workers and managers. Unfortunately for the newly arrived Shaws, theater owners in Singapore showed little interest in Tian Yi films, in large part because of the influence of Ming Xing in Malaya. Not easily discouraged, the two brothers built their own theater and soon added several more in the city. Then traveling the length of the peninsula by automobile, they went from town to town testing the enthusiasm of local audiences. Wherever the response was positive, they would purchase land for a theater and for related property development nearby, reasoning correctly that a new theater would raise land values in the immediate vicinity. For audiences in more rural locations, the Shaws developed a fleet of mobile projection units that toured rural villages, mining sites, and rubber plantations, screening movies for both ethnic Chinese and Malay audiences.

Tian Yi flourished in large part because it emphasized the Southeast Asian market at a time when its competitors in Shanghai were preoccupied with mainland audiences, a market that would shrivel as economic uncertainty, civil unrest, and warfare intensified throughout the 1930s. In shifting their focus southward, the Shaws developed a prosperous movie empire that by 1940 included 139 theaters (many of them joint ventures with local operators) and nine amusement parks in Malaya, Singapore, Thailand, Indonesia, and Indochina. Ethnic Chinese were a prime audience for the Shaw theaters, but the chain also drew Malays and European expatriates with a diverse roster of titles that included a healthy share of Hollywood features. With the regional economy booming from the growing demand for war materials, Southeast Asia became the most profitable market for Chinese movies, and the Shaws emerged as an industry leader. The company adapted to the arrival of sound technology by incorporating postproduction dubbing to its feature films, which made it possible to include dialogue in Mandarin, Cantonese, and other varieties of Chinese, as well as Bahasa Malay. Multilingual production techniques became standard operating procedure at the Shaw studios, with the exception of Cantonese musicals, which tended to appeal to audiences across linguistic boundaries and were especially popular in Southeast Asia. The diverse preferences of the Shaws' audiences and the growing demand for more titles encouraged the brothers to open new studios in Hong Kong (Nanyang Studio, 1934) and Singapore (Malay Film Productions, 1937), the former specializing in Cantonese titles and the latter emphasizing Bahasa Malay, as well as Chinese productions.

Yet this cycle of growth was undermined by the advancing Japanese military, which eventually caught up with the Shaws, first in Shanghai, then in Hong Kong, and finally in Malaya in 1942. After the Japanese army seized Singapore, the Shaws were forced to continue managing their cinemas under the direction of the occupation forces, which now added a significant complement of Japanese propaganda to each evening's program. After the war, the Shaws quickly bounced back, rebuilding their investments in theaters, amusement parks, and real estate. Industry lore suggests that the quick comeback was possible in part because Run Run had buried gold, jewelry, and other valuables immediately preceding the Japanese arrival in Singapore, a story that is not inconceivable, since concealing wealth in anticipation of such reversals of fortune was standard practice among wealthy overseas Chinese.

Indeed, the Shaws in many ways embodied the entrepreneurial style of overseas Chinese, a style that evolved in response to lessons learned over the course of some two thousand years. When merchants first emerged in mainland China, imperial regimes viewed them with suspicion if not outright contempt, because, unlike the landed gentry, who directly relied on the state's military and bureaucracy, the merchant class achieved a peculiar form of independence via commercial activities. As intermediaries in the social system, they wielded significant influence over the flow of goods, and they accumulated forms of wealth that were more easily concealed from tax collectors and government officials. Moreover, the merchant class was more likely to finance or participate in overseas trading ventures, which sometimes drew the enthusiastic support of the imperial regime and other times engendered xenophobic suspicion. Finally, merchants often lent money to Chinese rulers, and some would curry political favor through gifts and bribes, hoping that political influence might further enhance their fortunes. Consequently, Chinese leaders saw the merchant class as both necessary and something of a nuisance. One moment ruling elites might embrace them, and the next moment they might purge them. Most worrisome, state officials commonly offered up members of the merchant class as scapegoats during famines and periods of political unrest. These recurring fluctuations in status therefore encouraged business people to conceal their wealth and to exercise discretion in social settings. Generally, it could be said that status and power belonged to the government, while enviable pockets of wealth belonged to the merchant class. And even though both needed the other, the former often held the latter in contempt, sometimes subjecting merchants to penalties and seizure of property on little more than a whim.[2]

Secrecy therefore became an ingrained feature of many commercial enterprises, and family or clan members were often the only ones trusted with managerial power or with the secrets of company account books. Moreover, the uncertain social status of merchants encouraged many of them to move their operations south along the rugged coast of China, putting them at arm's length from imperial power. From Shanghai to Hong Kong—the area that has become the economic engine of China's recent modernization campaign—family- and clan-based merchant cultures emerged over time, each with its own distinctive language and social conventions. Yet even this distance from the palace was not enough for some merchants who felt constrained by imperial limitations on their seagoing ventures. In time, maritime merchants pushed even farther afield, setting up vigorous trading fleets in Nanyang (the South Seas) stretching all the way to the Strait of Malacca. Yet they, too, often plied their trade in hostile social environments, and, even today, ethnic Chinese sometimes find themselves the object of resentment, discrimination, and even violence in societies such as Indonesia and Malaysia. These ethnic tensions are in part attributable to the fantastic wealth accumulated by merchants and to the close ethnic ties maintained within Chinese communities. Ironically, close ethnic ties and familial enterprises are tied to the insecurity that Chinese merchants have experienced both on the mainland and in overseas locales. As Gordon Redding puts it, "The insecurity is that of an ethnic minority, generally non-assimilated and yet successful in wealth terms coming from a society in which the combination of totalitarianism and patrimonialism left a historical legacy of suspicion of any source of security except the family."[3] Although familial capitalism is a worldwide phenomenon, in Chinese societies it has often been rooted in suspicions about politicians, competitors, and even employees. Building relations of trust within the family and within a wider network of like-minded Chinese therefore became a crucial resource in the establishment of overseas enterprises.[4]

The Shaw brothers' decision to head south during the 1920s, therefore, made both cultural and commercial sense, since over the centuries millions of Chinese had migrated to Southeast Asia, and the region was comparatively stable and prosperous at the time, making it especially receptive to the novelty of motion pictures. The Shaws expanded their enterprise across national boundaries primarily in pursuit of ethnic Chinese customers, catering to them with films that drew from popular Chinese operas, featuring legendary characters in mythical settings. They invoked themes and narratives from the past as a way to tap into that which remained common among diasporic Chinese, but they also developed movies for ethnic Malay audiences, and they acted as regional distributor for several Hollywood studios, serving audiences across ethnic boundaries. As a Chinese family enterprise, they were discreet and even secretive, but they were also flexible, willing to exploit opportunities wherever they presented themselves.

Secret societies, or triads, also bear mention in this context, not because the Shaws owed their success to such associations, but because merchants and triads emerged out of a similar social milieu.[5] The origins of triad societies are diverse and complex, as are the histories that recount their development. Suffice to say that covert societies can be traced back to political reform movements in mainland China during the dynastic era. Early triads characterized themselves as patriotic organizations and self-help societies that arose in response to insensitivity and corruption among government officials. Providing support and shelter from abuses and misfortunes that were visited on their members, triads flourished at arm's length from the imperial court, many societies first emerging along the southern coast of China and overseas. The organizations were clannish in structure and clandestine in operation. Yet what began as mutual aid societies in some cases became protection rackets that shed the trappings of patriotism to become self-interested enterprises. Triads served, for example, as labor recruiters for the tin mines and tea plantations of Malaya and for railroad construction projects in the United States. Charging fees to both employers and employees, they grew wealthy facilitating waves of overseas migration, often at the expense of workers, who were lured into exploitative servitude. Triads further extended their influence overseas by setting up (or infiltrating) fraternal organizations and mutual aid societies from which laborers sought solace regarding their misfortune. In permeating the institutions of migrant communities, triads gained widespread influence, which made it difficult for many overseas Chinese to avoid contact with them.

Triads therefore bear mention when discussing the Chinese merchant class, because both groups established elaborate transnational networks in response to adversity inside China. Both groups furthermore relied on an extended web of fraternal and secretive loyalties. Accordingly, members of both thought it important to be influential—to have big face—among the right people but not to be so visible as to invite surveillance by competitors or state authorities. Over time both groups extended their networks beyond China to Southeast Asia and then to cities around the world. Triads and business people are not necessarily synonymous, but they can be under certain circumstances, and one is occasionally hard-pressed to distinguish between the two. Even today, people in the motion picture business will at times find themselves dealing with triads, sometimes as part of a legitimate business deal and sometimes because they are pressured to hire a particular star or to pay protection money to ensure the safety of a theater. Triads can range from small-time hustlers to very sophisticated business people.

What is intriguing about the Shaws, then, is that they navigated a spectacularly uncertain social and political terrain over the course of the twentieth century and yet were able to build a large and prosperous entertainment company that continually reinvented itself, sustaining its leadership under the most difficult of circumstances. Along the way, they expanded and transformed the scope of their enterprise, from theater exhibition to film production and distribution, then to real estate and amusement parks, later to television and music, and most recently to the Internet. They moved their headquarters from Shanghai to Singapore to Hong Kong, forged coproduction agreements throughout Asia, and pursued audiences around the globe. The Shaws began making movies during the silent era, but with the coming of sound they adapted to a variety of languages in response to changing audience tastes. They coped with the Shanghai film distribution cartel, the Japanese army, the Communist Party, the Nationalist Party, the British colonial regime, and triad societies. Through it all they sought to achieve control over production and consumption of popular entertainment, as well as every element of the business that falls between. In doing so the Shaws built a vertically integrated film studio unparalleled in the history of commercial Chinese entertainment, and they accomplished this with a centralized family enterprise. The youngest brother among the four, Run Run, increasingly took control of the company, providing crucial leadership during the expansion into Southeast Asia during the 1930s and again in the late 1950s, when he decisively shifted the company's center of operations to Hong Kong.

Shaw's decision to leave Singapore was no doubt motivated by a number of factors. First of all, his company was locked in competition with the Singapore-based Cathay theater chain, then under the leadership of the Cambridge-educated Dato Loke Wan Tho, whose family had made its fortune in the tin mining business in Malaysia. Loke was a patrician community leader and philanthropist with diverse business interests and a personal passion for ornithology and environmental conservation. Movies also fascinated him, but it's suggested that Loke fell into the business at the urging of his mother, who started buying movie theaters after Loke's father passed away when he was a child. On his return from college, Loke took charge of the family businesses and devoted substantial energy to expanding the Cathay chain throughout Southeast Asia. At its peak, Cathay matched the scale of the Shaws' theater circuit and studio operations, and in the 1950s Cathay's Yung Hua studio, a small but technologically sophisticated facility located in Hong Kong, started producing lavish Mandarin musicals and comedies with contemporary themes and settings. The British colony proved to be an ideal location for Mandarin-language film production, since many talented Shanghai filmmakers had sought refuge in the territory during the turbulent 1940s, creating a readily accessible pool of creative labor. Cathay's opulent feature films proved to be enormously popular with audiences in Southeast Asia and also, somewhat surprisingly, with theatergoers in Hong Kong, who previously showed a preference for Cantonese-language cinema.[6]

Taking stock of these trends, Shaw Brothers decided to expand its Hong Kong facilities, and Runde Shaw, the number-two brother, leased a large parcel of land at Clearwater Bay for that purpose. Yet Runde, an accountant who was nearing retirement, was cautious about breaking ground on the project, perhaps believing that market conditions were too unstable for such a substantial investment. Impatient with his brother's reticence, Run Run expressed concern that Cathay might outmaneuver the Shaws and pressed his brother to move forward urgently. If Loke's seemingly effortless rise as a movie mogul seemed suited to his patrician roots, Run Run was by comparison an aggressive Shanghai businessman who throughout his career seemed at his finest when rising to the challenge of a competitor. In 1958, he decided to move north, announcing with a flourish that Shaw Brothers was breaking ground in the construction of Movie Town, the largest, most technologically advanced studio in Asia.

For Shaw, not only did the shift to Hong Kong mark a new era in cinema style and technology, but also it represented a new conception of the Chinese cinema audience. During the post–World War II era, Hong Kong's population grew dramatically, with refugees from the mainland flooding into the British colony, doubling the population to more than two million in 1950, and swelling it yet another million over the ensuing decade. As the population exploded, the colony became an increasingly important theatrical market and a more diverse society as well, with close to one-fourth of the population hailing from parts of China that lay beyond the Cantonese-speaking Guangdong Province. Perhaps this diversity made Hong Kong more receptive to Mandarin movies, but the new trend was also stimulated by the emergence of Taiwan as an important nearby market, with its eleven million citizens now under the rule of Chiang Kai-shek, whose Nationalist Party declared Mandarin the official language of the new government. Though older Taiwanese struggled with the language, the younger generation used it at school, which in turn fueled the growth of the Mandarin movie audience.[7] By the middle of the 1950s, Hong Kong therefore offered numerous advantages for Chinese filmmakers. It was politically stable, had a wealth of émigré talent from the mainland, and had ready access to increasingly prosperous audiences in Hong Kong, Macau, and Taiwan. Although Southeast Asia remained an important theatrical market, Hong Kong now seemed an especially attractive location for the integrated film production facilities of Shaw Brothers.

Moreover, political changes on the Malay Peninsula introduced a note of uncertainty into the Shaws' Southeast Asian operations. After the British relinquished political authority to the Malaysian Federation in 1957, ethnic tensions erupted among Malays, Indians, and Chinese. Ethnic Malays, constituting more than 60 percent of the population, often expressed resentment about Chinese control of the film industry and pressed for more Malay-language film production. Such criticisms were most pointedly directed at Shaw Brothers and Cathay, which no doubt also felt threatened by calls to nationalize the film industry. The two companies furthermore must have been concerned about rumors that Singapore (75 percent Chinese) might secede from the Malaysian Federation, a development that would split asunder the peninsular theater chains they had worked so hard to establish.[8]

Such geopolitical shifts were also accompanied by generational changes. Rising levels of prosperity meant that many ethnic Chinese youngsters in Southeast Asia were now educated in schools where the language of instruction was either Mandarin or English, enhancing their interest in movies produced in those languages. And in 1965, when Singapore broke away from the Malaysian Federation, Mandarin and English emerged as the official languages of government and commerce in the new city-state, even though only 3 percent claimed Mandarin as their native tongue. Although most families would continue to speak different varieties of Chinese at home, the younger generation increasingly used these official languages at school and at work. When combined with the changes taking place in Hong Kong and Taiwan, such transformations in language policy made it possible for Shaw Brothers and Cathay to dream for the very first time of a transnational, pan-Chinese, Mandarin-language commercial cinema.

Yet the city where they could most easily ply their trade free from political and ethnic struggles was Hong Kong, which coincidently stood at the nexus of transnational Chinese commerce and migration. For Hong Kong was not only the destination of millions of migrants fleeing the mainland; it was also the point of departure for many more who would move to overseas locales. Hong Kong therefore remained an important site for commerce with the mainland and for sustaining ties to families and clans along the south China coast. Textile and apparel companies that fled Shanghai set in motion the territory's dramatic economic growth during the 1950s, as did financial institutions that lubricated the wheels of Chinese commerce around the globe. Hong Kong's star was rising, and Shaw no doubt sensed that it was time for his company to hitch a ride.

In 1961, Shaw Brothers celebrated the completion of Movie Town, a forty-six-acre compound of twelve sound stages, sixteen outdoor sets, a state-of-the art film laboratory, and a huge wardrobe of some eighty thousand costumes. With fifteen hundred contract employees working around the clock in eight-hour shifts, the studio produced an average of forty films per year during its peak in the 1960s, many of them low-budget comedies, melodramas, martial arts adventures, and contemporary action dramas. The centerpieces of the annual production schedule, however, were the lavish Mandarin productions released during school holiday periods. Like Hollywood studios during the 1930s, Shaw signed talent to multiyear deals, which helped the studio maintain control both on the set and at the payroll office.

Compliant actors were heavily promoted in publicity for Shaw feature films, and unruly ones were systematically marginalized. Many actors and craftspeople lived in a compound of modest dormitories and apartment houses on the studio lot. As if this didn't provide enough leverage over employees, Shaw also instituted training and recruitment programs, thereby ensuring a continuous supply of aspiring young talent that could keep the pressure on senior employees.

Over time, Shaw Brothers—whose corporate symbol emulated the shield of the Warner Bros. studio in the United States—established a tightly controlled circuit of cinemas with a dominant market share and a large-scale, integrated production facility to ensure a continuous flow of reliable product. It also ran a major distribution company that marketed and promoted Asian and American products. And it cultivated and monopolized key talent, allowing the company to manage audience demand for its movies and control costs. It adapted many of the managerial principles of the Hollywood studio system to the Asian context, but it also remained a familial Chinese enterprise in its style and objectives. As mentioned earlier, Shaw Brothers sought to control the land on which many of its theaters were situated, as well as controlling the surrounding real estate, where restaurants and shops catered to the growing foot traffic that cinema audiences generated. For one thing this provided a form of security for the theaters, and for another it gave the Shaws a stake in landownership, one of the most culturally attractive forms of investment in Chinese societies. In Singapore and Malaysia, comparatively inexpensive land prices encouraged the company to develop large shopping complexes that would come to constitute the major portion of the Shaw family's wealth. In fact, Run Run Shaw's two sons chose not follow their father to Hong Kong but instead stayed in Singapore with Runme, overseeing the family's vast theater and real estate holdings.

With family members situated in both locations, Shaw Brothers straddled the expanse of the Chinese film markets in Southeast Asia, from Taipei to Singapore to Penang, maintaining close control over every element of the its business empire. The Shaws used this control to dictate the quality, timing, and deployment of their films and also to dictate the context in which the films were screened. By comparison, Cathay had begun to falter in the early 1960s, and in 1964 the studio was dealt a devastating blow when Loke Wan Tho perished in a plane crash during his return to Singapore from the Asian Film Awards ceremony in Taipei. The company soon went into a tailspin, and several years later Loke's family decided to shut down the Hong

Kong studio and refocus their attention on the exhibition business, leaving the field of Chinese cinema production largely in the hands of Shaw and a few independent studios.

The golden age of Shaw Brothers ran from the mid-1950s through the early 1970s, and among its film production the studio turned out a healthy assortment of classics, although audiences also recall the many chintzy and self-consciously calculating feature films that checkered the studio's reputation, especially after competition with Cathay began to wane. Moreover, television would change Shaw Brothers forever, when Run Run shifted his resources and energies to the new medium. In 1967, Shaw became one of the first investors in TVB, a channel that would take the colony by storm within only a few years. During that time Shaw systematically grew his ownership stake until he gained effective control of Hong Kong's leading television station in the late 1970s. "Shaw made it clear that he thought film was a sunset industry," says one Hong Kong media executive who witnessed the transition. "He thought TV would make more money and dominate the scene for a longer time."

The transition to a new medium marked a significant change of orientation for the Shaws. Since the 1920s, the brothers had operated a transnational enterprise that grew even more international after World War II, when Chinese film studios lost access to mainland markets and therefore focused their attention on overseas communities. Yet even though these migrant audiences shared a cultural heritage, their diverse dialects and different social circumstances forced the company to adjust its strategies for each particular market. Kuala Lumpur, for example, was a very different market from Taipei and different as well from Hong Kong. Television, however, encouraged Run Run Shaw to recalibrate his media enterprise, focusing exclusively on the local Hong Kong market. This local emphasis was further solidified by the singularity of the British colony as the only territory that had a substantial Chinese audience and was open to commercial television investment. In Taiwan, Singapore, Malaysia, and elsewhere, television was then controlled by the government, and in mainland China, TV would not emerge as a popular medium until the 1980s and remains to this day an enterprise of the state. Consequently, Hong Kong provided Shaw's only chance to make the jump to television. In making the change, he narrowed attention to a single territory, focused exclusively on Cantonese-language production, and adapted his organization to an advertising-based mass medium. Although the logic of accumulation encouraged Shaw Brothers' film enterprises to expand transnationally and ultimately to establish its production center in Hong Kong, the government-regulated conditions of television broadcasting would securely anchor the company to the local market.

Despite this dramatic transition, Run Run seemed confident that Hong Kong would continue to thrive as a site of Chinese media and popular culture. Located on the south coast of China at the mouth of the Pearl River, the city had for decades been an entrepôt for commerce between Europe and Guangdong Province. Yet Hong Kong itself was not the center of economic or cultural activity in southern China. One hundred miles inland, the city of Guangzhou (Canton) was for centuries the main nexus of a lucrative network of agricultural and cottage manufacturing industries. It was also the cultural and intellectual capital of Cantonese society. In the mid-1800s, Hong Kong by comparison was a sparsely populated stretch of rocky headlands that was seized by British traders in order to establish a base for their commercial operations in East Asia. Most Chinese who traveled to the colony in search of jobs or commercial opportunities maintained their ties to a homeland elsewhere in China.

Cataclysmic events of the twentieth century, however, would forever alter the character of Britain's most distant imperial outpost. During World War II, the Chinese civil war, and resulting periods of economic misfortune, hundreds of thousands of people of all political stripes sought sanctuary in the colony. Most imagined the city as a temporary home, seeing their fortunes as ultimately tied to the villages where they had grown up and where their ancestors had lived for centuries. Yet the political tides of the modern era forced many to remain in the territory, where they found work, started businesses, and raised families. A city of little more than a million in 1949, Hong Kong tripled in population before Cold War tensions and government regulations began to restrict the flow of newcomers during the 1960s. Yet despite these political constraints and because of the city's central location in the Chinese diaspora, Hong Kong prospered as a nexus for financial and trade relations between mainland China and the rest of the world, serving as the conduit for well over two-thirds of China's international trade and investment during the last four decades of the twentieth century. Just as important, Hong Kong became a global banking and finance center for Chinese enterprises in such cities as London, Bangkok, and Vancouver. The city's growing wealth and influence during the 1960s and 1970s in turn fostered its status as a regional trade and finance center for all of East Asia, making it a central node in a vast and complex field of economic flows and transactions.[9]

Hong Kong's changing circumstances were further influenced by migrations of cultural institutions and creative talent. Prior to World War II, local performers and audiences looked to Guangzhou for leadership in matters of art and culture, with Cantonese opera serving as one of the most popular forms of entertainment. During the 1930s, nascent film studios happily appropriated the songs, narratives, and performance styles of the operatic art form. Indeed, many filmmakers simply recorded and exhibited opera performances via the new cinema technology. During this formative period, Guangzhou therefore reigned as both the center of Cantonese opera *and* Cantonese film production. But when military and political strife disrupted cultural activities on the mainland, many creative personnel sought refuge in Hong Kong. The Japanese invasion and the ensuing Chinese civil war also induced filmmakers and artists from Shanghai to flee south to Hong Kong, which offered sanctuary to members of these creative communities and thus emerged during the postwar period with a strong repertoire of creative talent that would continue to grow as the media industries prospered.[10]

Though the territory's status was on the ascent, its visibility on screen was often eclipsed by influences from the mainland and by attention to émigré audiences. Refugee filmmakers from Shanghai and Guangzhou often featured themes, stars, and topics that appealed to diasporic and pan-Chinese theatergoers, and some critics contend that, as a result, Chinese movies diminished in popularity among younger audiences in Hong Kong. For during the 1960s, immigrants were beginning to accept that their stay in Hong Kong might be longer than they had expected, and many were beginning to enjoy unrivaled prosperity. As incomes rose, so did the size of families, and young people came to constitute a larger percentage of the population. The youth culture that subsequently emerged in Hong Kong exhibited distinctive tastes, values, and life experiences. Many young people had absolutely no contact with life on the mainland and therefore did not share their parents' nostalgia for home. This cultural amnesia was compounded by the colonial school system's attempt to neutralize political tensions between the pro- and anti-Communist factions of Hong Kong society by eliminating twentieth-century Chinese history and civics from the school curriculum. Although the refugee generation of parents and grandparents still had their attention fixed on the fortunes of mainland society and politics, members of the younger generation harbored no such proclivities.[11] In many cases, this generation was more experienced with Western popular culture than with traditional Chinese culture and politics. Consequently, Hollywood movies and American music became quite popular in Hong Kong during the 1960s.

Yet even though young people embraced these cultural influences, they also seemed to be searching for cultural forms that were more proximate, more relevant to their everyday experience.[12]

It was at this juncture that local television was introduced to Hong Kong, and, consequently, its popularity grew with fantastic speed. By 1973, only six years after TVB took to the airwaves, the territory's first broadcast television service was reaching some 80 percent of Hong Kong homes. Wildly popular, TVB quickly became the leading advertising medium, reportedly attracting more than 50 percent of total ad revenues for the territory. TVB's dominant position allowed Run Run Shaw to adapt many of the same strategies he used in the film business. By monopolizing talent and distribution and by concentrating production at its studio compound in Clearwater Bay, TVB emerged as an unparalleled force in Hong Kong media. Although many criticized Shaw's tactics, TVB was a hotbed of creative endeavor during the early years of the medium. As former producer Cheuk Pak-tong points out, television was at the center of Hong Kong's "golden age" of popular culture during the 1970s and 1980s, functioning as a magnet for writers, actors, directors, and talent from all spheres of creative life.[13] It served as both a training ground for a new generation of locally born talent and a stepping stone for those who would move on from television to creative endeavors in film, music, publishing, and other media.[14] Although Shaw attenuated the geographical scope of his media operations during the television era, he retained many of the managerial principles that had guided the success of Shaw Brothers' movie empire, holding sway over an integrated production facility, monopolizing key talent, and controlling the circuits of distribution and exhibition.

Shaw Brothers, like its counterparts in Hollywood, was built on principles of rationalization, vertical integration, and star promotion. Unlike Hollywood, however, the Shaws never extended the circle of managerial control far beyond a small group of family members and never had access to a large and stable domestic market. The latter characteristic was perhaps the reason that in 1967 Run Run Shaw seemed so intrigued by the prospect of making a radical shift to the new medium of television. For it not only allowed him to focus on a single domestic audience; it also assured him a stable, dominant position in the market, because TVB had a first-mover advantage, a highly developed production infrastructure, and a wealth of talented people, most of them working under long-term contract. Rather than juggling the politics of Malaysian nationalism, Taiwanese authoritarianism, and Singaporean social engineering, Shaw could focus his attention on the

Broadcasting brought prosperity and organizational expansion to Run Run Shaw's enterprises. In the 1980s, at the height of TVB's prosperity in local broadcasting, Shaw House became more corporate in appearance and in practice. Author photo.

relatively stable, affluent, and rapidly growing audience for Cantonese-language television in Hong Kong. Although local commercial television proved dramatically different from the business of transnational cinema, Shaw throughout his career consistently pursued production economies, market hegemony, and workforce discipline, regardless of the medium. Deftly adapting to shifting conditions, he repeatedly refigured the geography his operations, thereby sustaining the profitability of Shaw Brothers' core entertainment enterprises despite dramatic social, cultural, and political changes throughout the twentieth century. Shaw's pessimism about the future of the Chinese film industry turned out to be premature, however. As we shall see, his transition to television opened the door for a new generation of filmmakers and a new ensemble of movie industry practices.

2 Independent Studios and the Golden Age of Hong Kong Cinema

The folklore of Chinese capitalism is replete with heartbreaking tales of those who work for a family enterprise and, despite their achievements and dedication, can never rise to the innermost circle of authority because they aren't members of the family that owns the business. Many stay on despite their frustration, but others leave to begin companies of their own, often in the same industry. Ironically, one reason that the patriarchs of Chinese enterprise rarely invite nonfamily staff members into the inner circle hinges on their suspicions that one day their trusted employee might depart, taking not only his or her expertise but also company secrets, perhaps even becoming a competitor. So goes the story of Raymond Chow and Leonard Ho, two of Run Run Shaw's top lieutenants, who eventually struck out on their own to establish Golden Harvest.

Their success story began at an unlikely moment in 1970, when the commercial Chinese movie industry was in the depths of one of its worst slumps. Cantonese film production in Hong Kong had ground to a halt, Mandarin moviemakers were complaining about competition from television, and the famous Cathay studio, Shaw Brothers' chief competitor, was closing down its production facility. Yet Ho and Chow believed that these setbacks created an opening for them, and they seized the opportunity to purchase the Cathay studio at a bargain price, furthermore negotiating a distribution deal that guaranteed access to theater screens of the Cathay cinema circuit, both in Hong Kong and throughout Southeast Asia. Much smaller than Shaw's Movie Town, the fledgling Golden Harvest studio, with its two soundstages, was wedged into a steep valley on Hammer Hill Road, leaving little room for expansion. Consequently, Chow and Ho forged innovative strategies for their new enterprise, involving a more moderate tempo of in-house production, more location shooting, and more collaboration with independent filmmakers. From such modest beginnings, Golden Harvest rose to become an industry powerhouse that would not only transform the look of Chinese movies but also dramatically alter the industry's production and distribution practices.

Key to Golden Harvest's success was a distinctive new mode of flexible production. As we shall see, the company played an important role as both financier and distributor of independent film projects, but it was cautious about the scale of its operation, focusing on production first and then expanding into distribution and exhibition. The company furthermore was the first Chinese company to make a major play in Hollywood, a move that solidified relations with major U.S. studios and paved the way for Western investment in Hong Kong productions. By the end of the 1970s, Golden Harvest was the dominant force in Chinese commercial cinema, not only as a producer and regional distributor, but also as a key conduit for independent film financing. If Run Run Shaw's enterprises benefited from his command of the managerial principles of the 1930s Hollywood studio system, then Raymond Chow's benefited from his awareness of American studio practices during the 1950s and 1960s, when Hollywood moviemakers pioneered new modes of disintegrated production.

Golden Harvest was not alone in embracing independent producers. Other theater chains and distributors did so too, some with notable success, as we shall see in the second half of this chapter. The Golden Princess theater circuit and its key supplier, Cinema City, forged a strategic alliance that fashioned films aimed specifically at the Hong Kong audience, despite Cinema City's reliance on overseas distribution to fund the greater part of its productions. Yet, interestingly, the company's resolute focus on local tastes proved to be a boon in its overseas markets as well, setting in place a system of financing that would fuel Hong Kong's surprising emergence as the world's second largest exporter of feature films.

When Golden Harvest opened for business in 1970, its first few films were rather unremarkable sword-fighting dramas, but the following year Chow and Ho struck gold when they signed Bruce Lee, a young Chinese-American performer who, after several years in Hollywood, left the United States in frustration, convinced that he would never play a leading role in American film or television.[1] When he arrived in Hong Kong, Shaw Brothers initially offered Lee its standard long-term contract, but Lee declined, hoping to sign with a studio that would allow him more creative control. As former executives at Shaw Brothers, Ho and Chow understood only too well Lee's aversion to the Movie Town star system, so they offered him both creative freedom and profit participation. Lee seized the opportunity, collaborating with Golden Harvest on four films that would prove to be among the most profitable in the history of cinema. Lee's innovations, in retrospect, seem relatively modest, for he tapped traditional martial arts themes and stylistic elements, recasting them in contemporary contexts with him as the protagonist. Yet the movies resonated with audiences, with Lee coming to symbolize an alternative action hero whose acrobatic screen performances evoked a visceral response from viewers around the world. For example, African Americans in the United States were especially receptive to Lee's portrayal of heroes who stoically endured the indignities of racial or social prejudice only to explode in an elaborately choreographed moment of retribution. Lee not only played the hero on screen; he also was influential in choreographing the action and positioning the camera to maximize the visual impact of his performances. Bruce Lee movies were some of the first Chinese films to draw significant revenues at theaters outside the Asian market, and global returns on *The Big Boss* have been estimated at more than five hundred times the initial production budget of $386,500, a multiple that continues to grow with each passing year.

Initially, Shaw Brothers tried to respond to Lee's popularity by promoting its own stars in similar roles, but none could compete with the on-screen charisma of the "little dragon." It is unclear whether Shaw Brothers' awkward handling of this new trend was due to complacency or to Run Run's growing fascination with television. Regardless, Chow and Ho seemed to be riding an escalator of success when each release drew enthusiastic responses from audiences, distributors, and theater owners. Consequently, Lee's untimely death in 1973 dealt a severe blow to the fledgling studio. Many wondered at the time if Golden Harvest could survive the loss or if the studio would turn out to be a one-trick pony.

Yet shortly thereafter, Chow and Ho scored another coup when they lured one of TVB's top comedians to the world of cinema. As part of the deal, Chow agreed to set Michael Hui up as an independent producer, offering him and his two brothers the opportunity to produce a series of comedy features. Comparing the movie deal with his restrictive contract at TVB, Hui took the jump, setting an example for other topflight talent who learned their craft and established their reputations at TVB during the 1970s and '80s, only to migrate to feature films when the chance arose. Hui, who graduated from the Chinese University of Hong Kong with a master's degree in sociology, produced a string of genre-bending social comedies that evoke comparison to the work of Jacques Tati, Peter Sellers, and Groucho Marx. The movies not only proved popular in Hong Kong but also scored strongly in overseas markets, especially Japan. Hui's transnational appeal was no

Action star Bruce Lee and CEO Raymond Chow during the early 1970s, when Lee's fantastically profitable kung fu movies helped to establish Golden Harvest as the leading studio in Hong Kong. Courtesy Golden Harvest Entertainment.

doubt attributable to his brilliant physical comedy, featuring a series of impeccably timed gags. Film historian Law Kar characterizes Hui's success best when he flatly asserts, "Michael Hui is to comedy what Bruce Lee is to the martial arts: they both reign supreme."[2]

Besides his comedic genius, Hui was also renowned for playing an important role in reviving Cantonese-language cinema and most especially for showcasing the Hong Kong variety of cosmopolitan Cantonese, helping to make it a new standard for the rebounding film industry. Although successful overseas, Hui's movies primarily focused on the changing nature of everyday life in Hong Kong. As such, his narratives often invert traditional character roles for comedic effect. In his early films, such as *The Private Eyes* (1976) and *Security Unlimited* (1981), Hui plays a mean-spirited, patriarchal boss who serves himself rather than his employees or his community. While navigating the tensions of modern city life, Hui's character abandons Confucian morals in a single-minded pursuit of sex, fame, fortune, and modern conveniences. Inevitably, the character's aspirations are dashed within the course of the narrative, which allows Hui to close the film with a comic moment of humility, pointing to the character's potential for redemption. Yet redemption is characterized not as a balance struck between East and West or between tradition and modernity but rather as a modern state of self-awareness. Hui's characters experience redemption not by simply reconnecting to a Chinese heritage or by blindly embracing Western modernity but rather by traversing the everyday pitfalls posed both by tradition *and* modernity. In the end, the character is an archetypal Hong Konger—a comedic representation of the dilemmas presented by living between cultures.

Film critic Jenny Lau argues that this ambivalence marked a break from Cantonese cinema of the 1950s and 1960s. "In the previous era, theater audiences, many members of whom were refugees from China, were generally China-centered. That is, they identified themselves more with the (romanticized) China than with Hong Kong and were quite willing to position Hong Kong as the 'Other.'"[3] In these earlier films, characters brushed up against greed and exploitation in Hong Kong, making them yearn for the social virtues of the life they left behind in the mainland. Lau suggests that the popularity of Hui's films signaled a shift in audience attitudes, since his characters don't find solace in the sacred virtues of traditional China. These audiences were beginning to see the territory as home and expressed enthusiasm about movies that explored the troublesome but often rewarding aspects of Hong Kong life.

Those actors and directors who followed Hui in making a career transition from Hong Kong television to film also addressed their work primarily to local audiences rather than to regional Cantonese or pan-Chinese audiences. This isn't to suggest that all Chinese content or references were emptied out of the films but rather to indicate the emergence of a distinctive new film style situated at the intersection of local, regional, and global flows. In the eyes of locally born audiences, Chineseness and Cantoneseness were no longer privileged points of reference. Young people—most of them educated in a British colonial school system—were receptive to movies, music, and television shows from abroad, but they were most enthusiastic about local popular culture that reflected on the everyday demands of life in a rapidly modernizing city. And perhaps somewhat unexpectedly, this local popular culture also proved fascinating to audiences in overseas Chinese communities, which were also experiencing a slowing of immigration and the emergence of hybrid identities. These overseas audiences, like their counterparts in Hong Kong, had grown up in diasporic communities, confronting new and complex identity issues that could no longer be salved by traditional Chinese melodramas or opera films. Even Cathay's comedies and musicals of the 1950s, with their modern settings and contemporary flair, would commonly resolve narrative conflicts with reference to traditional Chinese values. Michael Hui's films, however, marked a departure from such conventional homilies, participating in an ongoing transformation of popular cinema. These changes can be traced back to the 1960s, as film locations became more modern and more opulent, narrative more playful and irreverent, and visual style more fluid and more cinematic. By the mid-1970s, the generational shift began to coalesce as what would eventually be called New Wave.[4]

As for Golden Harvest, its fortunes blossomed even further in 1978, when it released *Drunken Master,* a Jackie Chan film blending martial arts, melodrama, and comedy. Playing the legendary folk hero Wong Fei-hung, Chan assumes the role of a young ne'er-do-well whose father packs him off to live with an uncle, who teaches an arcane martial art known as drunken boxing. Chan's unruly character ultimately redeems himself in the eyes of his family when he masters this traditional fighting style and subdues the forces of evil. Yet along the way, Chan adds contemporary humor and irreverence to a role that had previously been performed with conspicuous veneration. In many ways, the story mirrors Chan's own biography. Trained from a young age in a Peking Opera school, the particular genius of his on-camera performance style is based on his thorough knowledge of traditional art forms, which he then adapts to roles that feature him coping with modern job responsibilities, familial obligations, and generational tensions. Over time, Chan honed his character portrayals to appeal to all family members, making his films the flagship offering of the Golden Harvest studio and turning him into the biggest movie star outside Hollywood—by some measures the most popular film star in the world. For close to two decades, the studio's Chinese New Year release starred Jackie Chan in lavish productions underwritten by the biggest film budgets of the year.

The films of Lee, Hui, and Chan were the locomotives that pulled Golden Harvest along the tracks toward industry dominance, but many other films with much smaller budgets proved profitable as well. Working with a small staff, production chief Leonard Ho cultivated relationships with a growing number of independent producers in Hong Kong, and each year he allocated resources according to seasonal changes in the market. Jackie Chan productions for the Chinese New Year holidays were always a top priority, but Ho also lavished resources on films that were targeted at other holiday periods, and he had a deft appreciation for smaller, more experimental projects that might prove to be sleeper successes during the off-peak parts of the annual release schedule.

Accordingly, Ho deserves much of the credit for nurturing both the cre-

Jackie Chan with Leonard Ho (right), who was chief of production at Golden Harvest and executive director of most of Chan's classic hits. Ho's death in 1997 was seen as a transitional moment for the studio and for the Chinese movie industry as a whole. Courtesy Golden Harvest Entertainment.

ative and the commercial success of Golden Harvest films, but the company's ability to sustain its leadership role for over three decades was also attributable to the sophisticated distribution and exhibition infrastructure that Raymond Chow put into place. Drawing on the windfall from Bruce Lee movies, the company established a distribution unit in 1973, and one year later it began to piece together a local theater circuit called Golden Films. Peter Tam, who over the course of two decades rose to take charge of the exhibition business, recalls that by 1978 the company was operating seven cinemas in Hong Kong. "We also lined up thirty to thirty-five other independent theaters and would make a one-year agreement that gave us booking rights over their screens in exchange for a revenue split, which came out roughly to fifty-fifty. On normal weeks it would start fifty-fifty and go down 5 percent a week. So the second week they got 55 percent and we got 45 percent, and so on. But we were so strong that we usually could negotiate a deal for five blockbuster play dates that would start at a split of sixty-five and thirty-five. These would be the event films like Chinese New

Year or Christmas." Unlike Shaw or Cathay cinemas, which had direct ownership, the Golden Harvest theater chain in Hong Kong was largely a product of distribution agreements; nevertheless, this satisfied Chow, because it assured his films access to screens and gave him a share of the box office without forcing his company to make expensive real estate investments. Even the seven flagship cinemas operated by the company were leased facilities, thus avoiding entanglements with pricey commercial property in Hong Kong.

In Southeast Asia, it was a different story, however. "In Hong Kong we never bought any land," recalls Peter Tam, "but in Singapore we did. We built a freestanding multiplex and another one in a shopping mall. In Malaysia, we went into partnership with [the] Kwok family and [managed the] operations in return for a 40 percent interest in the cinemas, and some of these cinemas included the land." And in markets where Golden Harvest didn't manage a chain of theaters, such as in Taiwan, it set up distribution offices, which handled a broad range of titles from Chinese and Hollywood filmmakers. With Hollywood films, the company either bought the regional rights to particular films or developed long-term agreements with specific studios. For more than a decade, the company served as the regional representative for United International Pictures (UIP), a joint-venture company that handled overseas distribution for Universal, MGM, Paramount, and United Artists. This association with Hollywood majors not only gave Golden Harvest access to valuable feature films for its own theaters, but when those films were paired with blockbusters from Bruce Lee, Michael Hui, and Jackie Chan, it also gave the company enough clout to cut favorable revenue splits with local exhibitors.

Such was Golden Harvest's market power during its heyday that Chow felt confident enough to embark on a series of Hollywood productions beginning in 1975, when he opened an office in Los Angeles, focusing on grade-B film projects. Chow wanted to avoid gambling on big-budget movies, since losses from a single flop could jeopardize the overall fortunes of Golden Harvest. The company nevertheless achieved some notable successes. In 1981, *Cannonball Run*, budgeted at $16 million, grossed $168 million worldwide, and *Teenage Mutant Ninja Turtles*, a $10 million venture, grossed $135 million in North America in 1990 and probably an equal amount internationally.[5]

As the first and only Hong Kong studio producing films in the United States, Golden Harvest's strategy seemed to have three objectives: First, it wanted to promote some of its own stars, especially Jackie Chan, who made his first appearance on the Hollywood screen in *Cannonball Run* as a supporting actor. Second, it wanted to diversify into the American market for a hedge against potential reversals in Asia but also to enhance its status as a regional distributor. With its 1976 purchase of Panasia, Golden Harvest eclipsed Shaw Brothers and Cathay as the most important distributor of Hollywood product in the region. Third, the company's California ventures helped to establish relationships with U.S. investors, who over time would begin to provide financing for Chinese films.

Indeed, Raymond Chow turned his company into a financing conduit for many Hong Kong productions, which proved quite lucrative, according to one source familiar with Golden Harvest operations. For example, on the one hand the company would raise $1 million from U.S. investors, while on the other hand it would negotiate with an independent producer to make a movie for $600,000 to $800,000. Pocketing the difference, Golden Harvest would pay the producer a flat fee for all rights to the film, which it would then distribute and exhibit, both in Hong Kong and overseas. "They made money at each link in the chain," says one Hong Kong source. "They made money on financing, production, [and] licensing, and they made money showing the movie in their theaters. The original investors didn't make all that much money, and they certainly didn't see all the money that was being made. But what kept [Golden Harvest] going was that they always gave the investor a good movie. They didn't hold back or run off with the money or fail to deliver." And since Golden Harvest controlled publicity, release schedules, and cinemas throughout the region, the investors had a fairly high chance of enjoying a solid return. Indeed, given the company's brisk production schedules of three to six months, an investor could earn a 10 percent profit in a very short time. This was attractive to foreign investors, but it was less attractive to local investors, since during the city's boom cycles Hong Kong capitalists have been accustomed to making two to four times as much.

Thus, Golden Harvest successfully exploited its Hollywood connections to become gatekeeper for the flow of foreign capital into the Hong Kong industry. "Golden Harvest always got the lion's share, and they took money right off the top," says the same source, "but the other side of it is that if they weren't making all this money, there wouldn't have been any money to finance Chinese movies." Independent producer Peter Tsi agrees. "I've talked to a lot of venture capital people and merchant bankers about the film business in Hong Kong," he says. "For years they said that they didn't have enough information about our industry. Sure, a lot of them knew about Golden Harvest, but the other studios and the independents? Nothing." And without that knowledge, notes Tsi, they were reluctant to invest. As a known quantity, Golden Harvest was the exception, providing a gateway for international capital flows into the local industry.

Raymond Chow also used his considerable influence over financing and distribution to extract favorable terms from independent producers and to cajole directors to accept his staff's suggestions regarding casting, scripting, and editing. Some producers and directors felt the contractual terms were unfair; others simply didn't care. They just wanted to make movies, and if the budget was big enough to make a film they liked, then they were happy to tailor it to order. Interestingly, with far less overhead than Shaw Brothers, Golden Harvest was able to exercise substantial control over creative decision making. The company never established an elaborate studio, never maintained a large staff, and never built company housing. It could scale production to meet the demands of the market, cutting back on contracts with independents during a market downturn and supplementing its local productions with Hollywood titles during periods of short supply. In other words, its distribution and exhibition divisions always had enough new feature titles to feed the theater chain, but the company was not obligated to maintain a large production organization in order to ensure supply. It could produce what it desired and subcontract the rest. The public, the producers, and even the investors didn't know exactly how lucrative the business was, for Chow always kept his own counsel regarding the company's financial health. Figures released to the public showed only a small part of the picture, and the circulation of knowledge within the company was carefully controlled. Unlike Shaw, Chow didn't build a sprawling studio empire, but he did help to usher in the era of independents, an era that many refer to as the golden age of Hong Kong cinema, when dozens of producers and directors fundamentally altered the themes and stylistic conventions of commercial Chinese cinema. Yet Golden Harvest wasn't the only company spurring this transformation. Another major theater circuit played an important role as well.

The signature postcard of Hong Kong is a photograph of the financial district skyline soaring boldly above the bustling harbor, providing a striking contrast to a background of lush green mountains that rise inexorably toward Victoria Peak. At the center of this panorama, I. M. Pei's Bank of China slices dramatically skyward like a huge glass and granite knife. To its left, Steven Valentine's Hong Kong Convention Center presses into the harbor, its roof spreading like the wings of a gigantic seagull taking flight. For decades, architects from around the world have come to Hong Kong to ply their trade in this dramatic setting, making the skyline appear relatively indifferent to the city's setting on the coast of China. As one takes in this stunning vista from the waterfront promenade on the Kowloon Peninsula, few hints of the British colonial heritage remain, since Hong Kong has relentlessly reinvented itself, sweeping aside traces of the past as it goes. Located on some of the world's most expensive real estate, the city appears to have little time for nostalgia. Other than Victoria Peak—named in honor of the nineteenth-century British monarch—a visitor is hard pressed to detect anything distinctly British or, for that matter, Chinese about the skyline. Instead, Hong Kong's financial district presents itself to the harbor and to the outside world as a global metropolis.

Yet taking in this vista on the Kowloon waterfront promenade, one can turn about and walk only a few blocks north into a very different urban landscape. Here, a pantheon of glittering neon hovers above the raucous commotion on Nathan Road. If the skyline on the island side of the harbor seems barely distinguishable from other global financial centers, then Nathan Road, with its vibrant mix of Chinglish neon, illuminates Hong Kong's distinctive hybridity. As the main artery of the Kowloon Peninsula—a finger of land reaching out from the mainland toward Hong Kong Island—Nathan Road is the connecting link between residential and commercial sections of the city, as well as a geographical link between north and south and a cultural link between East and West. As you move away from the harbor, the side streets abound with Chinese shops, street markets, nightclubs, and restaurants. This area is also home to many of Hong Kong's leading movie companies, including Golden Harvest and China Star.

If you hop on a bus and keep traveling north toward the nine mountain peaks, or "nine dragons" (*kow loon* in Cantonese), you come to neighborhoods made up of the government housing estates that replaced the shantytowns that sprang up on the hillsides of the city during waves of immigration from the mainland. Catastrophic fires swept through two large settlements in 1953, leaving seventy-four thousand people homeless and prompting the colonial government to shed its laissez faire economic posture long enough to embark on a public housing initiative that over time would provide low-rent apartments to more than 40 percent of the territory's population. The policy has not only offered a shield against health and safety risks; it also set the stage for rising prosperity by guaranteeing widespread access to a modest middle-class standard of living. These densely populated neighborhoods north of the harbor fan out from the Kowloon Peninsula, heading east toward the old Kai Tak airport and west toward factories, warehouses, and shipping facilities that have fostered much of the city's economic development. Consequently, Nathan Road gathers and conveys traffic up and down the peninsula toward the harbor and the city center, making it one of the most heavily traveled urban thoroughfares in the world.

Before the construction of a subway system during the 1980s, tens of thousands of people commuted daily on this route, riding buses operated by the Kowloon Motor Bus Company. Many headed to a ferry terminal at the tip of the Kowloon Peninsula, where every few minutes a boat departed for Hong Kong Island, providing the primary transportation link across the harbor. As the territory flourished, so too did KMB, which was owned by Kowloon Development, one of the largest real estate firms in the territory. Under the leadership of Lawrence Louey, the company parlayed its transportation franchise into a lucrative set of strategic real estate investments along its major bus routes, including a chain of movie theaters, known as the Golden Princess circuit. From a purely economic standpoint, the Golden Princess circuit was one of the more modest investments that the firm made, but from a cultural perspective, this chain of theaters would rise to prominence during the 1980s as one of the leading entertainment destinations in the territory. Most theaters at that time featured a single screen, usually accommodating between one thousand and two thousand people. Except for the most popular films, titles changed frequently as theaters strove to entice return visits from regular clients. Thus, the demand for fresh film titles was consistently strong, requiring theater chains like Golden Princess to cultivate prolific and dependable suppliers. Yet having witnessed the decline of Shaw Brothers and Cathay during the 1960s and early 1970s, Louey was reluctant to launch a fully integrated studio of his own, so he turned to independent production companies for all of his Chinese movies.

Most prominent among Golden Princess's suppliers was Cinema City, a company founded in 1980 by film veterans Karl Maka, Dean Shek, and Raymond Wong. Like Golden Harvest, the fledgling company drew much of its young talent from the television broadcasting companies in Hong Kong, and its roster of filmmakers would come to include some of the biggest names in Hong Kong cinema, including directors Sammo Hung, John Woo, Tsui Hark, and Ringo Lam. Cinema City's house style involved a very calculated form of filmmaking, whereby Maka would draw together his collaborators for extended brainstorming sessions that lasted into the wee hours of the morning. Wong Kar-wai, then a young writer, remembers these sessions as especially grueling, saying that Maka "was a big believer in statistics, and everything had to be decided collectively. He had a room in an apartment, and all the seven heads of Cinema City [Maka, Shek, and Wong, plus Eric Tsang, Tsui Hark, Nansun Shi, and Teddy Robin Kwan] would meet there. We called them the Gang of Seven." They had a checklist of narrative and stylistic elements for each film and a clear sense of how they should be deployed throughout the movie.[6]

Clifton Ko, another writer-director, recalls, "We would divide the film into nine reels—each one ten minutes long—and then map out plot developments so that the first reel would provide an attention-grabbing opening, the fourth an important twist in the plot, the seventh a climax of some sort, and the ninth a resolution that would send the audience home happy." Within each reel, writers were encouraged to include a prescribed number of comedic or dramatic elements, as well as stunts and other gimmicks. One of the things that made Cinema City stand out during its prime was that it invested significant energy during the planning stage, unlike other independent production companies, which would often begin with a very vague story idea, developing the narrative as filming progressed. In all cases, however, it was common for Hong Kong filmmakers to plan in terms of ten-minute reels and to develop the elements within each reel in a collaborative fashion.

As David Bordwell rightly points out, collaborative scripting organized around the ten-minute reel evolved as a convention that allowed filmmakers to begin with overarching themes while leaving each segment open to improvisation.[7] With action films this made sense, since stunt sequences were often choreographed by a team of performers, such as Jackie Chan, Sammo Hung, and Lau Kar-leung, who had been trained in Chinese opera schools. Each chase scene or fight sequence might therefore be plotted out as a choreographed sequence of movements with an eye toward adapting the performance to available resources and immediate constraints at the shooting location. For example, a restaurant kitchen might lend itself to an elaborate food fight, featuring utensils and animal carcasses as impromptu weapons. Under these conditions, improvisation and teamwork were an outcome of the shooting circumstances and the professional backgrounds of the talent. Comedies used a similar logic of plotting by ten-minute reels, yet here the filmmakers were most likely influenced by their formative experiences in television work, in which sketch comedy sequences are played out in between commercial breaks.

With a careful eye on ticket sales, Karl Maka and his cohort fashioned a number of wildly popular features that drew enthusiastic audiences to the Golden Princess theaters throughout the 1980s. Perhaps most popular was *Aces Go Places*, a film that proved to be a huge sensation when first released in 1982. Four sequels turned it into the signature brand of Cinema City, with the principal roles played by Maka, Sylvia Chang, and Sam Hui, who had split from his brother, Michael, to pursue a very successful solo career. Besides being one of the top performers on the Cantopop music scene, Sam was a handsome, beguiling lead actor who played off Chang's youthful intensity and Maka's broad physical comedy. Each *Aces* release revolves around an intricately plotted caper involving jewel thievery, espionage, or kidnapping. Besides star performances and a madcap rhythm that mirrored the pandemonium of urban Hong Kong, the films traded on their familiarity with Hollywood movies, riffing on such films as *Rambo*, the James Bond series, and *Raiders of the Lost Ark*. Indeed, the first sequel features James Bond and Oddjob look-alikes playing the heavies in a kidnapping-espionage caper, with Peter Graves, of TV's *Mission Impossible*, performing an amusing cameo appearance to boot. The whimsical and sometimes cheesy special effects add to the ironic tone, making the films a string of in-jokes and winking references to the hybrid quality of popular culture in Hong Kong. Although Cinema City films were some of the most commercially calculating productions of the era, they nevertheless participated in a broader cultural discussion that was characterized by reflexive irony.

Directors of the 1980s have sometimes been referred to as the Hong Kong New Wave, in part because some of them self-consciously experimented with cinematic style and in part because many of them studied in the West and drew on influences from afar. Although the films lack stylistic coherence, the name quite correctly suggests that this generation departed from many of the conventions of the studio era. Whereas Shaw Brothers and Cathay were fully integrated operations that maintained an expansive capital infrastructure and a large production staff, the New Wave production houses were generally small independents that relied largely on a casual workforce. Where the studios pursued disasporic Chinese audiences across national boundaries, these producers focused first on feeding the local cinema circuit. Where the studios became renowned for formulaic filmmaking, the New Wave group earned its name no doubt because, in the midst of a very cash-conscious industry, Hong Kong producers found the resources for off-beat projects by directors such as Ann Hui, Tsui Hark, and Patrick Tam. Moreover, some of the most commercial films of this period exhibited traces of an improvisational exuberance lacking in films of the studio era.

What perhaps made the New Wave new was that demand for independently produced films was high, audiences were enthusiastic, and local society was in a dynamic stage of identity formation. For Hong Kong cinema of the 1970s and 1980s was a site in which residents of the territory began to imagine themselves as part of a distinctive social and historical formation.

Once or twice a month, the average Hong Kong citizen attended the movies in the company of one thousand to two thousand others, the vast majority of whom he or she would neither recognize nor remember outside the theater. Tracing their ancestry to different parts of China, these movie audiences were mostly from Guangdong, but quite a few were from Shanghai, Fujian, and Shandong—each region with its own distinctive cultural and linguistic traditions. Filmgoers also ranged broadly across generations, with those of disparate ages often attending as families. The grandparents might have spent their formative years in China, while the younger moviegoers would have had little or no experience of life outside Hong Kong. The challenge that filmmakers confronted, then, was to bring these generations together despite significant linguistic and cultural differences.

Cinema City, therefore, wasn't making movies for a particular segment of the population or for a particular age group; it was looking to entertain the whole family, an extended family at that. As one former executive put it, "We made the films with this in mind: Mother and father, usually meant the kids too, so you had four. Then, could you get grandmother and grandfather? That's six. Aunt and uncle? Eight." With this broad appeal in mind, a single film might tap a wide range of themes, genres, and talent; for example, a traditional Chinese ghost story might be reframed as a comedy set in a contemporary context, allowing it to draw on the star power of young Cantopop singing stars as well as Chinese opera performers. A private detective spoof that mimicked James Bond would expend much of its creative energy lampooning the new-fangled technologies of the West while solving a crime caper that involved an ancient imperial suit of armor. Audience members followed these hybrid narratives, imagining what it meant to be Chinese outside China and inside Hong Kong, one of world's the last colonial enclaves. They roared with delight at favorite actors riffing on characters drawn from folklore and Chinese opera, just as they thrilled to the antics of modishly attired swindlers, secret agents, and financiers modeled on Hollywood cinema. Not only did tradition and modernity collide on screen, but so too did the cultures of East and West, since foreign films, TV shows, and pop music were rapidly becoming part of the culture's everyday repertoire.

Movies therefore contributed to an ongoing public discussion of what it meant to be a resident of a very Chinese city in a very colonial context that was in the midst of very rapid modernization. Hong Kong theaters of this era could be likened to early cinemas in the United States, where filmmakers focused on local but culturally diverse audiences that were sharing the uncertain and stressful experience of modernization. Filmmakers experimented with narrative strategies that resonated with diverse audiences and that unexpectedly made the films attractive to audiences in other countries as well. Transnational appeal was not the first consideration, however, for seed financing always came from the local cinema circuit, but these local films nevertheless proved enormously popular with audiences in Taiwan, Singapore, and Malaysia, as well as with Chinatown audiences around the world. Despite this, Hong Kong movies eventually began to pay more attention to foreign audiences, largely because planning for new projects came to rely increasingly on overseas financing.

During its prime, the development process at Cinema City was similar to that of most independent production houses in Hong Kong, according Wellington Fung, who worked for the company throughout the 1980s, starting first as a scriptwriter and assistant director, then rising through the ranks to become a producer and ultimately the company's administrative manager. Fung explains that a film's producer would initiate projects by drawing up a proposal and a budget for presentation to a Hong Kong theater circuit owner, who would be asked to provide a cash advance. If a film was budgeted at $650,000, then the producer would be hoping to secure around $125,000 to launch the project. "Let's say it's April and you have two or three second-line stars, an experienced director, a story idea, and a budget. You pitch the film to the circuit owner and tell him you will finish the film by June." The circuit manager asks for a box office sales estimate and assesses the talent and story concept. He might also ask for some changes before agreeing to an advance figure that is usually paid in two or three installments.

With local distribution secured and cash in hand, the producer immediately hired a scriptwriter and used a portion of the advance to sign the lead actors. These agreements then became part of a package that the producer used to negotiate overseas presales of the film in key markets, such as Singapore and Malaysia, hoping to raise the rest of the money needed for production. Depending on the film, Japanese and Korean distributors might be contacted as well, especially if the film had a significant action component that would appeal to their audiences. Yet during the 1980s, the first point of contact was always a distributor in Taiwan, since, with a population three times as large as that of Hong Kong, it was the most lucrative single market for commercial Chinese films. If Hong Kong box office sales covered 15 to 20 percent of production costs, a presale agreement with a Taiwanese distributor could bring in two to three times as much, putting the project well on the way to covering anticipated costs. A Taiwan presale would launch the project into high gear, with the producer continuing to negotiate other presales in hopes of raising all the necessary funds in a timely manner. Should financing fall short, the producer might start yet another project in hopes of generating enough cash to pay off the current film and to get the next project under way.

By and large, this system of financing was quick and flexible, making it possible to move a project from concept to cinema screen in a matter of two or three months. It was not very transparent, however, because all parties made decisions on the basis of hunches, especially regarding overseas pre-sales. Distributors in Taiwan, for example, were rarely given a clear break-down of the production budget, and Hong Kong producers rarely received overseas box office data after the film was released. Distributors were buying a product sight unseen on the basis of their assessment of the producer, the concept, and the talent, and producers were selling all rights to a forth-coming film without any hope of participating in a share of the overseas ticket sales. Although revenue sharing might have been a better option, it would have required expensive systems for tracking costs and revenues, as well as a commitment to transparency. At the time, however, bookkeeping was informal, if not erratic, because of a small-business mentality among both distributors and producers and because it kept power in the hands of the owners and out of the hands of competitors, tax officials, and even col-laborators.

Most presale agreements were outright sales of the territorial rights to a film for five to twelve years or even more. From the producer's perspec-tive, the ultimate box office revenues of a movie in overseas markets re-mained largely a matter of speculation. "You don't ask and they don't tell," recalls Wellington Fung. "That was the general way. I would say 70 percent of deals were like that." Furthermore, many producers simply didn't care about overseas box office figures so long as they could come up with the money they needed to get their projects made. "Some talent-driven [pro-duction] companies were good at filmmaking," recalls Fung, "but they weren't good at business. So they'd rather say, 'Well, according to our cal-culation, Taiwan this much, Singapore this much, Korea—okay, whatever. You meet my price, it's yours for the next ten or fifteen years, or even life-long.' They didn't really care to build a distribution business. So their atti-tude was: I'm good in producing and you're good in distributing; this time maybe I win, next time maybe I lose. So it involved an averaging out of long-term relationships. Every time was like betting. If you bet high and you lose, next time, I give you a little bit more. It wasn't scientific, but it worked." And one of the reasons it worked was that producers with good track records would develop ongoing relationships with certain distributors based on reciprocal needs, each side seeking to keep the other in business without giving away too much, either in terms of money or information.

Similar relationships obtained in Hong Kong, where producers became associated with particular theater circuits on the basis of relations of complex reciprocity. "When you were finishing a film," says Fung, "you were always starting another one [and you needed to go back for more financing]; they're interlinked, interwoven in a certain way." For their part, theater circuits were loyal to their producers, because they needed a dependable group of suppliers to provide them with fresh films. Unlike a competitive market in which producers might shop their project around looking for the best deal, the Hong Kong film market was built in large part on personal allegiances. Producers sometimes changed circuits, but as Fung says, "If you go to one and then change to the next one, it would be more difficult to go back to the first circuit because they would think, 'You are not one of our producers.' The producers tended to be loyal to one particular circuit because it wasn't a one-deal thing."

In a society renowned for its commercialism, it's surprising that many producers and directors didn't think of themselves as business people. As long as they could find enough money for the next project, they showed little concern about bookkeeping or ticket sales. In fact, determining exactly how much a particular film cost was often hard, because cash flow problems were frequently resolved by launching yet another project. Film critic Sam Ho explains it by reference to a common Chinese saying about covering bottles: "You have ten bottles and nine caps, and you keep shuffling the caps to keep all the bottles covered as much as possible. A lot of small Hong Kong filmmakers do that. They need to keep coming up with new projects just to pay off the last one."

Such precarious economics affected not only the filmmakers but also the exhibitors. And even though Cinema City produced many of the most popular films during the 1980s, the company began to hit rocky shoals toward the end of the decade. One industry executive claims that part of the problem had to do with pressure from members of the Louey family who felt that Kowloon Development needed to focus on its core real estate and transportation businesses. Lawrence Louey had always championed the cinema business, but when he passed away in 1992, the family began to reconsider its involvement in the movie industry. As this executive recalls: "Eventually, the problem was that the Loueys were a family of business people, and they didn't like the way that the cinema people were handling their books. One of the owners was a professionally trained accountant, and he thought it was just too confusing. Their core business was running KMB, which also owned a lot of real estate, but movies—they just weren't that important." Consequently, in the early 1990s, the Louey family started pulling back from the entertainment business, slowly selling off theaters and in 1993 relinquishing the library of Golden Princess films to a new satellite television venture called Star TV.

But even without the backing of the Louey family, Cinema City might have survived if it had not begun to experience internal tensions of its own during the late 1980s. "I think it was human nature," says Wellington Fung. "When they founded the company, no one was too concerned with profit or how they were going to share it. But when the successful films came along, it was hard to determine who deserved what. How do you figure out each person's contribution? Effort? Talent? If you simply measure it by the number of shares you allocated at the beginning, then you might feel it's not fair. So things started deteriorating psychologically. They started to calculate, started to measure, and they started to realize there's a certain unfairness there, and that is human nature." Furthermore, success altered relationships among the founding members. Originally, Maka was the acknowledged leader, but when the company began to grow and the budgets became more lavish, different groups started to emerge, each with its own leader. As one insider from that era put it, "The only logical way out was to divide and diversify." Eric Tsang, Tsui Hark, and Raymond Wong each started independent production companies of their own, and the death of Laurence Louey further accentuated this trend, since he was a senior figure to whom all paid deference. Without Louey, relations among the partners were less certain, and ultimately each went his own way.

Cinema City was emblematic of a small production house that relied on a local exhibition chain to provide initial financing and on overseas distributors to provide completion funding. This was the structural foundation for the many independent production houses that flourished during the golden age of Hong Kong cinema, a time when the industry churned out hundreds of movies for an appreciative local audience that became renowned for the world's highest film attendance per capita. Surprisingly, these very locally inspired movies proved attractive to overseas Chinese audiences as well, which spurred Hong Kong's rise to become the world's second largest exporter of films after Hollywood.

Although the studio system pioneered by Shaw Brothers was superseded by an independent mode of production during the 1980s, centripetal spatial tendencies remained potent while Hong Kong solidified its status as significant site of financing and creative labor. Golden Harvest provided one model of adaptation with an infrastructure that situated the company at crucial nodes of the cinematic apparatus. It controlled access to cinema screens through revenue sharing agreements with exhibitors that ensured a steady cash flow, and it furthermore built relations with overseas venture capitalists who were willing to invest in Hong Kong productions. Golden Harvest also cultivated its access to creative talent through profit participation agreements, and it promoted its talent both in Hong Kong and via the regional distribution operation that it built for Chinese and Hollywood films. Chinese stars and directors needed Golden Harvest to gain access to audiences; exhibitors needed them to gain access to talent; and foreign investors needed them to gain access to investment opportunities with rapid turnover and tidy returns. Situated in the middle, Golden Harvest turned a healthy profit because each stakeholder was dependent on the company, knowing little about the business overall. Knowledge and capital concentrated at the very top of the Golden Harvest organization, allowing management to enforce standards of quality and efficiency unequaled by competitors. It was at once a model of post-Fordist (disintegrated) production and of tight managerial control, and its prominence helped to sustain Hong Kong as a central node in transnational Chinese cinema.

Cinema City, in contrast, is representative of an independent movie production company that lacked financial and distribution capacity, relying primarily on a local theater chain for seed financing and therefore focusing its attention on pleasing Hong Kong audiences with movies that were commercially calculating and highly reliant on insider jokes and hybrid genres. Dependent on the Golden Princess circuit for each film's start-up funding, Cinema City producers secured the balance of their production budgets through overseas presale agreements that were often fashioned quickly and haphazardly. Deal makers on both sides sought to sustain long-term business relationships while making short-term bets on the basis of limited information. Bookkeeping was sloppy, and organizations were small family-like enterprises that were redolent with personal tensions. Independent production companies like Cinema City saw themselves first as creative organizations that were highly reliant on local resources and personal networks, making it especially important for them to be located in Hong Kong.

Both Cinema City and Golden Harvest were strongly influenced by the independent production practices of Hollywood, but they were also shaped by mercantile practices common to Chinese capitalists. As Gordon Redding has observed, "Mercantile capitalism is essentially deal-making," involving opportunistic buying and selling.[8] It works best where negotiation and trading proceed at high speed and reliable information is a scarce and strategic resource. According to Redding, the concentration of decision-making power at the very top of the organization is a necessity, and personal relations are often key, since deals are struck quickly and rely on personal negotiations and trust. In most cases, one individual within the company becomes a magnet for capital on the basis of his (rarely her) reputation for deal making. In other words, mercantile capitalists tend to focus on seizing opportunities that appear under volatile trading conditions. Deal making occurs at the very top of the organization, since it allows the company to move quickly when necessary and to build social relations that may be crucial at forging cartellike arrangements that can help to stabilize market behaviors and provide long-term cash flows. Mercantile capitalism is common among Chinese enterprises of all sizes. Industrial (and postindustrial) capitalism on the other hand is predicated on a managerial revolution that tends to create distinctions between owners and managers. Rather than personal fiefdoms, these corporations are publicly traded entities whose managerial class shifts attention from short-term opportunism and cartel building toward the creation of complex bureaucracies. Such corporations seek to minimize the importance of personality and to regularize the return on capital through the establishment of rational systems at each link in the commodity chain. Although the Hong Kong movie industry during the 1970s and 1980s happily appropriated elements of Hollywood's poststudio mode of disintegrated production, it also retained many features of mercantile capitalism, and this has proven to be a crucial weakness of the industry.

In my conversations with movie executives and creative talent, I was often told that secretive behavior is quite prevalent in the Hong Kong film business. "Everybody wants to run their own little shop, and nobody thinks of it as an industry," explains one senior executive. Such expressions of concern reflect a frustration with the industry's inability to institute transparent practices that might regularize production, distribution, and financing, allowing the film companies to grow in scale and take advantage of opportunities in an era characterized by dramatic changes in technology, trade relations, and government regulation. So even though the logic of accumulation and the trajectories of creative migration helped to build and sustain Hong Kong as a media capital, business practices presented obstacles so serious that during the 1990s, as we shall see, they came to threaten the very survival of commercial Chinese cinema.

3 Hyperproduction Erodes Overseas Circulation

By the middle of the 1980s it was difficult for those in the Chinese movie business to imagine anything but good fortune as they looked to the future.[1] In Hong Kong, loyal audiences pushed per capita cinema attendance to stratospheric heights, engendering envy among exhibitors around the world. Citizens of the territory went to the movies on an average of once a month, outstripping their counterparts in North America and Europe by a factor of three or four. Hong Kong films also proved to be reliable box-office draws in overseas markets, performing especially well in Southeast Asia, and in Taiwan ticket sales for Chinese movies compared favorably with those of their Hollywood counterparts. Yet at this very moment of popularity and prosperity, cracks began to appear in the system, registering first in Taiwan but also unfolding in other overseas Chinese movie markets as well. Problems registered most dramatically in Taiwan, however, since it was the largest and most lucrative market for commercial Chinese films. Indeed, so prosperous was the island market that distributors competed fiercely for territorial rights to Hong Kong movies. With the introduction of the videocassette player and later cable TV, demand for Chinese movies escalated even further, because distributors engaged in frenzied bidding wars. In this chapter I explain how the systems of independent production and distribution unexpectedly crumbled during an era of growing demand. Ironically, the very technologies that boosted the prospects for Chinese films would contribute to the industry's undoing, because they sparked a cycle of hyperproduction in which the quantity of films mushroomed while the quality plummeted. As a result, audiences became less willing to risk the purchase of theater tickets for Chinese films and turned instead to cheaper alternatives: cable, video, and even pirated media. The situation became so dismal that in 1998 Golden Harvest closed its Taipei distribution office, and others soon followed suit. In 2000, during the Chinese New Year holiday—the most important release date of the year—not a single Hong Kong film had a successful theatrical run. *Tokyo Raiders* and *Purple Storm* both failed at the box office, and *2000 AD* was pulled from theaters after only a few days. This marked a dramatic reversal from only a decade earlier, when Hong Kong movies were the most popular draw of the New Year season. It also prompted a refiguring of the geography of distribution because it undermined the centripetal logic of accumulation that had catapulted Hong Kong movie business to the center of Chinese popular culture.

In 1990, Chinese movies seemed destined for a period of strong and protracted growth. For, in addition to theater demand, video rental stores were desperate to acquire Hong Kong titles in order to satisfy their rapidly growing customer base. Wellington Fung, manager of Cinema City in the late 1980s, remembers that video had a tremendous impact on the Hong Kong industry's core markets, which at the time included Taiwan, Singapore, Malaysia, Thailand, and South Korea. "Suddenly there were thousands of video rental shops around, and everybody wanted to fill their shelves with Chinese movies," recalls Fung. "Distributors were making a lot more money because of video rights, but the [number of available films] was limited, so all they could do was to push more money into the production of new movies." As a result, distributors began bidding wars during the negotiation of presale agreements, hoping to lock down the rights to forthcoming films. Some distributors went even further by signing output deals with independent production companies, agreeing to purchase a specific number of films over a period of twelve to eighteen months. Such agreements helped them to secure a steady supply of movies and also to assemble packages that could be marketed to video rental stores. "Let's say a store buys ten good films a year—what they call the driver films," explains Fung. "And then with these ten driver films, the distributor adds thirty grade-B or grade-C movies to make a package of forty films. At the retail shop they tell the owner, 'If you want the driver films with the famous stars, you have to buy the whole package.'" Of course, this meant that the video shops filled their shelves quickly, but the quality of production was uneven, and it began to skew the priorities of Hong Kong film producers, who started shifting their attention from local cinema circuits to overseas markets.

The cycle of hyperproduction that this demand spiral sparked started to have a negative impact on filmmaking practices and on the quality of the movies themselves. For example, multipicture output deals committed filmmakers to production schedules that were considered frantic even by the already brisk standards of the industry.[2] A successful director, who under normal conditions would produce four films a year, might produce twice that many, and topflight actors might be working on three or four films at the same time. In 1991, marquee idol Andy Lau was on call at four sets in a single day, reportedly sleeping in his car between shots. The gold rush mentality encouraged producers and creative talent to make as much money as possible before the vein of precious ore ran dry. Furthermore, everyone in the film community was well aware that the clock was ticking inexorably toward the 1997 handover of Hong Kong, and many were intent on making as much money as possible before the transfer took place.

Although such opportunism might seem crassly commercial, it is difficult to convey the sheer astonishment that most Hong Kong residents felt when, in 1984, the British government announced it would be returning the colony to Chinese sovereignty. The decision was completely unexpected and emerged out of closed-door negotiations between London and Beijing officials, without any input from citizens of the territory. Many Hong Kongers were outraged and immediately began to make plans to emigrate overseas. Others sensed a potential opportunity, anticipating that modernization of mainland China would give Hong Kong further entrée to a vast and growing market. In the film industry as well, feelings were mixed. At the time, the mainland entertainment market was growing rapidly, and Hong Kong media were enormously popular. Some hoped that the city's return to Chinese sovereignty might engender further opportunities, but this guarded enthusiasm gave way to a grim tension after the massacre of demonstrators at Tiananmen Square in the spring of 1989. More than a million people— close to a fifth of Hong Kong's population—took to the streets to protest the slaughter, and shortly thereafter another wave of emigrants began to relocate to Canada, Australia, and other destinations overseas.

Therefore, at the very moment when the frenzied bidding war for overseas film rights was at its peak, creative personnel were rethinking their future employment prospects. Many began to salt away their earnings, and others sought overseas residences that might provide refuge should the handover turn sour. Johnnie To, one of the most prolific and talented director-producers of the 1990s, signed an output deal with overseas distributors so that he could buy a house in Vancouver for his family. At the time, among applicants for permanent residency, Canadian law gave priority to those who invested over $500,000 in Canadian assets. To's presale output deal made it possible for him to buy a house in Vancouver, but it also put pressure on him to produce films at a frenetic pace. He adapted to these conditions in some cases by stepping back from hands-on filmmaking and delegating the actual directing duties to subordinates. Others followed similar strategies, such as Wong Jing, considered the most formulaic, but nevertheless financially successful, filmmaker of the era. Wong's assistants handled most duties on the set while he reportedly busied himself studying the horse racing form and talking on the phone with assistants at other filming locations. Considered Hong Kong's most calculating director, Wong excelled as a money-spinning machine during this era of hyperproduction.

By 1991, however, the frantic pace began to take its toll on the industry. "On any given day thirty or forty projects were shooting in Hong Kong," recalls Wellington Fung. "Can you imagine that? With our tiny talent pool here in Hong Kong, how could you support this volume of production?" But quantity and velocity weren't the only problems. Aiming to exploit the booming presale market, producers were tailoring stories, casting, and production elements to meet the expressed wishes of overseas distributors. Never before had overseas distributors wielded such influence over the content of Hong Kong films. Producer Peter Tsi remembers that in the early 1990s "it was pretty simple. Get an okay from Taiwan—which was 30 to 50 percent of your budget—then come back to Hong Kong and talk to a video distributor, and there was another 20 percent, maybe a little more."

As a result, says Tsi, Hong Kong movies began to change. "In Taiwan, with the exception of Taipei, you are really talking about large numbers of rural, low-income, less-educated viewers. Many of them are most comfortable with the Fujian dialect rather than Cantonese or Mandarin [and were therefore reliant on subtitles]. So they weren't looking for serious drama or even comedy; they wanted action." Advice from Taiwanese distributors dovetailed with advice from other markets, such as Thailand, Indonesia, Korea, and rural Malaysia. Although audiences in Hong Kong, Taipei, Singapore, and Kuala Lumpur generally preferred comedies, or at least action films with a satiric twist, their opinions were now pitted against the preferences of out-island audiences in Taiwan. And when presale negotiations turned from themes to casting, Taiwanese distributors would press for the biggest stars, even if they were expensive and incredibly busy. "Under this system," says Tsi, "action movies were safest, comedies came a close second, and some actors always ended up at the top of the list." Market pressures therefore skewed production toward hastily scripted action films headlined by a handful of overworked performers. Moreover, the preferences of Hong Kong audiences now mattered less, and the opinions of overseas distributors mattered more. Yet despite distributors' newfound power, it was unclear whether they truly understood their customers, since empirical marketing studies and viewer surveys were simply nonexistent. Instead, distributors relied on their feel of the market and their discussions with theater and video store managers. And since the stores were often buying films in packages of forty, it was difficult for them to provide specific feedback on anything other than the driver films. Indeed, the driver films became the object of intense rivalry, because distributors bid huge sums for films with topflight talent and in turn grew anxious to recoup their investment as quickly as possible. One industry insider in Taipei recalls, "The only thing that guy was thinking about was how to get back his $600,000, and you can't blame him—it's a lot of money."

Indeed, it was a lot of money and a lot of risk, but at the height of the boom there was a lot of money to be made, and, not surprisingly, that proved attractive to Chinese gangsters, whose involvement would become yet another factor in the downward spiral of the industry. One award-winning director estimates that fully one-third of the new production houses that sprang up in Hong Kong in the early 1990s were triad-owned. This remarkable spurt of criminal involvement was less a matter of latent creativity than of bold opportunism, for the triads had dabbled in the movie business for some time but had never before taken managerial control of film companies. Rather, many triads first became involved by providing "protection" services to crews that were shooting on location. In a classic shakedown scheme similar to those involving Chinese restaurant and shop owners around the world, Chinese filmmakers were offered protection against disruption and, under some circumstances, triads actually did perform a service since local governments paid little attention to the film industry and provided little in the way of location services during the 1980s and 1990s. If a producer wanted to shoot a sequence in a public place, the police rarely cooperated, and so filmmakers would have to make their own arrangements, surreptitiously setting up for their shoot and then often striking the set just before the police arrived. Under such circumstances triads helped to facilitate among the various stakeholders. "Let's say you wanted to shoot a scene on a small street in Tsim Sha Tsui [a densely populated neighborhood on the south end of the Kowloon Peninsula]," explains one director. "You need the cooperation of the shopkeepers and the people who live there, so you have to have someone to make the arrangements to make sure nobody calls the cops. Maybe they just need to talk to people, and maybe some people need some money because the shoot interferes with their businesses." Triads could take care of such negotiations, allowing the filmmakers to concentrate on the creative demands of the shoot.

But protection services aren't always voluntary. If a filmmaker is offered such assistance and declines, he or she runs the risk of inviting turmoil, even

In *Viva Erotica*, a satire of the declining fortunes of the Chinese film industry, Leslie Cheung (left) plays a hapless but talented director who is persuaded by his producer, played by Law Kar-ying, to make a pornographic movie. Courtesy Golden Harvest Entertainment.

on triad turf as far away as New York City. MGM found this out the hard way when it was shooting *Year of the Dragon* in 1985. Unaccustomed to the mores of the Chinese movie industry, the MGM crew thought they could get by with services of the New York Film Commission. Criminologist Ko-lin Chin, who has written several books on triads, recalls, "MGM tried to make the film in Chinatown, but didn't get clearance from the local gangs, so when they began to shoot, the gangs turned out a bunch of people in the neighborhood to protest, and things got really heated." Protestors complained that the film used racist stereotypes, but regardless of their publicly expressed concerns, what bothered them most was the gall of the Hollywood crew in making a movie about Chinese gangsters on their turf without paying protection money. "Finally," says Chin, "MGM decided to relocate production to North Carolina, where they spent $2 million building a set that looked like Chinatown in New York."

Protection services are a small-time hustle, but as triads became familiar with independent production houses (which tend to shoot much of their footage on location), triad bosses began to expand their services into film financing. As mentioned earlier, most film projects during the 1980s and 1990s were launched before financing was complete, and producers were therefore under tremendous pressure to find additional sources of money to keep the production going. As one explains, triads got into the movie business because they have a lot of cash, and they're always looking for places to launder it. Small production houses with casual accounting practices are therefore an ideal place for triads to invest, and during the boom years of the Hong Kong film industry, these investments played a small but important role in film financing. "If you start with a budget of $1.25 million," says one producer in Hong Kong, "you may be getting $250,000 from the video distributor, maybe $300,000 from Taiwan, and another $500,000 from your other presales. But then you still need another $200,000, and so the triads would offer to cover the rest and say, 'Make me a partner.' So they weren't financing the whole lot, but it was the piece that completed the picture." And with deadlines looming, many producers saw it as a quick fix.

As triad investors observed the machinations of the industry, some of them came to believe that film production was a lucrative and relatively simple scam. After all, if you came up with the idea for a movie and lined up a couple of big stars, you had a very good chance of scoring lucrative presale agreements, even before a script was written or a single frame of film was exposed. The most complicated challenges seemed to be securing contracts with star actors, but triads tended to have a gift for persuading others to work for them, and some triads decided to put those gifts to work by opening their own production companies and pressuring stars to sign on to their projects. Some of the biggest names in Hong Kong movies were targeted by triad producers. For example, Andy Lau's frenetic production schedule during the early 1990s was in part attributable to pressure to perform in films mounted by triad producers. Others such as Anita Mui, Stephen Chow, and Chow Yun-fat all had similar problems at this time. Some actors were even kidnapped or physically assaulted. But it wasn't just actors who came under the gun. One of the leading talent managers in Hong Kong, who at one time handled dozens of top performers, cut back his business dramatically after a pistol was put to his head by a triad producer who wanted to sign one of his clients. By January 1992, frustration with triad tactics reached a peak, and three hundred actors, directors, and film workers marched to the police headquarters in Hong Kong protesting criminal involvement in the industry. Led by Jackie Chan, Anita Mui, Andy Lau, and other well-known stars, the demonstrators presented a petition asking police to take a more assertive role in rooting out triad infiltration of the movie business. The event drew extensive media coverage and raised public awareness, but the police response seemed to have little effect.[3]

Although triad investors initially brought much needed cash to some producers, over time they tarnished the reputation of the industry, scaring off other potential investors. "Film has never really been legitimate in the eyes of Chinese business people," says director Peter Chan. "The film business is seen as something that is not professional, and with triad involvement, it was something that you don't want your children to work in. During the early 1990s, things were especially crazy with a bunch of fortune hunters who only wanted to make a quick buck and run little companies, a third of them triad related. As a result, nobody else wanted to touch the film business. Even the Hong Kong government took the attitude that they didn't want to deal with it. They just didn't want to hear from us." Producer Nansun Shi agrees, "Traditionally, if you came from a good family, you became a scholar or a government official, you never saw an ambitious man becoming an performer. Opera troupes then were like film companies are today. It's not the sort of business that gets respect from the government or from investors. That was bad enough, but the sensational triad stories in the newspapers made things even worse."

Despite problems posed by triads, opportunism, and hyperproduction, film critics and industry practitioners agree that during the 1990s Hong Kong continued to produce ten to twenty A-list films each year, but they became a smaller percentage of the total output, making it difficult for audiences to wade through the video fodder that was clogging cinemas across East Asia. For audiences, it became harder to recognize the good films. "In 1993, there were a total of 230 Chinese movies screened," recalls one distributor. "That's a tremendously high number for this industry. Before then it was 120 films or 130 films. From an outsider's point of view, it's great business, but when you divide it by fifty-two weeks and the total number of screens, it means each film gets a shorter run, and that made it harder to get the audience's attention."

Filmgoers became discouraged for other reasons as well. In the early 1990s, most Taiwanese cinemas were in such a serious state of disrepair that adults and families were reluctant to go to the movies. Only teenagers in search of social spaces they could claim as their own still attended the cinema in large numbers. A study done by the Motion Picture Division of Taiwan's Government Information Office (GIO) showed that, by 1994, 67 percent of theatergoers were under the age of eighteen. Not only was the audience getting younger, but it was also migrating toward Hollywood films with their high-tech special effects and glossy production values. Market researchers in Taiwan began to see the so-called net generation gravitating toward products with digital appeal. This audience was furthermore responding to a surge of new cultural products as the Taiwanese government lifted martial law following four decades of tight government censorship. Suddenly the number of newspapers and magazines grew dramatically, as did the promotional possibilities for new movie releases. Likewise, the entertainment press expanded, providing detailed reporting on media personalities from near and far.

Patrick Mao Huang, deputy managing director of New Action Entertainment, spends a lot of time thinking about audience preferences, the entertainment press, and the business of film promotion. His small distribution company handles products across the spectrum—Hong Kong, Hollywood, and art cinema. Thoughtful and articulate, Huang has a broad-ranging knowledge of the movie business in Taiwan, and he believes the end of martial law in 1987 was a watershed event for the industry. "For example," Huang muses, "I just watched an old Chinese film on TV the other day, a melodrama. It's twenty-five years old, and if I remember correctly, that film did very well at the box office, because in the old days, people didn't get many chances to see a Hollywood film, and the entertainment news about Hollywood didn't come across that fast. Of course we knew that Sean Connery was a big action star, and Faye Dunaway was a glamorous actress, but it's not like now when every detail of what happens in American entertainment instantly gets across to our audience through newspapers, TV, or the Internet. [Nowadays] whatever is on the cover of *People* magazine in the U.S. will soon be on the cover of our magazines and entertainment newspapers. In the old days, when people actually had a choice, they often chose films they were familiar with, even if they weren't as good. But now, Hollywood entertainment is almost as familiar as Chinese entertainment."

As Huang suggests, the psychic distance—the foreignness—of Hollywood product has been significantly eroded for the current generation of cinemagoers in Taiwan. The Hollywood studios now assume that by the time Taiwanese theatergoers step up to the box office window, they will know almost as much about a film and its stars as their American counterparts. Hollywood movies therefore became an attractive alternative when the overall quality of Chinese movies spiraled downward. "Maybe the government should force the theaters to show a certain portion of local films," speculates Huang, "but at the same time [Chinese] filmmakers have to change their style. They have to be more responsive to the audiences, and they have to think about the competition from foreign films. Everyone in this business tries to blame each other, but I think the audience is ultimately right. You can't force them to watch films that they don't like. If you try, they'll just do something else—go shopping, sing karaoke, or play video games."

Johnny Yang, the distribution manager of Long Shong Entertainment, agrees. We met at his company headquarters, located between Taipei's downtown theater district and the old neighborhoods that nestle along the east bank of the Tanshui River. The cluttered office has no apparent flow pattern and little in the way of interior design. Such appearances lend the impression of marginality, yet Long Shong is one of the most prominent film companies in Taiwan and was one of the leading importers of Hong Kong movies during the boom years. In addition to its film and video distribution businesses, it also owns a chain of theaters in Taipei and was one of the first companies to start a Chinese film channel on cable TV, a venture that proved to be an enormous success during the early days of cable.

On a dank winter day we retired to a trendy coffee shop in the theater district for an extended conversation about the film business. Sitting at an amoeba-shaped table in dappled blue and green lighting, we looked out over a busy intersection in Ximending, where streams of teenagers flow past boutiques, theaters, and restaurants. Yang explained that although Taiwanese teens are indeed quite familiar with Hollywood's output, they're also open to a range of cultural influences from abroad, especially from Japan and, more recently, Korea. Yang said his research shows that viewers in the thirteen- to eighteen-year-old range are the biggest audience for theatrical releases. "Kids usually attend in groups of two to five, and if it's a mixed group, the boys choose the movie. And they watch a lot of Hollywood films, which is a big change from ten years ago, but they also watch a lot of Japanese movies." Yang explained that Japanese idol dramas, which cast pop singing idols in TV soap operas, became a craze among young people during the late 1990s, which led in turn to a cycle of extremely popular Japanese horror movies. Young audiences developed a taste for Japanese movies by watching TV and following the music scene. "These kids don't read newspapers, but they do watch TV, and they read entertainment and fan magazines. They see a lot of things about Chinese singers and stars, but they also see a lot about Japanese and American entertainers." This is a stark contrast to twenty years ago, when access to American films was limited, Japanese stars were virtually unknown, and the Taiwanese entertainment press was comparatively diminutive. "Take a look through some of the shops around here," said Yang, motioning out the window. "You'll see Japanese fashions, magazines, and video games; American T-shirts, knapsacks, and movie posters. Of course, you'll also see Chinese stuff. But when someone stocks one of these little shops, what's the first thing he's thinking? He's thinking: Will it sell? Not: Where does it come from? It's the same with movies." Of course, Yang himself is not indifferent to the demise of Chinese cinema. He would love to see Chinese films flourish and has been actively involved with government efforts to promote them, but he thinks the future of Chinese cinema may rest with some sort of alliance between Chinese talent and American film studios. "I'd love to see a comeback, but right now my biggest ambition is for [Long Shong] to represent a Hollywood studio. That, plus some rights to Japanese and Chinese films, would put us on the right path."

Each of these factors—hyperproduction, triads, Hollywood competition, expansion of the entertainment press, and changes in teen culture—has contributed to the declining fortunes of Chinese cinema in the Taiwan market. Yet arguably the most significant factor is one of the least frequently mentioned, perhaps because it seems mundane and legalistic: the steady erosion of release windows for theatrical films. The concept of release windows dates back to the classical Hollywood studio system, when films were rolled out in sequential fashion, privileging picture palaces in downtown locations that would play a new feature film first before it moved on to theaters in city neighborhoods, outlying towns, and ultimately overseas. Theaters that played the movie first charged the highest prices, and thus at each stage of the release, a potential ticket buyer had to balance her willingness pay a premium price at downtown theaters against her ability to wait patiently for less expensive tickets at neighborhood cinemas. This encouraged some moviegoers to pay higher prices, but, just as important, it also made sure to exploit fully the value of a given feature film by marketing it to audiences with various budgets, in various locations, at various times.

Soon after television began, Hollywood studios adapted this logic to the new medium, guaranteeing theaters the first and second run of a film before releasing it to network TV and then to off-network syndication. These patterns became more elaborate as videotape, cable, and now digital video entered the picture, creating a complex international latticework of release windows.[4] Price discrimination is therefore situated at the very core of Hollywood's strategy for profit maximization as a result of a widely shared assumption that audiences are more likely to go to the cinema if they know they won't be able to rent a film for six months or see it on cable for nine months. Indeed, the global antipiracy campaign waged by Hollywood's Motion Picture Association (MPA) is probably less concerned with eradicating piracy than it is with protecting the integrity of release windows. For the economic value of this system to studios, investors, and distributors becomes only too apparent when considering the recent fate of Chinese films.

In Taiwan in the 1990s, Hollywood distributors commonly waited three to six months before releasing feature films for video rental and retail sales.

They waited another three to six months before selling their products to cable TV and perhaps as much as two years before marketing them to broadcast stations. When Hong Kong films started having trouble at the box office in Taiwan during the early 1990s, local distributors, having bid premium prices for film rights, started pushing Chinese movies onto the video rental market within one or two weeks of theatrical release, hoping that video revenue might compensate for films that performed badly at the box office. They were responding in part to the decline in theatrical revenues and in part to the growing demand in the video market, but they also were attempting to stave off competition from pirated video versions, which usually became available shortly after the theatrical premiere. Video rental stores, with their rapidly growing customer base, also felt pressure to get the authorized product on the shelf as quickly as possible and, failing that, were often tempted to stock pirated copies. They tried to convince distributors that long release windows did not work for Chinese movies, because adults, who have dominated the rental market, were unlikely to be lured into theaters regardless of how long they might have to wait for a Hong Kong title to migrate to video. According to this logic, adult rental audiences and teenage theater audiences were so different in their consumer behaviors that a short release window simply does not matter.

Release windows came under pressure on yet another front, as cable television grew increasingly popular, with the number of channels mushrooming from only three terrestrial stations in the 1980s to over one hundred licensed cable channels by the end of the century. In 1996, cable reached 80 percent of Taiwanese homes, and—perhaps ironically—Chinese movies were among the most popular programs during this period of fantastic growth. Although theatrical movie revenues were declining, video and cable licensing provided so much new income that some distributors bought movie theaters and established cable channels of their own. In doing so, they created an uncomfortable conflict, for in their video and cable businesses they were making substantial profits on Chinese films, but in their very own theaters, they were privileging Hollywood feature films in response to audience demand. As they watched ticket sales of Chinese movies plummet through the 1990s, their cable stations nevertheless remained almost entirely devoted to these products, which performed relatively well in television ratings and slightly better than Hollywood films (with the exception of blockbusters). By 2000, Taiwan had five channels devoted to Chinese movies (Long Shong, Star, Sun, Dongsen, and Scholar), and this intensified the pressure to move up the cable release window for Chinese films, so most titles began to appear on television only a week after their theatrical release.

Unexpectedly, this short window has put pressure not only on theater ticket sales but also on video rentals.

At one time the video rental market was the fastest growing revenue stream in the movie business, and perhaps no one rode that current more successfully than Garrie Roman, the founder and CEO of KPS, a video rental chain that began in Hong Kong in 1981 and expanded across Southeast Asia until the late 1990s, when it suddenly teetered and collapsed from the twin pressures of piracy and strong-arm distribution tactics. Roman has encyclopedic knowledge of the business, peppering his observations with statistics and examples when we met for lunch on a muggy Saturday only a block away from the KPS Video outlet I frequented when I lived in Hong Kong in 1997. At that time, video stores were still booming, and it's no exaggeration to say that this particular KPS store probably generated some of the busiest foot traffic in the city, and yet Roman says the shop struggled to make a profit. When I returned in the fall of 1999, the store was empty, a notice to creditors on the door explained that KPS had filed for bankruptcy.

Roman says that the company kept expanding as a way to spread the heavy costs associated with video rights, subtitling, tape duplication, and store maintenance. Furthermore, KPS's rapid growth had been motivated by a desire to have more leverage with distributors. "They'd come to us and say, 'If you don't buy this many, I won't sell you any,'" recalls Roman. "On top that the prices were too high, and then the quality of the movies began to decline, so we were buying packages with a lot of crap in them. Everything worked around their needs. They had no consideration for the end user. For example, when we would try to secure more copies of films that had done especially well, we would go back to the distributor and say, 'These films are strong performers. Can we get some more?' They'd say, 'No, we don't have any and we won't duplicate them. It's too troublesome. You should have bought more when we first released it.'" Roman throws up his hands in mock disgust and says, "Is it any wonder that the retailer can't make a profit in this business?"[5]

Such frustrations were only a prelude to changes that swept through the business in the mid-1990s with the arrival of VCD (video compact disk) technology. VCDs look exactly like DVDs but hold only one-tenth as much information, offering a picture quality roughly comparable to videotape. During the 1990s while much of the world was waiting for prices to drop on DVD players and disks, VCD players hit the market in Asia at one-fourth the cost of their DVD counterparts. "In June of 1996," recalls Roman, "we sold a thousand VCDs in our shops in Hong Kong. By December, it was thirty-four thousand VCDs per month, and we were only 18 percent of the market." At $10 a disk, the purchase price of a Chinese movie video was almost as low as the cost of a theater ticket, and pirated VCDs sold at half that price. With pirated copies putting competitive pressure on the market and distributors still charging hefty fees, video retail and rental shops were being squeezed. In Taiwan, the number of video rental stores plummeted from six thousand in 1993 to fourteen hundred only four years later. Roman says , "There was so little money going to the mom and pop stores because the distributors were raking off so much. Many of the little shops had to close, and even the chain stores were having a tough time making ends meet." Video was moving from a rental market to a sell-through market, and small shops were being squeezed out by mass-market retailers and street-corner pirates.

Video distributors in Taiwan began to feel squeezed, as well. Years of spirited competition for Hong Kong movie rights had driven up prices, and, as ticket sales were sinking and video rental revenues were shriveling, distributors began looking for new ways to contain costs and sustain income. In 1995, the leading Taiwanese distributors agreed among themselves to impose a price cap of $125,000 on the purchase of Chinese movie rights, hoping this would cool off the bidding frenzy that had sparked the era of hyperproduction. Previously, they had paid as much as five times that amount, so the price cap came as a staggering blow to Hong Kong producers. With the price of film rights now in check but the demand for quantity unabated, Hong Kong producers responded with cheap products that further eroded audience confidence in Chinese movies.

Increasingly anxious about the spiral of decline and worried about recouping their investments, distributors began to cast about for new sources of revenue. Some succumbed to temptation and began producing surplus copies of VCDs. Unlike videotapes, which must be recorded in a linear fashion, VCDs can be mass-produced, literally stamped out one after another at relatively low cost, and shipped to overseas markets. This practice of surplus production, however, has been a clear violation of the original purchase agreement, since the distributors purchased rights to only the Taiwan market. Unfortunately, this distinction has been lost on many, because historically the relationship between producer and distributor has been fraught with secrecy and intrigue. Rarely have they shared information, and even more rarely have they collaborated for their mutual benefit. As one industry insider puts it, many distributors "feel no obligation to report revenues, sales, or anything else. They think a movie is like a pair of shoes. I bought the shoes. Why should I tell you how many times I've worn them?" This attitude was less problematic when distributors circulated film prints only

Chinese movies have become cheap video curiosities, as indicated by the haphazard display of products and the discount prices, about US$1.50 per title. Author photo.

to theaters and TV stations, but VCD (and later, DVD) technology has increased the temptation to produce thousands of surplus copies and sell them to buyers overseas. According to industry sources, distributors throughout Asia participate in this illicit form of marketing. "We see it all the time," says one Hong Kong movie producer. "Whenever a film has an early distribution date in places like Taiwan and Malaysia, the minute it hits the screen overseas, copies are everywhere in Asia. And thanks to the technology, you now have different languages on the disk that make it easy to cross over to other markets. Of course," he smiles, "the distributors we sold the rights to always say they don't know anything about it." As if this weren't bad enough, triads expanded into the business and began shipping VCDs to gang members around the world, who then peddled the videos to small shop owners, video market stalls, and street vendors.

Just east of the city center in downtown Taipei, close by the headquarters of one of Taiwan's leading distributors, is a video market that spreads out on Ba De Road under a highway overpass, a jumble of small stalls that seem to have emerged in an urban crevice of Taiwan's media economy. One wonders if any of the vendors pay rent or if it's simply a squatters' zone, eked out on the margins of a public thoroughfare. Inside, narrow passageways wind through crowded stalls stocked with computer software, video disks, and other electronics gadgetry. Twisting through the crowd, I make my way back to a stall that stocks Chinese movies, music CDs, and porn videos. The collection is haphazard at best, as the shop seems to feature whatever is available from distributors at the right price. Yet among the assorted offerings, one can find some interesting titles for only a few U.S. dollars. Other shops are similarly outfitted, and although the prices are competitive, the products are treated as throwaway artifacts of popular culture—cheap, low-risk curiosities.

Emerging from the exit on the south end of the market, I walk diagonally across the street to a small plaza on the opposite corner, where a cluster of young men are gathered around a high-performance motorcycle, rakishly puffing on cigarettes and waving their hands while engaged in animated conversation. Video CDs, DVDs, and computer software are spread out on tables, and a small car is parked nearby, its hatchback open, seemingly at the ready should word come that it's time to pack up the goods and move on. In the market stalls, it is difficult to discriminate between legitimate videos and pirated copies, but not on this corner.

Such vignettes repeat themselves in Chinese communities around the world. According to historian Martin Booth, triads entered the video piracy business after the crackdown on the international heroin trade occurred during the 1980s.[6] Many were attracted by high profit margins and the comparative indifference of law enforcement officials, who saw video piracy as a victimless crime. And indeed, it's sometimes hard to see Hollywood studios as victims, but the impact of piracy on Chinese film producers has been tremendous, not simply because of lost revenues on the sale or rental of videos, but also because piracy puts pressure on Chinese distributors to push movie videos onto the market only a week after the theatrical release—effectively undermining the concept of release windows and sucking millions of dollars out of the legitimate distribution market.[7] With temporal boundaries lacking among theatrical, video, and cable windows, most prospective viewers see no reason to spend money on a theater ticket or a video of a Chinese movie that can be picked up cheaply at a night market or screened for free on cable TV.

In 2000, the Taiwanese video rights for an average Hong Kong movie sold for $45,000 to $50,000. Cable TV brought in a comparable amount, or, if one was able to sell the rights to a regional satellite service such as Star

TV, the film could fetch around $100,000. Yet the same title generated virtually no revenue at the theatrical box office, deriving all of its income from video and cable rights, which altogether yielded somewhere between $90,000 and $150,000. With few exceptions, a theatrical release is now seen as little more than a promotional ploy. In order to sell a Hong Kong title to a video distributor or a cable channel, the film distributor must release it theatrically to satisfy minimum advertising and promotion standards. It's almost a game. Distributors place the films in theaters in order to signify the premium value of a product that is then marketed through discount outlets, such as cable or video. Forget that nobody is actually in the theater. It's still a film—something more than a TV program—that can be rented cheaply or seen free of charge on cable TV.

Simon Huang, who has worked in the film distribution business since the 1950s, explains, "We have a saying about the Chinese film market over the past ten years: no money, no product; bad product, small audiences; small audiences, no investment. The market just keeps circling down. In 1999, according to our experience, Chinese films made up only 2.5 percent of the market islandwide. Absolutely horrible," says Huang, shaking his head. "Twenty years ago they had 60 percent of this market." To attribute this decline to Hollywood hegemony would be the crudest form of reductionism. Instead, a series of interlocking forces—new technologies, predatory distribution practices, hyperproduction, triad involvement, and piracy—many of them attributable to the secretive norms of the movie business in Asia, all converged to weaken the appeal of Chinese movies in the eyes of Taiwanese audiences, who during the post–martial law 1990s had more media choices than ever before. The forces of sociocultural variation that gave Asian audiences a multicultural cinema in the early years, a pan-Chinese cinema in the 1950s and 1960s, and a Hong Kong cinema in the 1970s and 1980s, seemed in the 1990s to be undermining the viability of the Chinese movie business, both at the center of production and creative activity, and throughout the centrifugal spheres of distribution. A lack of transparency, mercantilist opportunism, and short-sighted fixes to large problems only exacerbated the spiral of decline, creating a void that Hollywood was only too happy to fill.

4   Hollywood Takes Charge in Taiwan

On the east side of Taipei directly behind City Hall is one of the largest real estate development projects in the history of the Taiwan. Within an area of six city blocks, investors and urban planners put together an ambitious real estate project that now boasts the world's tallest building, Taipei 101. Without exception, gleaming steel, glass, and marble structures dominate this landscape, inhabited by businesses that consider themselves integral components of global capitalism. At the very center of the project is the China Trust Bank, established by Koo Chen-fu, who up until his death in 2005 was renowned as the most powerful banker in Taiwan, enjoying close connections to business and political leaders in both Taipei and Beijing. Next door to Koo's bank, the Mitsukoshi Department Store caters to the upscale shopping tastes of east side residents and points to continuing ties between Japan and many elements of Taiwanese society. China Trust and Mitsukoshi were two of the first projects completed in the development zone, and if these buildings signify important transnational links to Beijing and Tokyo, then the third major link was marked in 1998 by the grand opening of Warner Village across the street. During its February premiere, this seventeen-screen, state-of-the-art cinema boasted the world's record for multiplex ticket sales. More than a theater complex, Warner Village features thirty shops, restaurants, and related entertainment activities. A joint venture of Warner Bros. Theatrical and Australia-based Village Roadshow, it sold almost three million tickets during its first year of operation, grabbing a 25 percent share of the Taipei market and an estimated 13 percent of ticket sales islandwide. Over the next few years, the company opened five more complexes, allowing it to lay claim to more than half of all ticket sales in Taiwan. U.S.-based competitors Cinemark and UA Theaters also initiated their own multiplex campaigns around the same time, opening theaters in Taipei, Taoyuan, and Kao-hsiung and announcing plans for further expansion.

Why Taiwan? Theater executives point to rising prosperity and increasing leisure time among its twenty-three million people. In 1999, the government reduced the standard work week from six days to five, sparking an expansion in leisure-industry investment and an upgrading of existing entertainment facilities. Movie theaters were widely considered a prime candidate for investment, since most were in a state of serious disrepair. Seats were uncomfortable, ventilation was bad, and special effects on the screen were often caused by poor projection rather than authorial intention. Taiwan was not alone in this regard. Theaters in Japan, Hong Kong, mainland China, and much of the rest of Asia suffered similar problems, making these markets especially attractive targets for new theater construction. Yet it's surprising that multiplexes did not arrive in Taiwan until the late 1990s, since it is one of the most prosperous film markets in Asia and one of the ten largest film markets in the world.[1] For example, Warner Bros.' distribution divides Asia between two markets: Japan, which alone represents one of the top three markets worldwide, and Warner Bros. Asia, which handles the rest of the region, from India to Korea. Within this latter domain, Taiwan was the company's number-one territory in 2000, taking in 60 percent of all revenues for the region. It has also remained a very profitable market, garnering an estimated net income of $10 million per year for Warner Bros.[2] Indeed, because distribution costs are low and revenue splits favor distributors, profits from theatrical distribution in Taiwan are among the highest in the world. In 1999, Buena Vista International named Taiwan its most profitable market worldwide.[3] U.S. movies sold approximately $116 million in theater tickets in Taiwan that year, making an estimated $40 million in profits and a similar amount from television and video sales. That's $80 million in profits for the major Hollywood studios in the Taiwan market alone.

In the early 1990s, Chinese movies shared this market more equally, selling half of all movie tickets islandwide. Yet unlike the synergies implied by the proximity of Warner Village and China Trust, the relationship between Hollywood and Chinese cinema became horribly skewed as the decade progressed, with some contending that Hollywood's success came at the expense of Chinese filmmakers. By the end of the 1990s, Hollywood movies were taking in an estimated 93 to 95 percent of all box office revenues in Taiwan, while Chinese-language films had shriveled to a mere 2.5 percent. Taiwanese commercial film production, which virtually disappeared during the early 1980s, also seemed destined to be joined by its Hong Kong counterpart.[4] Many critics explained the decline by pointing a finger at the gov-

TABLE 1. Taipei movie ticket purchases, by film origin
(in millions)

	1992	*1996*	*% change*
Chinese films	8	1.3	−84
Non-Chinese films	8	11.9	+49
Total sales	16	13.2	−18

SOURCE: Government Information Office, Taiwan, 2001.
Reliable statistics are available only for the Taipei market. Film distributors in Taiwan presume that Taipei represents approximately half of all ticket sales for the island.

ernment's decision to eliminate movie import quotas in 1997, but others have suggested that the declining popularity of Chinese films was already well under way, with the box office share down to 10 percent by the time the government lifted the restrictions. Wolf Chen, head of film distribution for ERA Communications, is convinced that the decline had less to do with government regulation than with rational economic behavior by the moviegoing public. "Most of the audience in Taiwan is young—teenagers and single people in their twenties," says Chen. "A movie usually means going out with friends and spending money on transportation and a meal. Movie tickets aren't cheap, and at many theaters a Chinese film costs as much as a Hollywood film." Filmgoers therefore make direct comparisons between these two film categories, and according to Chen, "Audiences would see a Hong Kong film and think, 'Oh, bad luck.' They'd see another one and, well, maybe bad luck again. But then, after the third time, they decided they wouldn't waste their money on Hong Kong movies anymore."

Given the price of tickets ($9), such feelings are understandable. With a per capita income of roughly half that of the United States, Taiwan's moviegoing public is spending a big part of its discretionary income at the box office. For teenagers, a ticket purchase is a significant moment of choice, and for adults, a night at the movies is often compared with the cost of other forms of popular entertainment. A group of friends or family can, for example, enjoy a truly outstanding dinner at a restaurant or an evening at a karaoke lounge for about the same price as a night out at the movies. Thus, movies command a premium price, and they succeed to the extent that they deliver a premium entertainment experience. Consistent production values, marketable story lines, and well-recognized stars are all important factors, but equally important are distribution strategies that ensure prominent

TABLE 2. Taipei market share, by film category
(in percentages)

	1992	2000
Chinese films	50	2.5
Hollywood films	50	93.0
Independent films	<1	4.5

SOURCE: Government Information Office, Taiwan, 2001.

placement and promotion at theaters throughout Taiwan. In this chapter, I examine how the distribution business operates in Taiwan, showing that Hollywood distributors improved their distribution techniques over the course of the 1990s, while distributors of Chinese films failed to adapt to a changing competitive environment. As sociocultural forces shifted, the spatial contours of distribution changed as well, undermining the centrifugal power of the Hong Kong film industry.

Prior to 1990, relationships between distributors and exhibitors were quite traditional, according to Simon Huang, marketing manager for United International Pictures. A handful of distribution companies worked with independent theater owners around the island, securing screening facilities for their releases. Since theater chains then were relatively few and diminutive in size, distributors tried to put together a cohort of theaters that would guarantee broad exposure for each release. UIP—a joint venture that represented Universal, Paramount, MGM, and United Artists—was one of the most powerful players in the market, distributing twenty films each year, culled from a roster of some sixty titles on offer from the studios. Because UIP offered the largest menu of Hollywood movies, its executives were avidly courted by theater owners, but Huang says he has preferred to establish long-term relationships rather than jumping among theaters with each new film: "Once we do business with a theater, we do business forever, unless we have a very, very unpleasant experience or an argument." Huang says the most important goal was to ensure the financial health of both parties over the long run. Nevertheless, such seemingly symbiotic relationships were not without their power valences. "For the past thirty or forty years," says Huang, "we would tell the exhibitors when we would release the films and what would be the revenue split [for the opening week]. Seventy-thirty? Sixty-forty? They would just accept the terms without any objection. That's the traditional way. So they trusted us to give them a good supply of films at a fair price, and we trusted them to give us access to their screens."

Currently within the city of Taipei, where box office figures are accurately reported, Hollywood distributors generally begin their negotiations with theater owners by asking for 70 percent of the box office takings during the first week of a film's release. Each subsequent week, the distributor's share drops by 5 percent and the exhibitor gains 5 percent, with most films ending their run by the end of four weeks. With a population of seven million, the Taipei metro area is one of the most lucrative movie markets in Asia, and revenue reporting systems conform to global standards. Outside Taipei is another story, because box office figures provided by theater operators are notoriously unreliable. As a result, rental negotiations usually begin with the distributor asking for a fee based on data derived from Taipei ticket sales for a comparably sized theater. This extrapolation might seem equitable; however, as one studio representative puts it, "most Hollywood films don't work in the non-Taipei market. Audiences are less sophisticated, so dramas and romantic comedies—films with a lot of dialogue—usually won't work. Action movies, disaster movies, larger-than-life movies" are most popular, but ticket sales can sometimes vary dramatically throughout the island. Thus, neither the box office numbers provided by the out-island theater owner nor the calculation suggested by the distributor provides an accurate basis for setting a rental fee. Instead, the negotiations involve elaborate attempts by both parties to secure financial benefits while sustaining an appearance of social harmony. "It's not very scientific," concedes one distributor, and given the unpredictable returns on many films, a distributor sometimes needs to accommodate theater owners who say they took a loss on a previous title by offering better terms on the next title. "What we try to do along the way is to make adjustments that keep everybody happy."

Like many business transactions, the relationship between buyer and seller cannot be reduced to simple mathematics. Instead, it's a complex negotiation of finances and face, requiring each party involved to feel the relationship is mutually beneficial over the long term. Historically, however, the distributor, who controls access to the film prints, has held the upper hand, and this makes the exhibitor especially reluctant to provide accurate box office information, since this local knowledge constitutes the one bit of leverage an exhibitor enjoys. The less the distributor knows about the actual popularity of specific films, the more he or she must rely on a relationship of trust. And even though distributors may bristle at this lack of transparency, they consider it not worth their while to send employees to out-island theaters to keep track of attendance figures.

This complex interface between global Hollywood and local culture manifests itself in other ways as well. Entering the main office at UIP, I look left down a hallway toward the marketing department and see Simon Huang, a robust man in his early sixties with a full head of gray hair, squinting in my direction and gesturing to his assistant with his left hand while cradling a telephone to his right ear. Huang takes pride in his seniority, saying, "These days, nobody talks history but me. Everybody else talks about the future." And even though he acknowledges that the film business in Taiwan is changing rapidly, he contends that traditional values and practices remain at the heart of the business.

Take, for example, his office, which is situated at the northwest corner of the UIP suite. In 1996, when the company was shopping for new digs, it hired a feng shui master to inspect the energy paths and spatial arrangement of the fifth-floor suite. The master explained that on entering the main gate of a traditional Chinese house, the most important location is always to the left. Pointing down the hallway, he declared that whoever occupies the northwest office will play a very important role in promoting harmony and prosperity, but the power of the office could be fully realized only if UIP were to place a stalactite stone in the corner by the window. Mounted on a traditional Chinese pedestal, in precisely that location, sits an off-white, three-foot-high stalactite, remarkably reminiscent of the Matterhorn mountain-peak logo of Paramount Pictures. Only a few feet away sits Simon Huang, seemingly living up to his designated role, as he continues to take phone calls, receive guests, and consult with his staff throughout our interview. Unlike Western executives, who are often secluded from the traffic flow of the office, Huang multitasks with his door wide open. Dressed in a gray tweed jacket, he nurses a Rillo cigar burned down to the very end, a fresh supply stashed at arm's length on a credenza, strategically situated next to a bottle of Excedrin. Every available surface, as well as most of the floor space, is piled high with boxes of tie-in merchandise, marketing files, and promotional artwork. Squeezed into a far corner is a director's chair emblazoned with *The Truman Show* logo, and on the bookshelf behind it is a *Babe* interactive doll. On the opposite wall hangs a 007 film poster, commemorating one of the most profitable film franchises in the Taiwan market.

As marketing manager, Huang is in charge of advertising and publicity for most films. Yet the overall strategy of each campaign—the artwork, the trailers, and the copy lines—is designed initially by the headquarter staffs in Los Angeles. Huang's job, therefore, is to adapt global materials to the local market. Most important, he is responsible for the translation of each title, which is a rather complex affair. "After screening *American Beauty* about three months ago," says Huang, "I decided this is the best film of the year, and I wanted to give it a title that would be typical for an Oscar-winning film." He came up with *Meiguo xin, Meigui qing.* Directly translated, the Chinese characters are "American Heart, Rose Love," but Huang explains that it would be interpreted by audiences as "Rose American Dream." He beams at me conspiratorially and says, "It's a very high-class name." With furrowed brow, I prod him, "Why not Meiguo Meili?" (literally, American Beauty). Huang scoffs at my clumsy translation with a good-natured wave of his hand, "This doesn't sound like a *title.* It means nothing." Huang explains that the actual characters are less important than the associations they evoke. *Meiguo xin, Meigui qing* sounds as if it leapt off the pages of a famous Chinese novel, and he points out that such inferences are difficult to explain to executives in Los Angeles.

Paramount's 1990 romantic melodrama *Ghost* is a good example of the perils of direct translation. In Chinese, a single character, *gui,* is the closest corollary, but when Huang suggested *Diliu Gan Shengsi Lian*—literally, "The Sixth Sense, the Love with Life and Death"—he recalls that UIP headquarters and the studio both responded incredulously, asking, "What's this?" Phone calls and cables shot back and forth across the Pacific. "We tried to explain, but they wouldn't accept it. They wanted 'Gui.' I said, we can't do that. It looks like a horror film." Much anticipated by audiences, the film was scheduled for an October play date, but negotiations over the title and marketing dragged on for two months. Finally, the studio relented, but only after the Taipei office agreed to guarantee the box office take. "It was a big success," gloats Huang. "The first drama over $3 million. We did almost $4 million just in Taipei." Huang claims that promotional campaigns are most successful when they convey a set of expectations about a film, and the best way to do that is to associate the film with familiar images, stories, or emotions. "When [audiences] go to the theater, they have to have a *feeling* about the title. The title is even more important than the trailer."

Eric Shih, general manager of Warner Bros. distribution, agrees. Although his Taipei office rarely tampers with the artwork on ads and never edits the trailers or TV spots, it is responsible for setting the tone of the ad campaign and, perhaps just as important, for heading off potential gaffs that might arise from translation. For example, Shih explains that *You've Got Mail* literally translates as "Xin laile," "but we told them in L.A. that we wanted to change it because it didn't sound right." Warner resisted until finally Shih explained that *xin* could mean letter or it could mean sex. "In a way, it fit with the movie, but it was also a bit racy and didn't really fit the characters or the stars [Meg Ryan and Tom Hanks]. It might work in Taipei but not in Kao-hsiung or Taichung, so we changed it to 'Love E-mail' (*Dianzi qingshu*)."

Sometimes it's difficult for Shih to anticipate the reactions of audiences in other parts of Taiwan, since his staff is based in Taipei and spends most of its time working in the capital city. Indeed, the Warner Bros. office has one of the most cosmopolitan addresses in the business, a stylish two-story loft overlooking the trendy Ximending theater district. An oversized fishbowl sits in front of a huge picture window in the lobby, a dozen exotically colored goldfish languidly swimming about. The office atmosphere is casual and hip but quietly intense. One could be in Hollywood, SoHo, or Silicon Valley, which perhaps explains why the staff finds it easier to anticipate the tastes of metropolitan moviegoers in the urban north of the island.

Shih says that, unlike UIP, his office has less discretion with film selection, accepting the entire slate of major titles that Warner Bros. releases internationally each year. "They usually let us know the release date six months to a year ahead of time," and the L.A. office solicits input only on films that might prove controversial, such as *South Park*, which Shih says he personally enjoyed but worried that ticket sales would be modest. "We never actually refuse a film. We just give them our estimates of ad/pub costs and box office. Then they make the decision." Most often the Taiwan premiere is a month or two after the U.S. release. This helps to capitalize on the American promotion of the film, including the box office record, which is often a very important way to create buzz. "People want to see blockbusters, films that do well in the U.S.," says Shih. "They're curious about them. They're also curious about films that get nominated for awards, so sometimes we'll adjust the premiere date to take advantage of this, and other times we adjust the date because of competition here in the Taiwan market." Yet distributors generally try to align their release with the U.S. premiere, because cable TV and the local entertainment press create a pervasive awareness of the latest Hollywood buzz. If Taiwan lags too long, say, several months, then "it's a season and you've had a whole change of wardrobe," argues one distributor. "In the case of women, you've been through winter, you're into spring. It's like going back to last year's styles: it's not fashionable. Taiwan is certainly not as label-conscious as Hong Kong, but people are very conscious of what's current. It's not fashionable to be playing Backstreet Boys when Enrique Iglesias is hot; it's just not the thing to do."

Like UIP, Warner Bros. aims for a seventy-thirty revenue split from theater owners. "During the first week of a film's run, we try to recoup our advertising and promotion budget," says Shih. "We also try to cover the cost of the prints and office costs. The rest becomes income." Releasing thirteen to fifteen films each year, Warner Bros. has done exceptionally well, averaging an estimated $10 million in annual profits, which makes it a leading distributor in Taiwan and one of Warner's most lucrative territories worldwide. Yet, until the early 1990s, the major Hollywood studios had a rather casual attitude toward Taiwan, believing that government import quotas and limited promotional opportunities artificially constrained the market. "Under martial law," says Shih, "there was no Internet, no cable, and not so many newspapers and magazines. That put limits on the kind of promotion you could do." For example, newspapers were licensed by the government, which meant advertisers competed for a limited amount of space among officially sanctioned publications. That same small circle of newspapers published movie reviews by an equally small circle of critics. Once restrictions were lifted, however, the number and variety of newspapers and magazines exploded. Major distributors no longer dominated access to advertising space, and new publications, such as entertainment and lifestyle magazines, offered fresh perspectives on movies and popular culture.

Independent movie distributors were the first ones to take advantage of these new opportunities. Then it dawned on the major Hollywood studios that they too might increase their returns through more aggressive marketing. Yet change didn't come easily or quickly. In fact, Rudy Tseng, one of the most successful distributors in Taiwan, used to work in the Warner Bros. office as a junior executive during the early 1990s, until he was terminated because his brazen ideas irritated some of his superiors. Tseng moved over to ERA Communications, a rapidly growing independent. Then in 1995 when Buena Vista International (BVI) decided to open a Taiwan office, the company recruited Tseng as the general manager, despite his relatively young age. "[BVI] put a guy in charge who was less than forty years old," says Shih. "At the time, it was unheard of, but Rudy deserved it because he was bringing new promotion concepts to the market." Other studios followed suit, and in 1997 Warner Bros. named Eric Shih general manager at a similarly young age. He embraces many of the same strategies that Tseng pioneered at BVI. "Foreign film companies now have specialized marketing and merchandising teams [in Taiwan]," observes Shih. "It's not like the old days, when film promotion was just doing some publicity and showing the film to a few critics. It's not that easy. You have to create a whole chain of activities that lead up to the premiere." Given the proliferation of newspapers, magazines, and cable channels, successful distributors now target promotional messages and media buys, aiming especially at teens and young adults.

BVI Taiwan with its four divisions—theatrical, video, ancillary merchandise, and the Disney Channel—is now considered a distribution powerhouse, handling Disney, Touchstone, and Columbia films. At the time of my visit, theatrical marketing manager Tom Wang and his staff had just completed a successful run of *Toy Story 2*, which scored a dramatic improvement over the original, in large part as the result of an elaborate promotional campaign. Anchored by a global tie-in agreement with McDonald's, *Toy Story* dolls, drink cups, and theme meals were featured at chain outlets during the month leading up to the premier. BVI complemented the restaurant tie-in with a promotion by Mitsubishi Motors, featuring posters, banners, and television advertising that encouraged customers to take a test drive in exchange for free tickets to the movie. Overall, the Mitsubishi campaign cost $500,000, significantly more than the $350,000 that BVI itself spent on the movie's promotion. Likewise, China Trust Bank, the largest commercial bank in Taiwan, offered free movie tickets to new credit card customers.

BVI follows a similar formula with all its family movies. "*Dinosaur* is our summer release this year [2000]," confides Wang, "and we've already confirmed Mitsubishi, China Trust, and McDonald's. Combined they will contribute $1.5 million in media spending, but our own media spending will only be $300,000. It's almost like a formula now, and Rudy [Tseng] is the one that perfected it in this market." Overall, the *Dinosaur* budget of $1.8 million represents a very significant amount of advertising, considering its primary market of seven million in the Taipei area and the islandwide population of twenty-three million. With most of the costs borne by its partners, BVI leverages its own rather modest ad-pub budget into a collaborative campaign that thoroughly saturates the market.

BVI enjoys another successful partnership with 7-Eleven convenience stores, an island franchise operated by the President Corporation. With twenty-three hundred stores—roughly one store for every ninety-five hundred residents—7-Eleven is a pervasive presence in most cities and towns. Although the shops are modeled on their American counterparts, product selection varies significantly—instant noodles instead of bread, dried squid instead of tortilla chips—and so do the services: one can pay a phone bill, water bill, or traffic ticket, or make a photocopy, or send a express mail packet. In urban areas, the foot traffic at 7-Eleven is brisk and continuous, with two or three clerks working the cash registers at most times of the day. One month before *Toy Story* 2 opened, 7-Eleven offered a theme-related drinking cup and two movie tickets for $15. "That's about 70 percent of what you would pay if you just went to the theater," chirps Wang. "So they put up *Toy Story* posters in their twenty-three hundred stores and manufactured a cup with Woody and Buzz Lightyear on it and sold tickets to the movie—and we didn't spend anything on it. That's humongous POP [point of purchase] exposure, and that's everyday exposure," exults Wang. "So we had something at restaurants, something at the bank, something in the media world, and something at the corner store. If you just had the TV commercials, it's not complete, because some people don't watch TV, and even if they do, they might not watch your ad."

Although tie-in promotional campaigns are common in the West, they have become especially popular in Taiwan. The free gifts featured in most campaigns are important, because institutional retailers must compete with a barter culture that is still very much alive in small shops, produce markets, and outdoor night markets, where vendors regularly haggle over quality and cost, providing discounts to volume purchasers, to repeat customers, or simply to those with an entertaining or persuasive bargaining strategy. Sometimes I felt that vendors were giving me a break simply because they were amused that I dared to bargain in faltering Mandarin. Other times, it's likely that I thought I was getting a good deal when, in fact, the vendor was simply reconfiguring the mix to make a marginal deal look more attractive. Moreover, it's not unusual for a vendor to close a sale by throwing in another small item to encourage return business or to introduce the customer to a related product. So, for example, the owner of one of the vegetable stalls that I frequented would sometimes conclude a sale by adding a turnip or a pear to my satchel, which was perhaps a product I might like to try or one that had just come into season.

Given this context, department stores, supermarkets, and movie theaters are sometimes perceived to be at a disadvantage because they operate with set prices. Consequently, they sometimes respond by offering free gifts with each purchase. Even at upscale Cartier or Hermes, regular customers receive small tokens of appreciation. "This simply doesn't happen in the U.S.," notes one American movie executive. "When you walk into Cartier [in the States], they say, 'Oh, thank you,' and take your money and that's it. But in Taiwan it *has to happen*, because people are used to shopping in the street markets, and they're used to getting something extra in value each time they make a purchase." Thus, the tie-in campaign—a globalized promotional technique—resonates especially well with local cultural norms in Taiwan.

Yet even though film distributors in Taiwan now make extensive use of tie-ins, some movies present particular challenges. "When we acquired *Scream*," recalls ERA's Wolf Chen, "we wanted to do a tie-in with a convenience store chain, but they weren't interested, because they thought it was just a gory horror movie. This kind of movie is very difficult to pitch to a tie-in partner." And perhaps a mass-appeal retail outlet was not the right company to approach, says Chen, since some films, such as *Scream*, require that executives at the tie-in company are knowledgeable about Hollywood stars, genres, and trends. Of course, Disney enjoys major advantages in this regard, since it is a widely recognized brand with a well-known pantheon of characters.

A box office track record also makes it easier to pitch films to prospective tie-in partners. "After *Scream* became a big box office success," says Chen, "things changed. With *Scream 3* we are doing a tie-in with a cell phone chain store that gives new customers a *Scream* phone cover when they sign up." It's a shrewd campaign, since teenage life in Taiwan in many ways revolves around the mobile phone, a technology that is at once a crucial communication link and a self-conscious fashion statement within the social networks of young people. A *Scream* cover no doubt conveys the user's pop culture competence, but, just as likely, it situates the phone user as part of the larger circle of teens who can share jokes and recollections of the film, no doubt encouraging attendance by the uninitiated as well, so that they, too, might be able to enter the circle of discussion. One can imagine a group of teens riding on a crowded bus when someone's phone rings, drawing everyone's attention to the *Scream* casing, a scenario that no doubt has launched thousands of conversations about the film.

Although new marketing and promotional techniques have served Hollywood distributors well, they were less commonly used for Chinese films during the 1990s. Wolf Chen, the head of film distribution for ERA Communications, reports directly to CEO Chiu Fu-sheng, an ambitious and enigmatic media tycoon who has been a significant player in the world of commercial Chinese cinema, both distributing and financing Hong Kong productions, including several films by one of the industry's hottest directors, Johnnie To. The company has furthermore provided funding for numerous art house productions, such as Chen Kaige's spectacular allegory of the Cultural Revolution, *Farewell My Concubine*, and Zhang Yimou's *Raise the Red Lantern*. Chiu has tried to play a role in fostering the Chinese film industry throughout East Asia, and according to Chen, ERA would like to play a role in the future of commercial film in mainland China as well, having opened offices in Beijing and Shanghai. But for now, the company is cautious about its investments in Chinese films, and, in Taiwan, it is also cautious about theatrical distribution of them.

It wasn't always that way, however. Soon after martial law was lifted, ERA was notably enthusiastic about local talent, with Chiu providing substantial financial backing for Hou Hsiao Hsien's renowned masterpiece, *City of Sadness*. "In 1989, when *City of Sadness* got the Golden Lion Award in Venice," recalls Chen, "it was the first time that a Taiwanese film had won such a major award. The box office in Taipei was over $3 million, and it was the number-one movie in both Taiwan and Hong Kong. It did even better outside Taipei, because it was one of the first times that people could touch the horrible memories of 2–28 in public," says Chen, referring to the February 28, 1947, massacre of thousands of Taiwanese shortly after the Chiang Kai-shek government took power. Chen says *City of Sadness* succeeded because it dealt with topical issues in an accessible way. "People really liked the film because it was a family saga," he says. "It was a story they could follow, and it had a lot of meaning for them, because [at the time of its release in 1989] martial law had just been lifted two years earlier, and that same year the [PRC] government attacked demonstrators in Tiananmen Square. So a lot of special things happened to make that movie a very big event."

Indeed, the film seemed to herald a renaissance in Taiwanese cinema, sparking a wave of new titles, many of them seeking to follow Hou's distinctive style. This popularity was short-lived, however, because Hou repeatedly avowed his aversion to commercial imperatives, declaring that he makes films only to please himself. That declaration proved only too true, as popular interest in his subsequent films plummeted. For example, *The Puppetmaster* was hailed by critics abroad and received numerous international film festival awards, yet its Taipei box office was miniscule compared with *City of Sadness*. Ironically, Hou's films now sell more tickets in Paris and New York than they do in Taipei.

Just as vexing, says Chen, is the fact that the current generation of Taiwanese directors embraces Hou's defiant attitude and cinematic style: "For the last ten years, local films have been too arty for the audience. The directors always want to make movies that will win awards at Cannes or Berlin or Venice. They forget the entertainment element. They just want to show their personal style or their personal philosophy, but this just makes the market for local movies smaller. Now the major problem is that the audience feels that watching local movies is a burden." Despite Wolf Chen's admiration of Hou's work, he worries about the fate of Chinese cinema, saying that ironically the industry seems headed in two directions at once: on the one hand, Hong Kong films have deteriorated under the pressures of commercialism, while on the other hand, Taiwanese films have declined because they resisted commercialism. Chen and others, however, also believe that distributors share some of the blame.

As Eric Shih, of Warner Bros., puts it, "One of the reasons that Chinese films have gone into a slump is because the distributors who handle these titles have not adapted to the new era of competition." Throughout the 1980s, Chinese films enjoyed an edge because of an elaborate web of formal and informal constraints on the movie business. Hollywood imports were subject to government quotas, while Chinese films produced in Hong Kong and Taiwan benefited from subsidies and tax policies. This not only limited the amount of available product, it also made it possible for a small circle of distributors to monopolize the supply of theatrical titles in a cartel fashion that is characteristic of Chinese mercantile capitalism. Consequently, exhibitors had to curry the favor of suppliers in order to ensure that they would have access to the movies they needed, and distributors didn't have to concern themselves too much with the mechanics of marketing. Furthermore, government controls on publishing and broadcasting meant that this circle of distributors had the upper hand in securing access to limited advertising space in government-sanctioned newspapers and magazines. This cartellike environment began to break down after martial law was lifted in 1987, as new distributors (such as ERA and BVI), new channels of promotion (in publishing and cable TV), new promotional strategies, and an influx of new films from around the world undermined traditional market relations. "Movies that were built on old relationships, built on small circles of insiders, built on bribery and blackmail, suddenly faced new competition," says Shih. "You had to face the crowd and face the new and different voices from the media."

Shih is not alone in making this assessment. Producers and directors in Hong Kong often complain that their very best movies usually fail in Taiwan, largely because they are handled by an older generation of distributors, who continue to promote films the same way they have for decades. "That doesn't mean that tradition is bad," says Shih, "but they're using the bad parts of the traditional ways. The old traditional way is: they shoot a movie and spread a press release. Right before the film premiere, they'll gather all of the talent and get them on a TV variety show, where they play some games and joke around with the host. Sometimes they will also try to organize some sort of press junket for the journalists and try to give them money to say something favorable about their film. Then they spend a lot of money on TV commercials, but the ads aren't well thought out. All of this happens just three days before the opening." Although such strategies may have been viable in the 1980s, they are sorely lacking in today's more open and competitive environment.

Shih believes that some distributors are beginning to change their ways, especially as the reins of these companies pass from father to son. This is happening at both Scholar and Long Shong—historically two of the biggest distributors of Chinese-language films—with a younger generation of distribution executives beginning to employ many of the same marketing techniques as their Hollywood counterparts. In fact, companies like Long Shong may be changing their ways in part because they hope someday to land a contract representing one of the major Hollywood studios.

Interestingly, at the very moment that distributors of Chinese films are expressing their interest in Hollywood films, executives representing the major U.S. studios are saying that they would like to play a role in the revival of Chinese cinema. Eric Shih says that he thinks *Crouching Tiger, Hidden Dragon* is only the most obvious example of the enormous talent pool in East Asia and the relative cost advantages of producing in the region. Indeed, when I hand him a magic wand and ask him what he would do if he had complete control over Warner's Asian operations, he barely skips a beat before replying, "First of all I would want to guarantee that we have enough [Hollywood] films to do our distribution job. Secondly, I would like to produce and finance some local movies. You have to have a healthy balance between local and foreign movies," he contends. "The demand is there. It's a question of putting together the resources. Local movies have a greater potential to reach a broader audience, not just the young and educated."

Tom Wang, of BVI, agrees: "Around 1996 the trend was to bring Chinese talent to the U.S. and do action movies cheaply. But now the trend is shifting towards, 'Let's recruit the finest talent, put together some financing, and let them make their own movies in their hometown, because that is where their creativity will fully blossom.' That's why Columbia set up a production center in Hong Kong, and that's why they're financing directors like Ang Lee, Zhang Yimou, and Tsui Hark. In the U.S., there are a lot of action directors who can fill the pipeline in Hollywood, but a film like *Crouching Tiger* or *The Wedding Banquet* can only be made in Asia. And if they are done well, these films will bring new audiences to the theater both here and abroad." Wang's and Shih's assessments are shared by many other distribution executives in Taiwan, all of whom grew up locally and say they feel strong ties to the culture.

It's perhaps surprising that another supporter of Chinese film is the general manager of Warner Village. "There is nothing wrong with the Chinese

Jackie Chan's *New Police Story* and Wong Kar-wai's *2046* enjoyed ample production budgets and high-profile marketing aimed at theatergoers in Ximending, the heart of Taipei's movie theater district. Author photo.

film industry," says Steve Kappen. "The only thing that's happened to it is that it has been transferred to Hollywood, and now it's coming back to Asia with the tools that Hollywood uses to make global films." Kappen is proud to point out that Warner Village hosted Ang Lee for the Taiwan premiere of *Crouching Tiger,* and he presumes that the future is bright for coproductions that tap global financing and creative resources from Asia. Kappen argues that the economies of scale in the film business make it virtually impossible for regional and local filmmakers to compete with global product on their own. That doesn't mean, however, that local and regional films can't find a niche at multiplexes such as Warner Village. With an annual demand for two hundred films, Kappen says those in his organization have to keep their eyes open for a diverse range of product. "It's very beneficial for an exhibitor to have a healthy independent film market," explains Kappen, noting that the demand for new titles at his Taipei multiplex outstrips supply from the major Hollywood studios by a factor of more than two to one. Furthermore, he observes, "If you only play major product, like all good things that come from America, it eventually will cost you more." And even though Warner Village has corporate ties to one of the major studios, it constantly battles to bring down the price of film rentals in the Taiwan market.

A disarmingly chatty Australian, Kappen is well suited to the job of wrestling with distributors over film rental fees. Quick with both quips and statistics, he engineered Warner Village's entry into the Taiwan market, focusing his first few years on theater construction and promotion. He then turned his attention to wringing price concessions from suppliers, such as Warner Bros.' distribution manager, Eric Shih. Many presume that global media conglomerates such as Time Warner operate like well-oiled juggernauts, but they are in fact permeated with internal competition among various divisions and ventures. Although Warner Bros.' international *exhibition* division has a huge stake in the success of Warner Village, the *distribution* division treats it like any other exhibitor, asking for a seventy-thirty revenue split during the first week of release. "From our perspective," says Shih, "we want to maximize the revenues for our division. We have no special access to Warner Village theaters, and we give them no special deals. In Chinese we have a saying, 'Even with a brother, we calculate precisely.'" For his part, Kappen passionately criticizes the practices of Hollywood distributors in the island market. "If I am paying 70 percent for film rental in Taiwan, why am I paying 55 percent in Singapore for the same film, released at the same time with an identical ticket price? Or 50 percent in Malaysia? Or 60 percent in Hong Kong or in Korea? We are indeed looking forward to the years when we have more screens [in Taiwan], when we have more leverage. Like all good businesses, if you are big enough, you will buy cheaper. And that ultimately will assist in stabilizing prices, improving facilities, improving technology, but most of all in satisfying patrons." Unmentioned is the historical shift in power from distributor to theater chain manager that would also occur.

Consequently, Kappen would be delighted to see a resurgence of in films from Hong Kong or Taiwan. "The Chinese film industry has never charged 70 percent for anything," he observes. "You can buy Chinese film for as low as 40 percent today; ten years ago, 50, 55 percent." Standing on the side of the angels, Kappen argues for a more open, diverse, and transparent film market, saying that Hollywood distributors have monopolized the industry in Taiwan for too long. I ask him point-blank if his concern for Chinese movies grows out of a philosophic commitment to diversity or a strategic desire for price concessions. Kappen feigns offense at the question, purses his lips and pouts, "*That* would be an unfair statement." Then an impish grin cracks across the corners of his mouth, and he proceeds in a gleefully ironic tone, "It would be really *cruel* for me to do something like that—really, *really* awful." Yet Kappen's lighthearted banter barely conceals his competitive desire to transform the movie business in Taiwan.

Kappen is also challenging what he sees as an artificial limit on the availability of product. Historically, film rights have been sold by territory, and distributors exercise monopoly power within each market. Such practices ensure distributors exclusive control over their titles, but such licensing practices can also lead to abuse. By limiting the supply of movie prints in Taiwan, for example, a distributor can enhance his or her bargaining position with exhibitors who are competing for product. Of course, limiting supply might also affect the distributor, since it could depress total ticket sales. Yet the value of such a strategy is that it allows distributors to wield power over exhibitors when it comes to the negotiation of rental fees, play dates, and screening times. "Talk about archaic business practices," Kappen avers, "[the majors] graciously distribute eighteen prints [in Taipei] for a metropolitan area of four million people. In Melbourne there are forty screens showing the same film, but here the distributors say, 'The government won't allow us to bring in any more.' Taipei could easily support forty screens showing a James Bond film," he declares. Such limitations not only disadvantage Kappen in film rental negotiations, but they also prove worrisome while Warner Village considers its expansion plans for the future. Should the major studios continue to ration the number of prints parsimoniously, it could seriously hinder the company's ultimate ambition to operate fifteen multiplexes in Taiwan.

Before moving to Taiwan, Kappen worked for Village Roadshow in Australia, which was founded in 1954 by Roc Kirby, who made his initial fortune in drive-in theaters and subsequently led the multiplexing wave as the company grew to become the largest theatrical chain down under. Then during the 1980s, like its counterparts in the United States and Europe, the company began to look overseas for growth opportunities. Roadshow executives first turned to Taiwan, visiting in 1988 with prospective partners from Golden Harvest. Problems arose, however, regarding building codes and real estate limitations in city centers and regarding government import quotas for Hollywood films. The partners reasoned that their multiplex strategy could succeed only if there were enough prints to satisfy demand at their theaters. On the basis of their reconnaissance, they bypassed Taiwan, choosing instead to invest in a string of theaters in Singapore and Malaysia in 1992 and 1993. Other joint ventures with Golden Harvest in Thailand and South Korea followed, but the Taiwan project never got off the ground, and Golden Harvest began to lose interest, shifting its attention to mainland China. Consequently, Roadshow went looking for another partner and linked up with Warner Bros. around the time that Taiwanese officials were deliberating about lifting quotas on Hollywood imports. Between 1998 and 2003, Village Roadshow built half a dozen multiplexes in Taiwan and laid plans for three more, featuring more than a hundred screens overall.

Kappen says that the company does extensive market research on all of its prospective sites and that even crude estimates suggest that the demand for cinema in Taiwan far exceeds supply. "Somewhere in Taiwan there are twenty-two million people, which means, by an international standard, there should be sixty-six million admissions each year." With ticket sales only half that much in 2000, Kappen foresees plenty of room for growth. "Our business is very much driven by the nature of available facilities. The equation is really very simple: If you build it, they will come. That is, if you take movies to people, if you provide them with comfortable theaters and good films, more people will go." The company hopes to sell over ten million tickets a year, which could represent more than a third of all tickets sold in Taiwan. Ultimately, the figures could run much higher, since Warner Village in Taipei alone sells three million tickets for only seventeen screens. And outside Taipei, Kappen contends that industry conventions grossly underestimate movie attendance, since they assume that out-island sales are roughly equal to the Taipei box office. Kappen furthermore disputes the conventional wisdom that audiences outside Taipei are significantly different from those in the capital metro area. "Our experience has been, if you do the job right, if you educate, if you appreciate the audience in terms of concessions, screening times, and customer service, people will come. It's almost a *Field of Dreams* mentality, but research supports that." Kappen claims that most theater owners outside Taipei have invested little in promotion or facilities, and consequently the out-island market is ripe for development.

Some distributors agree with Kappen's criticisms, and they especially welcome the installation of computerized sales reporting systems at theaters outside Taipei. Says Patrick Huang of New Action Entertainment, "Most important is having accurate information so that we can know how effective our promotional efforts are and whether we need to spend more

Warner Bros. and Village Roadshow partnered in the development of the largest theater chain in Taiwan, anchored by the Warner Village multiplex in Taipei. Author photo.

money on advertising or whether we need to spend less on a particular film." Indeed, the lack of data regarding ticket sales discourages distributors from running promotional campaigns outside Taipei, and that in turn discourages the growth of ticket sales. "I really appreciate the Warner Village system, because I can know how many tickets were sold to adults, how many to students, how many tickets on promotion," says Huang. Indeed, independent distributors often find it easier to deal with multiplexes than with traditional single-screen cinemas. "Theaters owned by the older generation are more difficult for us to get our pictures in, largely because they aren't multiplexes and they don't have as much flexibility," says another independent. "They just want to work with the majors, and they don't want to do any promotion." By comparison, Warner Village is trying to cultivate relations with alternative suppliers by helping them to promote their films and by showing their films side-by-side with the majors.

Yet distributors like Chen are well aware that Warner Village is playing the independents against the majors. "Their business strategy," he says, "is to use us to force the majors to lower their terms." For some independent distributors, this strategy suits them well for now, but others are skeptical about Warner Village's commitment to a diverse menu of titles. "It's like any chain store," says one. "When they first come to the neighborhood, they try to convince everyone that they bring more choice, not less. But over time, you begin to feel that everything on the shelf looks the same." Although it is difficult to tell whether such an assessment will prove to be true in the long run, one could sense the tension between Warner Village's "global standard" and local cultural expectations at the Chinese New Year grand opening in February 1998. Traditionally, the lunar New Year is the most important holiday of the Chinese calendar and also the most important play date of the year for film exhibitors. Quite often family banquets are preceded or followed by a trip to the cinema, and, given the surfeit of delicacies that are prepared for the holidays, families usually take leftovers with them. Yet breaking with tradition, Warner Village staff discouraged this practice and tried to convince families standing in line at the box office that they should jettison their holiday treats in favor of beverages and popcorn at the concession stands inside. Arguments broke out in the ticket line, causing quite a stir in the local media. Holiday traditions were at stake: prior to the multiplexing of Taiwan, movie fans were thoroughly accustomed to bringing boxed meals with them to the movies, since most theaters are located in city centers, where street vendors hawk such popular treats as fried tofu, hot yams, noodle dishes, barbecued meats, and warm buns stuffed with sweet bean paste. For about two dollars one can buy a delicious dinner that clearly outshines the overpriced popcorn and hot dogs sold at theater concession stands.

Management not only banned boxed meals; it also began an earnest campaign to retrain customers by offering incentives and promotions. "In the very beginning," says operations manager Jessie Chou, "not even 20 percent [of ticket purchasers] bought something at the concession stand, and right now it's over 30 percent, sometimes at 35 percent," which is a figure that compares favorably with those of theaters in Australia and the United

States. Indeed, despite its outspoken support of alternative movies, Warner Village holds fast to its "global standard" of for food consumption in the theaters. In the end, Kappen argues that such changes are necessary if theaters in Taiwan are to become profitable operations that can support a greater diversity of movies, better access for moviegoers, and higher-quality facilities that will be attractive to audiences of all ages. Left to its own devices, says Kappen, a cartel industry protected by government regulations would be unlikely to undertake the necessary changes that might reverse a declining market. In the process, however, some things will be lost, and, perhaps most worrisome, one wonders whether Chinese movies will be among the casualties.

The movie distribution and exhibition businesses provide telling examples of how the centrifugal spatial logic of distribution interacts with forces of sociocultural variation. One might reductively argue that the declining popularity of Hong Kong movies during the 1990s was attributable simply to the elimination of import quotas that subjected the Chinese movie business to overwhelming competition in one of its most important markets. Since import quotas are one of the clearest expressions of political will in the domain of popular media, it seems reasonable to conclude that the elimination of this particular contour of sociocultural variation would clear the way for the logic of accumulation to operate more fluidly, thereby exposing the Hong Kong movie industry to the superior capital resources of Hollywood.

Yet, as we've observed, the decline of Chinese film had already occurred before quotas were lifted, in large part because of hyperproduction in Hong Kong and a resulting deterioration in movie quality. Audiences abandoned Chinese films because they were priced as a premium product that competed with Hollywood counterparts and with other forms of entertainment as well. Movies that seemed satisfactory as a rented video or an inexpensive VCD were woefully incapable of drawing audiences into the theaters. Chinese films also suffered because of deficient marketing practices that were forged in an earlier era when a distributor cartel held sway over a limited number of theaters and promotional outlets. Distributors milked their cash cows with the opportunistic enthusiasm of mercantile capitalists, jealously guarding their monopoly and never bothering to tinker with the system itself. By dint of custom, patronage, and political favor, they built empires that readily seized on the easy fortunes offered by video and cable but were unable to adapt to the challenges posed by a younger generation of distributors who brought a new wave of independent movies to the market after the martial law era had ended and promoted them successfully through alternative media outlets using techniques adapted from abroad. Inspired by these examples, the major Hollywood distributors began to alter their practices and to reshuffle their Taiwanese marketing personnel, promoting young executives well versed in modern managerial and marketing practices. Yet distributors of Chinese films lagged behind, no doubt lulled by a false sense of optimism engendered by exploding new revenue streams in the video and cable markets. By the time they refocused their attention on theatrical marketing, the spiral of decline had already set in. As the market grew more competitive, Chinese movies seemed less attractive. As promotional techniques grew more sophisticated, distributors of Chinese movies held fast to practices that were haphazardly designed and casually executed. Now confronted with direct competition from global media conglomerates, the Chinese movie industry remained a collection of small enterprises guided by a shopkeeper mentality.

If lifting import quotas did have an impact on the Taiwanese market, it was in the realm of exhibition, as global theatre chains moved forward with multiplex plans, increasingly confident that they could secure prints to supply their growing phalanx of theater screens. Confident that global standards for tickets sales, theater construction, and operational practices could revolutionize Taiwan's movie industry, Warner Village executives pressed to change the behaviors of their movie suppliers and audiences. Yet even without quotas, the major Hollywood distributors held fast to past practices, keeping the number of prints in check as they tried to exert pressure on the exhibitors so as to sustain the premium rental prices to which they were accustomed. Interestingly, tensions between the distribution and theatrical divisions of Warner Bros. reveal the complex relations within global media conglomerates themselves, showing how large-scale organizations can be subject to conflicting customs and interests. In an attempt to gain leverage, Warner Village managers have made overtures to independent and Chinese film distributors, hoping to expand the pool of available titles and to subvert the market dominance of Hollywood distributors. Whether this represents a short-term strategy or a long-term commitment is unclear. Even less clear are the fortunes of Chinese commercial cinema in what was formerly its most lucrative territory. With products that seem less distinctive, audiences that are more discriminating, and a market that is now flooded with a diverse menu of movies and entertainment alternatives, the Chinese movie industry can no longer survive on past relationships and practices. The future will require new perspectives and a willingness to explore new organizational structures and new possibilities for cross-media convergence. It will require that film producers and distributors begin to see themselves as part of a larger media industry and, likewise, that television companies expand the scope of their activities as well.

5 The Globalization of Hong Kong Television

In most countries of the world, broadcasting emerged as an adaptive response to the centrifugal tendencies of media distribution, especially with regard to the transnational influence of Hollywood entertainment. When public service media were first launched in Europe during the 1920s and 1930s, governments invested in radio partly as a foil for the growing popularity of American music and movies. During the 1960s, as television swept into Asian territories such as Taiwan, Malaysia, and Hong Kong, government regulators expressed similar concern about the productive and marketing power of Hollywood, but this time they pointed the finger at Hollywood's vast syndication libraries of American TV series as well as its feature films. In countries such as Malaysia, they also expressed concern about the cultural influence of Hong Kong movies and music. Like most other parts of the world, the television economies of Asia emerged as protected oligopolies with government public service mandates.[1] This is not to say that the principles of media capital did not obtain but rather to say that the logic of accumulation and the trajectories of creative migration evolved within geographical spheres that were delimited by the state. In Taiwan, Singapore, Malaysia, and other Southeast Asian territories, television emerged as a medium that was closely protected, monitored, and regulated. In some cases television operated as a wholly owned government institution, while in others a clientele relationship obtained. The centripetal and centrifugal tendencies of media capital unfolded within the context of national broadcasting systems, allowing the state to exercise influence over flows of information and culture in public as well as private contexts.

By the late 1980s, these territorial monopolies grew more problematic as state subsidies waned and as advertising growth within particular markets began to level off. TV executives were forced to look for new opportunities in other media and other markets. Meanwhile, influential Chinese capitalists who had never shown much interest in media began to take notice of the growing importance of information and entertainment, especially when the industrial tigers of East Asia began shifting toward service economies. With new technologies such as VCR, satellite, cable, and computer becoming more widely available, some entrepreneurs began to anticipate a media gold rush. So even though the Chinese film industry seemed headed into troubled waters during the 1990s, the television industry throughout Global China seemed to be moving into a new phase characterized by deregulation, new technology, transnationalization, and political realignment. Hong Kong was at the leading edge of these developments in a number of ways: Run Run Shaw's TVB escalated the overseas distribution of its programming; a Hong Kong property mogul established the territory's first high-tech cable system; and the son of another mogul, Richard Li, launched Star TV, a pan-Asian satellite platform with expansive ambitions. In this chapter I compare these corporate ventures, each of them shaping the transition to a new era characterized by diversification of content and transnationalization of industry strategies and practices.

Originally chartered to operate both Cantonese- and English-language stations, TVB by necessity became a substantial importer of foreign television series during the 1970s. This in turn led to the establishment of a small international division to purchase regional program rights, allowing this Hong Kong station to broadcast shows locally and then resell the remaining territorial rights to broadcasters in such places as Taiwan, Singapore, and Thailand. Syndication was a profitable but relatively minor part of the company until the mid-1970s, when TVB launched its own Chinese drama productions and itself became a significant exporter of series on telefilm. Although the move to drama production was both costly and perhaps risky given the small size of the Hong Kong market, several factors encouraged this pathbreaking initiative. First of all, TVB faced growing competitive pressures when ATV (Asia Television) and Commercial Television came online during the mid-1970s, creating a heated ratings race that forced all three companies to expand from variety and talk shows to far more expensive drama productions. Second, TVB's shift to drama worked to its particular advantage, since the station could tap the resources of Shaw's expansive movie studio to produce programs that were likely to trump the offerings of its much smaller competitors. Finally, the move to drama dovetailed with TVB's growing syndication business, which became so profitable that in

1982 the company set up TVB International (TVBI), devoted solely to the distribution of English- and Chinese-language programming.

TVB seemed destined for long-term prosperity both locally and abroad until suddenly in 1984 the colonial government announced that Hong Kong would revert to Chinese sovereignty in 1997. The impending transition cast a particularly grim light on TVB's prospects, since the station's resolutely capitalist practices and values seemed dramatically at odds with mainland media, which at the time revolved around state radio and newspaper propaganda. Other developments generated further uncertainty for TVB when satellite and videocassette technologies loomed on the horizon. Already popular in Europe and North America, these technologies would, it seemed, eventually affect the Chinese TV industry as well. Moreover, these developments came at a time when the initial enthusiasm for television was beginning to wear thin. TV receivers were now in every home, and the period of sustained and rapid growth was over, but perhaps more worrisome was the fact that the audience was beginning to splinter. Once a city with an expansive Chinese middle class, Hong Kong was by the 1980s becoming a segmented society in which the myth of upward mobility was fading. What had been a truly mass medium during the early 1970s was increasingly becoming a service for older, less affluent audiences. Television was no longer at the center of everyday life. Gone were the days when it gave Hong Kongers a pretext for sharing dreams, aspirations, and emotions. Instead, wealthy and younger citizens began to seek out alternative modes of entertainment, such as movie videos, karaoke, and video games.[2]

Many critics furthermore contend that the medium's declining popularity in the local market was a logical outcome of the TVB's strident campaigns to vanquish all competitors. "Its programming became stale," says media executive Nansun Shi, "because when you are the dominant player for too long, you start to think that people will watch whatever bullshit you produce. TVB had high standards at one time, and they had to, because they faced tough competition, but then when the competition went down, so did the standards. As a [TVB] producer, you begin to ask, 'Why should I try that much more? I don't need to. Even if I drop a little bit, we still have the same ratings. Why should I bother?'" According to Shi, this created a factory mentality, in which innovation took a back seat to the company's primary concern, which was to keep churning out fodder for the local advertising market. Media critic Winnie Chung agrees that TVB's factory mentality began to undermine its appeal to local audiences. "They save money by producing in house and keeping control of distribution rights, but it becomes a very inbred system. It's very fortresslike and the results are very formulaic." Consequently, TVB began to see wealthy segments of its audience gravitating to other forms of entertainment, leaving behind a broadcast audience of "housewives and senior citizens," says Chung. TVB had always won ratings battles against other stations, but by the late 1980s, it was losing the war against competing forms of entertainment. Management then began to explore new opportunities, but government cross-ownership rules prevented the company from moving into other local media.

These converging factors prodded TVB to globalize its operations, exploring new markets and bringing aboard new investors, among them Robert Kuok, a Chinese-Malaysian business magnate renowned for his connections to the Beijing leadership and the overseas Chinese business community. In 1993, Kuok's Kerry Holdings took a 15 percent share of TVB, second only to Shaw's 35 percent controlling interest. The British media conglomerate Pearson bought another 10 percent, significantly altering the ownership structure of the company. Other suitors came and went, including News Corporation, Time Warner, and Sony, each expressing interest in taking control or at least buying a substantial share. Although these deals eventually fell through, TVB management seemed aware that its future would quite crucially rely on transnational operations and linkages.

Armed with the world's largest library of Chinese TV programs—containing more than seventy-five thousand hours of domestic dramas, kung fu epics, musicals, and feature films—TVB also began to explore a diverse range of new ventures. Spearheading the expansion overseas was a video rental enterprise that grew rapidly in markets that had been part of the Shaw Brothers cinema circuit. TVB series about ancient dynasties and kung fu heroes tended to attract ethnic Chinese viewers in Southeast Asia, but dubbed versions also performed well among Malay, Thai, Cambodian, Vietnamese, Korean, and Japanese audiences. By the end of the 1980s, TVBI was operating wholly owned video rental chains in Malaysia, Canada, and London, and it also forged exclusive licensing agreements with retailers in dozens of other territories around the world. Unlike their counterparts in the film industry, who failed to track the ticket sales of Hong Kong movies in overseas markets, TVB managers scrupulously compiled video rental data from each licensee. Such data were used both to calculate revenue splits between distributor and retailer and to develop new marketing strategies. Moreover, like its Hollywood counterparts, TVBI carefully managed the release windows on its programming so as to maximize profitability.

Taiwan became one of the first and most lucrative overseas markets for TVB videos after the company forged a long-term partnership with Chiu

Fu-sheng, the owner of ERA Communications. During the early 1980s, Chiu operated as a program distributor and packager, buying territorial rights to foreign TV shows and then purchasing time slots from Taiwanese broadcasters to air the programs, along with commercial spots that he sold to local advertisers. Chiu's TVB acquisitions proved extraordinarily successful, with the first two series drawing a seventy share in the three-station market.[3] Soon after a third series premiered, Taiwanese station managers met to discuss the new programming phenomenon, worried that it might smother the local drama production industry. After they imposed a broadcasting ban on Hong Kong series, Chiu nevertheless decided to distribute these series on videocassette, enhancing the popularity of the new technology.

Chiu therefore caught the earliest swell of the video rental wave in Taiwan, and his exclusive contract with TVB afforded him control over what would become some of the most popular programming of the 1980s. With Taiwan still under martial law and TVB programs banned from the airwaves, Chiu was able to offer renters the forbidden fruit of television imports from a cosmopolitan city with the most liberal free speech legislation in East Asia. The programs proved enormously popular, and at the end of the 1980s, when cable TV emerged, TVB programs would again play a significant role. "When the pirate cable systems came along," recalls Michael Chan, general manager of TVBI, the operators "would rent videos from ERA, put them in a VCR, and play them over their channels. At the time, there was no way to stop them, and [Chiu] could see that, so when cable got into about 40 percent of homes and it was beginning to affect the video rental market, we put together the TVBS [TVB Superstation] channel. This helped us in two ways: it was a new window, and it arrested our decline in revenues. Then as the government cracked down on piracy [in the mid-1990s], the situation began to look even better: one channel expanded to three channels within a period of four years, and they all became leaders in their respective categories."

The TVBS channels furthermore became foundational programming for a regional satellite service that was fed to cable operators in Indonesia, Singapore, and Malaysia. As these services matured, they in turn became the basis for the global Galaxy satellite platform, serving Asia, Australia, Europe, and North America with news, entertainment, variety, and talk shows. Galaxy both distributes satellite feeds and initiates program production aimed at increasingly diverse international markets. Local operators then select from the Galaxy offerings and package distinctive services for their local audiences. "The idea," says Chan, "is to tap a Greater China market and to provide a service that is adaptable to many variations. In North America, we will probably end up with a Thai channel, a Korean channel, and a Japanese channel. There, it's more than just a Chinese platform; it's an Asian service," with TVB providing the distribution infrastructure that many other Asian TV companies lack. "It's no longer the case that you can say, 'I control the network; I control the technology.' The world has changed and we might as well recognize that. Galaxy positions us initially as the gatekeeper for Chinese news and entertainment and eventually [as the gatekeeper] for the distribution of other people's products. So we're moving from a broadcast model to a position as a major producer and distributor of content for what some people are calling personal TV."[4]

Yet Chan is quick to point out that TVB's true strength as a global distributor lies not with its technology but with the organization itself. "Look at the key markets," he insists. "North America, we're there. Europe, we're there. Taiwan, we're there. Malaysia and Singapore, we're there. Thailand, we're there. Indonesia, we're beginning to be there. We're not just up in the air with satellite footprints like Star TV. We actually have ground forces doing the necessary work with research, programming, and marketing." Chan believes that the future success of TVB will depend on its ability to globalize its reach and to localize its appeal.

The success of TVBI's far-flung ventures was in part fueled by satellite interconnection of Chinese newspapers during the 1990s, allowing Hong Kong- and Taipei-based publishers to deliver stories to subsidiary editions around the world on the very same day. This means that movie premieres, record releases, and pop music concerts now receive near synchronous global exposure to Chinese readers, helping to feed demand for television services that provide the latest in entertainment. With this in mind, TVB managers strategically craft release windows for each TV series, with the Hong Kong broadcast and worldwide video release acting as the premiere window, followed three to six months later by pay-per-view, then cable TV at six to twelve months, and finally terrestrial syndication one year after the initial telecast. "If you're crazy about Hong Kong entertainment or if you're reading one of the satellite versions of the Hong Kong newspapers, you may want to see the program in its first window," explains marketing manager Helena Lee, "but even if you wait for the second or third window, newspapers have helped to create an awareness of the product."

Moreover, the expanding circulation of entertainment news via the Internet, along with the development of Chinese-language software and search engines, has cultivated overseas audiences for TVB products. Those who log on to the Web searching for information about particular stars or series are likely audiences for overseas rental and premium cable products. In the late 1990s, TVB therefore started to develop its own Internet services, including news, talent profiles, program listings, chat rooms, and online games. TVB.com also became an important site for publicizing international promotional tours that provide fans with the opportunity to meet actors and singing stars from TVB programs. As digital technologies further develop, Chan envisions an even more elaborate set of services. "Now the move is to multiple channels and digital interactive platforms," declares Chan. "We're getting ourselves ready for personal media, so whatever we do is content-based. It's more about distribution formats, more narrow-cast, more niche. We need to create new resources and products to fill these niche markets that are appearing all over the place."

To Chan, "all over the place" means exactly that: tying together local niche audiences with TVB's international reach. Unlike the days when virtually everyone in Hong Kong watched TV on a daily basis, Chan observes that today only 40 percent of the local population regularly tunes in, while the rest have fled to other forms of information and entertainment. He believes many of them could be lured back by niche services but cautions that it wouldn't make sense to produce programming for minority audiences in a city of only six million. Yet by linking niche audiences in Hong Kong with overseas audiences for specialty programming, TVB now has the opportunity to expand both the scope of its content and the geographical reach of its services.

Such a shift in the company's distribution strategy also entails a transformation of TVB's production operations. In the past, producers and directors rarely paid attention to the needs of international audiences. Like Hollywood producers, TVB talent attended to domestic viewers, and only afterward would the international division cull items from the local schedule for overseas syndication. During the 1980s and 1990s, Hong Kong performers and programs were enormously popular with Chinese audiences in many parts of the world, and, as we've seen, TVBI had a first mover advantage, so it was able to distribute many of its prime-time dramas to markets in which television services were expanding. Recently, however, foreign markets have become significantly more competitive, especially as a result of the growing sophistication of Mandarin-language TV services that now compete for airtime. It was therefore necessary for TVBI to reassess its production and distribution strategies, looking for synergies between local and global operations. So, for example, the company is now producing shows that might have only niche appeal locally but may prove to be durable performers in transnational markets. "Hong Kong is too small," says Chan.

"We're only six million; Taiwan is four times the size; and in China, one provincial or even one municipal TV station, such as Shanghai, might have an audience of thirty to forty million." Consequently, TVB now caters to its local mass audience, its transnational niche audiences, and, interestingly, to a very large and loyal audience in adjacent Guangdong Province, where studies show that the number of people viewing TVB dramatically exceeds the size of the Hong Kong audience itself.

Indeed, the population of Guangdong Province is eighty-six million people, more than the combined population of California, Texas, New York, and Pennsylvania. Inhabitants of the province, which was hailed as the engine of China's modernization drive under Deng Xiao-ping, are comparatively well-off, and the province was the first to experience the mass diffusion of television during the 1980s. At the time, TVB's "spillover" signal proved enormously popular with Cantonese-speaking residents. Riding through the lush Pearl River Delta, one sees remnants of this past: large, dishlike antennas on rooftops of apartment buildings, all of them pointed toward Hong Kong. Most of these antennas are now neglected relics of the era before cable television, when one could access TVB only by pulling in distant terrestrial signals, but the antennas nevertheless serve as a reminder of the enduring popularity of Hong Kong television throughout the region.[5]

Unfortunately, TVB found it difficult to capitalize on this popularity, because until recently it was impossible to calculate the number of Guangdong viewers, their consumer preferences, and their access to consumer goods. Consequently, it was hard for TVB to convince its advertisers to pay for the spillover audience. In the mid-1990s, when the Chinese government began to encourage low-cost cable hookups, the situation seemed destined to improve, but cable operators refused to pay license fees to the Hong Kong stations and furthermore refused to respect the integrity of TVB transmissions, replacing Hong Kong commercials with their own local advertising. National and provincial officials sympathized with TVB managers during more than a decade of protracted negotiations but claimed difficulty in spurring reform, since local cable operators were heavily dependent on the revenue generated by their illicit advertising inserts. Cable carriage in the Pearl River Delta nevertheless allowed TVB to build a powerful brand identity and to achieve an enviable position in TV ratings, regularly dominating the top ten slots. So even though piracy of the TVB signal was a source of irritation throughout the 1990s, it nevertheless signaled a lucrative possibility for the future, especially because China continued along its path toward marketization and Hong Kong moved inexorably toward re-unification with the mainland.

TVB's successes abroad during the 1980s grew ever more valuable when regulators in Hong Kong began to scrutinize the company's monopolization of the local television market and implied that it was time to take action. Yet regulators confronted a peculiar dilemma, since it would be difficult to take action against TVB without clear documentation that the company had engaged in anticompetitive practices. Although performers and advertisers often grumbled about the restrictive contracts they were pressed into, no one dared to step forward publicly and file a grievance with the Television Licensing Authority. Artists feared that such a move would be tantamount to professional suicide, and advertisers were loath to jeopardize their standing with the single most important promotional medium in the territory. Lacking documented complaints, government action against the station would appear to be "punishing TVB for its success." Moreover, the company's market power was not exceptional when compared with that of other local industries such as banking, real estate, and supermarkets, which were likewise dominated by only a few large-scale competitors.

Consequently, the Broadcast Review Board imposed only modest constraints on the company in 1985 by limiting cross-media ownership, restricting its local operations to the television business. It furthermore decided the best way to enhance competition would be to encourage the development of cable television, thereby multiplying the number of competitors. At the time, Hong Kongers had access to only two Cantonese- and two English-language stations. Concerned about market concentration and anxious not to be left behind other high-tech societies, the government decided to solicit bids for an exclusive fifteen-year license to build the territory's first fiber optic cable network. Regulators justified this monopoly charter by projecting that cable technology would spur the proliferation of new channels and provide an alternative telecommunications infrastructure that might someday compete with the territory's local telephone monopoly. Numerous companies immediately expressed interest, but the scope and scale of the undertaking seemed to call for more resources than any single firm could muster. It wasn't until 1986 that two consortia finally materialized, one led by Hong Kong Telecommunications (HKT), the colony's existing telephone monopoly, and the other led by Li Ka-shing, of Hutchison Whampoa, one of the wealthiest tycoons in East Asia.[6]

Hutchison Whampoa seemed an unlikely bidder, since it had no experience with media and little experience with telecommunications. The company's patriarch, K. S. Li, began his rise to power during the 1950s, manufacturing plastic flowers in a small factory amid the shantytowns of the British colony. As Hong Kong flourished, so did Li's business, expanding into shipping, petroleum, and real estate. In only two decades, Li rose to become one of the territory's wealthiest capitalists and something of a local folk hero. Reputedly, his meteoric rise to riches was predicated on his ability to turn around floundering enterprises that had been abandoned by other investors. Li bought low and sold high, earning him a devoted following among small- and large-scale investors. In 1978, he consolidated his status as one of the preeminent tycoons of East Asia when he boldly bid for control of Hutchison Whampoa, making him the first Chinese capitalist to take command of a venerable British hong, or trading house.

Just as boldly, in 1985 Li formed Hutchison Cable Vision (HCV), a consortium that included British Telecom, the Hongkong Bank, and TVB. Although TVB was precluded from making a bid of its own, the company was allowed to take a minority position in Li's venture, and Shaw's considerable programming resources no doubt loaned an air of legitimacy to the fledgling enterprise. Yet Li's interest in the fiber optic cable license was perhaps sparked less by television than by telecommunications. Investing first in a paging service during the early 1980s, Li shortly thereafter moved on to cellular phones, a domain in which his company quickly captured the imagination of Hong Kongers when it ran a series of newspaper ads featuring photos of the boss icing yet another deal on his cell phone. Given Li's folk hero status, the phones quickly became a sign of aspiration, if not necessity, among local business people, from small shop owners to well-heeled financiers.

What started as a diminutive paging service soon grew into a sprawling telecommunications empire that expanded onto three continents, becoming one of the biggest players worldwide. Li's bid for the Hong Kong cable license was therefore part of a larger strategy to develop a fiber optic backbone for his proliferating communication enterprises. As the deadline for proposals neared, a consulting firm hired by the government dramatically tilted the bidding process in Li's favor by raising concerns about a conflict of interest posed by the competing Hong Kong Telecommunications consortium. Noting that telephony, not television, was seen by both bidders as the jewel in the cable crown, the consultants pointed out that a successful bid by HKT, the territory's telephone monopoly, would undermine the ancillary purpose of the cable license, which was to foster competition in the telecommunications market. With the deadline fast approaching, it looked as if Li's group would secure the license. Yet regulators worried that a single bidder would undermine the government's negotiating leverage. Moreover, many critics contended that a cable monopoly would extend Li's already expansive control over a range of strategic local businesses, from real estate to retailing to utilities. As complaints mounted, the colonial government dramatically shifted course, reopening the process and inviting bids from foreign investors. Within six months a new consortium was formed under the leadership of Wharf Holdings, a company owned by Pao Yue-kong, another of the city's great tycoon's.

Like Li Ka-shing's, Pao's biography resembles a Horatio Alger tale. Born in 1918, the son of a cobbler in the port city of Ningbo, just south of Shanghai, Pao fled to Hong Kong after the revolution and began a modest import-export business before buying a rusty, second-hand steamer in 1955, an investment he would eventually parlay into the world's biggest cargo fleet, Worldwide Shipping. By the 1970s, Pao's oil tankers had the capacity to carry twenty-one million tons of fuel, dwarfing his closet competitor, Aristotle Onassis, whose ships could transport a mere three million tons. Pao was perhaps the first Hong Kong tycoon to achieve truly international status, but he remained quirky and unassuming in a number of ways. He was a fitness enthusiast who packed a jump rope in his luggage on business trips, and he rarely carried cash, preferring instead to borrow from his chauffeur. His business philosophy was similarly frugal: "Take a thin profit," he said, "and never accept an escalation clause in a shipbuilding contract."[7] Such was his stature that Pao was invited to join the board of directors of the Hong Kong and Shanghai Bank. As a board member, Pao used his influence to pave the way for another historic transition when he championed Li Ka-shing's bid for a controlling share of Hutchison Whampoa in 1978, a move that reportedly established a close personal bond between the two men. Only two years later, Pao himself would follow Li's example, taking charge of another British trading house, the Hong Kong and Kowloon Wharf & Godown Ltd., later renamed Wharf Holdings. Yet having achieved preeminence in the Chinese business community, Pao abruptly decided to retire in 1986 and relinquish control to his four sons-in-law, among them, Peter Woo Kwong-ching, then thirty-eight, the husband of his second daughter, Bessie.[8]

Woo's parents, like Pao, fled Shanghai on the eve of the Communist Revolution, arriving in Hong Kong when Peter was a small child. Although the transition was difficult for the family, its fortunes improved quickly, and Peter was able to spend his teenage years at a private boys school. Reflecting on his past, Woo once referred to his prep school as a "country club" that instilled an enthusiasm for sports and no doubt also benefited him by providing social connections and English-language instruction, preparing him for future commercial endeavors. After taking a degree in math and physics at the University of Cincinnati, where he was senior class president and a varsity cheerleader, Woo completed his MBA studies at Columbia University in only one year, followed by three years with Chase Manhattan Bank. He returned to Hong Kong at the age of twenty-seven to wed Bessie Pao in what was gushingly referred to by local newspapers as the social event of the year. Lean, polished, and dapperly dressed in designer-label suits, Woo worked as Pao's assistant for several years before assuming executive responsibilities. As he took control, Woo seemed anxious to make a distinctive contribution to the Wharf conglomerate, and cable television seemed to offer just such an opportunity.

Yet stepping into the bidding process in 1989 was sure to raise the hackles of Pao's friend Li Ka-shing, who was already disturbed by the government's decision to alter the tender rules only a year before the deadline. An ambitious Peter Woo nevertheless seized the moment, putting together a consortium with US West, Belgium's Coditel, local property baron Sun Hung Kai, and, oddly enough, Run Run Shaw, who now was lined up on both sides of the bidding. Woo's larger strategy was to move Wharf out of the shipping business and into real estate, telecommunications, and the hotel industry, all of which put him on a collision course with Li's companies, instilling a competitive resentment that reportedly continues to this day.

Finally, in July 1989, only a few weeks after the Tiananmen massacre, Li Ka-shing abruptly withdrew his application for the cable license, sparking rampant speculation among investors and critics. Some viewed it as a strategic retreat, instigated by events in Beijing. With the impending transfer of Hong Kong's sovereignty in 1997, the slaughter of civilians in Tiananmen Square cast a sobering pall over the British colony during the summer of 1989, and overseas migration picked up pace, especially among well-educated, upscale families who are a key target for cable TV and premium telecommunication services. Moreover, the uncertain political situation raised questions about the security of future investment in Hong Kong's infrastructure. Just as likely a reason for Li's pullout, however, may have been that the terms of the contract simply didn't meet his expectations for profitability, as he stated at the time. HCV was offering to build the cable system for roughly $500 million, but the government wanted a system that would cost $700 million. Li was offering an 8 percent royalty on turnover, but the government wanted 10 percent. Moreover, Li was reportedly miffed by the bidding process. But perhaps most important, as one inside source claims, the government made it clear to Li that cable TV should not be seen as the opening move in a telecommunications endgame. Television, rather than telephony, was the government's key concern, and regulators warned that the licensee would be responsible for delivering a robust menu of programming, something that Li probably perceived as troublesome and expensive, if not risky.

In the end, Wharf was the only company that tendered a bid, and it too seemed shaken by the government's emphasis on cable TV, negotiating only a three-year license to develop a very modest system. Ironically, Wharf was no more enthusiastic about the television business than Hutchison, which is why it turned to media executive Nansun Shi to write the programming portion of its application. "Cable was the Trojan horse for the telephone service," recalls Shi. "[Wharf] saw Hong Kong Telecom making huge profits on its fixed-line service, and that's what they were after." The appeal of telephony was furthermore grounded in cultural biases of the entrepreneurial elite. "Hong Kong is very much built on real estate," explains Shi, "so they really *believe* in real estate. And they believe in manufacturing, too, but cable TV, well, that was television, entertainment. It's changing, but the people who were making these bids all came from the elite businesses in Hong Kong. They had no experience with television and no real interest in it." Consequently, Wharf rolled out a minimal cable system, hoping the government would allow it to expand into telecommunications after the initial three-year license. They cobbled together twenty channels of free programming and delivered them via MMDS (multipoint microwave distribution system), using microwave transmitters on the mountain peaks of Hong Kong to deliver signals to receiver dishes on top of buildings that served as the head ends of cable loops in neighborhoods and apartment complexes. It was a tentative solution and certainly not the sophisticated fiber network that government planners originally envisioned. Yet until Wharf received clearance to move into telecommunications, company managers said they were reluctant to lay fiber optic trunk lines. As a result, the early years of cable in Hong Kong were largely a disaster.

Besides technological limitations, the system suffered from a lack of compelling programming. "One of the key problems was content," observes Shi. "If we had been operating in an English-language environment, we could have acquired lots of programming from around the world. Even then, you still have to develop some of your own shows, because everyone knows that cable is driven to some extent by local programming. But here's the problem: the Cantonese market is so small. If you produce your own, it's expensive. If you try to buy it from somebody else, they turn out to be your

Nansun Shi, cofounder of Film Workshop, developed the programming plan for Wharf's bid for the cable television franchise in Hong Kong. Author Photo.

competitors [like TVB or ATV] and they don't want to sell to you." And although the television industry in nearby Guangdong Province was growing rapidly, its programming lagged far behind the glossy production values of the Hong Kong market. In addition to building a network, Wharf would therefore need to produce hundreds of hours of original programming each year and expend further resources on repackaging content acquired from overseas. Marketing the new cable service proved difficult as well, since most potential customers lived in housing complexes, many of them built and managed by real estate firms that were reluctant to allow a competitor's cable lines in their buildings. In other complexes, the company needed to gain approval from tenant committees, an equally difficult and time-consuming process. Consequently, Wharf initially chose to focus on public housing estates where approval could be secured from the central housing authority. But this had its drawbacks as well, since residents often weren't interested in the added expense of cable TV, declaring themselves highly satisfied with TVB.

After several rocky years of development, Wharf Cable finally began to find its feet when it started rolling out a broadband service and refining its programming and marketing strategies. Peter Tsi, former head of programming, says that during the 1990s, Wharf shifted its focus back to upscale families, constituting less than 40 percent of local households. In Wharf's average household, "both parents work and family members spend only ninety minutes each day watching television, but when they do watch, they want more than the broadcast stations have to offer," explains Tsi. Wharf caters to these needs by providing a range of programming, including children's and women's channels, documentaries, news, movies, and sports. Yet, says Tsi, most families sign up for one of two reasons. The first is access to sports programming, especially the World Cup soccer matches. Starting in 1994, Wharf bid aggressively for exclusive rights to World Cup telecasts in Hong Kong, setting off a firestorm of criticism that the popular championship, which previously was shown on free-to-air broadcast channels, was being privatized. Government regulators refused to intervene, however, and the championship series became one of the company's enduring promotional devices, generating a dramatic uptick in subscriptions with each championship. Some of these sports fans continue their cable subscriptions, especially in public housing estates, because, says Tsi, they "are drawn to both World Cup and European league play, and they want to have access to all the games, not just one or two. The [broadcasting] stations would never play this stuff except on weekend mornings. They wouldn't even run it late night. The soccer audience is a very strong one." Feature films are the other major attraction for Wharf. "The movie watchers don't really care what you are playing," observes Tsi. "They feel they are watching for free and don't mind what it is, so long as it's watchable. The ratings are very stable, except for big movies—recent titles that you spend time promoting—but most of the time it's like they have cable TV instead of a fish tank."

Other than high profile movies and sports events, Wharf's strategy is less an entertainment strategy than a common carrier strategy. That is, Wharf cable executives are not trying to shape audience tastes or inspire loyalty with a discerning mix of marquee attractions. Instead, they provide a diverse combination of channels for a modest amount of money, carefully weighing costs and revenues. When they invest in expensive programming, such as big-ticket movies or World Cup soccer, they base it solely on cautious market calculation rather than on inspiration. "Wharf looks at TV just like another one of its shopping arcades," says Peter Tsi. "They want certain shops like DKNY because they want the image, but they're not really interested in the shop itself or even what's in the shop. They're interested in the rent." Tsi's assessment is shared by other TV executives, who say that Wharf was an odd choice to run the territory's first cable service. "They have no big vision for the future of media and may not even be in the business in ten years," comments one executive. "Of course, if they were asked by a journalist, they would act as if they had some sort of vision, but their real objective is to build up the par value in case they want to sell it. They have no attachment to the media industry per se."

In keeping with Wharf's bias toward tangible capital assets, management slowly but surely expanded the fiber optic network until cable lines passed most businesses and homes in the territory. In the late 1990s, when broadband coverage reached critical mass and when the city became enamored of the dotcom economy, the asset value of Wharf Cable began to rise rapidly. In 1999, near the height of dotcom fever, the company rebranded itself as i-Cable, an interactive service connected as much to the future of the Internet as to the business of cable television. Listing itself on the NASDAQ, i-Cable offered 18 percent of its shares to the public, raising close to $400 million in fresh capital, most of which helped to pay down the $900 million in debt owed to the parent company, Wharf Holdings. Peter Tsi says that with that stroke, Wharf came close to realizing the first phase of its business plan—to break even. And indeed, at the time of the initial public offering, the company was returning a modest yearly operating profit, and the net asset value of i-Cable stood at close to $1 billion.

Most of that value resides in the network infrastructure, says Tsi. "To them, that's Tara: home, land, something tangible; that's still the most important thing to them. Just take a look at *Gone with the Wind* and you know their mentality. Wharf is sticking very, very tightly to its network, because they believe this is the one thing that will keep them in competition." Tsi claims this is especially important given the volatility of the digital economy. "To them, it's good to have flashy content, it's good to have interesting portals, but at the end of the day, network access is what will bring you reliable income and market position." Tsi, who has since moved on to other ventures, observes that Wharf has a very conservative, very modest strategy, built around the notion that content is a mercurial business with some very big winners and lots of bright, dynamic losers. As services proliferate, management holds even more tenaciously to the notion that others can provide the content, so long as i-Cable provides the connection. "I don't think Wharf wants to beat anybody, actually," says Tsi. "It's a very, very *Chinese* concept. They would be happy enough if they could stay as, let's say, one of the three survivors in the market. They wouldn't say it, but I think that's more or less the strategy. Because they believe if that other guy spends a hundred bucks to be number one, wouldn't we be smart if we just spent thirty to be number three? They look at profitability and longevity." The emphasis, says Tsi, is not so much on the service as it is on the investment. "It's sort of an asset-building strategy. If you stay in the market long enough, you're worth something. And what they think is, the only thing that matters is to have something with tangible value. And if I put myself in their shoes, maybe this is not a bad strategy. Because connection is something that Wharf has and not everybody else has. So to ride on that is sensible. My only concern is: don't be too cheap with your content, because you still have to do that." According to Tsi, content is important both to attract audiences and to keep them happy when other competitors enter the market.

It was probably no surprise to Peter Woo that Li Ka-shing would reappear as one of those competitors only a year after he withdrew his cable bid. Heading up a satellite communication consortium, Li seemed to be searching for a back door into the Hong Kong television market, and satellite technology offered a promising gateway, since satellite and cable have been at turns complementary and competitive technologies throughout their histories. During the 1980s, satellite services expanded rapidly around the world, spreading signals across vast footprints. Nothing short of a comprehensive global treaty could stop these proliferating transmissions, and, as the cost and size of dishes decreased, seemingly nothing could stop audiences from purchasing the receiving equipment. By the end of the 1980s, viewers in Bangkok, Riyadh, and Belgrade could buy a sixty-inch dish for as little as $600. As sales exploded upward, industry executives began to promote these audiences as promising targets for advertising and pay services. Yet the debates over satellite TV continued, centering not only on technology and commerce but also on issues of national sovereignty. In Europe, Jack Lang, the French minister of culture, famously decried the encroaching influence of satellite channels by conjuring up the loathsome specter of "wall-to-wall *Dallas*" as the future of European television. Throughout the 1980s, such flamboyant hyperbole colored policy debates across the Continent as public broadcasters witnessed their television monopolies succumb to pressures exerted by rising costs, new technologies, and growing competition. Up until that decade, the technical constraints of terrestrial broadcasting had limited the number of available TV channels within any given territory because of signal interference problems, creating a condition known as signal scarcity. With only a few channels available to each nation, many governments entrusted the medium to public service institutions, while others carefully vetted and regulated commercial providers. Satellite channels miraculously overcame the problem of signal scarcity by employing an underutilized part of the electronic spectrum well above the frequencies used by existing technologies. This new frontier allowed many more channels to operate without interfering with one another and therefore promised a cornucopia of programming that would make it difficult to justify artificial limits on the number of channels.

Satellite technology therefore seemed to trump a fundamental rationale for public service broadcasting, but it did not ameliorate concerns about the impact of foreign media on local populations. That would have to wait until the dramatic events of 1989, when popular uprisings unfolded across the globe from Manila to Tiananmen to Gdansk. Each of these events seemed intimately tied to the spread of new communication technologies, leading ABC's Ted Koppel to expound enthusiastically about the democratic potential of satellite TV during a U.S. network news special entitled *Revolution in a Box*. Koppel, like many others at the time, contended that dramatic changes in electronic media would hasten the march of democracy, ushering in a new era in human history. Indeed, Marshall McLuhan's "global village" now seemed within reach, as a stratospheric rhetoric of satellite TV saturated newspaper and magazine articles with breathtaking accounts of signals transcending national boundaries, overriding restrictive government policies, and connecting villagers in remote parts of the world to the flow of global events.

The vaunted prospects of satellite TV also attracted the attention of investors such as Li Ka-shing, who was approached during the late 1980s by a group of entrepreneurs that had purchased Westar VI, a communication satellite launched in 1984 that wandered off course, requiring a NASA shuttle crew to retrieve and repair the wounded bird. Li was intrigued both by the discount price of the satellite and by the prospect of expanding his telecommunications empire. In conjunction with Cable & Wireless (the British Telecom giant) and CITIC (the Chinese government's official investment arm), Li purchased the satellite and relaunched it into high orbit over the Indian Ocean, creating a satellite footprint that stretched from the Middle East to Japan and Indonesia. Renamed AsiaSat I, it could carry both telecommunication and television signals. And even though Li was primarily interested in the former, it was his Star TV venture that would draw far more attention, for it seemed to usher in the bold prospect of pan-Asian television.

Yet governments within the region, like their European counterparts, were less sanguine about the prospects of satellite TV, accustomed as they were to sovereign control over the circulation of images and ideas within their borders. Satellite television promised to change that, opening a new window onto the outside world for millions of viewers. Even more dramatically, in India and China, the satellite era dawned at the very same time as the arrival of television for the masses. In 1980, fewer than a million PRC citizens owned televisions, but by the end of the decade the figure had soared to over eighty million. India was likewise experiencing a television revolution, and transnational media companies looked to these countries as promising new markets that were also undergoing a period of trade liberalization and deregulation.

In early 1990, Hutchison Whampoa launched Satellite Television Asia Region (Star), headed by Li Ka-shing's twenty-three-year-old son, Richard Li Tzar-kai. With the company conceived as a competitor to Wharf Cable, Star staffers busied themselves preparing to file for access to the Hong Kong market after Wharf's exclusive three-year license lapsed, but the company also entertained more expansive ambitions, proclaiming itself a pan-Asian service aimed at innovators, trendsetters, and decision makers. "People who fly first class when they travel abroad," trumpeted one of Star's promotions. "People familiar with global lifestyles and the latest technology." People like, well, like Richard Li, who was groomed for leadership from a tender age, when he and his elder brother, Victor, first began attending company board meetings. Packed off to prep school in Palo Alto, California, Li later attended Stanford to study engineering for several years before departing for Toronto, where he worked a short stint with an investment bank. In January 1990, he returned to Hong Kong at the behest of his father, who put him in charge of a venture capital portfolio at Hutchison Whampoa. It wasn't long before Richard latched on to the exciting prospect of satellite TV, promoting the idea to his father and personally taking charge of the fledgling company.

Although some expressed admiration for Richard's leadership, others considered him an ill-mannered and abrasive boss who put impossible demands on employees. Having hired some of the best executive talent in the Asian television business, Richard reportedly bullied and berated them, apparently hoping to realize the expansive expectations that he and others were circulating to investors and news reporters regarding pan-Asian satellite TV. Noting his seemingly affected British accent, one Star executive referred to him as a "pompous little [expletive]," while another observed, "Either he's going to be one of the great successes of twenty-first-century capitalism, or a colossal crash-and-burn failure."[9] Richard's immaturity proved to be the focus of press speculation during the early years of Star, and many wondered if his drive to succeed grew out of a desire to step out from under the shadow cast by his father. Richard dismissed this possibility, claiming instead that the pressure to succeed came from the market-place, and indeed Star became one of the most flamboyant new enterprises of the 1990s and one of biggest news stories in Asia.

The most immediate challenges confronting Li's staff were cash and content. In search of programming, the company cast about for services that were seeking to establish a presence in Asia and were therefore available at a discount. BBC's World Service Television and Prime Sports Network out of Denver, signed on to the new venture, since it allowed them to lay claim to an expanding presence in Asia. Likewise, MTV, which had pioneered one of the most successful satellite services in Europe during the 1980s, was looking to expand eastward. And Star itself cobbled together a Mandarin-language service, redubbing programs acquired from ATV in Hong Kong and movies culled from a film library it established under the name Media Assets. In all, Star's initial operating budget was estimated at $80 million a year, besides the more than $120 million in start-up costs.

As the premiere date approached, Star's marketing staff began to peddle charter advertising subscriptions to longtime business associates of the Li family. For $250,000 one could purchase two years of ad time and receive preferred status in a future flotation of Star shares. Institutional ads therefore prevailed initially, but ad spots for consumer goods soon took off as well, in part as a result of Star's market research, which claimed in 1992 that its channels were reaching eleven million homes in forty-seven countries. These figures were impossible to verify given the rudimentary quality of audience measurement then available in most Asian countries. More persuasive evidence was derived from promotional ploys that, for example, invited viewers to subscribe to a free programming schedule. In 1993, the company delivered 365,000 schedules each week via fax, almost a third of them to China, with others spreading from Yemen to Korea.[10]

Equally compelling evidence of Star's impact seemed to come from governments protesting the intrusion of satellite signals from afar. Indian officials were early and passionate critics, challenging the company's right to operate in a gray zone created by the absence of international satellite regulations. Faced with enormous social and economic development challenges, the government worried that the unbridled commercialism and sensuality of channels such as MTV Asia would undermine the public service mission of Indian television. In a different vein, the Japanese government criticized Star's attempt to skim prime advertising revenue from its national broadcasters, and Singaporean bureaucrats complained about the ideological content of Star, banning private receiving dishes and fashioning a highly sophisticated (and highly regulated) cable system to compete for the attention of audiences.

Such anxieties only fueled Star's mystique and encouraged the sale of ad time. And no one was stoking the fires of controversy more assiduously than Richard Li, who in his midtwenties fashioned himself as something of a visionary, making bold pronouncements about the dawn of pan-Asian advertising and the twilight of mass broadcasting. "Ultimately, niche channels could be supported by specific industries," opined Li. "An automobile channel, for instance, could be financed by car companies. Indeed, television of the future will enlighten, entertain, and uplift us in surprising new ways. It's an inexpressibly vital form of liberty that we are to gain: the freedom of choice."[11] Regardless of what limited enlightenment one might expect from an automobile channel sponsored by car manufacturers, Li was avidly participating in the very same stratospheric discourse that had spurred the new technology in Europe: satellite TV promised to erase spatial barriers and national frontiers, helping to bring together far-flung audiences and specific shared interests. Although available to many, satellite TV targeted the affluent consumer, who, it was suggested, deserved the basic human right to choose. Japanese regulators might fulminate and Indian authorities might fret, but the stratospheric discourse of satellite TV made it seem that little could be done to stop the growing momentum of Star and the upwardly mobile middle class that it served.

Nevertheless, significant problems festered. For one thing, the company still lacked adequate market research to inspire advertisers to pay premium rates. Levi's jeans might be flashed on television screens across Asia, but the size and location of audiences remained vague. Did viewers, in fact, have access to stores that carried the product? Was it truly within their means? And how did the cost of Star's advertising compare with local forms of promotion? Perhaps even more troublesome was the competition that Star's seemingly bright prospects were beginning to attract; by 1993 some 350 transponders were beaming signals at the Asian continent, including new services sponsored by global media conglomerates. Such pressures exacerbated concerns about Star's modest menu of programming. Although management had assembled enough channels to draw the attention of millions, the novelty was beginning to wear off, and the future seemed likely to include direct competition from the likes of ESPN, HBO, and TVB. Star was now on the threshold of the big-time media industry, a terrain littered with the carcasses of upstart novelty acts that couldn't sustain themselves over the long haul. Pan-Asian rhetoric aside, it needed programming strategies that were targeted at specific time zones, cultures, languages, and competitors. That meant program costs were sure to rise, and the Li family would have to assess the depth of its commitment to the television business.

As early as 1992, there were numerous reasons for the Lis to begin searching for satellite partners or even outright buyers. Chief among them were the financial reversals suffered by Hutchison enterprises in the early 1990s. After Hutchison purchased the Alberta-based Husky Oil in 1986, a soft global oil market and the collapse of the Soviet economy forced Husky to write off $200 million in losses. Similarly, Hutchison's aggressive expansion into the European cell phone business started to founder, as the $1.3 billion rollout of Hutch Telecom in the United Kingdom showed only faint signs of health, with management anticipating ongoing losses until the end of the decade. Other projects were slated to launch in Australia, Greece, and Germany, but then Li Ka-shing suddenly reversed course, deciding to withdraw from all three places. As one securities analyst in Hong Kong speculated, "They are so deeply involved in the U.K. that they can't pull out, so they have to pull out elsewhere." For many years, Li Ka-shing had been accustomed to operating in markets in which his firm dominated and the barriers to entry for new competitors were high. The senior Li's penchant for owning infrastructure—real estate, utilities, port facilities, and retail chains—shows why he was initially interested in telecommunications. Not everyone could own and control satellite, cellular phone, and fiber optic cable networks. The world of entertainment was different, however, with far more competitors, many of them more experienced than Li and some with even deeper pockets than the Hong Kong billionaire. Perhaps with this in mind, Star TV executives started shopping for partners, first opening talks with Pearson, but soon broadening their discussions to include other suitors, among them Rupert Murdoch, then the world's most aggressive satellite television operator and chair of the News Corporation media conglomerate.

Up until the mid-1980s, television in Hong Kong was a government-regulated oligopoly, dominated by Run Run Shaw's powerful TVB, a company that alone commanded more than half of all advertising expenditures in the territory. Earnings from this lucrative franchise began to plateau, however, when television ownership reached most households and when the audience began to fragment into smaller market segments. Government protection that at one time assured market dominance and profitability had now become a constraint on accumulation, with regulators seeking to rein in TVB's attempts to expand across media platforms. With profit growth diminishing, TVB was in need of a "spatial fix." This might have involved the reorganization of its production facilities, but they were already highly concentrated and refined, so much so that programming was often criticized as formulaic. The centripetal logic of accumulation therefore seemed fully exploited, leaving the centrifugal realm of distribution as the focus of management's attention. Pressed to explore new areas for growth while restricted from cross-ownership in the local market, TVB began to look overseas, initially developing video rental services before expanding to cable and satellite TV, first in Taiwan and then throughout Asia and even farther afield. Commercial Hong Kong television, which had been focused on local identity, now needed to reinvent itself using new technologies to complement its local programming with niche-market fare that could be targeted at audiences around the world. This new emphasis on "personal TV" sought to take advantage of new delivery technologies and media convergence, allowing TVB to refashion itself as a transnational conglomerate rather than as a licensed local broadcaster.

Such transformations were further stimulated by government regulators who sought to encourage broadband communication technologies, which they saw as crucial to sustaining Hong Kong's stature as a global financial center. Focusing first on television, government regulators solicited bids for an exclusive cable franchise, attracting the attention of the territory's business elite, who had previously shunned what they saw as the crass, volatile, and ephemeral world of entertainment. Yet the prospect of building a broadband network for both television and ultimately telecommunications drew interest from two of the wealthiest and most influential capitalists in Hong Kong, both of them heavily invested in real estate and shipping but looking to migrate into the unfolding information economy of the late twentieth century.

Peter Woo, who built Hong Kong's Wharf Cable system, saw television as a Trojan horse for his company's strategic interest in telephony, a utility that he hoped would at first provide an exclusive government franchise and in the long run turn into a capital-intensive network with tangible asset value. Woo had little interest in television programming per se, seeing it largely as window dressing to attract subscribers, who could provide ongoing streams of rental revenue that could then be plowed back into capital development. Wharf's strategy was strongly influenced by its previous experiences in real estate and shipping, and the company invested only marginally in program production, focusing instead on the network infrastructure. The strategy proved unexpectedly successful when the dotcom boom allowed Wharf to rebrand itself as i-Cable and float shares in the red hot speculative fever of the late 1990s NASDAQ.

Likewise, Li Ka-shing entered the satellite business with a common carrier strategy, hoping to control capital-intensive infrastructure that could be used by a host of communication services, including his burgeoning telecommunications business. He was no doubt surprised that a motley pan-Asian television channels run by his son would engender eager enthusiasm and speculation. Despite this, as Richard scrambled to amplify Star's first-mover advantage and build its brand identity, he and his staff still encountered emerging competition from experienced media conglomerates with far greater creative resources. Unlike Woo's cable franchise, Li's satellite system had neither an exclusive monopoly nor a territorial infrastructure to hold competitors at bay. Lacking such advantages, the Hutchison enterprises either had to plunge into the competitive world of content production and fully embrace the logic of media capital or needed to unload the brand they built before it began to unravel. Either way, the Lis seemed acutely aware that Chinese capitalists could no longer ignore the media business, and, like Shaw, they seemed to sense that the future of the industry would be transnational rather than local, a lesson that was being learned in other markets as well.

6   Strange Bedfellows in Cross-Strait Drama Production

Although Hong Kong was the undisputed capital of the Chinese commercial media production during the 1990s, Taiwan was still the largest single market for movies, music, and television. After the end of martial law in 1987, however, new challenges and opportunities arose in Taiwan when the government relaxed restrictions on media, spurring the emergence of dozens of fiercely competitive new television companies. Unlike the martial law era, during which three state-controlled channels monopolized the airwaves, the new media economy offered the average viewer more than a hundred cable channels, featuring a broad range of programming and political opinions, making Taiwan an increasingly open, if also unruly, media environment.

In this chapter I explain the pervasive impact of media privatization and liberalization during the 1990s, focusing on the fortunes of terrestrial television services. I show how shifting forces of sociocultural variation profoundly affected the strategies and operations of these media institutions as tight government controls on media imports and local production gave way to an increasingly diverse and competitive market. Accordingly, major television services were pressed to look for new markets, new partners, and new production resources. Surprisingly, in many cases these partners turned out to be stations in the PRC that were themselves experiencing dramatic competitive pressures and audience fragmentation. In their bid to survive and prosper, the big three Taiwanese terrestrial TV services began to place greater strategic emphasis on the logic of accumulation and trajectories of creative migration, both of which encouraged them to consider transnational strategies as some of the brightest prospects for the future of these enterprises.

The early years of Taiwanese television were strongly influenced by Chiang Kai-shek, who dominated most aspects of the island society from the 1950s to the 1970s. After World War II, many residents were hoping to be granted independence after fifty years of Japanese colonial rule. Instead U.S. leaders prodded the United Nations to transfer governing authority to the retreating Chinese Nationalist army, allowing Chiang to install his regime in the former Japanese colonial capital of Taipei. Those who accompanied him into exile would come to constitute less than 15 percent of the island's population, yet they controlled the army, the state apparatus, and the only political party. Local Taiwanese administrators, intellectuals, and businesspeople were shouldered aside while the government doled out jobs, subsidies, and political favors to exiles from the mainland. Clustered in the northern part of the island around Taipei, this generation of exiles became known as *waisheng ren* (people born outside), yet ironically it was the Taiwanese who found themselves living as outsiders on their own island. The regime callously slaughtered its opponents, imposed martial law for more than three decades, and engaged in a thorough program of ideological indoctrination that proclaimed Chiang's government as the only legitimate representative of all Chinese people. The regime dismissively treated Taiwan as a minor province, as little more than a temporary haven until the Nationalists could rejuvenate their military forces and mount a campaign to reclaim control of the mainland.

Yet for all its nefarious activities, the government also realized that it needed to cultivate the island population if only to muster a new generation of soldiers. Consequently, universal education was instituted, and children began each school day singing songs glorifying President Chiang and spent much of their time studying the history, culture, and geography of mainland China, learning little about their own island. Mandarin became the language of instruction, governance, and big business, even though few Taiwanese could speak it fluently. Overall, the regime's ideology was a mixture of sinophiliac nostalgia, virulent anticommunism, and Nationalist Party republicanism. Schools, newspapers, and movies were all closely monitored, and when television arrived in the 1960s, it too was fashioned as an ideological tool of the state. Broadcasting largely in Mandarin, one station was controlled by the provincial government (Taiwan Television, TTV, established in 1963), another by the military (China Television Service, CTS, 1971), and a third by the Nationalist Party, or Kuomintang (China Television, CTV, 1971).

Pressed to appear strong in the face of invasion threats from the PRC, the government sought to modernize the economy and the military, which in turn required ideological mobilization of the local population and support from the United States. Consequently, the regime fashioned itself as the democratic alternative to communism, even if, in fact, it was thoroughly corrupt and autocratic. When American support began to waver after Richard Nixon's trip to Beijing in 1972, reform elements within the Kuomintang (KMT) began to press for further democratization, and with Chiang's death in 1975 and the ascendancy of his son to the presidency, the government began to open its doors tentatively to Taiwanese participation in politics and government. This process culminated in the lifting of martial law in 1987, the emergence of an oppositional Democratic Progressive Party (DPP), and the election of native-born Lee Teng-hui as president in 1988. It also sparked a cautious movement toward media liberalization, which laid the groundwork for the cable television revolution of the 1990s when the number of stations mushroomed from three to more than one hundred licensed operators.[1]

Wholly owned by the Kuomintang, CTV provided a lucrative source of income and played an influential role in shaping public opinion for more than two decades, but during the 1990s, as martial law began to wither and new media outlets began to flourish, KMT leaders reluctantly decided to release their grip on the station for a number of reasons. First of all, reformers within the party believed the commercial objectives of the station would be best realized by breaking explicit ties with the KMT. Second, as competition from cable television intensified, financial planners worried that the value of the station might decline, so it would be best to float a public stock offering in the near future. Finally, some party leaders feared that, should the KMT ever lose power, the station might be seized by the opposition DPP or rendered worthless by government regulatory action.

Accordingly, in 1996, the CTV board of directors hired Su Ming Cheng to prepare the company for an initial public offering (IPO) that would pave the way for a transition of ownership. A former television news professional and cabinet official, Cheng swiftly spun off nine subsidiaries and established ten joint-venture companies in computer graphics, digital gaming, and telecommunications. With the company now known as the CTV Media Group, Cheng also engineered a change in its corporate culture, which is exemplified by her office atop the CTV complex. Conspicuously absent are any traces of the company's connections to the ruling party: no pictures of KMT leaders or even of Chiang Kai-shek. An ikebana-inspired floral arrangement in one corner adds a splash of color, and a Chinese calligraphy brush painting crisply contrasts with the teak wall paneling, but overall the décor is modern and corporate. Cheng's ready smile and telegenic appearance in her smart black suit recall her prior career as an evening news anchor. Yet these days industry professionals are more likely to comment on her managerial performance at CTV, a company often referred to as the "brightest of the terrestrials." Cheng's diversification strategy worked well initially, with more than half of the company's profits now coming from nonbroadcast revenues.

Cheng believes that TV advertising sales cannot keep up with the rapidly rising costs of program production, especially since TV ad revenues are now spread among more than eighty channels rather than the original three terrestrials. Indeed, between 1998 and 2001, ad income at CTV plummeted from $147 million to $88 million, dropping more than 40 percent.[2] Cheng contends that the company must diversify and globalize, repositioning itself as a multimedia content provider with a strong focus on Chinese language and culture. "We're talking about transforming Chinese culture into something modern that can be accepted by the whole world," she explains. No longer a propaganda tool of the ruling party, CTV fashions products to suit diverse audiences: mass and niche, domestic and foreign. Yet the core identity of the company revolves around its distinctive association with Chinese arts and culture. "Whether fortunately or unfortunately, we were ruled by Chiang Kai-shek," says Cheng, "and at that time everybody thought that we were the rightful heirs to Chinese culture." Chiang's regime nurtured and sustained traditional arts during the era when the PRC was undergoing the Cultural Revolution and Hong Kong and Singapore were living under colonial rule. In her estimation, CTV can tap its deep connections to Chinese culture to produce captivating media products in a contemporary Chinese vernacular.

"A modern language is something that can be accepted worldwide," says Cheng. It maintains distinctive cultural traces and yet at the same time is capable of addressing audiences that come from a variety of backgrounds, especially young audiences. "Last night at the movies," she explains, "I saw the trailer for an animated mainland movie called *Lotus Lantern*. You can really see the difference between it and Disney's *Mulan*. You look at it, and you can immediately tell: no, it's just too Chinese. Not only too Chinese for Taiwan, but too Chinese for Hong Kong and a lot of other places. It's just too *old*," she chuckles. Interestingly, our conversation was taking place only a month before the July 2000 premiere of *Crouching Tiger, Hidden Dragon*, which succeeded precisely because its Taiwanese director, Ang Lee, was able to produce a film that paid homage to romantic dramas and swordplay films of the past while also producing a very contemporary, transnational blockbuster using global talent and resources. Likewise, Cheng believes that CTV should be at the center of content development for a global market, providing financing and organizing resources on a regional basis.

As an example, she points to *Splendid China*, a CTV documentary series that capitalizes on Taiwan's growing tourist trade with the mainland. For many citizens, especially *waisheng ren* and their children, trips across the strait have become increasingly popular since both the PRC and Taiwan governments began lifting travel restrictions during the 1990s. Many who venture to the mainland wish to reconnect with family and friends, whereas others are intrigued by the opportunity to visit sites they could only imagine while studying Chinese history and culture during their school years. CTV cashed in on this trend by fashioning a long-running series of travel programs and by producing a host of related products and services that include publications, videos, a Web site, and a travel service, all of them owned by CTV Media Group. "A lot of people want to travel in mainland China," says Cheng, "but they don't know where and what and how. There are dozens of agencies that provide these services, but we use the name *Splendid China* for our program, our travel agency, and our Web site. The brand has become quite famous, and the name makes each of these products stand out in their own markets." Such products both complement one another and multiply the profit opportunities generated by core programming. "We're also dubbing it into English to sell overseas to National Geographic or Discovery or other English-speaking services." Other genres are also ripe for synergistic development, according to Cheng. A popular game show called *The Matchmaker* expands its appeal to young audiences via an audience-participation Web site, as well as several e-businesses that focus on gifts, weddings, and honeymoons.

While both travel and game show genres seem especially ripe for transnational, multimedia development, prime-time drama is perhaps the most important form of core content that the station produces. Traditionally, eight o'clock dramas have been a keystone of the evening TV schedule, forming a bridge between the nightly news and variety programs. A strong drama series not only attracts a large audience but also helps to carry the audience through prime time. Moreover, since each drama series is usually telecast five nights a week over a period of eight or more weeks, it also serves as an important promotional vehicle for terrestrial stations. By comparison, cable channels find it difficult to finance original dramas, so they usually purchase dramas from foreign suppliers, or they rerun series that were originally produced by their terrestrial competitors. When cable stations do venture into the realm of original prime-time series, they usually produce low-budget studio dramas, often with contemporary themes. The original three terrestrial stations, therefore, distinguish themselves by mounting lavish historical dramas, but interestingly, they now have difficulty financing the programs, and so they must look for coproduction partners overseas. Moreover, they must, from the very outset of the production process, take into consideration the international distribution of each series, since Taiwanese ad revenues can no longer support original productions. Consequently, the competitive economics of the *local* market are now driving CTV toward *transnational* coproduction and distribution.

In the spring of 2000, Su Ming Cheng was quite proud that CTV productions were playing in prime time on the leading terrestrial stations in Hong Kong and the PRC. And she was furthermore delighted that in the preceding year *Huanzhu Ge Ge* (*Princess Huanzhu*, aka *Princess Pearl*), another CTV coproduction, scored record audiences throughout Global China, especially among young viewers, who Cheng sees as prime users of ancillary products and services. "With all of our dramas we now target young audiences, and we try to develop computer software to go with them," enthuses Cheng. "We have a joint venture with Soft China, the biggest video game company in Taiwan, so now every one of our evening dramas is aimed at audiences who might be interested in these games."

Of the terrestrial stations, CTV has moved most aggressively to reposition itself in a changing media universe. It was able to do this because the station was "privately" owned and operated by the ruling KMT rather than the government. When the party decided to mount an IPO, the decision was made internally by shareholders and the KMT leadership. In comparison, efforts to reform the other broadcast stations, CTS and TTV, have presented a far more complicated set of issues, because both are government-owned, and any attempt to reorganize them has to be vetted by the legislature, a process fraught with political conflict and maneuver. Nevertheless, all three stations feel the pressure to reform while the competitive crush in cable TV continues to drive down advertising revenues, thus stimulating the search for new ways to attract audiences. The extent to which CTV can realize its ambitions as a transnational, multimedia enterprise with a contemporary Chinese identity is still up in the air, but the institutional dynamics provide a good example of the macropolitical and economic pressures that are driving Taiwanese broadcasters to look overseas for production and distribution opportunities. In the realm of production, creative personnel look especially to historical drama as one of the few genres that can succeed transnationally.

During the late 1990s, TTV's Eric Yang emerged as one of the most successful young producers of television drama, scoring six hit series over the

Vicky Zhao skyrocketed to fame in her portrayal of the main character in *Huanzhu Ge Ge*, a cross-strait coproduction renowned throughout Global China. Courtesy China Television.

course of two years. His achievements were all the more remarkable, since TTV, Taiwan's first television broadcaster, was in a downward spiral, especially with its eight o'clock dramas, which were then drawing ratings in the 2 to 3 range, a little less than half those of the other terrestrial stations. In 1999, Yang spectacularly reversed that trend with a series that more than tripled the station's eight o'clock audience. Titled *First Lady and the Officer*, it's the story of a Chinese general during the Qing dynasty who serves as the first imperial governor of Taiwan and marries a strong-willed young woman from the island. The story premise is gimmicky but also rich with possibility, explains Yang: "This was the first time that China ruled Taiwan, and he was the first governor, but at home it's a different story: he seems to have all this power, but he's scared of his wife. It's a story about their marriage, but it's also a story about different kinds of power." As with many Chinese TV dramas, the series refracts contemporary concerns through the prism of historical narrative, setting the program more than three hundred years in the past but fashioning a story line that is remarkably contemporary. At the time of its broadcast, identity issues were the subject of widespread discussion in Taiwan, as was deliberation over cross-strait relations with China. Interestingly, mainland audiences were likewise intrigued by the series, since at the time, the Beijing government was avidly promoting a policy of reunification that would bring Hong Kong, Macau, and Taiwan back to the motherland.

Yang further explains that the couple's ongoing attempts to sustain domestic harmony are complicated by a shrewd narrative device in which the first lady speaks in her native Taiwanese and the governor (a mainland actor) speaks in Mandarin. As in real life, one's expressive abilities in a native tongue surpass those in one's second language, and the series invokes this device to subtly suggest the difficulties of communication between mainlander and Taiwanese, as well as to highlight distinctions between imperial culture and local culture. Although this contrivance resonates with contemporary concerns over cross-strait relations, it also evokes memories of Chiang's occupation and sino-fication of Taiwan from the 1950s to the 1970s. Issues of difference—played out at the level of language, culture, and gender—are therefore central narrative concerns, made all the more intriguing because the first lady is portrayed as a match for her husband in many ways, perhaps implying an equal status between Taiwan and the PRC or between native Taiwanese and *waisheng ren* or between contemporary men and women.

Although Yang acknowledges that the series' premise was formulated to attract coproduction partners in the PRC, another rationale for this cross-cultural drama grew out of his calculation of TTV's problems in the Taiwan market. At the time, he recalls, "our ratings were low, even for a terrestrial, and it had been two years since TTV had the number-one prime-time drama. *First Lady* was only my second series [as executive producer], but I was convinced that the reason we were failing was that too many people in the business still see Taiwan from a Taipei perspective, and they forget the rest of the island." As noted earlier, *waisheng ren* tended to settle in the northern part of Taiwan, near the capital, Taipei, and consequently the area became dominated by the Mandarin language and a sino-centric worldview. Meanwhile, the Taiwanese language (a Min variety of Chinese) continues to be widely used in the southern and central parts of the island, even by those who have been educated in Mandarin. Therefore, Yang's linguistic device was fashioned to appeal to viewers outside the northern metropolitan region, and he also aimed his promotional efforts at southern and central cities, such as Kao-hsiung and Taichung, buying radio spots and newspaper ads and staging promotional events with the leading actors. It paid off handsomely; he explains, "The series before *First Lady* had a 2 rating, but our first episode got an 8, and it went up to a 10.4 rating overall, and in central Taiwan we got a 14 rating, which is very high these days."

During one of our interview sessions, Yang and I met at the Living Bar in Taipei, a Japanese-owned, Western-style restaurant set on a quiet lane just behind the major department stores that line Chung Hsiao Road. It was a cool, rainy, February evening, and Yang arrived in a navy peacoat, with a Nike knapsack casually slung over his shoulder. Tall, slender, and thirty-something, Yang spoke energetically, describing the mechanics of drama production in Taiwan. At the outset, his programming department develops a story line and makes initial casting decisions either alone or in consultation with an independent producer. The station then makes a financial commitment to the independent producer in exchange for territorial rights to Taiwan and overseas markets, such as Malaysia, Indonesia, and Korea. Taiwanese stations usually provide most of the financial resources for such series, for example, $1.4 million for the first forty episodes of *First Lady*. With an agreement in hand, the producer then shops the concept around to provincial and municipal TV stations in the PRC. Most of these stations tend to be cash poor, but they are attractive partners because they can provide facilities, services, labor, and shooting locations that would otherwise be very expensive or, in the case of locations, unavailable in Taiwan. Historical settings and stunning terrain are two key attractions that mainland partners bring to the table. Moreover, labor and technical costs in the PRC are significantly lower than they are in Taiwan. In exchange, the mainland coproduction partner secures series rights for the PRC, allowing a premiere telecast on its own station and then sales to other provincial and municipal broadcasters around the country.

Although most deals follow this well-established pattern, the negotiations are very fluid. For example, the Taiwan station may decide to limit its financial commitment to the series by bidding only for the island rights, requiring the producer to find another investor who is willing to pick up the international distribution market. Likewise, the mainland partner might provide only studio time in exchange for rights to transmission on its own station, leaving the rest of the PRC markets in the hands of the producer, who must then line up a distributor for the remaining provinces. Overall, the Taiwan station usually plays a substantial role in financing and creative development, essentially acting as executive producer, while the mainland partner is primarily involved in staging and shooting the production. The independent producer is responsible for putting together the overall package, negotiating territorial rights, and hiring appropriate talent. Obviously, stars from each market enhance the appeal of a series, but producers also try to select appropriate writers, directors, and videographers from each territory. For example, mainland scriptwriters are widely revered for the depth of their historical knowledge and the intricate plotting of their story lines, leaving many Taiwanese television executives expressing exasperation at the paucity of such talent in their own market. On the other hand, mainland writers and actors are also known to write and perform in a plodding style that doesn't appeal to viewers in Taiwan, Hong Kong, and overseas markets. As a result, Taiwanese writers are often hired to generate snappier dialogue and wordplay. They're also considered especially adept at romantic plots, while mainland writers are considered best at imperial court intrigue.

Each partner shares significant responsibilities and takes calculated risks, but none is more vulnerable than the independent producer, whose very survival may rest on the success of a single series. Profit margins are often thin, and losses can sometimes be substantial, but successful producers generally make money by developing strong reputations that can be parlayed into long-term contracts with stations in the PRC, Taiwan, and Hong Kong. A well-established producer, such as Yi Ren Media, can increase its profits by extending the run of a series (economies of scale) and by negotiating performance bonuses with stations. Producers can also negotiate for a share of the income derived from syndication. This combination of strategies can prove quite lucrative, as with the series *Huanzhu Ge Ge*, which performed well in all markets, allowing Yi Ren Media to bid for much higher fees when it extended the series beyond the first forty episodes. Despite such successes, however, many production companies in Taipei live on the edge, moving from project to project, sometimes using income from a new project to pay off past debts and assuming new debts to keep a current series running. Staffing is kept lean in order to control overhead costs, so the production team for each new series is assembled on a project-by-project basis.

Taiwan's independent producers are especially interested in historical dramas, because they are durable performers in syndication markets throughout Global China. Although contemporary dramas often attract higher ratings in local and national markets, historical dramas are easier to sell transnationally, because they are less controversial and less culturally specific. "That's why so many prime-time dramas are set in the Qing dynasty," says Yang. Among Chinese audiences around the world, "there's no conflict over that part of history, but after the Qing dynasty, each government has a different interpretation of history." These ideological differences are compounded by other differences as well, notes Yang: "The closer you get to our time, the more likely you are to notice cultural differences. Taipei's lifestyle is different from Hong Kong's lifestyle and also different from the mainland." Historical dramas successfully negotiate such diversity, because they take contemporary concerns and displace them to a mythical past that is open to interpretation from a variety of perspectives. Moreover, the programs are attractive to audiences in rural as well as urban areas, and their appeal also tends to cut across class boundaries. The use of historical characters and settings furthermore lends legitimacy to these series, making them appear educational in the eyes of many parents. And although critics regularly question their accuracy, audiences draw lessons from what they assume is based on characters and events from China's past. In a broader sense, the programs allow viewers to rehearse their thoughts regarding what it means to be Chinese.

Such series can be divided into two main categories: one is the palace drama, which focuses on the political and personal intrigues within a specific dynasty, and the other is the martial arts genre, in which legendary figures do battle on behalf of a particular group or a set of moral principles. Palace dramas can be made more cost efficient by restricting their focus to inner chambers of the court, or more ambitiously they can be ratcheted up to a grand scale, featuring elaborate locations, action sequences, and large casts. Yet not unlike Hollywood programs such as *Dallas* or *Dynasty*, the defining feature of these series is the intricate web of relationships among family members of a powerful clan.[3] *Huanzhu Ge Ge* and *First Lady* fall into this category, since both focus on familial and romantic relationships within the context of imperial households. Yet interestingly, both proved exceptionally popular because they dwelled on the romantic fortunes of young women who seem to be exploring feminine power and identity, themes that clearly resonate with young female viewers today. *Yongzheng Dynasty* is an example of another type of palace drama that offers an elaborate tale of a strong and righteous young heir who rises to power amid the corruption and intrigues of the imperial court. The heir's struggles with bureaucracy are as much a study of statecraft as they are of family politics.

Palace dramas tap a wealth of historical, operatic, and literary sources, yet they also draw on the traditions of Chinese cinema, in which such stories flourished, especially during the 1960s. Li Hanxiang, a leading director of the palace-chamber dramas *(gongwei)* for Shaw Brothers, argues that *gongwei* faded from popularity because they were costly to produce.[4] Yet Li makes no mention of television, which is where Shaw Brothers redirected most of its production capacity when it began to produce palace dramas for the small screen during the 1970s. Stations in Taiwan and Singapore followed, with producers learning to scale *gongwei* to budgets small and large, producing a steady stream of series up to the current day. In fact, the accessibility of such TV narratives may have been what made the genre less attractive to cinema audiences.

Equally popular on the small screen is the martial arts genre *(wushu)*, which subdivides into kung fu dramas and swordfighting dramas *(wuxia)*. The latter revolve around a group of warriors, or sometimes a single warrior and his comrade, who for some reason have fallen on hard times. The lord to whom they pledged allegiance has been slain, corrupt officials have taken over the government, or they have been banished into exile after an invasion by outsiders. They are now "rebels without a cause," living on the margins of society, but they remain pure of heart and bound by deep ties of honor and brotherhood. The action is usually set in the distant past, reaching back to as early as the seventh-century Tang dynasty. Members of the group may have quirky personality traits or fighting styles, but all are exceptionally dedicated warriors. A crisis inevitably emerges, and they prevail after protracted and bloody fighting, thereby restoring the legitimate ruler to the throne or peace to the community or both.

The other subgenre, kung fu, focuses on characters that represent a particular fighting style, but more important they represent a worldview associated with their school of kung fu. The heroes generally tread a path of ascetic restraint but invariably find themselves pulled into a conflict on behalf of an oppressed community. Despite their efforts to resolve problems peacefully, they ultimately are left no alternative short of physical force, allowing them to exhibit their well-honed skills while subduing the forces of evil and restoring community harmony. Sometimes these stories involve conflicts between kung fu schools, but, keeping with formula, one school is generally cast as an evil aggressor and the other is a more humble and righteous ensemble under the leadership of a benevolent master. Although kung fu stories can be set in the distant past, many of them take place during the late Qing dynasty or the early twentieth century, at times when traditional Chinese values were threatened by corrupt rulers or foreign invaders. Legendary kung fu masters often practice traditional arts, medicine, or philosophy and may also possess mystical powers, since they must overcome spectacular odds in the pursuit of justice.

The formula for the martial arts drama is in some ways similar to the Hollywood Western during its halcyon days, when it provided a pretext for reflections on tradition and modernity. But as John Cawelti suggests, one of the signal characteristics of such popular fiction was the abstract diegetic terrain of the "Wild West," which provided a tableau for action that was far from the experience of modern audiences. Moreover, he argues, Westerns needed to resemble games with clearly defined boundaries of action. "This game-like aspect of the formula permits anyone who knows the 'rules'— and in our culture children are instructed in the rules of the Western from a very early age—to enjoy and appreciate the fine points of play, as well as to experience the sense of ego-enhancement that comes when 'our side' wins."[5] Chinese martial arts dramas are, like Westerns, rule-bound stories with clearly defined opposing players, a sequence of moves that must happen in a particular order, and an abstract social structure and physical landscape on which the game is played out. The "game" is one that draws on Chinese legend, novels, and opera from the past, as well as on today's thriving mass-fiction industry, whose authors have refashioned these stories with a more contemporary inflection.[6]

Eric Yang points out that in Taiwan a substantial audience can be readily tapped for martial arts dramas, chiefly because a large reading public is already presold on the genre. The programs perform particularly well during school vacations, when teenage boys—a core audience—gravitate to the programs, especially if they are based on stories by popular novelists, such as Jin Yong, Gu Long, or Liang Yusheng. Yang says, "According to my research, any [martial arts] drama gets at least a 4 rating, so it's a guarantee of basic survival, because students like to watch them and older male viewers in general are attracted to them." He says that most of his kung fu series have pulled ratings in the 5 to 9 range, making them impressive performers among their peer group. They also prove effective as counterprogramming opposite another popular genre, the contemporary family saga, which tends to draw women and older viewers during the heart of prime time.

As mentioned above, historical dramas succeed on both sides of the strait because they are seen as uncontroversial, even though they may, in fact, raise very relevant issues in an allegorical fashion. In 1999, *Yongzheng Dynasty* drew fans throughout Global China and was reportedly a favorite of PRC premier Zhu Rongji and Taiwanese president Lee Teng-hui, making it one of the few things the two could agree about. Both reportedly admired the lead character because he was able to make difficult policy decisions without being swayed by flattery, familial pressure, or personal gain. Indeed, both Zhu and Lee are widely seen as calculating leaders who have weathered adversity because of their political principles. Yet their principles and their political circumstances are very different, with one battling an entrenched government bureaucracy in hopes of modernizing mainland society and the other struggling to sustain the independence of Taiwan in the face of exorbitant pressure for reunification. Though regular adversaries over a number of explosive political issues, both leaders were captivated by the televised tales of politics and power offered up by daily episodes of *Yongzheng Dynasty*.

On the other hand, TV dramas with contemporary settings don't enjoy the polysemic range of interpretation characteristic of their historical counterparts. Rather than fantasizing about a vague yesteryear, audiences for contemporary dramas tend to be quite sensitive to the social differences they discern in the characters, narrative, and mise-en-scène of contemporary series. For example, when viewers watch a domestic scene, most seem to feel that it should be furnished in keeping with what they understand to be contemporary design. Likewise, clothing, autos, and consumer goods all should resonate with their immediate experience. "Since 1949," observes Yang, "Taiwanese people have had a very different lifestyle [from their counterparts in the PRC]: different celebrities, different novels, different authors." Consequently, contemporary Taiwanese TV dramas don't fare especially well in the PRC, nor do PRC series do well in Taiwan. "When I was in China recently," recalls Yang, "I watched a drama with beautiful scenery and good-looking actors (two of them from Taiwan), but it didn't look Taiwanese. The dress style was not very chic, and the lifestyle didn't seem familiar." Executives from otherTaiwanese TV companies agree, one suggesting that different consumer behaviors and fashion trends are quick to register with viewers: "The actors [in mainland dramas] are very label conscious, and they tend to flaunt expensive jewelry, but they aren't the labels or the kinds of jewelry that are popular now" in Taiwan.

Ironically, adds Yang, Taiwanese viewers are often more comfortable with contemporary *Japanese* dramas than they are with dramas shot in Beijing. "When we see a Japanese drama, we see very similar lifestyles." This assessment is widely shared among programming executives in Taipei, who compete ferociously for the rights to Japanese "idol dramas," which are so named because they feature pop singing idols as their lead actors. TV executives find the series attractive because they are easy to program, running only ten to thirteen episodes, and because they are especially popular with teenage girls, college students, and young working women. Idol dramas are revered for their topical concerns, glamorous actors, and steamy love stories. Just as important, audiences are attracted to the programs because they provide a showcase for the fashions and lifestyles of Tokyo, a trendsetting capital of East Asia. "It's not only Japanese programs but Japanese culture that has swept into Taiwan," says a stylish female programming executive. "Young people are kind of crazy about it. It isn't Hollywood any longer, and it isn't Hong Kong. It's Tokyo." Another young programming executive adds, "My parents would never watch the idol dramas, because they aren't familiar with the idols and don't know the language and they don't want to read subtitles." Yet interestingly, *grandparents* who were schooled in the Japanese language during the colonial occupation of Taiwan will often watch idol dramas with their grandchildren, largely because they can more easily follow the dialogue of Japanese dramas than Mandarin dramas, creating a curious cultural bridge across generations.

Indeed, as islanders search for an independent identity, they look back to Chinese legend, they reflect on native Taiwanese customs, and they consider the lingering influence of the Japanese colonial regime that modernized Taiwan. Although largely seen as niche programming, Japanese dramas invoke a sense of cultural affinity. "We still have connections that go back to the occupation, so in some ways our cultures are very similar" says Vivian Hsieh, an acquisitions executive with a leading cable channel. Like many of her colleagues, Hsieh also believes that the popularity of idol dramas derives from their glossy production values. "Japanese shows are considered the best quality," she declares, "Chinese shows next, then Southeast Asian shows. I'm not sure where to put Korea but probably somewhere between Japanese and Chinese TV shows." Consequently, Hsieh contends that Japanese stations would not buy from Taipei producers, nor would Taipei broadcasters buy from Southeast Asian broadcasters. "I think the hierarchy of quality is real," she asserts. "It's not just a perception." Given their slick production values and their cultural proximity, Japanese shows have become strong performers among niche viewers. And after 2000, as the competition for Japanese imports escalated, stations also began to purchase Korean dramas, finding them less costly but nevertheless surprisingly popular with audiences. Although Korean series don't enjoy the cultural cachet of their Japanese counterparts, the style of familial interactions makes them attractive to all age groups. Says one executive, "The Japanese shows are very trendy, and the drama is very sophisticated, but the characters in the Korean shows are very warm with their families. The relations between generations are very similar to here in Taiwan, and you don't see that with the Japanese dramas." High production values, cultural proximity, and perceived trendiness are features that help Japanese and Korean dramas transcend national and linguistic differences.

Interestingly, Hollywood imports have suffered significantly since Taiwanese television has become more open and competitive. When the three terrestrial stations used to dominate the market, they regularly relied on shows like *Cosby* and *MacGyver*, but as the cable era ushered in an expanded range of programming choices, Hollywood series began to look overpriced. American programs also began to suffer from a drift toward irony in scripted series. The lifestyles, topical humor, and polysemic banter on programs such as *Friends* or *Will and Grace* are difficult to translate, both linguistically and culturally. Self-referential talky comedy does not fare as well as family comedy or physical comedy. Likewise, high-context dramas such as *West Wing* or *Desperate Housewives* tend to have difficulties compared with the more visual storytelling style of, for example, *CSI* or *The X-Files*, the latter of which had the further virtue of centering its narrative on government conspiracy and the supernatural, themes that resonate with audiences around the world. Buoyed by extensive press coverage in the United States, *The X-Files* scored strongly for a season, but then its popularity also began to sag. According to ratings researchers, part of the problem was that the core audience for such series tends to be younger and more highly educated. "They spend the least amount of time with television," says A. C. Nielsen's Tina Teng, "and when they want to see an American entertainment product, they are more likely to prefer a movie. They're very busy people, and they don't want to schedule their lives around a show that only comes on once a week."

This matrix of cultural and institutional preferences registers in the pricing structure for imported programming. In 2000, the average one-hour drama cost $2,000 to $4,000, and the Japanese idol drama commanded a premium price of $4,000 to $8,000, which according to distributor James Chang, vice president of Tempo International, is high but reasonable because of their strong ratings and youth-oriented demographics. On the other hand, U.S. dramas have been forced to recalibrate their asking prices. "I used to be able to sell U.S. dramas for $6,000," says Chang, "but now they're down in the $2,000 to $4,000 range. Some [Hollywood] syndicators are trying to make U.S. shows more attractive by offering them in bundles at a cheaper cost per unit, but it's too risky for us. It's hard to make such a large purchase when the demand is so low."

Although American dramas are now less attractive, the trade in foreign TV shows is nevertheless brisk, largely because of the costs and uncertainties associated with original production. For example, TTV dramas are produced for $30,000 to $40,000 per episode. During the 8 P.M. telecast, advertising is sold for $6,000 per minute, running up to ten minutes of advertising per hour. At the very most, TTV is taking in $60,000 per hour and spending as much as $40,000 on production costs alone. Given the additional infrastructure, marketing, and personnel costs, profit margins are slim. For a cable station, the accounting considerations are even more forbidding, since these stations charge only half as much for prime-time ad slots, although the gap has been closing since 2000. Consequently, most cable executives consider the cost of drama production to be prohibitive unless the series is a modestly produced contemporary drama shot in Taiwan. Such series tend to forgo location shooting, elaborate costumes, and special effects, and it's often difficult to attract topflight talent on a modest budget, making the prospects of such ventures highly uncertain. Given the improbability of overseas distribution, even a successful program offers only modest returns. Accordingly, producers of glossy, prime-time dramas must be willing to explore coproduction opportunities, which in turn encourage an emphasis on historical drama, even if many of these series are only average performers in the ratings.

The biggest challenge that producers confront, however, is the volatility of the local industry. During the martial law era, the three main terrestrial stations established a stable set of expectations for programmers and advertisers. With only three competitors, projecting the audience size for most programs was comparatively easy, and therefore stations could anticipate substantial and consistent profits from most of their prime-time programs. The end of martial law in 1987 and the rise of cable television during the 1990s disrupted that confident arithmetic. They not only transformed practices within the industry; they also transformed the expectations of viewers. "I remember the day that martial law was over," recalls Eric Yang. "I was in the army at that time, working at the missile control headquarters. To celebrate, I took the day off and got on my motorcycle and went for a ride. It seemed that everywhere things were different—fresher, freer—and soon there were new magazines and newspapers, and then came the changes in TV. It all happened so fast, and the changes seemed so dramatic."

The end of martial law in Taiwan spurred a dramatic multiplication of television channels, creating an intensely competitive environment that forced the three terrestrial broadcasters to reorganize their corporate structures and seek production alliances outside the island in order to respond to new pressures in the local market. For CTV this meant a shift away from its previous focus on KMT political patronage and TV ad revenues toward a multimedia conglomerate structure in which series like *Splendid China* and *Huanzhu Ge Ge* are launched as key pieces of intellectual property that are then strategically spun out to ancillary media, both in Taiwan and abroad. Moreover, the end of the Cold War and the increasing liberalization of transnational trade made it possible—indeed, necessary—for television companies to pursue cross-strait collaborations, despite the ongoing political struggles between leaders on either side. TTV's *First Lady and the Officer* provides a model of such collaboration, resulting in a polysemic historical narrative set in an abstract diegetic world in which contemporary concerns are raised allegorically. Issues such as corruption, tradition, gender, and identity are prominently addressed, but perhaps the most pervasive concern of this series and others like it is to reflect on the meaning of Chineseness in a rapidly changing modern world. To situate such tensions figuratively within the intimacy of a Qing dynasty household—in which language, culture, politics, and gender clash—is as much a pragmatic textual gimmick aimed at responding to the exigencies of the industry as it is an interpretation of themes broadly circulating in the culture at large. The popularity of *First Lady* was less the result of its historical accuracy than of its strategy for interpellating diverse audiences on the mainland and within Taiwan itself.

Such strategies are a significant departure from the logics that governed the television industry from the 1960s to the 1980s, when forces of sociocultural variation established a clearly but narrowly delineated market that supported only three television channels under close government supervision. Within those parameters, the forces of production concentrated in the capital city of Taipei largely as a by-product of political patronage, and the geography of distribution reached only to the shores of the island, largely because the broadcasting oligopoly had little incentive to move beyond its protected market. As in Hong Kong, however, television in Taiwan had penetrated most every home in the market by the end of the 1980s, and after more than two decades of consistent revenue growth, the television oligopoly began to experience competition from other forms of media and from emerging cable TV channels. Thus, market liberalization and government deregulation converged during the 1990s, significantly refiguring the conditions of production and distribution. Under these circumstances, the terrestrial broadcasters needed to experiment with new relations of production and new markets for distribution. The new sociocultural configuration now exposed broadcasters more fully to the logic of accumulation. Likewise, as we shall see, several of the successful new cable competitors in the Taiwan market soon grasped the inevitability of a transnational strategy as well.

7 Market Niches and Expanding Aspirations in Taiwan

In 1990, it would have been difficult to imagine that in little more than a decade newly emerging cable services would completely erase the dominant status of Taiwan's three terrestrial broadcasters. For most cable systems during the 1980s were little more than mom-and-pop operations that skirted the boundaries of the law. Someone would buy a satellite dish and, to defray costs, would hook up neighbors to their system. Some started informal movie channels, renting videotapes at local shops and playing them for subscribers, while others began to produce their own offerings, especially political shows that became quite popular during the post–martial law period. Facing a groundswell of popular enthusiasm for such ventures, government officials tread cautiously when they tried to regulate the growth of cable TV. It wasn't until 1993, when cable was in more than a third of all TV homes, that the government finally established a licensing process and formal regulations. This brought an end to the mom-and-pop phase of cable TV, ushering in a period of consolidation, with the number of cable operators diminishing from more than six hundred to fewer than seventy by the end of the decade. Two powerful conglomerates, United Communications (part of Koo's Group) and Eastern Multimedia (part of Rebar), emerged as the most active applicants for government licenses, often buying up small operators or squeezing them out in the regulatory licensing process. Now in control of more than two-thirds of all cable systems, these multiple system operators (MSOs) also established a programming cartel that represents channel providers in their negotiations with cable operators. Thus, the biggest operators not only own the hardware; they also run a company that represents the software providers, an arrangement that allows them to control programming prices, since their representatives sit on both sides of the bargaining table. Despite such anticompetitive practices, many industry executives agree that signal quality and channel selection improved during this period of consolidation and that cable subscription rates for consumers have remained comparatively low. Such improvements are, however, largely attributable to government oversight and the duopoly's desire to avoid public criticism while it was taking control of the industry.[1]

Both United and Rebar are connected to the KMT power elite, and both are controlled by families that, like the Lis and the Woos in Hong Kong, take an infrastructural approach to empire building. Rebar is a sprawling conglomerate that emerged out of the structural steel and construction industries under the leadership of Wang Yu-tsung, a member of the KMT's leading policy committee. His son, Gary Wang Ling-lin, head of the family's media operations, was formerly an influential legislator in the national assembly. The younger Wang is renowned for employing political connections and unconventional business practices. When interviewed off the record, executives at successful cable channels are quick to enumerate the many times they have been pressured to sell an ownership share to the Wangs, so as to maintain favorable standing in Eastern's cable systems. Those who refuse such "offers" subsequently experience a range of "technical difficulties" that affect the quality of their signals and ultimately their ratings. Although the victims of such persuasive techniques sometimes complain, the Wangs successfully used their political influence throughout the 1990s to derail government investigations of such practices. They furthermore were able to push through a relaxation of ownership rules, allowing the major MSOs to expand their control from 20 percent to 33 percent of all cable systems. Covert business agreements have further extended their influence to an estimated 40 percent of the market. In 2000, the election of the Democratic Progressive Party's Chen Shui-bian heralded the beginning of a new era, when government officials began to aggressively investigate "black gold" crimes, which were common under the KMT, and Gary Wang was one of the first suspects held up to such scrutiny. Cable industry practitioners claim that cronyism and corporate manipulation played a significant role in the rise of the Wangs' Eastern media conglomerate *(Dongsen)*, which in the fall of 2002 claimed a market capitalization between $1.6 billion and $2.4 billion.

Although United Communications has likewise used political influence, its parent company, Koo's Group, has a reputation for managerial expertise and financial integrity. Led by Koo Chen-fu, a prominent KMT policy maker and former presidential adviser until his death in 2005, the family is reputedly the fourth wealthiest in Taiwan.[2] It is further distinguished for its patronage of the arts, as indicated by an elaborate Chinese opera theater located in the China Trust headquarters building in Taipei. Hosting visiting performers from around the world, the resident troupe operates under the patronage of one of Koo's daughters who is widely respected in Taiwanese arts circles. Thus, the corporate styles of the two major MSOs vary dramatically. The Koos entered the cable business at the urging of the eldest son, Chester Koo Chih-yun, who grew enamored of the visionary possibilities of cable TV during the early 1990s. An MBA from the Wharton School of Business, Chester trained as a branch manager at the China Trust Bank before being put in charge of China Life Insurance at age thirty-five. Not unlike Hong Kong's Richard Li, Chester reportedly longed to move out from under his father's shadow, and cable television seemed to provide such an opportunity. Yet to Koo's Group—with $36 billion of assets in banking, real estate, insurance, plastics, and cement—the cable venture must have seemed positively loopy. Chester nevertheless persisted and soon began buying small cable systems while he attempted to cobble together an islandwide MSO. At the time, triad societies either owned or extorted money from many cable enterprises, and they didn't respond warmly to Chester's initiative, exposing him and his fledgling company to sabotage and threats along the way. Still, Chester soldiered on despite triad troubles, mounting losses, and public criticism of the emerging cable duopoly.

By the late 1990s, the intoxicating growth of the Internet and telecommunications industries encouraged Chester to morph his enterprise into a sophisticated broadband delivery system, giving a new complexion to Koo's Group. If his father's generation had focused on basic infrastructural enterprises—finance, plastics, cement—during Taiwan's industrialization, Chester would pioneer a new breed of enterprises for Taiwan's increasingly informational economy. On numerous occasions Chester declared that he wanted to build Taiwan into a global hub for Chinese-language media. Like others, he envisioned an emerging Global China media market as the endgame of the twenty-first century and contended that Taiwan could sustain its prosperity only if it were positioned to take advantage of digital opportunities. Ironically, this fledgling media mogul was conspicuously averse to media publicity. In an industry that thrives on glitzy ideas and strategic posturing, Chester was uncharacteristically shy and unassuming. He rarely made public pronouncements on behalf of his companies, leaving that to managerial subordinates. A heavy smoker who walked with a slouch, Chester was both cerebral and unconventional according to business associates. Although he grasped ideas quickly and brought fresh vision to a conservative family business, associates said he was also free-spending and impulsive. When he liked or wanted something, Chester's calculation of its value sometimes ran awry. Industry insiders claim his bids for local cable systems often were higher than necessary, saying he occasionally got swept up in a competitive frenzy with the Wang family.

Koo's Group spent somewhere between $700 million and $1 billion building a media empire that today includes a cable MSO, a platform of TV channels, an Internet portal, and a wireless telecommunications provider, all of which contributed to United's rising stature among global media companies. In 1999, Koo's Internet business, Gigamedia, attracted a $35 million investment from Microsoft, and a 2001 IPO on the NASDAQ raised another $270 million in capital. Likewise, in May 2001, China Network Systems (CNS) was formed as a joint venture of United Communications and Rupert Murdoch's Star TV, with Star investing $240 million in exchange for a 20 percent ownership stake. With CNS rolling out digital TV islandwide, Taiwan is quickly becoming an important broadband market. Yet despite these ambitious ventures, Koo's Group faces numerous obstacles in recouping its investment and turning a profit in the near future. Key among them are the general slowdown in the global economy and the collapse of the astronomic valuations of digital media companies. Further complicating the situation is the taint on the Taiwanese cable industry for its continuing reputation for shady practices, such as advertising theft, underreporting of subscription figures, and cartel behavior in pricing and services. These problems unexpectedly burst into the open at a cable industry conference in 2001, when James Murdoch, CEO of Star TV, referred to Taiwan's cable TV operators as "thugs and thieves—bandits on the super highway."[3] Murdoch expressed strong displeasure with "ad masking," a practice that involves a local cable operator bumping ads from a channel such as Star TV and replacing them with spots sold to local businesses. In such cases, the local operator maintains the integrity of the programming content but tampers with the advertising slots, turning them to its own benefit. In addition, cable operators often fail to report accurate subscription numbers, allowing them to pocket a share of revenues that should go to content providers. Yet cable operators respond to such charges by saying that they are hemmed in by a regulatory cap on basic cable rates at $19 per month, forcing them to seek creative solutions to their financial problems.

Such problems have moved United and Rebar, formerly bitter rivals, toward an era of guarded cooperation while they lobby for regulatory changes that will pave the way for digital TV. Arguing that broadband technology is crucial to Taiwan's future economic development, the duopoly pressed for the introduction of set-top boxes and tiered subscription services in 2002, a proposal that is important not only to MSOs but also to cable program providers, who hope to supplement their advertising income with new subscription revenues. Tiered services will allow the MSOs to offer premium packages that include movie channels, gaming, erotica, video-on-demand, and Internet access. These revenues should, according to industry analysts, provide a crucial step toward profitability, which in turn could spark greater investment in content production.

Chester Koo would not live to see these changes, however. After undergoing cancer treatment in 2001, he died in December at the age of forty-nine. Although Koo was clearly an important figure in the development of the Taiwanese cable industry, his mixed legacy also attracted fierce criticism, especially from stockholders of enterprises such as Gigamedia, who saw the value of their investment plummet more than 90 percent during the dotcom collapse. Some of these losses were obviously due to forces beyond Koo's control, but some critics explain the collapse of Gigamedia by citing a Chinese proverb: prosperity rarely lasts beyond three generations. It is perhaps still too early to know whether Gary Wang's or Chester Koo's legacy will be fashioned by such folk wisdom, but some observers would suggest, conversely, that United and Eastern—both tied to large family conglomerates with powerful political and economic connections—are now positioned to play an influential role in the development of Chinese media. And although both companies spent most of the 1990s establishing their base of operations in Taiwan, they envision their future in transnational terms, saying in the words of one Koo's Group executive, "Greater China is where we're going. That's what it's all about." Yet it's unclear whether such infrastructural monopolies are seasoned enough in the domain of content creation to compete transnationally. Other competitors in Taiwan have, however, built their businesses through popular programming, and it's therefore useful to compare their fortunes with those of Eastern and United.

Chiu Fu-sheng's TVBS headquarters rises out of a shopping district next to the main east-west highway that cuts across the heart of downtown Taipei. Its sixteen floors of aluminum and glass betray the effects of its location, a layer of grit turning the building from shiny metallic to sooty gray. At street level, a warren of small shops and underground markets sell videos, software, and computers, often for a fraction of the price that they might fetch if piracy laws were effectively enforced. Chiu was one of the first and most noteworthy victims of video piracy, so it's ironic that his skyscraper is situated in the heartland of his nemesis. As mentioned earlier, Chiu built his media empire in collaboration with TVB, first as a syndicator of its programming on the government-run terrestrial channels and then—after

TVB dramas were banned from the airwaves—by distributing the series on videocassette. They proved enormously popular at video rental shops, but when piracy skyrocketed during the late 1980s and early 1990s, profit margins took a tumble. Chiu then adroitly sidestepped into the world of cable television by launching a joint venture with TVB and turning his already substantial media enterprise into an even more powerful force in the Taiwan market. By the end of the 1990s, Chiu was head of the three TVB Superstation (TVBS) channels, five ERA channels, a film distribution company, and an advertising agency.

Of all Chiu's media ventures, TVBS is the jewel in the crown. In 1993, when the station first took to the airwaves, Chiu's Hong Kong partner provided managerial advice, technical support, and TVB programming in exchange for a 70 percent ownership share. Chiu, with a 30 percent share, took responsibility for daily management of station operations. It was a productive alliance, with imported drama series helping to establish the channel's brand identity, which Chiu then leveraged into a more diverse range of services. Most prominently, TVBS pioneered talk shows and news programs that lifted the company to a leading position in the Taiwan market, putting it on par with the terrestrial stations. A key figure in this success story has been Lee Tao, general manager of TVBS. Lee also plays host to one of the station's most popular talk shows, fashioning himself as the Larry King of Taiwan or, in his more expansive moments, as the Larry King of Global China. Ruggedly handsome, Lee is generous with both facts and anecdotes, strategically punctuating his observations with a photogenic grin. Stylish suspenders pulled over his blue checked shirt, Lee consciously courts the Larry King analogy at every turn. Before joining TVBS, he hosted a talk show during the 1980s on CTS, the government station run by the military and the Ministry of Education. At that time, guests had to be screened in advance, and topics had to be cleared by censors three to four weeks ahead of each show. Moreover, station staffers were socialized to observe unspoken guidelines, and, as a result, the programs generated few surprises, either for the interviewer or for the audience. Shortly after the end of martial law, Lee Tao launched a radio talk show that began to test the boundaries of censorship, but he still remained wary of government surveillance. By 1993, however, it seemed evident that the trend toward democratization was irreversible, and even television, the most conservative medium in Taiwan, might be ready for change. Lee met with Chiu Fu-sheng and pitched a self-consciously provocative talk show for TVBS, noting both a ratings opportunity and the relatively modest costs of production.

Only ten days later, on August 1, 1994, Lee settled behind the anchor desk at a makeshift studio in a rented warehouse on the outskirts of Taipei. "I remember the first night," Lee muses. "It was raining hard, and the roof was leaking, and the engineers hadn't finished laying the phone lines. The first two guests I tried to invite [declined] because it was too far away, and the ones I was able to line up were having a hard time finding the warehouse. Right before we went on air, one of the engineers came up to me and said, 'Mr. Lee, I'm sorry, but you have to use your hands to hold together these two wires.'"

With seconds to air, only two of the three guests had made it to the studio. One was a taxi driver representing hundreds of cabbies then campaigning for wider access to government-controlled radio channels. The other was a media executive who likewise was pressing for more channel allocations. Up to that time, government officials had tightly managed all radio frequencies, with military and strategic services receiving first priority, followed by state-run radio and TV stations. But taxi drivers, a vocal and volatile group, brought the issue into the arena of public debate when hundreds of them marched to the Government Information Office to petition for wider access to the airwaves for their radio dispatching systems. It was the first time that anyone dared to challenge government control of the radio spectrum openly, and now they planned to argue their case before a national TV audience, another unprecedented challenge to the KMT. Meanwhile, as the clock ticked toward the premiere telecast of 21:00, the deputy minister of the GIO was still out on the rain-drenched streets of Taipei, searching in vain for the studio. When the show began, the cab drivers' representative gleefully seized the moment, boisterously asserting the public's right to the airwaves and dominating the discussion during the early part of the show. Much to the delight of call-in guests and the viewing audience, it was one the first times that the government literally found itself out in the cold during a discussion of broadcasting policy. Finally, during a commercial break, engineers were able to hook up the hapless GIO official by cell phone, so that he could participate in an unrehearsed and surprisingly frank exchange of ideas.

The show not only made history but also scored a remarkable 10 rating, a record for cable TV and fully competitive with the ratings of terrestrial stations at that time. Lee chuckles when he recalls that the audience had "never experienced a real, live talk show like this," adding that "taxi drivers can be pretty colorful characters." Viewers were just as enthused that phone-in comments weren't screened in advance and topics weren't vetted by censors. "They called in and heard their own voices," notes Lee, "and, even more important, they also could hear the government official responding." As a result of the program's strong rating, TVBS management trumpeted it as a significant break from the past, and in subsequent shows Lee kept probing other taboo subjects, becoming the channel's signature attraction. The 21:00 program captured the temper of the times, and the format became one of the most popular offerings on cable TV, generating dozens of imitators. As one cable executive puts it, "People are eager to express their feelings on TV and to debate with people from other parties. Some call-in programs get a 1+ rating, which is a good performance [since the average cable program scores only a .5 rating]. The programs don't have any value for resale [overseas], but they're cheap to produce, and Chinese people in other countries will watch if they can get them by satellite; sometimes they'll even call in from overseas."

The passion for talk shows is perhaps one of the leading characteristics of Taiwanese TV, and their popularity extends to radio as well. It's not uncommon for hosts to field calls from listeners in restaurants and shops, as well as from audiences at home. Although at first they provided a refreshing break from the past, the topics and formats have grown more formulaic and some say more sensational. Lee concedes that the increasing competition has made his job more difficult. "The Chinese actually don't prefer to watch people talk," he observes. "They can be very impatient. Maybe in the U.S. people will listen to someone speak for a minute or even three minutes. But here, they will switch channels. The first thirty seconds—kind of interesting, draws attention—then, bye-bye. So, it's very high stress when I'm on the air. I keep thinking to myself, keep pushing myself: this five seconds, is it going to hold the viewer? I have to change topics and look for gimmicks." When asked to compare his show with *Larry King Live,* which Lee watches regularly, he says, "I think [21:00 is] more exciting, more fast paced, more complicated and controversial, a lot of things going on. It's like *Larry King, Nightline,* and even some parts of the *Late Show with David Letterman.* It has to be. Taiwanese or Chinese, it's very hard to hold their attention."

Shortly after the talk show format took off, TVBS broke new ground again with the island's first twenty-four-hour news channel. Chiu reasoned at the time that the station's growing reputation for current affairs programming would require an ongoing expansion of the news staff, so in 1995 he launched TVBS-N, a channel that branded itself as a fashionable and informal alternative to the terrestrials, relying heavily on the drawing power of its presenters, such as the former TTV anchor Chang Ya-chin, who was described by one TV executive as "flamboyant, alluring, more like a variety show hostess." The channel also benefited from dramatic news events during the 1990s: several close elections, two showdowns with Beijing, and sev-

After the end of martial law in Taiwan, the explosion of cable services during the 1990s was spurred in large part by popular demand for news programming outside official government channels. Author photo.

eral sensational kidnappings, one involving the daughter of Pai Ping-ping, a famous Taiwanese singer and actress. Such events became a pretext for ongoing news coverage with frequent updates, turning TVBS-N into the leading source of island news.

As the company matured, Taiwanese news and infotainment shows began to crowd out syndicated dramas, so management decided to float a general entertainment channel, TVBS-G, which specializes in imported programming from Hong Kong as well as from Japan and the United States. TVB's kung fu series holds down the 8 P.M. slot, targeting viewers in their twenties, while contemporary family drama draws a broader spectrum of viewers at 6 P.M. Although not as popular as its other two channels, TVBS-G generates solid ratings on a modest budget. "We're very cost effective," explains Lee. He says there's little incentive for TVBS to venture into the risky world of original drama production, since it has privileged access to the TVB program library in Hong Kong. And once it acquires a program, it can use that program multiple times. "In fact, right now our 8 P.M. soap opera is a rerun," Lee confides with a wink. "We don't pay, since we already paid once, and the ratings are still very good, no cost at all. Our competitors spend sometimes $30,000 to produce one program for one night. We buy programs from TVB for several hundred U.S. dollars, something like that, a couple thousand dollars at the most." Lee estimates monthly revenues from the three TVBS channels at around $13 million in 2000, whereas the terrestrial networks each gross around $10 million. But taking production into account, TVBS's advantage over the terrestrials is even greater, since its programming costs are much lower.

Despite the success of Chiu's joint venture with the Hong Kong-based TVB, tensions between the partners emerged over time when Chiu began to feel he wasn't being remunerated in proportion to his contributions. Certainly, TVB helped to establish the venture, but it was Chiu and his local staff who had made it a leader in the very competitive Taiwan market. Chiu longed for more control, and he therefore began to develop his own cable services, known as ERA Communications, offering sports, financial news, and entertainment channels. In part, Chiu sought greater autonomy, but he also sought to expand his overall presence among the competition. TV executives in Taiwan commonly assert that once a cable channel establishes its identity, it takes tremendous resources to push ratings higher in a market crowded with competing channels. The most cost-efficient way to add new viewers is to expand the number of channels in one's platform, providing more opportunities to capture the grazing cable viewer and to cross-promote programs. Thus, Chiu reasoned that six channels—three TVBS and three ERA—was better than redoubling his efforts to improve the existing TVBS platform. Yet it's difficult to secure carriage for new channels unless one has leverage over the system operators. Using the popular TVBS channels as both a cudgel and a carrot, Chiu was able to persuade local operators to carry his new services, expanding the TVBS-ERA platform to eight channels—five of them ERA stations—by the end of the 1990s. At that point, Chiu could claim close to 10 percent of the total channel lineup on most cable systems throughout the island.

Despite this steady growth trajectory, the original joint venture was beginning to unravel, with the two partners starting to tussle over managerial and strategic issues, such as a joint venture in an expensive DTH (direct-to-home) satellite service that ended up costing ERA more than $20 million in losses. Shortly thereafter, the advertising economy in Taiwan hit the skids, and disputes emerged over operational costs and profit statements. "Sometimes it's hard to tell which is which, who should take what percentage" says Lee. The two companies differed in other ways as well. "TVB is a slow-moving organization," Lee confides. "Maybe they are too happy, too fat. Here, everything moves very fast. And the chairman—he can foresee things. If we have any success, it's because of this. Maybe we're not fully prepared and the planning isn't always done, but the industry moves so fast that we have to be this way to stay in the market. Everything is image, and people see us as a pioneer. We have to move fast to protect that image." TVB by comparison is an established broadcaster that has dominated its local market for close to four decades. With its well-tested protocols and managerial hierarchies, decisions grow out of research and consultation. Layers of bureaucracy provide slow but patterned responses to changes in the organization and in the market. This corporate style clearly diverges from Chiu's more intuitive, entrepreneurial style

During the late 1990s, as Chiu began to develop his ERA channels, TVB managers grew increasingly uncomfortable with potential conflicts between the two services. They felt, for example, that ERA's twenty-four-hour financial news channel might someday compete with TVBS-N. Likewise, its general entertainment channel seemed poised to compete with TVBS-G. Moreover, it was rumored that TVBS resources and equipment were being "shared" by Chiu's new cable stations. These tensions escalated further while both companies contemplated their future ambitions. Both saw the limits of their respective home markets, and both were strategizing about Global China. In 2000, Lee Tao told me that the long-term survivors in the Taiwanese TV business "will have to move out of this market. It's too small. We can't depend on it to keep us going further or stronger in the future."

"Where would you go first?" I asked.

"Mainland China," Lee replied. "We're ready, any minute." Then gesturing with his right hand like a jet taking off, he let out a big "whoosh" and shot me a conspiratorial smile. "When the opportunity comes, we're there." Lee said the company had already set up a production house in Shanghai, news crews in three cities, and was training and recruiting talent for both entertainment and information. "That's our bread and butter in the future. Financially, China could be our most important market." Lee believes the PRC is on the verge of many of the very same changes that fueled the emergence of Taiwan's free-wheeling television market. The big challenge is to navigate the political intricacies of mainland TV, and this is where issues of corporate culture become especially important.

Throughout its history TVB has taken a very guarded approach to politics, trying to ply the choppy waters between the British and Chinese governments delicately while serving local Cantonese and transnational Chinese audiences. Chiu, on the other hand, immersed himself in politics. Even before the rise of cable TV, Chiu worked the KMT hierarchy for necessary favors to benefit his growing video empire. Then after the end of martial law, he skillfully navigated the shifting political shoals, making appearances at power events and playing golf with the right people, including president Lee

Teng-hui. Like Chiu, Lee himself has been a bit of a maverick, becoming the first native-born Taiwanese to rise to a position of leadership in the KMT during the 1980s. Named vice-president under Chiang Kai-shek's son and successor, Chiang Ching-kuo, Lee wisely cultivated his own power base, and, after the younger Chiang's death in 1988, Lee's allies in the legislature elevated him to president. While the 1990s unfolded, Lee was reappointed to a second term but was facing the prospect of Taiwan's first direct popular election in 1996, competing against James Soong, the popular provincial governor, who by law had authority to appoint the directors of Taiwan Television. With TTV in Soong's camp, CTS in the hands of the military, and CTV controlled by a divided KMT, Lee Teng-hui turned to TVBS as a station that might offer balanced, if not sympathetic, coverage. During the 1996 campaign, which began shortly after TVBS launched its twenty-four-hour news channel, Lee Teng-hui and Chiu Fu-sheng reportedly developed a close personal relationship, and after the election the relationship grew even tighter when Lee publicly criticized the government TV channels, declaring TVBS news more independent and more responsible. Consequently, government officials began to open their doors to TVBS reporters, and the station's ratings began to soar. Thus, the fortunes of Lee and Chiu rose in tandem throughout the 1990s, but eventually Lee's political agenda would prove problematic for Chiu, since it increasingly hinged on Taiwanese independence.

Although Chiu's alliance with Lee made strategic sense during the mid-1990s, mainland Chinese officials began to criticize Chiu during the early 2000s, citing his links to Lee. What seemed like smart politics in the 1990s was now stifling the future development of ERA Communications, with mainland bureaucrats undermining Chiu's attempts to expand across the strait. One high-ranking TVB official in Hong Kong observed, "Chiu had 30 percent ownership and operational control of TVBS, but that wasn't enough. He wanted something more: he wanted to dabble in Taiwan politics and cross-strait politics. But he played too close to the candle, and now he's getting burned." Indeed, the Chinese government has repeatedly turned down ERA's applications for "landing rights" in the PRC, which means that the company is not allowed to market its services to viewers, advertisers, or cable system operators.

Chiu also began to experience political problems on the island when his association with Eastern's MSO boss Gary Wang began to turn sour. In 2000, Wang was indicted for rigging a real estate sale to a government investment bank, and Chiu, a member of the bank's board of directors, was named as a coconspirator for using his influence to push through the sale at an inflated price. According to one informed source, Chiu wiggled out of the scandal by having one of his subordinates take the rap for him, "but not without losing a lot of money and creating some very bad feelings."

TVB executives in Hong Kong were keeping a close eye on these political developments and on Chiu's ERA cable channels, which had technically violated a noncompetition clause in their joint-venture agreement. After the real estate scandal unfolded, Run Run Shaw's wife, Mona Fong, who has for several decades played an influential role at TVB, made a surprise visit to TVBS headquarters with a team of auditors in tow. While her accountants pored over the books, Fong privately interviewed top executives, asking them, among other things, to declare their loyalties. Like most others, Lee Tao cast his lot with TVB, sensing that operational control was shifting hands. As for Chiu, he retains his 30 percent ownership interest, but as one TVB executive explained, he has been encouraged to "sit quietly" and learn to become a team player. According to this executive, "We've worked very hard to develop a company in which no single person is more important than the organization. And part of that corporate philosophy is based on our desire to stay independent and not get too involved in politics. It's a very delicate situation. We're in many markets, and we have a very large news organization as well as entertainment. We can't be seen to be meddling in politics, especially when there are some very explosive issues involved."

For almost a century, Run Run Shaw's political neutrality and commercial sensibility allowed his media enterprises to cobble together Chinese audiences throughout Asia, but in Taiwan it's unlikely that the TVBS platform would have become one of the strongest competitors during the 1990s without local partners who were willing to build a network of political connections. The station's success was in large measure due to the idiosyncratic, entrepreneurial style of Chiu Fu-sheng, who cleverly positioned the station as a leading news and information source during a tumultuous decade of political change. Yet as the constraints of the highly fragmented island market became more apparent, Chiu began to focus increasingly on the prospect of transnational expansion, a move that generated friction with his Hong Kong partners regarding both corporate style and strategic ambition. Although Chiu's eventual showdown with the Shaws was putatively triggered by his political and financial entanglements in Taiwan, it was just as likely engendered by his burgeoning ambitions regarding the Global China market, ambitions that put him on a collision course with TVB.

If ERA provides a good example of why many Taiwanese media enterprises must eventually begin to look outward, then Formosa Television (FTV) provides a counterexample of a service that is resolutely retaining a focus on the local market. Taiwan's fourth terrestrial station, Formosa Television was formed in 1997, when, under the leadership of Trong R. Chai, two groups of investors from the Democratic Progressive Party decided to launch a station aimed at providing an oppositional perspective on news and entertainment. Targeting the Taiwanese-speaking population in the southern part of the country, FTV further sought to promote awareness of local history, myth, and legend, to serve as an antidote to the many years of indoctrination under the Nationalist government of Chiang Kai-shek. On more than a few occasions, when I queried TV executives about why entrepreneurs are willing to take a chance on the hotly competitive Taiwanese market, I was told repeatedly that the owner believes "media is power." Whether Gary Wang, Chiu Fu-sheng, or Trong R. Chai, the new media moguls of Taiwan are, unlike Run Run Shaw, keenly interested in the broader social influence of television. Moreover, some station executives believe that their bosses wish to wield political power even more than they wish to make money, as indicated by a fist-flying donnybrook that erupted at one cable station in 1999 when a dispute between owners escalated into a struggle over who would take control of the money-losing operation. With studio cameras still on-air, one faction stormed the station, only to be met by a bare-knuckled defense of the facility and its precious cable license.

Television generates such passion because owners believe the medium plays a significant role in framing political debates, shaping social behaviors, and influencing consumer preferences. This perception is largely based on decades of experience under the ruling KMT, when government stations controlled both the flow of ideas and advertising dollars. At that time, broadcasters dutifully respected the KMT party line, and they furthermore loaned their creative expertise to government officials and ministries. Television employees also worked in subtler ways to foster the KMT's version of Chinese cultural consciousness by broadcasting Beijing opera, calligraphy lessons, and historical documentaries about Chinese dynasties, while giving short shrift to local history and culture. Indeed, during the first three decades of television, the Taiwanese language was suppressed, and indigenous perspectives were marginalized.[4] Memories of the martial law years are especially painful for members of the Democratic Progressive Party, since many of them suffered imprisonment and assassination, little of it acknowledged, much less covered by the mainstream media.

It's therefore easy to sympathize with Trong Chai's desire to operate a station that owes specific allegiance to the DPP. Yet FTV's initial ratings proved disappointing, and after a rocky first year, the owners conceded that survival in the marketplace would have to take precedence over political symbolism. In an explicit departure from the founding principles of Formosa Television, the owners therefore decided to recruit executives from competing broadcast stations, offering them a mandate to focus on profitability before politics. New management jettisoned much of the prime-time schedule in favor of contemporary family dramas, such as *Grace in My Heart*, a nightly series about a self-sacrificing mother who attends to the needs of her extended family.[5] Premiering in the fall of 1998, the story line was not particularly unique, but FTV programmers reasoned that two elements would make it especially attractive. First of all, *Grace* would be produced in Taiwanese, making it readily accessible to older viewers, who usually had to suffer through Mandarin-language drama series. Second, the lead character would be played by Pai Ping-ping, a singer and actress who is extraordinarily popular with audiences in the southern part of the island. Even more, the series was to be the first time that Pai had performed since the kidnapping, torture, and murder of her seventeen-year-old daughter, a crime that drew sensational news coverage during the spring of 1997. "Pai was the perfect actress for the role," one FTV executive told me. "She suffered so much during the kidnapping, and people felt that the role was true [to her experience]."

Within ten days of the premier, *Grace in My Heart* topped the 8 P.M. ratings and became FTV's signature program, averaging close to a 7 rating and helping to establish a loyal audience over the course of 120 episodes. Station executives furthermore took the unprecedented step of rerunning each episode the following afternoon, when it averaged a very strong 2 rating. *Grace* rocketed FTV to prominent status, and the following year FTV solidified these gains with another drama, *Two Families, One World*, drawing even larger audiences. Like *Grace*, the new series was produced on a local sound stage, keeping costs low in comparison to historical dramas. In general, FTV's family dramas are dialogue-driven, with inexpensive sets and contemporary costumes. Produced entirely in Taiwan, they obviate the need for a transnational coproduction partner, but they are likewise limited in appeal, aimed largely at island audiences with little chance of overseas syndication, especially since most of the series are produced in Taiwanese. The programs nevertheless perform well during the heart of prime time, allowing executives to build a successful nightly schedule around news and family drama.

"I think retired people, especially the grandmother, make most of the decisions about the family's [viewing]," says Vivian Chien, a programming executive with FTV who previously worked for United and ERA. "In my family's house, during the time news is on, my father controls. But at eight o'clock my mother takes over and chooses the drama, and a lot of times my dad and I will watch too." Having established itself with mature female viewers, FTV began to shift its attention to holding on to its younger viewers after their elders retire for the evening. "Advertising agencies say these [young] viewers have more buying power," notes Chien. "They say their clients look at the ratings, but they also look at who that audience is. Most desirable is the thirty-four-year-old working male, and we need more of those viewers. At first it bothered me that we were going away from our loyal audience. In the beginning we put emphasis on getting high Nielsen ratings, because that's what attracts some advertising agencies. We needed to do that to survive, but now we want to improve the audience composition. The drama series [aimed at older viewers] was a way to establish our brand, but now we have to make the brand grow."

Chien is a member of the demographic that FTV is now courting: young, middle-class, and willing to experiment with new programs and new products. We meet at the company's headquarters, situated between one of the most cosmopolitan neighborhoods of Taipei and one of the most traditional. To the west of FTV, the streets are dotted with upscale department stores, fashion boutiques, nightclubs, and trendy restaurants. Brightly lit shops—lavishly appointed with products from Tokyo, Paris, and New York—beckon shoppers with imaginative wordplay from near and far, such as the Ozoné coffee shop, My de Girl boutique, and the Jazz Your Mind restaurant. Yet walking in the opposite direction on Pateh Road, the signage is almost exclusively in Chinese—Good Fortune Jewelers and Double Happiness Restaurant—and less than a block from the FTV headquarters, one plunges into a crowded street market with vendors selling everything from fresh fish to sweaters to calligraphy brushes. FTV's location is emblematic of the broad register of cultural differences that the station needs to navigate in its pursuit of audiences—differences between East and West but also between the north and south, between Chinese and Taiwanese, and between generations.

The challenge for Chien and her colleagues is to exploit the popularity of FTV's family dramas while also attracting new audiences. An initial solution was to program drama series for young women at 9:30, when older viewers retire for the evening, but the strategy failed to draw audiences away from the popular variety shows on competing terrestrials. Next, FTV tried to develop its own variety show, but that too met with limited success, in large part because it's difficult to secure topflight talent. "When a show is popular, everybody tries to copy it," says Chien. "At those times we feel the shortage of talent in Taipei. We feel we can't come up with enough good writers or actors to compete. If you look at variety shows, you notice the stars are almost the same, just different combinations. So tonight they are on TTV, maybe Wednesday on CTS, maybe Saturday on CTV."

Consequently, says Chien, new channels find it difficult to cultivate innovation. "We have lots of cable stations, lots of channels. I think there is plenty of *opportunity* for talent, but the problem is, can they get good training? Cable stations don't have much budget. Maybe they can give you an opportunity, but they can't really train you." By comparison, Run Run Shaw's enduring success is attributable in part to the extensive training his Hong Kong studio provides by conducting recruiting drives and training workshops and by offering talent contests aimed at attracting fresh creative prospects. Taiwanese TV stations have, in contrast, relied on independent producers for much of their entertainment programming, and these producers, given their often precarious financial status, have not cultivated talent as systematically. Moreover, this deficiency was exacerbated by the shift from the three-channel cartel of the broadcasting era to the hundred-channel universe of the cable era. Today, stations scramble to sign hot new prospects, but they generally fail to *cultivate* homegrown artistes. Shortages are especially vexing when a channel is trying to alter its programming strategy, hemmed in on one side by modest budgets and on the other by a very competitive ratings environment in which shows rarely have time to find their audience.

Indeed, ratings have dramatically changed the decision-making process for television executives. Before the cable era, broadcasters enjoyed a government-sanctioned monopoly, which allowed them to make programming decisions with little concern for the ratings outcome. One way or another, viewers were tuned to a station that served the interests of the ruling government and its associated enterprises, so there was little need to worry about competition. Moreover, an artificial scarcity of advertising time made it possible for the big three to set rates with little concern regarding audience size or characteristics. In fact, it wasn't until the late 1990s, when broadcasters saw their share of viewers dramatically erode, that the big three turned to independent research companies.

A.C. Nielsen is now the dominant ratings firm in Taiwan, gathering data in fifteen-minute increments from meters placed in six hundred homes around the island. Tina Teng, senior manager of media research at Nielsen, says over 70 percent of households have more than one television, and virtually all have remote controls, fostering a trend toward personal viewing and rapid channel changes. The watershed mark for the industry, according to Teng, was 1995 when cable TV penetration broke the 70 percent barrier, giving the average home access to more than eighty channels and making cable ratings an important part of the television economy. Although advertising sales volume has continued to grow since then, ratings have consistently slid downward as audiences have begun to graze among programs, rarely resting on the same station for more than a few minutes. The exception is when families view together. At 7 P.M., for example, news programs draw viewers across generations, and adult males usually choose the channel. The 8 P.M. drama also tends to pull a family audience together, but choice usually passes to the senior woman of the household. Interestingly, viewers over fifty-five, especially in south and central Taiwan, make up the largest viewing segment for prime-time drama, which FTV capitalized on in its rise to prominence. When seniors retire, however, overall ratings drop significantly, and audience composition takes a radical turn toward younger viewers, who prefer variety shows.

Teng says that ethnicity and geography tend to correlate with program choices. "In south and central Taiwan, local drama is most popular, especially dramas that are very emotional." Teng observes that the popularity of Taiwanese drama is largely attributable to the resurgence of identity issues after the end of martial law and to the impact of older audiences on ratings data. Audiences in the south and central regions, especially rural areas, tend to skew older, with many retirees returning to the same neighborhoods in which they grew up, after spending much of their working lives in big cities. By comparison, in the north of Taiwan, especially around Taipei, viewers prefer Mandarin-language series with more elaborate production values and more complicated narratives. The plot lines tend to move quickly, and the dialogue is more stylish, more contemporary. "For example," says Teng while pointing to a ratings sheet, "you can see that the CTV series with very high ratings has a very modern style, even though it deals with very traditional *wuxia* [martial arts] themes." Such programs are attractive to advertisers because younger audiences have higher incomes and tend to be more fashion-conscious and more receptive to novel products. For decades, the Taipei region has been a magnet for young people seeking their fortune in the big city, many of them competent in Mandarin as a result of government education policies.

Nevertheless, Teng cautions that these generalizations don't always obtain. She points out, for example, that cities throughout the island have their share of the youth demographic and that preferences among young viewers tend to converge regardless of ethnicity or geography. "Ethnic differences are strongest among the older generations," observes Teng. "In

Hsinchu [a city on the west coast known as the Silicon Valley of Taiwan] audiences are split between young high-tech workers—many of them educated overseas—and Hakka, who are very, very traditional, even a little more traditional than Taiwanese viewers. But I don't think the younger generation strongly identifies as Hakka, and the same is true for Taiwanese people, because of intermarriage, education, and popular culture." Teng claims that the biggest differences are not among ethnic groups but among generations and that age magnifies one's tendency to identify with a particular ethnic group. With this in mind, Teng says she can discern some fairly clear patterns: Taiwanese seniors prefer local dramas, while middle-age viewers are attracted to movies and infotainment, such as travel, geography, and science programming. The youngest cohort, the "Net generation," likes movies, variety shows, and trendy Japanese and Korean dramas. Teng observes that FTV succeeded by programming for an underserved population, but she suggests that in the future it may be difficult for a station so strongly identified with Taiwanese drama to build a bridge to younger late-night audiences.

FTV isn't alone in its attempts to negotiate the divide between generations and ethnicities. Sanlih television likewise built a popular service by appealing to audience tastes in southern Taiwan, but, unlike FTV, it eschewed drama and built its reputation with musical variety programs. Like the talk show, the variety genre is one of the most popular in Taiwan, featuring musical and dance routines as well as guest appearances by entertainment celebrities. Influenced from the outset by Japanese television, many shows also include audience participation and wacky competitions, for example, guest celebrities playing a tag-team ping-pong match while the host quizzes them with ludicrous trivia questions, or audience members eating exotic foods and guessing their origin, only to discover they had feasted on marinated camel's cheek or raw ostrich egg. Such high jinks obviously resemble recent reality shows in Western societies, but interestingly they have been part of East Asian television for decades.[6] Taiwanese variety shows also rely crucially on the improvisational talents of the host, who most often plays the role of trickster—teasing, tormenting, and cajoling guests—thereby giving the show an informal quality that makes it seem part of the family circle. Many hosts are also renowned for their ability to tell racy jokes, and, here again, trickster qualities are crucial, for the joke must seem to come from inside the family circle at the very same time that it transgresses the rules of propriety.

On weekday evenings, the programs usually begin at nine o'clock, after the prime-time drama, and on weekends the programs begin as early as eight. Weekend shows are more elaborately conceived, with one program during the 2003 season relying heavily on sketch comedy, as *Saturday Night Live* does, and another featuring a weekly "Super Mission" to find long-lost friends and relatives, reminiscent of *This Is Your Life!* In such cases, the game or the gimmick may be as important as the host, and the credit for such innovation lies not with the broadcast stations but with independent producers, who both create and produce the shows. These producers act as program packagers, developing concepts and competing for key programming slots on the top broadcast stations. They design the format, line up the talent, and in many cases sell the advertising time, splitting the proceeds fifty-fifty with the station. Although the shows were relatively tame family fare during the martial law era, cable competition has upped the stakes, resulting in some frantic ploys to attract viewers. Sexist jokes and lewd banter have come under fire from critics, and one show drew especially heated condemnation when, in a cynical bid for ratings, it furnished the set with bikini-clad young women.

As durable ratings performers for more than forty years, variety shows initially provided a crucial advantage to terrestrial broadcasters over their emerging cable competitors, since producers usually pitched their shows first to the big three terrestrials, believing that would earn them the biggest ratings and the highest ad rates. Counter to this, Sanlih television, a cable enterprise launched in 1996 by Chang Rong-hua, built its reputation on a variation of the variety show that specifically catered to audiences in the south. During the late 1980s and early 1990s, Chang made a small fortune producing music videos of restaurant *(canting)* shows that featured singers in southern Taiwan performing in their native language. As the business grew, Chang also set up nightclubs, formed a record company, and began to produce videos for karaoke, an increasingly popular pastime during the 1990s. In an era when the KMT controlled broadcast TV, Chang's video business paradoxically benefited from broadcasting regulations that marginalized the Taiwanese language, allowing him to exploit an alternative market niche. But the arrival of cable undermined Chang's success, because unregulated operators rented the latest Sanlih videos at local shops and telecast them to subscribers. Like Chiu Fu-sheng, Chang was forced to set up his own cable channel in response to such unauthorized use, and he counterprogrammed with live *canting* shows, thinking they would be less susceptible to piracy. During the first year of operation, 56 percent of Sanlih's schedule was composed of such shows, and another 22 percent were live singing competitions, in which winners earned a recording contract and were then cycled into the regular program line-up. Both formats were inexpensive to produce, making Sanlih as one of the more profitable cable enterprises of the late 1990s. The channel furthermore bolstered the visibility of its stable of performers and enhanced record sales at Chang's music company.

Interestingly, the variety show, the *canting* show, and the nightclub performance share not only a generic connection but also an association with organized crime. Nightclubs have long been attractive to triads, because they provide a convenient front for underworld enterprises, such as prostitution, gambling, and drugs. Although clubs flourish in many cities, the Taipei municipal government has made numerous attempts to crack down on them, most famously in the mid-1990s, when then mayor Chen Shuibian outlawed prostitution and banned dance shows from the city. As with most attempts to regulate organized crime, the restrictions merely transformed rather than eliminated the nightclub performance, which soon morphed into medicine shows that would set up in open fields on the outskirts of the city, drawing male audiences for an evening of laughter and lurid entertainment. In fact, Jacky Wu, one of the top variety show hosts in Taiwan, launched his career as the emcee of one of these shows, telling jokes, bantering with the audience, and pitching medicinal products that reputedly enhance sexual performance.

It is not surprising that triads would be influential purveyors of such bawdy fare. For centuries they have exploited popular fantasies about wealth, beauty, and sexual fulfillment via such vice operations as gambling, prostitution, and video piracy. Yet it's also important to note that when the opportunity presents itself, gangsters are just as likely to extend their services to "legitimate" forms of entertainment, and their presence is sometimes felt in the most unexpected places. As explained earlier, those who work in Chinese entertainment may or may not be consciously consorting with triads, but all understand that it's difficult to succeed in the business without brushing up against triad society members. This is especially true within the nightclub industry. Although Chang Rong-hua has been circumspect about his associations with triad societies, his former collaborator, Yang Teng-kuei, a renowned gangster and nightclub operator, has been less so. After years of working together, Chang and Yang had a falling out in the late 1990s, and Yang set up his own competing cable channel, Ba Da. Both companies therefore grew out of the nightclub milieu in the south, but over time Sanlih dramatically transformed itself into a modern corporate enterprise and markedly distanced itself from past associations.

Unlike Ba Da, which is very opportunistic, Sanlih became one of the first

Taiwanese television services to employ systematic audience research in its programming and marketing strategies. Yvonne Chang, a team leader of media research, is one of the few executives I interviewed to arrive at our meeting armed with charts and diagrams of programming trends and audience viewing patterns. She acknowledged that Sanlih's original hook was a combination of music, humor, and Taiwanese, but as the service grew and as competition became more ferocious, Sanlih's managers decided they needed to diversify operations, so they opted to add a Mandarin-language channel targeted at audiences in the north. "Music shows are good for some advertisers," she observes, "but not for others, and we wanted to reach both." So, toward the end of 1996, Sanlih launched the City Channel, featuring entertainment news and syndicated programming, such as Japanese animation, Mandarin drama, and infotainment shows that repackage wild footage of sensational crimes, disasters, and oddities of nature. Aimed at younger and more upscale audiences, the City Channel also uses its entertainment news shows (which constitute 25 percent of the programming) to interview pop stars and telecast feature stories about musical trends. Its solid ratings attracted substantial new ad revenues, especially from Taiwanese music companies that target young consumers.

Yvonne Chang reports that Chang Rong-hua then considered a third service, saying, "Without news, we really aren't a TV company." So in 1997, Sanlih launched SET-N, self-consciously replacing the company's brand name with a more contemporary-sounding acronym SET (Sanlih Entertainment Television) and adopting the N to denote "national" as well as "news." According to Y. Chang, "We thought it was time to put away the local," time to develop a strategy aimed at the islandwide market. Chang observes that it would be illogical to develop a commercial news service aimed at only one part of the island. "We had two very important election years in 1996 and 1997, and we knew that more elections were coming," she says. As democratization swept through Taiwan in the 1990s, the number of political parties proliferated, and the number of hotly contested elections grew as well. Parties and candidates besides the KMT now had a genuine chance to succeed, and consequently, spending on election advertising grew dramatically, most of it lavished on news and public affairs programming.

"We really don't need so many news channels [in Taiwan]," concedes Chang, "but media executives want the influence that comes with news, and they want to attract advertising from the political parties. If you don't have news programming, they aren't as interested in you. If you interview their politicians [for your news show] and you invite them on your talk shows, then they are more likely to remember your station when they are thinking about advertising. News is necessary for sales, not just for political influence. It's the same with record companies. If you interview their singers and you do reports on their stars, then they are more likely to advertise on your station." Such shrewd calculations have helped SET to grow its news operation despite a very crowded and competitive market. Besides broadcasting political news, SET-N distinguishes itself by presenting feature magazine programs with biographies of celebrities, politicians, and ordinary people. It also produces tabloid news shows, such as *On the Spot*, modeled on the popular U.S. reality program *911*. Overall, the SET news channel offers a journalistic mix that is slick, salacious, and political, not unlike the mix one finds among New York or London tabloid newspapers.

With three channels (SET-1, -2, -N) on the air, it seemed that the company had reached maturity, but toward the end of 1999, executives decided it was time to revisit the programming philosophy of the first service. "The era of the *canting* show has passed," explains programming executive Tiffany Sheu, "and we're looking for new types of shows." As the core audience of the restaurant shows aged and the media environment grew increasingly open, the original appeal of the programs began to wane. Consequently, SET started to retire the *canting* shows and experiment with original drama production, scoring successes with contemporary series aimed at younger audiences, a move that again targeted an underdeveloped genre and an underserved audience. As FTV and TVBS did, SET entered the television business through a market niche but quickly discovered that it would need to grow its audience and expand to a cable platform if it was to survive. Despite its initial focus on audiences in the south, it soon fashioned services for the island as a whole and ultimately began to contemplate the prospects of transnational operations and opportunities as well.

By 2000, Taiwanese cable subscribers were paying $15 to $19 per month for services that reached 82 percent of all homes, one of the highest rates of penetration in the world. With over a hundred licensed channels on the island, most homes receive at least eighty channels, creating a hotly competitive environment that eroded the KMT broadcasting oligopoly. Nevertheless, political connections and favoritism still played a significant role in electronic media when United and Eastern, the two leading MSOs, consolidated their holdings and positioned themselves for the introduction of tiered services. Having invested hundreds of millions of dollars to achieve duopoly influence over cable infrastructure, the MSO giants are now rolling out premium services and hoping to increase basic monthly charges. Yet a more open and contentious political and regulatory atmosphere in Taiwan has stalled these developments, generating uncertainties for both companies. For now, they must content themselves with the knowledge that they achieved a first-mover advantage in an industry both see as central to the new economy. Still, the costs of consolidation and technological development have been massive, encouraging both to consider a broader frame of reference that includes expansion into other parts of Asia and into such distant markets as North America, where Eastern TV (ETTV) now offers satellite and cable channels.

Likewise, successful content providers such as TVBS and SET have also run up against the limitations of the Taiwan market. With only 10 percent of cable channels turning a profit as of 2000, many companies seem to be digging in for an industry shake-out. This determination to survive despite dismal short-term prospects is no doubt attributable in part to a fascination with the power of media, but it is just as likely that the pressures of heavy investments in programming and infrastructure are equally compelling. As channels develop their long-term strategies, they tend to move away from the niches in which they first succeeded and gravitate toward additional services that will attract new viewers and complementary revenue streams. Even Formosa Television, which by many measures succeeded at attracting large audiences of mature viewers with strong ethnic and political identities, has had to recalculate the value of its core audience under pressure from advertisers who are hoping to attract younger and more cosmopolitan consumers. Under such circumstances FTV has had to reassess its notions of the audience, since younger viewers do not exhibit the strong and distinctive ethnic identities of older generations. Similarly, SET arrived at a crucial moment when it had to "put away the local" in hopes of rebranding itself to attract ad revenues from pop music companies and mass-appeal political parties. Having migrated away from an underground music economy and nightclub culture, SET executives have embraced audience research that pointed toward the cultivation of new markets and expanded distribution. Such considerations have pressed both SET and FTV to continually refigure their brand identities, probing for a balance of services that most fully employ the logic of accumulation. Yet both have run up against shortages of talent, a problem that neither has been able to resolve, given significant the costs of cultivating and training new performers and writers. Taiwan's legacy of media oligopoly and political censorship for years discouraged transnational trajectories of creative migration toward Taipei, and now with the emergence of the new informational economy, the island's media industries have been suffering from the resulting talent deficit.

What Taiwan has encouraged since the end of martial law, however, are vibrant political discussions, which TVBS has exploited thoroughly in its talk shows and news programs, deftly courting on-air controversy and off-air connections to the political establishment. Its platform furthermore has capitalized on the advantages of low-cost genres, such as talk and news, making it one of the most profitable ventures of the cable era. Yet these advantages also presented their own set of limitations when political alliances and a reputation for controversy began to undermine strategic aspirations to expand overseas. Consequently, forces of sociocultural variation that had at one time provided advantages have started to undermine opportunities for geographical expansion based on the logic of accumulation. Moreover, the alliance with Hong Kong's TVB began to seem burdensome when Chiu sought to develop his own branded services, putting him on a collision course with a seasoned adversary. TVB, having its own transnational ambitions, exploited a moment of vulnerability to reassert control and pull its Taiwanese operations back into a more conducive orbit around the corporate parent, hoping that it can continue to harvest revenues from the island market and at the same time be able to proceed with its global strategies.

The history of cable television in Taiwan therefore provides an enlightening example of Chinese capitalism in which firms solicit the patronage of party leaders and use media properties to cultivate and sustain influence over political and consumer behaviors. Unlike the British colonial government in Hong Kong, which showed little interest in television and film, Taiwanese politicians and leaders have been especially fascinated with the power of media and have been closely involved in shaping the them through broadcast licensing and censorship, as well as movie import and production quotas. Whereas in Hong Kong the logic of accumulation and the trajectories of creative migration have played a leading role, in Taiwan the forces of sociocultural variation have prevailed, even when the competitive market logic of the new cable economy took hold. Yet the future prospects of Taiwanese media, which seem to point increasingly to overseas locales, may require new strategies that will distance media institutions from the state, thereby opening the door to transnationalization of production and distribution. Such strategies might furthermore make Taipei a more attractive location for the agglomeration of creative labor.

8 Singapore: From State Paternalism to Regional Media Hub

International airport arrivals in Singapore involve one of the smoothest and most efficient border crossings anywhere in the world. Unlike most other ports of entry in Asia, where immigration officials sit behind high desks in military-style uniforms, Singapore's multicultural immigration staff, attired in colorful tropical garb, greets passengers while sitting eye-level beside a low counter, casually scanning passports into an unobtrusive database.

"Welcome to Singapore," a fifty-something woman of Indian ethnicity greets me. "Would you like some candy?" she asks warmly, taking my passport with one hand while gesturing with the other toward a well-stocked bowl of sweets in colorful, assorted wrappers. Somewhat taken aback, I decline the invitation but notice this gesture has been institutionalized across twenty inspection stations. Indeed, even the supervisor's station, which is where the problem cases are referred, is equipped with a bowl of sweets.[1] Furthermore, the air of suspicion that one expects in these situations seems to be lacking. Perhaps the government is confident that it can track the movements of visitors within its borders, or perhaps it is attempting to counteract Singapore's police-state image with a dose of tropical hospitality. This tension between openness—indeed, a *need* to interact with outsiders—and a common desire for internal security has been a prominent feature of Singaporean society since its earliest years.

The rise of the Malaysian Federation after the departure of the British in 1957 was fraught with tensions between the Malay and Chinese populations, creating conflicts at many levels of education, business, and government. Although millions of ethnic Chinese remained in Malaysia after independence, others migrated to Singapore, which in 1965 became an independent state, portraying itself as a society that favors political pragmatism and transnational commerce. Yet at a de facto level the city was also a refuge for Chinese fleeing Malaysia and Indonesia, where nationalist campaigns often targeted them as unwelcome aliens or ethnic interlopers. Searching for a place in the global economy and hoping to insulate the tiny island society from its precarious status in Southeast Asia, Singaporean leaders emphasized employment, education, and social planning.[2]

Lee Kwan Yew, who took power in 1959, instituted long-term government planning that touched many realms of social life, from industry to education to public works. Not only were the policies popular, but according to most Singaporeans they also worked well, helping Lee to hold power for more than three decades. Compared with the smog-choked, gridlocked cities elsewhere in Asia, Singapore today is clean and well manicured, with broad boulevards, pedestrian shopping districts, and public parks crisscrossing the island, many of them beautifully landscaped with tropical flora. Likewise, office buildings and shopping malls in the downtown are relatively spotless, and a gleaming mass transit system makes movement around the island relatively easy, which is especially important given the tight restrictions on private auto ownership. Although public prohibitions on chewing gum have been the butt of jokes around the world, many Singaporeans embrace the regulation of daily life, saying that they may not agree with all the rules but that the alternatives are worse. They contend that prosperity and security are the legacy left to them by President Lee, and some wax nostalgic about the firm guidance he provided during the first few decades of the country's history. Indeed, from the many people interviewed throughout the course of this research comes a recurrent aphorism: the Chinese people prefer a strong leader because they have seen the other side: the chaos, famine, and warfare that have marked periods of tenuous leadership. In Singapore this viewpoint is augmented by the suggestion that democracy is gradually being bestowed on the population as it grows more responsible and mature. They claim that, like a child, the public must be carefully cultivated so that it will blossom with an awareness of the rights and responsibilities of maturity. After several decades of Lee's guidance, these proponents of the status quo claim that the country is now ready for more openness and democracy. Critics, on the other hand, suggest the government is being forced to loosen its grip as a result of pressures exerted by globalization and the country's transition from a manufacturing to a service economy. In the new global order, Singapore must represent itself as a modern, cosmopolitan center if it is to attract strategic service industries such as finance and biotechnology. After years of orderly stability, it's not surprising that many Singaporeans embrace the regulation of everyday life, but the challenge for the new economy is to encourage creativity, spontaneity, and serendipity despite decades of meticulously managed social engineering.

This challenge manifests itself most tellingly in Singaporean television, which developed as a heavily subsidized service closely controlled by the government. At its inception in 1963, a core objective was to promote interethnic harmony in contrast to the nativist nationalism in neighboring Malaysia and Indonesia. The population of Singapore, at 3.5 million, is described as 77 percent ethnic Chinese, 14 percent Malay, and 8 percent Indian, with government officials claiming that an additional million reside in the city on work visas, a category that ranges from domestic helpers to construction workers to global corporate executives. Consequently, government TV channels were developed along cultural and linguistic lines, with one service focusing on English and Malay and the other on Chinese and Tamil. Yet English and Mandarin Chinese have been privileged among these four languages because the government has calculated that they give the city's workforce an edge in global finance, shipping, and commerce. Mandarin is further privileged in hopes that it might unify the diverse Chinese populations of Singapore, since it is considered a "neutral" language, with less than 2 percent of the population claiming it as their native tongue. Instead, Hokkien, a dialect of coastal China, is far more common, followed by Tew Chow and Cantonese, largely because these ethnic groups have constituted the largest numbers Chinese migrants to Southeast Asia since the 1700s. Accordingly, these regional varieties of Chinese are the languages of home and hearth, but they were officially banned on television and in movie theaters for close to four decades.[3]

Singapore added a third TV channel in 1984, providing an expanded range of cultural, sports, and educational programming, but the biggest changes came in the mid-1990s, when the government reorganized electronic media with an eye toward corporatization and globalization. This strategy was part of a broader campaign to instill commercial discipline in a number of strategic industries, among them transportation, telephony, and utilities. In the case of electronic media, this campaign was also spurred by an emerging consensus that the island country could not become a global financial and informational hub unless it developed a state-of-the-art communication infrastructure that was open to services from around the world. A newly established private entity, Singapore Cable Vision (SCV), therefore began laying a sophisticated fiber optic network, linking homes and businesses throughout the island. In addition to carrying government TV channels, SCV carries original programming of its own and a host of international offerings, such as Disney, ESPN, and MTV. It also delivers high-speed interactive services that provide a wealth of information and imagery from around the world. The network generated tremendous enthusiasm among policy makers and business leaders during the 1990s but less excitement among everyday users. By the beginning of the new millennium, cable was available to every citizen, but fewer than 20 percent of households had subscribed, and by 2003 the percentage had risen to only 35 percent. Slow penetration was something of a relief to broadcasters, yet it's widely believed that cable subscriptions will rise and media competition will intensify over time.

To prepare for this eventuality, policy makers established MediaCorp in 1994, terminating public subsidy to broadcast TV stations and urging a reorganization that would emphasize balanced budgets and entrepreneurial initiatives. Currently, the company is divided into seven divisions ranging from television to publishing to new technologies, and instead of three TV channels, it now programs five, targeting audiences according to demographic groupings and viewing preferences. Dedicated news, sports, and children's channels have not only expanded the number of services, but, for example, they have also allowed Channels 5 and 8 to shed their children's programming, so as to emphasize core strengths in drama and entertainment. What was once a centralized mass medium has now become a platform of services aimed at niche as well as mass audiences.

In order to further stimulate entrepreneurial initiative, the government also licensed two new television channels to the government-owned publishing conglomerate, Singapore Press Holdings (publisher of the *Straits Times*). This expanded the universe of local program possibilities, but it also divided TV ad revenue between two companies. SPH Television, headed by former MediaCorp executive Lee Cheok-yu, began contending for top ratings with its popular Chinese-language channel, but the English-language service has languished, with an audience share of only 3.5 percent compared with 14 percent for its MediaCorp counterpart. Nevertheless, competition has altered the strategies and practices of media enterprises in Singapore. In the words of one industry insider, the government sent a strong message, "The barriers are down. Do whatever you have to do to survive in the market: increase the competition, increase the quality."

Despite these changes, most of MediaCorp's attention still focuses on its Chinese- and English-language services, Channels 8 and 5, respectively, which aim their programming at middle-class families, known as heartlanders. Heartlanders are ethnically Chinese, but, as noted above, they may speak different varieties of Chinese in the home. Most have been educated in both Mandarin and English, with one serving as a primary language of instruction. Thus, a Mandarin-educated person may be conversant in English as well, perhaps using both official languages at work, while speaking Hokkien at home. Heartlanders typically have one or two children, and it's not unusual for grandparents or other relatives to live in the household, often helping to sustain unofficial languages in everyday domestic interactions. Heartlanders are also homeowners, since the government made it exceptionally easy for workers to save the down payment for a flat through its Central Provident Fund.

On Channel 8, news begins the evening, followed by game shows and situation comedies that in turn give way to Chinese historical dramas during the heart of primetime from eight to ten o'clock. According to one programmer, it doesn't matter whether the shows are locally produced or purchased overseas, viewers are drawn to quality historical dramas, with 40 percent of the audience tuned in on any given night. Programmers for the English-language channel are well aware of the powerful appeal of Chinese dramas, and they counterprogram with local productions and high-quality imports, drawing 15 percent of the audience, most of them teens and young adults. By targeting eighteen- to thirty-five-year-olds, Channel 5 tends to skew toward more educated viewers with higher disposable incomes, but the channel sometimes attracts fairly broad-based audiences, especially with its locally produced situation comedies. Because of limited production resources, imported programming plays a significant role on both channels and is often used to muster audiences as a lead-in to local programming or to build a bridge between popular local productions. Consequently, viewers in all age groups are accustomed to foreign media products and are likely to migrate toward offerings on the basis of personal tastes and perceptions of quality. Local shows with talented actors and high production values always outdraw imported fare, but homegrown locations and talent don't necessarily guarantee popularity.

In an attempt to improve program quality and address challenges from new competitors, MediaCorp executives are trying to enhance overseas co-production alliances and expand program exports. In charge of this initiative is CEO Franklin Wong, who began his career working for ATV and Radio Television Hong Kong (RTHK), with a subsequent stint at stations in Australia. MediaCorp has a reputation for hiring senior executives with scholarly backgrounds, and indeed Wong has a bespectacled, somewhat owlish appearance, and he speaks pensively and precisely about the studio's strategy. "Our annual output is eighteen hundred hours in all genres," he explains and points out with some pride that MediaCorp Studios now sell

TV dramas throughout Asia, even in the highly competitive markets of Hong Kong and Taiwan. Foreign sales grew threefold during the late 1990s, pushing to over $10 million, and Wong contends that program quality is the key to further expansion. "The visual narratives of our programs are smooth and upmarket," he observes. "We have a strong pool of directors, so the visuals are very sophisticated, but we still need to bring our scripts up to an international standard."

Script quality is a common concern among television producers throughout Global China, but it's a distinctive challenge in Singapore, where Chinese cultural influences are relatively attenuated. "You can't compare Singapore with Hong Kong or Shanghai or Taipei, where they read the classics, the novels, and the newspapers everyday in Chinese," explains Wong. "They live in an environment where there's Chinese history and literature and art. That's why our scriptwriters have a difficult time competing with them in period drama or classical adaptation." Yet Wong hopes that training workshops and collaborations with producers from other parts of Asia will compensate for this deficiency. He is also quick to point to the distinctive geographical opportunities at the tip of the Malay Peninsula. Sitting at a confluence of Southeast Asian flows, MediaCorp has extensive experience producing in Mandarin, English, Tamil, and Bahasa Malay. Consequently, Wong is keenly interested in regional markets, saying that recent sales to India and Malaysia point the way toward a diverse range of possibilities.

Two floors below, Michael Woo is in charge of coproductions, the most important component of the company's overseas strategy. For more than a decade Woo produced and directed Chinese dramas and in the late 1990s became manager of Chinese productions. Campaigning to enhance quality, Woo scaled back annual program output from six hundred to four hundred hours, focusing resources on fewer shows. Audience tastes are changing, he says, because viewers are exposed to more entertainment options. "They appreciate good product, so we can't fool them with low-budget drama." Rising costs and increasing competition put MediaCorp producers in a bind, since government regulations cap the number of TV commercials at twelve minutes per hour, constraining the revenue pie in the local market. As a result, investments in program quality may not generate significant increases in local ad revenues, which in turn means that MediaCorp must pursue overseas syndication if it is to sustain the quality of its productions.

Like Wong, Michael Woo is a Hong Kong native, and although his small office is crammed full of furniture, he cheerfully waves me in while he continues chatting on the telephone in a rapid-fire blend of Cantonese, Mandarin, and English. Speaking with an expansive flourish, Woo waves his hands as words trip off his tongue in a rapid patter. To some, his appointment as head of distribution may have seemed an odd choice, since he has little experience with program sales, yet he explains that his contacts with creative talent throughout the region uniquely qualify him to broker co-production agreements, which are a key aspect of MediaCorp's overseas strategy. "I worked with a lot of different TV talent, and we are global people," he explains, "so after twenty years, if you're still in this line, you are part of a network. Michael Mak, Star TV controller, we are good friends, and we were colleagues back in Hong Kong; Li Hui-wan, film director; Yang Pei-pei, producer; Pan Wen-jie, of China Star; and so on. It's easy for us to just pick up the phone and say, 'Hey you guys, I need a producer, I want to do this show.' We will quarrel and bargain, but we are good friends, and if we can make a deal, then great, but if not, we still go for a drink or whatever, because we were buddies before. I worked at ATV and TVB. This is an advantage. Sales people don't have that kind of friendship. The people in this network can talk about everything openly."

Like producers in Taiwan, Woo finds it easiest to build transnational co-productions for martial arts and palace dramas. "With historical dramas," he grins, "we all come from the same root: Sung dynasty, Ming dynasty, swordfighting, fly here, fly there, everybody's happy. Okay?" He lets out a mischievous laugh and then notes that, by comparison, layers of cultural difference make it difficult to produce contemporary series that resonate with Chinese audiences in several markets. For example, in Hong Kong, "you have a lot of criminal cases," he explains. "You have M-16 or AK-47 or whatever in the street—*ga-ga-ga-ga-ga-gah*—just like a movie," he says, spraying the air with imaginary machine gun fire, "but it's the real thing. Here you can't see that. Triad societies in Hong Kong, Taiwan—although we don't say it, we know [they are a] common phenomenon. Here, we can't say we don't have them, but it's minimal. Corruption. Here, we don't say we don't have it, but it's minimal. I know this for a fact." Consequently, Singaporean viewers don't tend to show the same enthusiasm as audiences in Hong Kong and Taiwan show for triad dramas. Indeed, local film exhibitors make a similar observation, noting that Singaporean audiences tend to like romances and comedies, but even within these genres, tastes diverge, says Woo, and again it has to do with the social experience of the audiences. Woo points to the successful Beijing author Wang Shuo, whose many novels have been adapted by TV producers in the PRC. With the roiling changes of mainland society as his backdrop, Wang is renowned for weaving social commentary into his romances. "As an industry worker,

I appreciate his stories," remarks Woo, "but the common audience [in Singapore], they don't appreciate it, because they don't come from that culture. They don't understand that the change from a closed economic system to an open market economy can cause a change of mindset that can create conflicts in a love story, and maybe the Taiwanese don't understand this either. It's a type of contemporary culture, but you have to be part of it. It doesn't matter if you speak Chinese and you are Chinese, you still might not understand it."

Interestingly, audiences in Singapore more readily accept such narrative tropes if the characters are from a non-Chinese culture. "We like James Bond; we like Indiana Jones; we like Titanic," declares Woo. Japanese screen stories are similarly attractive, in part because of glossy production values and in part because Japanese society is seen as both foreign and a trendsetter for Asia. "We see computer war, high-tech things—and then, wah! What a good-looking Japanese actor! You see a lot of very handsome guys and good-looking ladies. So this is their selling point." Yet paradoxically, Japanese dramas are also popular because they often pit innovation against tradition and desire against duty. "You know Japanese, they yell all the time. Very dramatic. And then they go and they bow, and when they eat they just kneel down; it's just—you can feel that it's part of their tradition; you can see the art inside it. You can see the artistic light. Among Chinese we all sit at a big round table, that's family, but Japanese families kneel down on the floor around a small table, and especially those paper doors . . . ," his voice trails off pensively. "When you see a program like that you say, *that* is their culture."

Foreign productions are therefore acceptable if they are culturally distant, and Chinese productions can win over audiences if they are historically distant. Contemporary drama is more complicated, requiring a deft mix of local relevance and overseas allure. With such productions, Michael Woo says it's his job to cook up a dish that seems local with just a dash of cosmopolitan flavor. "For example," he explains, "if I go to India, I add some curry; if I go to Hong Kong, I use some of their seafood or whatever. So that means, if I coproduce with Hong Kong, I use some of their artists or some of their directors to make it more Hong Kong-like. And I will deliver something Singaporean, so we can share the program in both markets." The ideal program appears as a local product to viewers in both markets, and at the same time it brings new talent, new techniques, and new story lines to MediaCorp's series. Rather than producing TV programs for the local market and then trying to sell them overseas, coproductions attempt to secure foreign exhibition from the very earliest planning stage.

Moreover, the economic benefits of such a strategy are easily grasped from the following hypothetical example: MediaCorp dramas cost approximately $100,000 per episode, and they bring in roughly $70,000 in local advertising. Previously, the company sought to reduce this production deficit by marketing the programs overseas, but when sales agents made their pitch, there was no guarantee that a foreign buyer would find the series of interest or have an appropriate place for it in the station's schedule. Even if the programmer were interested, a sale would be made only after substantial negotiation over the price per episode. If, say, the program could be sold to a Hong Kong station for $5,000 per hour, that would still leave a production deficit of $25,000, and so one would continue to search for other stations that might be interested in the series. On the other hand, a coproduction deal with a Hong Kong station usually involves an equal division of production costs, which would lower MediaCorp's share to $50,000 per episode while keeping local ad revenues constant at $70,000. Instead of realizing a net deficit, it then would realize a net profit of $20,000 per episode. Moreover, the coproduction agreement would guarantee that the series would make it to air in Hong Kong, in contrast to the previously described practice of simply hoping to generate revenues through syndication sales. And if, because costs were now lower, MediaCorp were to decide to inject more resources into the project (say, $60,000 per partner per episode), it could still turn a profit, and the final product would be of higher quality and an even more likely candidate for syndication to other markets.

Coproductions also generate other benefits, such as talent exchanges that enhance the expertise of one's staff and increase the exposure of one's stars in other markets. "Our programs formerly carried our artists overseas," says Franklin Wong. "Now it is the reverse track, where our well-known artists can carry our programs. Fan Wong [no relation], in particular, is very popular [both in Hong Kong and Taiwan]. We are concentrating on improving our artists and marketing them, because right now in Hong Kong, for example, some of the superstars are too expensive and their schedules are so tight, very busy." As MediaCorp talent gains greater exposure through coproductions, it further enhances the value of other programs in the MediaCorp catalog, since programs are often marketed on the basis of star appeal.

In all, the emphasis on coproductions represents a new strategy: ambitious but also cost-conscious, unlike earlier attempts to expand overseas. During the 1990s, when government policy makers first signaled that broadcasters were headed toward privatization, Singaporean TV executives borrowed a leaf from Star TV and TVB in trying to set up their own satellite services in hopes of repurposing local productions for overseas markets. Attempts at launching an entertainment channel for Taiwan and a Southeast Asian news channel both failed, in large part because of monthly costs associated with satellite technology and the ongoing expense of deploying sales staff to other markets. Coproductions have the merit of containing costs while also providing guaranteed access to another market. They furthermore tend to enhance the quality of productions and help to develop the library of programs that can be marketed overseas. Such series also launch creative talent into broader circulation, which makes them not only more productive but also, paradoxically, more satisfied with their careers in Singapore.

This, in part, was the motivation behind MediaCorp's decision to launch a film studio to complement its TV production operations. Daniel Yun, head of Raintree Pictures, explains that "once a TV series succeeded, people wanted to move on." In the past, that meant leaving the Lion City for other locations, which in turn contributed to the shortage of creative people, especially writers, directors, and actors. "When I talk to people in Hong Kong movies and say, Where did you start? They say, 'Oh, my first ten years was with TVB. My first whatever years . . .' Stephen Chow, Chow Yun-fat, Andy Lau, all these big names started at TVB and then they moved on, but many of them also return to television, which helps to build the appeal of their series. We would like to show creative people here that you can find other opportunities to grow your career here in Singapore, that you can do television *and* film *and* music. You can do it locally, and you can do it in other parts of Asia, too."

Founded in 1998, Raintree is Singapore's only film studio but certainly not its first, since both Shaw Brothers and Cathay ran profitable studios there for almost twenty years. After the demise of Shaw and Cathay as local producers, Hollywood and Hong Kong films have dominated Singaporean theater screens, and over the years, the core of experienced talent has dwindled, until now, as one local filmmaker remarked, "you can count them on the fingers of one hand." Another problem has been government regulations on thematic content and restrictions on language use, privileging English and Mandarin Chinese. Yet another challenge is the discouraging economics of the market. Widespread media piracy in Malaysia as well as a complex set of political sensitivities make it difficult to reestablish the peninsular market that prevailed during the glory days of Shaw and Cathay.

Yet in 1998 it seemed that the conventional wisdom was subverted when television star Jack Neo released a breakaway comedy feature film about a group of down-and-out heartlanders who were suffering from the fallout of the Asian economic crisis. *Money No Enough* brought in a stunning $9.3 million at local theaters, setting a box office record and smothering its Hollywood competition. In part, the film traded on its topicality, since audiences could identify with the misfortunes of the leading characters, but just as important it flagrantly transgressed government censorship restrictions, casually mixing Hokkien with Mandarin and English, just as Singaporeans do in their daily lives. "After two decades of suppression of the Hokkien language, suddenly this film made it seem as if the dam had burst," declares film critic Kelvin Tong, of the *Straits Times*. "Besides the typical [teenage] cinemagoers, you suddenly saw three generations going to the theater together." Yet the film's remarkable success only served to emphasize the problems confronting local filmmakers. For even with $10 million in box-office revenue, the producer's share was only 25 percent, with the rest going to the distributor and exhibitor. After production costs of $1.3 million and profit shares to the stars, that left the producer only $650,000 in profit for a blockbuster movie. Because of the enormous risks involved in film production, such a profit could easily vanish with the producer's next movie venture. In other words, audiences may have a hunger for local films, but the economics of the market, even in a prosperous city-state such as Singapore, simply do not justify the risks of production.

Nevertheless, in the wake of Neo's success, others tried to cash in on audience enthusiasm for local films, many of them crude take-offs that proved to be box office disasters. Even more serious efforts suffered by comparison, and as a result, the flood of new venture capital evaporated almost as quickly as it had appeared. Yet despite such grim economics, filmmaking was suddenly on the agenda again in Singapore around the turn of the century. Kelvin Tong scripted one of the more interesting films of this period, titled *Eating Air*. Although it was considered a flop at the local box office, taking in only $320,000, the film performed well at overseas film festivals, including festivals in Hong Kong, Taipei, and Manila. Tong contends the movie suffered from poor distribution and that he had trouble getting it into local theaters frequented by his target audience: teenage heartlanders, many of whom hang out on Orchard Road, a spacious, tree-lined boulevard north of the downtown. Orchard Road is the country's premier leisure destination, where families, tourists, and local teens congregate in a shopping and entertainment district that bears the marks of scrupulous government planning. Clean, orderly, and well-manicured, Orchard Road is home to fashionable department stores and trendy shopping complexes, as well as sidewalk cafés, theaters, and coffee shops. Gaggles of teens stream along the boulevard, in and out of stores and arcades, buying little but lingering throughout the afternoon and evening. Orchard Road is also one of the city's feature attractions, obscuring the often bleak uniformity of the public housing estates, where most teenage heartlanders actually live.

The film's title, *Eating Air*, refers to late-night motorcycle rides around the island, which provide the lead characters with a sense of release from their otherwise tedious lives. According to Tong, these lower-middle-class kids are what policy makers glibly refer to as the country's most important future resource, since their labor will serve as the backbone of Singapore's service economy. The film explores the rhythms of their daily lives and the complex identity issues that register in their language. "People ask what language the film is in, and I say, 'Orchard City Leisure Language,'" explains Tong. "When I was writing the script, I would hang out there just so I could eavesdrop on the kids. When you listen to the way they speak, you hear them move from English to Mandarin, with a smattering of Malay or [Chinese] dialect when it suits their purpose. It's a very fast, efficient style of communication, but not grammatically correct. They're comfortable with English and Mandarin, but they are also very creative with the language, which some say has created problems in communicating with foreigners." In fact, *proper* English has become a subject of serious concern among government policy makers, who contend that a high level of English competence is one of the core advantages that Singapore enjoys over other Asian economies. Since the island lacks natural resources or a large population, it is dependent on the reputation of its workforce as reliable, educated, and fluent in the lingua franca of global commerce. In the late 1990s, bureaucrats therefore launched the Let's Speak English Correctly campaign, which included public service announcements, classroom activities, and efforts to clean up the language of popular TV characters. In part, *Eating Air* subtly interrogates the value of language orthodoxies imposed from above and obliquely questions the relevance of a whole host of orthodoxies that structure the lives of young Singaporeans. Order and prosperity have brought dramatic material benefits within the span of only a couple of generations. The challenge now confronting teenagers is whether orderliness and prosperity can foster creativity and spiritual well-being. Although these issues confront many societies, the film's resolutely local focus was unlikely to prove profitable in the regional film market, and it was therefore of little interest to MediaCorp's Raintree Pictures. For if *Money No Enough* demonstrated the box office potential of local movies, films like *Eating Air* made the limitations only too apparent.

Since Raintree was founded with an eye toward profitability, it tends to focus on films with transnational appeal and is cautious about investments, because the seed money it received from MediaCorp could easily be squandered by one or two failures at the box office. Absent a large domestic market and lacking experience in transnational distribution, Daniel Yun has tried to leverage his resources through a series of strategic partnerships. Luckily for him, Raintree was launched in the midst of a downturn in the Hong Kong film industry during the late 1990s. At a time when it was suddenly difficult for filmmakers to find financial backing, Raintree appeared on the south horizon looking for entrée to a business that others were fleeing. "It opened doors and made it possible for us to talk to key people in the industry," recalls Yun. "In 1992, no one would have had time for us, but in 1998, things were different." A whirlwind series of meetings with Hong Kong movie executives was serious enough to generate speculation that Raintree was preparing to make a purchase offer for Golden Harvest, but Yun dismisses that speculation, saying he was interested in developing a diverse collection of coproduction deals that would provide Raintree needed expertise and visibility. Although Golden Harvest was at the time still a preeminent force in the movie-making business, Yun found Media Asia to be more compatible with his vision. "I was not very interested in Golden Harvest, but I was very keen to work with an up-and-coming company like Media Asia, then doing *Gen-X Cops* and all that. I was also very interested to work with Peter Chan and Teddy Chen. When they formed Applause Pictures, it was like, this is the group of people who don't have a fixed mindset about what Hong Kong movies should be."

Teaming with Media Asia for its first major coproduction, Raintree released *2000 AD*, a computer-terrorism thriller, helmed by Gordon Chan, a leading Hong Kong director, and headlined by two prominent Hong Kong stars, but also featuring a number of Singaporean actors in leading roles. The film's high-tech theme and special effects gloss come across as visually appealing, indeed competitive, with most Hollywood films, but the narrative gets a bit muddled at points, and the character played by Francis Ng, the film's strongest actor, dies tragically in a hail of bullets about one-third of the way into the story. Nevertheless *2000 AD* should have proven attractive to young audiences if it had premiered at the right time. Unfortunately, production delays pushed the release date back past the midwinter school holidays into the Chinese New Year period, when demand is high for movies with comic and family appeal rather than thrillers aimed at young moviegoers. Although the film stumbled at the box office, Media Asia nevertheless benefited from a coproduction partnership that contributed sig-

Hong Kong heartthrobs Aaron Kwok *(left)* and Daniel Wu *(right)* star with Phyllis Quek in *2000 AD,* a high-tech thriller coproduced by Raintree Pictures and Media Asia. Courtesy Media Asia.

nificant financing, a fresh pool of acting talent, and a feature film that fits logically with the studio's syndication catalog. For Raintree it was a learning experience that put the company's talent at the center of regional production and quickly elevated the profile of the studio. Succeeding projects with Media Asia—*The Eye; Turn Left, Turn Right;* and *Infernal Affairs II*—scored box office successes, and coproductions with several other studios further solidified the Raintree's reputation.

Yun believes that Raintree's distinctive strength is that, even though it lacks long-term experience in the feature film business, the company has access to MediaCorp Studios, which are the best equipped studios in Southeast Asia, having turned out thousands of hours of television programs. The executives of MediaCorp and its Raintree division, which have an extensive track record in producing TV dramas and comedies in a variety of languages, including English, believe their companies are uniquely positioned to take advantage of the increasing velocity of media and talent flows in Southeast Asia. As film critic Kelvin Tong puts it, the success of MediaCorp and SPH will crucially rely on their abilities to tap talent throughout the region and weave them into productions with broad appeal. "If you're not too xenophobic about where you get the talent," he says, "the potential is tremendous, but you have to move fast because the competition is growing."

Between the 1970s and 1990s, rigorous government planning helped to launch the "miracle" economy of Singapore when the island society first carved out a competitive niche in world markets with its low-wage factory workforce and then sustained its advantages by adapting over time through systematic investments in education, job training, and technology. Most recently the transition to a high-tech service society has encouraged Singaporean leaders to self-consciously reposition their city as an important node on the global communications grid, investing heavily in transoceanic cable and satellite technology. This further encouraged planners to spur institutional reform in the media sector, initiating the rollout of a sophisticated broadband cable service and forcing television and publishing monopolies to diminish their reliance on government patronage and diversify their product lines with an eye toward regional and even global distribution.

No longer a monopolist, MediaCorp undertook a series of initiatives aimed at improving the quality of its programming so as to confront new challenges in the local advertising market and to make its dramas attractive to audiences overseas. At first it sought to distribute its creative output via syndication and through its new regional satellite network, but neither strategy proved financially viable, so it shifted focus to coproductions, hoping to find partners who might share financial and creative resources, including opportunities for mutual learning effects. The strategy also aimed to ensure that such programs would at the very least be distributed in the production partner's market, a significant improvement over the vagaries of international distribution.

Nevertheless, coproductions presented distinctive challenges of their own because of shades of variation in audience preferences regarding television programs marked by foreign cultural influences, a problem that has commonly affected all types of transnational media circulation. Scholars and industry practitioners have commonly noted that foreign programs can improve their prospects in particular markets to the extent that they seem culturally similar in the eyes of viewers. That is, Peruvian audiences are likely to prefer a Mexican telenovela as opposed to a Hollywood drama because of linguistic and cultural similarities between the two Latin American countries.[4] Yet, as we've observed both in Singapore and in Taiwan, cultural proximity can under certain conditions have the opposite effect, inviting critical scrutiny from viewers. That is, a contemporary Singaporean TV series may spark discomfort among, for example, Taiwanese viewers, who are likely to perceive subtle linguistic and cultural differences as alienating. In contrast, Chinese historical dramas set in the distant past (temporal distance) or programs imported from distinctively alien cultures, such as Japan or Korea (spaciocultural distance), often tend to be more easily accepted, in many cases because of their abstract or exotic textual qualities. For their part, successful Chinese coproductions seem to require a deft mixing of local talent and scenery with exotic elements provided by partners or abstract tableaux on which to fashion more culturally neutral narratives. Although such mixtures offer cost efficiencies and assured distribution, they are unlikely to satisfy audience interests in emphatically local and topical concerns.

MediaCorp therefore faces a complicated challenge. On the one hand it must coproduce programming with glossy production values that will be abstract enough to travel into overseas markets and familiar enough to be popular in the local market. On the other hand it has to sustain its commitment to emphatically local shows so as not to surrender its Singaporean identity to emerging competitors in the island market. What had once been a resolutely national monopoly has transformed its operations in response to changes in the global political economy. Forces of sociocultural variation that had at one time dominated the city's media now have given way to an increasingly transnational market logic that forces companies not only to refigure their spheres of distribution but also to reconsider the city's potential to sustain itself as a site of creative endeavor that might prove attractive to talent from the region as well as from the city itself. Yet, even though capitalist pressures are reconstituting the geography of Singaporean media, forcing the local to go global, a counterexample, which we will observe in the next chapter, shows how global media have been forced to localize.

9 Reterritorializing Star TV in the PRC

Dramatic changes in Chinese media began as early as the mid-1980s with liberalization and reregulation in Hong Kong, Taiwan, and Singapore, as well as the People's Republic of China. In the PRC the introduction and diffusion of television technology proceeded at a frenetic pace. In 1980, only a tiny percentage of homes owned TV receivers, but by mid-decade a majority of urban households had purchased their own sets. This enthusiastic embrace of the new medium was commonly linked to Deng Xiao-ping's "Four Modernizations," and therefore many observers anticipated that it was only a matter of time before PRC media, like many other industries, would commercialize their operations.[1] As political and economic pressures combined with a technological shift toward satellite, cable, and VCR, they fueled the rising aspirations of citizens, who now had access to more information and imagery than would have seemed imaginable only a few years before. If Richard Li's claims about the promise of Star TV seemed inflated and pretentious, they nevertheless were inspired by epochal changes then taking place on the ground. The promise of Asian television therefore appeared boundless, but as mentioned earlier, Richard Li became anxious about the fortunes of Star as early as 1993, worried that global media conglomerates with greater expertise and programming resources might expand their operations in Asia and thereby diminish the value of Star, despite its first-mover advantage. When the Li family began to probe for partners or buyers, Rupert Murdoch emerged as one of the most likely candidates, given his expressed ambition to build a global media empire and his extensive experience with satellite television in Europe. Yet News Corporation was also in talks at the time with TVB, certainly the most prominent Chinese-language media enterprise in the region. Interestingly, Pearson was talking with TVB, too, as were Sony, Disney, Turner, and Time-Warner. The maneuvering by global conglomerates seemed to be escalating daily, and speculation proliferated about which parts of the mainland China market would open first and which commercial television service would be in the best position to take advantage of this emerging opportunity.

TVB appeared to hold a pivotal position, but as negotiations with News Corporation unfolded, it became clear that government ownership regulations would factor into any merger or acquisition plan. That is, a foreign investor could take up to a 15 percent interest in a Hong Kong station, but a conglomerate such as News Corporation or Pearson could not take a controlling interest without securing a waiver from the territory's Executive Council. This proved to be a significant obstacle for News Corporation, since Murdoch was widely perceived, both in Hong Kong and London, as a marauding investor bent on building a global empire at the expense of local media enterprises. Londoners, who were especially sensitive to this issue, irreverently referred to Murdoch as the Dirty Digger, an Australian interloper who had taken over major newspapers, such as the *Sun* and the *Times*, turning the former into an overheated tabloid and the latter into a middlebrow shell of its former self. To critics of the increasing conglomeration and globalization of media, Murdoch was the most nefarious example of the new media barons that Ben Bagdikian dubbed the Lords of the Global Village.[2] Critics in Hong Kong were no less concerned, for allowing Murdoch to take control of the crown colony's only profitable TV station seemed antithetical to regulations aimed at sustaining local voices on the airwaves. Making matters even more complicated, Beijing officials expressed misgivings about Murdoch, and with the 1997 handover looming, their opinions carried weight with many Hong Kong officials. If the colony's Executive Council were to waive the residency stipulation, not only would it be an affront to the Beijing leadership, but it also would make it difficult for local regulators to resist future takeover attempts mounted by mainland investors.

With these complications rising to the fore, Murdoch abruptly terminated his courtship of TVB in June 1993, much to the relief of the Li family. From the Lis' perspective, a News Corporation–TVB alliance would have brought together the world's most prominent satellite TV firm with the most formidable force in Chinese commercial television, and such an alliance would surely threaten Star TV's tenuous status as the leader of Asian satellite TV. Furthermore, the collapse of Murdoch's negotiations with TVB meant that he would likely turn his attention to other prospective acquisition targets, and the Lis made it known that they were ready to talk.

Negotiations began with News Corporation offering $425 million for a substantial stake in the Asian satcaster, but the Lis demurred, saying the offer simply wasn't rich enough. Executives from the two companies haggled for weeks, until finally Richard Li accepted an invitation to negotiate face-to-face with Rupert Murdoch aboard his yacht, moored off the island of Corsica in the Mediterranean. Emerging from the six-hour meeting, Murdoch announced that News Corporation would pay $525 million for a 63.6 percent stake in Star TV, leaving the remaining portion of the company and the ownership of AsiaSat in the hands of Hutchison Whampoa. The deal was a bonanza for the Li family, providing a sizable cash return on their investment and relieving them of the burden of running a multichannel television service. For their part, News Corporation executives crowed that the sale price was a bargain, and they continued to tout the merits of Star two years later, when they bought the rest of the company for an additional $345 million, bringing the total purchase price to $870 million. Murdoch claimed that the future promise of commercial TV in Asia made Star worth more than three times what News Corporation had paid. Others, however, weren't so sure.

Although Star remained Asia's leading satellite telecaster, it still suffered from all the problems that had beset the Lis: it needed better market research, more advertising, and more subscription revenue. And even though News Corporation made its vast inventory of English-language content available to Star programmers, Chinese and Indian resources were still in short supply. Moreover, Murdoch soon made matters considerably more difficult when, in a London speech only a month after the 1993 acquisition of Star, he enthused that satellite television was breaking down borders and proving to be "an unambiguous threat to totalitarian regimes everywhere."[3] Without specifically mentioning China, he continued, "Satellite broadcasting makes it possible for information-hungry residents of many closed societies to by-pass state-controlled television channels." Murdoch's hyperbole, which interestingly was telecast around the world by satellite, immediately raised eyebrows in Beijing, where officials perceived it as a direct challenge to party supremacy.

In a swift and calculated response, Chinese leaders banned private ownership of satellite dishes, prohibited newspaper advertising for foreign satellite services, and selectively showcased the prosecution of violators. Even more creatively, the government began to promote cable TV, making services available at such low cost that satellite dishes no longer seemed worth the bother. Paradoxically, Chinese leaders chose to *proliferate* access to government cable systems in order to *limit* signal flow, reasoning that cable would be easier to regulate than satellite signals from afar.[4] Taken together, these steps initially proved so successful that News Corporation managers realized they had a crisis on their hands, and it would take years of concerted, almost obsequious, effort for the company to regain even limited standing with the Beijing regime. This contretemps furthermore emphasized—Murdoch's remarks notwithstanding—that infrastructure on the ground was just as important to Star TV as high-speed conduits in the sky. That is, government relations and marketing personnel inside the PRC would prove crucial to Star's attempts to access government cable systems and promotional opportunities in local print media. The seemingly inexorable logic of distributing high-quality Hollywood programming via satellite throughout the PRC proved to be quite vulnerable to forces of sociocultural variation marshaled by the Chinese state.

Murdoch's management team discovered it had other problems as well. Initially, Star was developed as an English-language, pan-Asian platform aimed at upscale households across the continent, but it soon became clear that the company would have to multiply the number of channels and target them more specifically along linguistic, cultural, and national lines. For it became evident to Star executives that a transnational elite audience was not large enough to sustain the costs of operation, let alone to turn a profit. Moreover, the dispersal of elite viewers across the vast expanse of Asia proved to be a programming and marketing nightmare. Time zone differences alone made a single program service untenable, and, as it turned out, less than a third of Star's advertising clients were interested in synchronous continental exposure. Instead, most clients preferred to buy ads that would promote particular products in specific media markets. In order to serve these customers, Star needed to produce and acquire programming crafted to the tastes of such audiences. This realization caused a major shift in company strategy, according to John O'Loan, the chief of network operations who oversaw Star's transition to News Corporation control. "After we bought Star we realized that what [the Li family was] doing was wrong. It would be nice if you could get some economies of scale. It would be nice if you could squeeze another 1 percent out here and there. And like any other business, you'll look for places where you can get those economies, but not if they're going to put you out of business by losing touch with your audience." Star's pan-Asian strategy would have to be recalibrated in light of local preferences.

Program acquisition and scheduling therefore proved to be much more complicated than anticipated. Although the Fox film and television libraries are among the most extensive in the world, Star soon found that it needed access to programs that would generate buzz among its diverse audiences.

In some cases that meant access to a hit Hollywood show that had gone into global syndication, and in other cases it meant access to locally produced programs. Yet from the outset, TVB refused to sell to Star, because the two companies competed in Taiwan, China, and India. Likewise, Taiwanese broadcasters were reluctant to supply programming to Star, because they too were beginning to think transnationally. Only ATV, the hapless competitor of TVB, agreed to do business with Star on a regular basis.

Global media firms were only slightly more cooperative. Warner Bros., Sony, and Paramount each sold Star some programs, but they were reluctant to feed too much content to the News Corporation subsidiary, because each was laying plans for its own Asian satellite services. Moreover, companies such as Warner Bros. Television worried that satellite transmission would undermine the value of programs they were selling to local broadcasters. As O'Loan explains, "If a program fetched $1,000 an hour in six markets across Asia, why put it on Star, which cuts across those markets?" If the syndicator sold the program to Star for $3,000, it would jeopardize the $6,000 the syndicator might make by selling the show in six separate markets. Star tried to argue that satellite audiences and broadcast audiences were distinct, but this failed to console local broadcasters, who countered that whenever they telecast American dramas, they too were targeting the very same niche audience as Star. Consequently, Star spent much of the 1990s patching together its programming schedule with content from Fox, BBC, ATV, and to some extent Sony. One of the most common criticisms of Star during this period was the unevenness of its telecasting schedule. Although its Western programming proved somewhat attractive, Star struggled to acquire compelling content in local languages and to deliver services that would meet the needs of non-English-speaking viewers.

At first Star's new management thought it could cope with these challenges by splitting the service in two, creating a northern and a southern beam, which would be pan-Chinese and pan-Indian, respectively. Yet before long management discovered that these markets were further complicated by prevailing taste hierarchies *within* them. For example, a viewer in Fujian Province, directly across the strait from Taiwan, is likely to be interested in Taiwanese television shows (especially those broadcast in the southern Min dialect), but the reverse is highly unlikely: Taiwanese viewers are not apt to be interested in programs from Fujian, since most viewers in Taiwan already have access to more than eighty channels that compete ferociously for their attention. Moreover, a Hong Kong viewer is unlikely to be interested in programs from either Fujian or Taiwan because of linguistic, social, and cultural differences, although a (Cantonese-speaking) viewer in nearby

Guangzhou might be interested in the same sorts of Mandarin programming that interest viewers in Fujian Province or even Shanghai.

Cultural biases proved to be just as important. For example, residents of both Guangzhou and Hong Kong speak Cantonese, and Hong Kong TV programs are quite popular in Guangzhou, but not the reverse. The reason for this particular pattern of cultural flow is best expressed in temporal terms: Guangzhou looks to Hong Kong as its future, while Hong Kong looks inland toward its past. As Koichi Iwabuchi has observed, such valences are at work throughout Asia, and they significantly influence patterns of cultural exchange.[5] Given these complexities, Star decided that the only way to move forward with its Chinese TV services was to develop two distinctive Mandarin-language platforms, one for Taiwan and one for the eastern region of mainland China, while largely ignoring such lucrative but competitive markets as Hong Kong, Singapore, and Malaysia.

By 1995, management had all but abandoned ambitions for a pan-Chinese, let alone a pan-Asian, service, since both approaches simply lacked enough advertiser support. John O'Loan explains that transnational advertising works best for companies that are trying to build a brand identity with consumers who are unfamiliar with their product. "The people who are the biggest spenders on pan-European advertising are the Japanese, who are furthest from the market, followed by the Yanks," observes O'Loan. Establishing a brand identity is important to these companies, either because they are just beginning to develop a new distribution infrastructure or because they have a product (often a luxury product) that does not rely on mass distribution systems. Advertisers in such cases aren't especially concerned about the competitive dynamics of particular local or national markets, since they see themselves as distinctive or even exotic brands. Likewise in Asia, says O'Loan, "we sell a lot of pan-Asian advertising, but not to Asians. We sell it to the Americans, and we sell it to the Europeans—Volvo, for example—but we couldn't survive on that type of advertising. The money that keeps television going is soap, toothpaste, and consumer products, which is national advertising that's tied to a distribution network on the ground."

Yet within the borders of the People's Republic of China, Star found that even national advertising is problematic, because, like many other parts of Asia, distribution networks are rarely national in scope. Infrastructural constraints, personnel limitations, banking idiosyncrasies, and complex social networks all militate against national product distribution. "If you have a toothpaste factory," observes O'Loan, "you've got to have a way to get your product around the country. In China, right now, there's no way to do it. The obstacles are severe, because the road and rail infrastructure can't handle

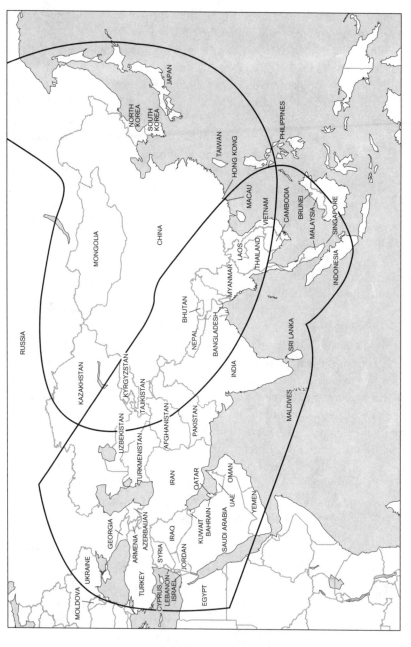

Star TV shed its pan-Asian aspirations soon after News Corporation took control, dividing its services into a northern and a southern beam, aimed, respectively, at Chinese and Indian audiences. The area of overlap had access to both services.

this kind of thing. Then if you open up different factories in different parts of the country, you have to be careful about quality control, staffing, and you also have the problem of getting supplies to the factories. China is hardly a unified market. Now consider the problem of calling Asia a unified market."

Such uncertainties and reversals beleaguer global media conglomerates that aspire to expand their operations into the growing markets of Asia. Between 1993 and 1995, Rupert Murdoch invested close to a billion dollars in a venture that was losing money at the rate of over a million dollars a week.[6] Murdoch soon learned that, besides the problems he encountered with Chinese officials, the idyllic image of three billion Asian consumers was attractive to only a limited number of global advertisers and financiers, many of whom had only vague plans for future involvement in the region. Far more important were the advertisers with existing products and distribution systems in the numerous, diverse, and often underdeveloped markets of the region. As one senior Chinese media executive puts it, "Asia is a hell of a big place, and a lot of people come from outside, and they make one big mistake: They assume that it's a melting pot like the United States or even a confederation like Europe. In fact, it's a collection of tiny places, and you have to keep your focus; otherwise you will be lost." For Star to reach audiences in such diverse locales, it had to multiply its channels and narrow the focus of each service. So News Corporation managers found that, instead of having a pan-Asian satellite platform beaming Western programming in from the outside, they were saddled with a growing number of channels and markets, each with distinctive features and each requiring the painstaking cultivation of personal relationships with local businesspeople and government officials.

By 1995, Star's Indian and Taiwanese services were off to a capable start, but the PRC channels were in deep trouble. They had effectively been frozen out of the market by Chinese government regulators, who made it clear that they would not allow Star to bypass state-controlled television channels. Taking the cue, Murdoch initiated discussions with a number of potential joint-venture partners, among them, Liu Changle, a former officer in the People's Liberation Army and, during the 1980s, a military affairs reporter with Central Radio, one of the most powerful media services in pre-TV China. Liu seemed an especially good prospect, because he had expansive contacts and reputed managerial expertise. Moreover, many of his top staff members were also from the PRC, and consequently they understood what audiences had been seeing on television and what they had been missing. Moreover, Liu's group had participated in the development of mainland broadcasting institutions, and its members had a deft sense of the political and entrepreneurial nuances of the system.

Yet, perhaps most important to Murdoch was Liu's backing by an influential political faction within the ruling government. Speculation on this issue abounds, but two theories are often repeated and seem most feasible. According to several sources, the first theory suggests that a group aligned with President Jiang Zemin supported Phoenix TV in preparation for the 1997 transfer of sovereignty in Hong Kong. This event was to be one of Jiang's enduring legacies, and his supporters were anxious to ensure that it enhanced his status both in Asia and around the globe. Consequently, this group sought to create a commercial satellite service outside the state broadcasting system that would provide favorable coverage of the 1997 event. One media executive explains, "They needed a service that looked independent, but one they could trust." And since Liu Changle had been "nurtured" for many years during his service in the PLA and at Central Radio, he looked especially attractive to the Chinese leadership.

A second theory suggests that Phoenix was envisioned with a more expansive set of objectives. According to a media consultant with extensive contacts throughout Asia, "Liu probably went to some key figures in the State Council and pitched the idea for Phoenix and probably—as with most important decisions in China these days—some pockets were lined. It's not clear exactly who is behind Liu at this point. What is clear is that Liu was given the remit to feel out what is acceptable on TV. This serves the interests of the reformers inside the government and of the people at CCTV [the government's national TV network], but it's safe. It's arm's length. There's plausible deniability if an ideological backlash should emerge."

In either case, all agree that Liu has served the interests of powerful factions inside the Chinese government, and certainly Phoenix exhibits the very same traits as other Chinese enterprises that mix capitalism with party politics (enterprises known as "red chips"). Yet Liu protests that Phoenix is not simply a product of political favoritism, and indeed, from the very beginning, Murdoch was reportedly impressed by Liu's programming and marketing proposals, convinced that he understood the intricacies of both Chinese politics and audience preferences.

In 1996, Murdoch and Liu launched Phoenix as a forty-five and fifty-five joint venture that would complement the Star platform. While Star would continue to beam English-language sports and entertainment channels to the mainland, Phoenix would have exclusive rights to develop Mandarin-language movie and general entertainment channels, with the latter emphasizing news and information programming. Just as important, the

Phoenix staff would take on the time-consuming task of building a marketing organization inside the PRC and cultivating relations with advertisers and government officials.

In charge of this effort was Howard Ho, the general manager of distribution and marketing. When I visited him at Phoenix TV, Ho invited me to be seated in his office near a promotional poster for *GTO*, a Japanese TV drama series. *GTO* is about the adventures of an unconventional young teacher who suffers from bad manners and a bad college education but who nevertheless wins the hearts of his students, because his brash, honest, and ultimately righteous behavior provides a stark contrast to the forces of institutional sloth and indifference at their high school. Known as Great Teacher Onizuka, or GTO, the hip young educator is familiar to television audiences in many parts of East Asia and was introduced to China on the Phoenix satellite signal. A slickly produced series, *GTO* offers both cosmopolitan gloss and allegorical episodes about the shortcomings of bureaucracy, a topic that no doubt appeals to many Chinese viewers who might draw connections to their own experiences in the PRC.

The *GTO* poster, featuring a glamour portrait of its star, Takashi Sorimachi, is mounted on the wall in Ho's office right beside a large map of the People's Republic of China featuring conspicuously unglamorous thumbnail portraits of provincial officials accompanied by brief biographical data. Published by one of Hong Kong's biggest trading companies, the map is perhaps among the most important documents in the office, for one of the marketing department's prime responsibilities is to convince provincial officials throughout China to allow cable operators within their jurisdiction to carry the Phoenix channels. Such approvals take place beneath the radar of national politics, since the government in Beijing has granted Phoenix only limited rights to transmit to upscale hotels and expatriate housing complexes. Yet, in fact, thousands of cable operators around the country, with guidance from provincial and municipal officials, exercise local discretion in selecting the cable services they offer in their locality.[7] As a result, an ironic pattern of uneven exposure has emerged in Chinese television: The closer one lives to Beijing, the more cautious the local cable operator. As one moves away from the capital, however, the variety of channels expands significantly, often providing provincial viewers with broader access to cosmopolitan TV fare than those living in the capital city. It's up to Howard Ho and his marketing staff to convince local officials that programs like *GTO* are distinctive, edgy, and attractive but at the same time are unlikely to create a stir that might draw the attention of leaders in Beijing.

An effervescent personality, Ho seems amply suited to the task, alternately exhibiting a flair for corporate promotion and a gift for philosophical reflection on subjects ranging from Chinese culture to corporate strategy. For example, Ho points out that the Phoenix name and company logo actually have great significance. "To Westerners," he says, "Phoenix suggests a rare bird that has been reborn. In Chinese, however, the word *fenghuang* is a compound of two characters, one meaning male bird and the other female bird. But the interesting thing," observes Ho, "is that you don't know which is the male and which is the female. Is *feng* a male or a female? No one knows." Thus, the company logo features two lavishly plumed birds, swirling head-to-tail around a central point. "And if you look at the logo more carefully, you see that it also looks like the iris of a camera. And it looks as if it is rotating and it will never stop. And it also looks like a *feng-shui bagua*," which is an amulet representing the fortune-telling sticks of the I-Ching arranged around a tai chi symbol, again suggesting a swirling complementarity of life forces, or the yin and the yang.

"We spent a long time designing this logo, because it represents the meaning of our brand," Ho continues. "Phoenix represents something that is brand new but also something that is very Chinese. It's new and old, Western and Eastern. It also tries to represent a merging of the northern and southern parts of China and of their cultures, which are very, very different. The southern part of China is always creating, looking forward, and extending outward. But," he leans forward for emphasis, gazing emphatically above his black-rimmed spectacles and slowing the cadence of his delivery, "the *real* culture of China comes from the north, thousands and thousands of years of history and culture. And the mixture of these two areas is a major part of our thinking as we develop the programming strategies for Phoenix."

Engineered into the Phoenix identity from the very outset was this version of Chineseness that embraces the conservative cultural and political philosophies preferred by the party leadership in Beijing. It acknowledges the northern part of China is as the "middle kingdom" (the political, historical, and cultural center of the country), while the south is portrayed as a complementary source of dynamism and experimentation, an image that jibes with popular perceptions of Guangzhou, Hong Kong, and Shanghai—the engines of economic modernization. In describing the brand, Ho makes no explicit mention of the global or foreign elements of the company. Rather than portraying Phoenix as an intrusive or exotic presence, Ho describes it as a domestic service that fits into every home: a window looking out rather than a signal beaming in. The distinction, he says, is that Phoenix is run by Chinese for Chinese. Yet, at the same time, Phoenix works hard to

Liu Changle, CEO of Phoenix Television at the company
headquarters in Hong Kong. Over his right shoulder is the
Phoenix logo. Courtesy South China Morning Post.

distinguish itself from other television services in mainland China. Uplink-
ing from Hong Kong, the brand intentionally plays off the city's reputation
as a cosmopolitan center of China and regularly invokes the glitter of the
city's entertainment industry, much as Hollywood media do in the United
States.

The Phoenix brand plays on these multiple meanings. Yet such ambiguities are not solely a product of corporate calculation; they also result from
the company's status on the margins of Chinese television. Not yet fully
recognized by the PRC government, Phoenix seeks tacit acceptance of its
presence on local cable systems by positioning itself within a dominant
framework of Chineseness and at the same time invoking a cosmopolitan
gloss that might distinguish it from its competition. Not unlike the city of

Hong Kong itself, Phoenix exploits its marginality while obscuring its links to global capital.

In part, this strategy seeks to appease leaders in Beijing, but, just as important, it assists the marketing department in its efforts to get Phoenix onto cable systems that don't currently carry the service. Marketing executives must therefore come up with strategies to ingratiate Phoenix with local officials and to generate popular demand for a service among people who have never had the chance to view its programs. Since it is banned from advertising in newspapers and magazines inside China, the company relies on a combination of promotional events and word-of-mouth recommendation. For example, in 1997, to celebrate Hong Kong's return to China, the company invested over $1 million in promoting a stunt driver's jump across the Hukou Falls of the Yellow River. Working with local officials, Phoenix executives spent close to a year organizing celebrations and festivities that would surround the June 1 event. The jump was emblematic of the gap being bridged between Hong Kong and the mainland but also was designed to build relationships with officials in the two provinces on either side of the river. "One year of promotion and a ten-second jump," enthuses Howard Ho. "In that one year, the penetration of Phoenix in those two provinces rose dramatically, all because of mouth-to-mouth promotion."

Similarly, three years later, the Phoenix marketing team organized a road rally to commemorate the new millennium. Starting from Athens and traversing the Middle East and Central Asia, four-wheel drive vehicles raced across six provinces of China before reaching their destination at the Great Wall. Wherever they stopped along the way, Phoenix arranged festivities—arrival ceremonies, welcoming parties, and musical performances—each event aimed at promoting goodwill and popular buzz. The rally was further designed to maximize visual appeal (from the departure at the foot of the Acropolis to the arrival at the Great Wall), so that the entire road rally might be covered continuously on the Phoenix Channel. Like the Silk Road travel routes of ancient times, the journey emphasized connections between China and the outside world, and at the same time it elevated the country's status by establishing the Great Wall of the Middle Kingdom as the destination of the winners.

The ultimate objective of all these marketing activities has been to increase audience penetration figures. *Penetration* and *viewership* are the two most important indicators that advertisers use when negotiating the purchase of airtime from a satellite telecaster. In markets like Taiwan, viewership is more important, because advertisers already know that most channels have complete penetration. In China, however, penetration figures are more important for services like Phoenix, which try to demonstrate their growing visibility in a vast and complex media environment. As of 2003, Phoenix claimed to reach forty-two million households, or 13 percent of the total. "Compared to CCTV, we're just a small child," observes Howard Ho, "but with our market surveys we can prove to our advertisers that these households are more affluent and more socially influential."

Indeed, by 2000, Phoenix's audience profile was impressive enough to attract close to $65 million in revenues from a roster of three hundred advertisers, fewer than 30 percent of them international firms. Equally important, total ad sales more than tripled during the late 1990s, generating a profit of close to $5 million in 2000. Moreover, Phoenix executives express confidence that the company's growth potential is tied to the overall growth potential of the advertising economy in China. "The total ad-spend in China compared to the total GDP is still really low [.5 percent] compared to Hong Kong or the USA [1 percent]," observes Ho. "Secondly, if you look at the ad-spend in these other countries, you'll see that the TV is about 45 percent of the total—that's an average—but if you look at China, it's about half that. So there's a lot of room for growth."[8]

Apparently, investors agreed with such estimates. An initial public offering in 2000 valued the company at $700 million, but investors quickly bid it up to a $2 billion valuation before it settled back to a figure closer to $1 billion. Yet despite Phoenix having proven itself to be a capable operator in a large and growing market, its profitability since the IPO has been erratic. Revenues have grown to over $90 million, but costs have also spiraled, generating a loss in 2002 of $21 million. In large part, these fluctuations stem from its recent expansion to a third channel—a financial news service, Phoenix Infonews, which at the time was losing money at the rate of about $1 million per month. Expansion into Europe and North America is also a drag on the bottom line. Yet perhaps the biggest worry is debt collection from advertising clients in the PRC, an issue that may not be resolved until national regulators grant Phoenix official status as a mass-audience television provider.

Exactly when that might happen remains unclear. The central government tacitly acknowledges Phoenix's presence while continuing to withhold official approval, expecting Phoenix to prove it is earnest about its stated intentions to provide a complementary service that will not undermine the PRC television system or challenge the authority of the Communist Party. The government has effectively turned Phoenix to its own purposes by controlling access to cable systems, prohibiting newspaper advertising for foreign satellite services, and explicitly punishing Murdoch for his display of hubris in 1993.

Yet Phoenix also *benefits* from government regulations in a number of ways. For one thing, broadcasting services inside the PRC were developed with the aim of fostering national unity, requiring that all channels broadcast in Mandarin. Despite the many different varieties of spoken Chinese, this policy made it possible for Phoenix to fashion a service aimed at viewers who were accustomed to Mandarin programming. Another regulation that benefits Phoenix is the fact that local and provincial stations—many of them quite popular—are discouraged from covering national and international news, a domain reserved for CCTV, the Beijing-based national network that is closely monitored by government censors. Ironically, this forbidden terrain has become Phoenix's programming preserve. "Dangerous topics are Phoenix TV's strength," declared Liu Changle in a toast to Hong Kong journalists in 2001.[9] "When you turn on Phoenix, no matter whether in Sichuan, Hunan, or Yunnan, it looks different from all of the other channels," adds Howard Ho. "When you look different, people will spend time watching you, if only because they are curious. We are very lucky at this moment. It won't be the same in ten years. There will be more competition, and we may have to regionalize our services within China, but right now we are very lucky because, wherever we are, we look different from the competition."

Indeed, Phoenix current affairs programs tackle issues that provincial and municipal broadcasters conspicuously avoid. For example, in 2000, the Beijing leadership aggressively criticized the presidential election campaign in Taiwan, because the political party of a leading candidate, Chen Shuibian, openly proclaimed its support for Taiwanese independence. The election was clearly marked as a sensitive issue, since the PRC government considers Taiwan a renegade province of China rather than an independent country. Consequently, mainland stations have a longstanding policy of deferring to CCTV, which cautiously toes the Communist Party line in its coverage of Taiwan.

Yet Phoenix TV drew widespread attention by not only providing live coverage of the election but also by promoting news specials and talk shows on the topic as a prominent part of its schedule. Estimated audiences averaged thirty-five million, and viewership was especially high on cable systems farther afield from the direct oversight of Beijing officials. In Fujian Province, little more than a hundred miles from Taiwan, Zhong Pengtu, a tax collector, gathered with friends regularly to follow the coverage on Phoenix and reportedly became so engrossed in the political drama that he and his friends placed bets on the outcome. "We were so happy when Chen Shui-bian won," Zhong recalls. "He was the underdog, and he speaks our dialect, Minanyu. We understood every word of his victory speech in Taiwanese. It was great entertainment."[10] Meanwhile, in Beijing, where cable operators dare not carry the Phoenix channel on their systems, the signal was available only in upscale international hotels and in the residential compounds of government leaders. But reportedly, university students were so intrigued by the democratic transfer of power in Taiwan that groups of students pooled their money to check in to five-star hotels, where they could follow the campaign even if they couldn't afford the room service.

According to Howard Ho, "As long as we said, 'Taiwan election' and not 'the Republic of China' election, we knew we were safe. And we'd say, 'Chen Shui-bian got elected.' We didn't say he was elected president of the Republic of China.[11] CCTV only ran very short, one-minute reports on election day, but we went in depth and did analysis of what was going on. People in China, even [Premier] Zhu Rongji, like to watch Phoenix. People like to have that kind of information. And for more than three months, we were the only station broadcasting that kind of news about Taiwan, and we enjoyed very good ratings."

This was not the first time that Phoenix trumped CCTV, the national Chinese network. One year earlier when NATO bombers destroyed the PRC Embassy in Belgrade, killing two reporters, Phoenix lavished extensive attention on the event. Indeed, British press reports criticized Phoenix for pandering to officials in Beijing. Other observers noted, however, that Phoenix was probably as much concerned with audience sympathies as it was with government favor. Says one Chinese media critic, "Phoenix was trying to do what CCTV was not allowed to do, which was to tap into popular outrage and fervent nationalism. The Chinese stations were not allowed to do this, because the government worries about stirring up nationalist feelings. The government is afraid of any kind of popular movement that it doesn't control, even a nationalist movement, because once the genie's out of the bottle—" He shrugs and waves his hands, as if to suggest a loss of control.

Howard Ho dismisses the notion that Phoenix was catering to PRC censors or trying to whip viewers into a nationalist frenzy, but he doesn't deny that the channel's coverage sought to elicit audience sympathy for the victims. "If you take a close look at the coverage, we never said anything subjective, such as the U.S. government is to blame. We never said that," he declares as he taps the table top lightly for emphasis. "If, however, you look at our coverage compared to the coverage of the Western news services—that particular picture of the demolished building and the removal of the bodies—you'll see that it only happened once on CNN, but with Phoenix you saw those images on and on. But we never tried to promote a political line. If we did so, we might get in trouble with the government. Instead, we were trying to promote sympathy [for] those who suffered a loss of their friends and families." Indeed, the Phoenix coverage was not so different from the sort of coverage one might expect from U.S. cable news channels in the wake of an American tragedy. Yet, it is difficult to overlook the irony of a marginal TV service plucking the heartstrings of a country in which the government is exceedingly cautious about appeals to popular emotion. Here again we see Phoenix testing the boundaries of possibility in Chinese television while allowing those inside the ruling regime and the government media who benefit from such experimentation to maintain a plausible distance.

Clearly, Phoenix news and public affairs programs are dancing close to the fire, but they have not yet been burned, in large part because many Phoenix executives have experience inside mainland broadcasting organizations. Liu Changle spent five years as a chief editor at Central Radio during the 1980s. "He knows what can be said and what cannot be said," observes one Chinese media executive. "I think he understands what the government would like to hear, but more important, what they can tolerate and what they cannot." Liu himself refers to it as risk management, saying, "We have a team of professionals who constantly measure our programming for sensitivity."[12]

Such awareness makes Phoenix rather successful in the mainland and yet at the same time precludes it from attracting audiences in places like Hong Kong or Taiwan, where viewers are accustomed to even more freewheeling news coverage of Asian politics. Consequently, Phoenix benefits from its ability to negotiate the complex shades of political discourse on the mainland, but, interestingly, that same sensitivity limits the scope of its address. Although the company's Internet home page represents Phoenix as "a Global Satellite Television Group Reaching Chinese Communities around the World," it must constantly balance the economies that may be achieved by broader appeal with the need to position itself in relation to mainland competitors and government policies.[13] Although it has the technological potential to reach a Global Chinese audience, Phoenix in fact focuses most of its effort on only a portion of the viewers in the PRC, a far cry from what was imagined only a decade ago by executives at Star TV.

Maps of satellite footprints were perhaps one of the most intoxicating yet deceptive representations of the early satellite era. In the case of Star TV, they suggested blanket coverage across Asia, from Lebanon to the Philippines and south to Indonesia. In fact, however, the development of Star and Phoenix has been shaped by numerous sociocultural forces on the ground: infrastructural, political, and textual. In the infrastructural realm, government regulation and market forces significantly influence the configuration of delivery systems for satellite TV. Rather than bringing a totalitarian regime to its knees, Star TV has been forced to accommodate Chinese officials in an attempt to gain carriage on government cable systems. Moreover, Rupert Murdoch's dreams of exploiting a pan-Asian market were dashed by the cultural diversity of audiences and the logistical demands of competing with local and national television broadcasters. Likewise, the complexity of product distribution networks on the ground has undermined the possibility of expansive advertising strategies in the sky. And finally, the promotional chores associated with building services inside China have been exacerbated by restrictions on newspaper and magazine advertising.

In the political realm, Murdoch found that the Beijing government is far more complicated than popular conceptions of authoritarianism might suggest. On the one hand, Chinese leaders can initiate sweeping changes to media policy on relatively short notice. On the other hand, these policies can be executed with significant discretion at the local level, a phenomenon indicative of the devolution of power in China over the past two decades. Moreover, within the national government various factions vie for power. Among the manygroups involved, some are reformers bent on experimentation and are often connected to transnational commerce, whereas others are guardians of Mao's peasant revolution and are suspicious of foreign threats to the supremacy of the Communist Party. In such a context, global capital can be figured either as an exploitative force that seeks to extract value from Chinese society or as a productive force that can be put to use for the development of a national media system. Yet even those who perceive positive benefits from a global enterprise such as Star or Phoenix do not necessarily believe that satellite TV will democratize China or enlighten its citizens. As we have seen, such services can incite nationalist passions just as easily as they can stimulate reasoned deliberation on important social issues.

Finally, in the textual realm, each satellite service must establish a style or a brand that can earn a niche among competing forms of information and entertainment. Accordingly, Phoenix intentionally represents itself as a service transmitting from an electronic elsewhere on the margins of China. With its headquarters in Hong Kong, Phoenix appears at once familiar and proximate to Chinese viewers and also edgy and cosmopolitan. And like CCTV, it presents itself as a national Mandarin-language service, but it focuses on upscale, influential audiences in the eastern part of China. In so doing, the Phoenix brand invokes both a locality (eastern, cosmopolitan) and a temporality (innovative, modern) to suit its commercial purposes, but this also restricts Phoenix's appeal to audiences within the PRC, since Chinese residents of Hong Kong, Taiwan, and Vancouver see little in its programming that is especially familiar or provocative when compared with other television services at their disposal.

Such complexities no doubt surprised Rupert Murdoch when he first ventured into East Asia, and one still wonders if his gamble will pay off. Murdoch's stated ambition is to put together the first global satellite network and then float a public stock offering in hopes of recouping his initial investment. An important part of that portfolio will be Star and Phoenix, but many media executives in Asia wonder if either service will ever turn a consistent profit, and estimates of News Corporation's total investment range as high as $3 billion, making it still a high-stakes gamble with no guarantee of longterm success. Indeed, to witness Murdoch kowtowing to Chinese leaders, currying the favor of provincial bureaucrats, and pandering to nationalist sentiments of Chinese audiences invites us to reconsider presumptions that the logic of accumulation inevitably prevails in its encounters with the forces of sociocultural variation.

10 Global Satellites Pursuing Local Audiences and Panregional Efficiencies

Dramatic changes in Singaporean media policy during the 1990s helped to make Singapore Cable Vision one of the most robust broadband services in Asia, delivering dozens of channels from around the world and providing high-speed Internet access to homes and businesses throughout the island. Just as important, the very same policies encouraged global satellite services to establish their regional headquarters in the "media hub of Southeast Asia." HBO was the first to arrive in 1993, followed by MTV, Sony, ESPN, Discovery, and Disney. In all, thirteen out of sixteen global media divisions established a headquarters and uplink facility in the Lion City. Most executives for these companies concede that their initial strategies were based on a diffusion model of programming, whereby they would deliver to Asian audiences the same shows that were available to audiences in North America and Europe. They believed the superior quality of their services would stand out in comparison to local television, outweighing the relative foreignness of their programming. Indeed, most saw cultural difference as a positive characteristic that would distinguish their products, attract large audiences, and ultimately transform Asian media markets, bringing local competitors more in line with "global standards." Some, however, didn't worry much about local competition or mass audiences, believing that low distribution costs would make their services profitable, even if they turned out to be little more than niche channels for cosmopolitan elites.

HBO Asia—a joint venture of Warner Bros., Universal, Paramount, and Sony—is a good example of the latter perspective, since it fashions itself as a provider of global products that require very little adaptation to the local market. "Our service transcends all cultural boundaries," says vice-president Jim Marturano, explaining that his job is simply to create a secure pay-TV window in Asia for the major Hollywood studios. According to the terms of the joint venture, each partner owns an equal share of HBO Asia, and each agrees to deliver a minimum number of films for play on the channel each year, receiving in return license fees that are based on theatrical box office sales in the United States. Sometimes studios are reluctant to deliver their best movies because of concerns about piracy or because they have conflicting distribution arrangements,[1] but Marturano contends it's ultimately in the interest of partners to supply a steady stream of attractive films in order to maximize return on equity and fully exploit the pay-TV window of their products. Although the quality of films from each studio may vary from year to year, differences tend to even out over time, and potential tensions among studios are further mitigated by the relatively low number of subscribers in Asia, which, as of 2001, was a mere 3.9 million homes, a diminutive audience in comparison to markets in Japan, North America, and Europe.

HBO's strategy enabled it to become the first regional satellite service to turn a profit in Asia, largely because it is simply extending the distribution of existing movies (prototypes) and because the company's costs are carefully managed, according to Marturano. Covering territories across the continent with the exception of Japan, HBO Asia telecasts a fairly uniform product, and the only concession it makes to local markets is subtitling—Thai, Chinese, and Bahasa Malay—as well as some adaptation of scheduling and content, including the elision of controversial representations of sex, violence, and religion. Unlike some international operators who might be leery of Singapore's renowned media censorship, HBO actually takes advantage of its uplink location to screen programming with government censors. "We have two feeds for HBO," explains Marturano. "The Singapore censored feed, for lack of a better term, is a regional feed that is reviewed by the censors here, and then we have a Malaysia feed, which is reviewed by censors up north. [The Malaysians are] even more demanding right now, but we hope that will change in the future. The beauty of it is that Singapore censorship standards give us a nice entrée into markets like China, and the Malaysia standards set benchmarks for Islamic markets." Overall, the company toes a cautious line when preparing its feeds, hoping to anticipate and address conflicts that might emerge at the local level.

Launched in 1992, HBO Asia performed well in many territories as a niche service, but growth began to slow during the late 1990s, when the company wrestled with signal piracy and contractual disagreements with local cable operators. Although available in more than twenty countries, HBO Asia is a premium service in only seven because of limitations of policy, technology, audience income, and market dynamics. For example, throughout the 1990s it was a premium offering in Hong Kong but a basic channel in the much larger Taiwanese market, where tiered services were unavailable. Marturano says he is hoping that recent changes in Taiwan's cable policy will help "unlock the value of our channel." Yet, that could take time, since viewers have grown accustomed to a free English-language movie service as part of their basic package. This problem also exists in other markets in which HBO initially sought to be part of the basic cable package in order to claim "shelf space" but eventually found itself confronted with the delicate challenge of transforming its identity to a premium pay-TV brand. In general, local cable operators are reluctant to shift channels from the basic lineup to the premium tier, arguing that, if they do so, audiences will demand a price reduction or other forms of compensation.

Couple these marketing challenges with issues of political control and public access, which have surrounded Taiwanese television for over a decade, and one begins to understand why rebranding is such a delicate question. During the transition HBO needs to be sensitive to the concerns of both cable subscribers and government regulators. Just as worrisome, says Marturano, angry operators have at times threatened to delete channels from their systems. During the 1990s HBO was available to a very small number of early adopters, but now, as cable households increase in numbers, debates over the mix of available services are intensifying, as are debates over content. Therefore, one's identity as a global brand is just as likely to raise suspicions as it is to generate enthusiasm.

Like HBO, Discovery Asia also positions itself as a global brand, aiming to realize economies of scale by producing programs with an eye toward global distribution and by purchasing the worldwide rights to programs it acquires for broadcast. Yet, unlike HBO, Discovery is an advertising-supported service that aims to grow its audience quickly and therefore prefers to be bundled with basic cable services. This requires the deployment of sales reps to local territories and the development of a worldwide marketing infrastructure. According to Penny Chan, marketing director of the Asian region, the channel's brand identity is similar across territories. "One tunes in to Discovery to have a learning experience—a personal discovery. It's someone who likes adventure, wants a challenge, and wants to be entertained at the same time. We see ourselves as educational but approachable." Yet that very identity also invites competition, since the format is relatively inexpensive to produce and adaptable to local themes, interests, and concerns. In Taiwan, for example, Sanlih makes extensive use of the genre, and other channels produce similar programs focusing on local and regional topics. Moreover, Japan's NHK and Hong Kong's TVB likewise syndicate glossy educational fare throughout Asia. Initially, the Discovery niche seemed fairly exploitable, but over time local competitors and other global brands, such as the BBC, have increasingly crowded the market.

Indeed, global competitors can be especially troublesome, since they fragment what is already a relatively small niche in cable markets. Such was the experience of Star Sports, which began as a regional service that was part of the pan-Asian Star TV platform. Just when the channel was becoming financially stable, ESPN entered the Asian market in 1995, and the two services began to cannibalize each other's audiences. Star Sports tried to distinguish itself by providing local flavor that included on-camera commentators from various locales. ESPN, by comparison, offered a more American mix, acting as a direct conduit for ABC/ESPN programming and emphasizing its status as a global brand. Yet within a year, the two services grew closer as each sought to broaden its appeal, with Star drifting toward a more global presentation and ESPN migrating toward a more local appeal. Furthermore, they began to compete for the same commentators and sporting events, and they began cutting ad rates in an attempt to grow their respective client bases. Competition intensified, and the sports television niche grew more slowly than anticipated, forcing them to call a truce after only a year of heated rivalry. Toward the end of 1996 they formed a joint venture that consolidated all aspects of their operations but sustained some distinctions between the brands. Four years later the combined enterprise was delivering eleven satellite feeds, featuring two pan-Asian services and nine subregional channels aimed at such markets as India, Taiwan, Singapore, and the Philippines. With a staff of more than five hundred deployed throughout the region, ESPN/Star became the dominant satellite sports channel.

"In Taiwan, we run the same thing we run in greater Asia for seventeen hours a day," says Russell Wolf, senior vice-president of programming, "but for seven hours, especially during prime time, we run programming specifically for Taiwan, where the preference is for baseball, basketball, NFL, billiards, snooker, bowling, and during the Asian games, we ran live coverage of the Taiwanese national baseball. We've also customized the promos to match the look and feel of the local advertising market. The programming hasn't changed drastically—we haven't bought a lot of new programming—but we've taken the programming we have and made it much more appealing to the Taiwan audience. We also made sure that the commentary is specifically the Taiwanese version of Mandarin, which is very different in terms of tone, accent, and especially slang [expressions] used in sports."

Although ESPN/Star Sports is premised on the notion that sports programming should easily cross national boundaries, the company must nevertheless adapt to different tastes and team allegiances, as well as time zones, programming schedules, and market competition. The economies of scale that seemed so apparent to Star and ESPN executives when they first entered Asia now seem more difficult to realize. "You can go in and buy rights to cricket in India," observes one industry insider, "but maybe [cricket's] not popular in Malaysia or maybe that league isn't popular there. Soccer is very popular in Singapore, but not in Taiwan. U.S. baseball may do well in Taiwan, but not anywhere else." Moreover, in order to reach audiences in highly competitive markets such as Taiwan, ESPN/Star Sports must take into account the flow of programs on competing stations in order to counterprogram when necessary, and it must develop promotional spots that fit seamlessly with the look and feel of local advertising.

Russell Wolf concedes that global media brands, such as ESPN, must constantly adapt to local conditions, but the more significant question is, how much should they adapt? "It all boils down to panregional efficiency versus local appeal," says Wolf. "I think that's the challenge that exists for everybody. Asia does not exist. There is no Asia. If you say to someone in Bangkok, 'You're Asian.' They'd say, 'No, I'm not; I'm Thai.' This is a functional reality. You come to Asia, and you put up one service. Then you realize India's different, so you buy some cricket and you realize that you have to separate the channels, so you go to two services. You think you've solved the problem, and then you start to wonder, how do we make this more profitable? It's is a learned philosophy. Panregional is the opening play for many services, then subregional, then local. The question is, how local do you get? And that depends on developments in each market. As [cable] penetration grows in each market, the market grows more appealing, so you start to consider ways to improve your position in that particular market."

In other words, global satellite services localize over time as penetration grows, as advertising revenues increase, as market competition intensifies, and as audience viewing options multiply. Global and regional services initially seem viable, because their broad geographical reach allows them to pull together what would otherwise be considered very small, very elite, and very dispersed pockets of viewers, delivering them to transnational advertisers. Yet the amount of transnational advertising revenue is limited, and as satellite services seek to expand their mix to include national and local ad revenues, they must increase their presence within particular territories, forcing them to multiply the number of channels and adapt their programming to accommodate the distinctive features of local markets.

Nevertheless, some media content—such as Hollywood blockbusters and

World Cup soccer—proves popular despite local considerations, a dynamic that continues to intrigue companies with access to the technology of satellite TV. These programs offer "panregional efficiency," and during the 1990s, musical artists such as Madonna, Michael Jackson, and Whitney Houston were likewise believed to have broad appeal among teenagers around the globe.[2] Such calculations provided the original rationale for MTV's expansion into Europe and then to other parts of the globe, arriving in Asia as part of Richard Li's Star TV platform in 1991.

When they were first telecast in Asia, MTV's music videos seemed to cross national boundaries with relative ease, encouraging extensive buzz, both positive and negative, among industry insiders and the popular press. In fact, one of the most common tropes in newspaper stories about the spread of satellite TV during the 1990s was character portraits of remote Asian villagers tuning in to music videos by Western artists. MTV seemed to be emblematic of the transnational and transformative power of satellite television. So when Star changed ownership in 1994, MTV seized the opportunity to develop a stand-alone service, reasoning that a pan-Asian music channel was destined for success. This was also a moment when Viacom, MTV's parent company, was emerging as one of the world's largest media conglomerates after purchasing Paramount Pictures in 1993. With their company now on equal footing with Rupert Murdoch's News Corporation, Viacom executives self-consciously started to chart the company's course as a *global* competitor, and its MTV Networks reflected this shift, expanding into Latin America and Asia as well as Europe.

After splitting with Star and moving its regional base of operations to Singapore, MTV Asia relaunched in 1995 with two channels, one dedicated to the Taiwan market and the other aimed at a regional market. In 1996, it added a third service, this one to the Indian market, but none of these channels was proving to be the money spinner that executives had originally envisioned. For example, the Taiwan service performed well on the island but failed to develop a substantial pan-Chinese following because of market conditions and government regulations. The station's music rotation, which was based in part on album sales and music stars specific to the island, did not perform especially well in Hong Kong, Singapore, or the PRC. Moreover, the mainland ban on foreign satellite services forced the company to repackage content for the PRC into hour-long blocks that could be sold to local stations, an added expense that undermined the economies of scale envisioned at the outset and also weakened the company's control over content and scheduling.

The national service for India encountered a different host of problems.

Originally positioned as a channel that would bring the best of global talent to the Indian market, it tried to distance itself from the musical traditions of the Bombay film industry. Offering a mix that was 80 percent global and 20 percent local, MTV hoped to achieve cult status as a cosmopolitan musical alternative. Augustine Tan, a U.S.-educated Singaporean who programmed the channel at that time, recalls that "it was very Western," in part because of MTV's business strategy and in part because there wasn't much local product to mix in. "I would have maybe three Indian music videos to choose from, and there were only so many times that you could play them." Tan says the channel was then losing a million dollars per quarter and was being solidly trounced in the ratings by more locally oriented satellite music services, such as Zee TV and even Star's Channel V, both of which played a heavy dose of songs from Bollywood musicals and both of which tried to promote and develop the careers of performers in the emerging Indian pop music industry.

MTV on the other hand, was trying to develop a more distinctive identity with its international mix, but the results were disappointing, recalls Frank Brown, president of MTV Asia. "We started with a blueprint that was supposed to be predominantly international, but I think that in the beginning the product was too Western; it was too rock 'n rap," he says. "It was adhering too much to the American brand image. It was very fast-paced, very cool, very hip. People would tune in and go, 'Wow, that's incredible. I've never seen anything like that. Click.' It's like you go into a club, and it's full of wild music, trendy fashions, and cool people: stars over there, transvestites over there, and cool kids over here. Your response is, 'Wow. This is really an amazing club, but it's not where I really belong. That's what was happening with some of our consumers. It was just too overcooked in a way."

After dismal midyear results, MTV began to restrategize in August 1997, reversing its mix to feature 75 percent local content. Tan explains that a shift in company culture as well as a commitment to the development of local artists and events helped the company recover and at the same time contributed to the emergence of a distinctive Indipop industry. A similar narrative unfolded in other markets, such as the Philippines and Indonesia, where audiences showed more interest in local musicians than in warmed-over rock and rap from the West. MTV soon learned to insinuate itself into these vibrant local music scenes and to play a role in the development of television services that complemented an already existing cultural repertoire. This shift in strategy yielded dramatic results, and by the following August, as Brown recalls, the network's "audience multiplied by a factor of forty."

Another contributor to change was the arrival of compression, encryption, and multiplexing technologies in the mid-1990s, allowing MTV to carry eight channels on each satellite transponder. "One of the biggest single overhead costs in our business is transponder costs," notes Brown, "so along comes digitization, which we didn't expect when we started, and suddenly the costs of localization dropped dramatically." Instead of four signals on four transponders, MTV suddenly had thirty-two signals available to cover its Asian markets. And instead of feeding sixteen hours of programming from its headquarters in Singapore, it cut back to eight, with the rest of the programming shipped in from locations throughout the region. John Wigglesworth, MTV's creative director who runs the Singapore facility, says, "The whole idea of a media hub makes less and less sense as technology gets cheaper. Now that we have more channels, it allows our talent to be more dispersed and therefore more in touch with local audiences." It also allows programmers to tap material from localized services in order to remix them as regional programs. For example, Singaporean audiences might not be interested in a direct feed of the Taiwan service, but they might be very interested in a local channel that includes a Taiwanese pop music hour or a round-up program of Chinese music hits from around the world.

The MTV strategy in Asia, which Frank Brown refers to as a multimarket model, eventually evolved along the same lines as MTV Asia's European counterpart. Brown contends that tribalism, or the need to belong, proved to be an important factor in audience responses to both services. "I'm from the north of England, from Blackpool," he says. "I'm a Manchester United fan, and when Manchester United is playing a London club, there's a fierce rivalry between the north and the south. But when England is playing France, suddenly north and south are united. If tomorrow the world found itself engaged in an intergalactic war, we'd suddenly discover that the differences between people on this planet are very small." Brown's notion of tribalism is both flexible and multiple. That is, one embraces multiple loyalties, but one experiences them differently and assigns them different priorities according to circumstances. And although some affinities are geographically defined, other factors can be influential as well. Especially important to MTV is generational affiliation. Brown explains, "We even have a saying that a twenty-year-old in Paris has more in common with a twenty-year-old in Beijing or Singapore than he does with his own parents. He's at a stage in life that, wherever you are, you're going through certain things—angst around career, the future, dating, as well as a shared passion for music and movies, very often the same movies—that give you a bond with young people elsewhere."

Consequently, the extent to which MTV is able to build a transnational brand image and realize economies of scale derives from its ability to tap generational concerns and forge collective responses to those concerns. But even at this most expansive level, MTV's brand image plays differently around the world. Brown recalls a creative meeting in 1996, when MTV brought together new Asian staff members with key executives of MTV International in order to brainstorm about the brand identity of the new Asia service. "Of course, the first people to speak up were the Westerners, partly because they're more vocal and partly because they had more experience with MTV. So it was like, 'Frank must be asking us to educate our Asian colleagues.' All the usual stuff came dropping out: we should be rock 'n roll, we should be edgy, we should be hip. Finally after things cooled down a bit, a Filipino guy speaks up and says: 'Something that's kind of missing here is that, in the Philippines, it's very important to have a good relationship with your parents, and not only that, it's very important to be *seen* as having a good relationship with your parents.' And the Westerners are looking at me like, 'He can't be serious.' And then someone else from Asia spoke up and said, 'We haven't mentioned anything about career or about the future. We haven't talked about education.' At this point my Western executives are falling off their seats, because in the West we wouldn't have touched that stuff at that time." Brown recalls it as an important learning experience for everyone involved, especially since these valences were so different from those at work in Europe and North America. It led them to develop programs like *MTV English*, which features a Chinese-American comedian, David Wu, giving language lessons with a hip irreverence that nevertheless informs while it entertains. Code switching between English and Mandarin at the speed of light, Wu's short drop-in segments helped to reposition the channel to match the aspirational outlook of its young Chinese viewers.

Channel executives also reassessed core values that were assumed to be part of the MTV brand. "In Asia," observes Brown, "rebelling doesn't necessarily mean rejection of traditional values, whether moral, religious, or social values. Instead, they *keep* the old values whilst rebelling *to* some new values. We call it a dual passport. They're very comfortable with contemporary values: consumerism, success, technology, new media, a Western style of dress. Young people on the streets of any major city in Asia, you'll see them with jeans and a T-shirt, sneakers, and the cap turned backward—okay, the cap turned backward is kind of out these days, but you know what I mean—then they may go home and change into traditional dress for the family meal. Underneath the cosmopolitan look, the values that they have inside are often very traditional, and this shows up in our research all the time." Thus, for the global brand, edginess means a willingness to reinvent oneself, but in Asia it carries a different inflection, embracing tradition and family while also embracing the newest technologies and fashions. And although Brown, like ESPN's Russell Wolf, is skeptical about an "Asian identity," he nevertheless points to what he sees as certain commonalities. "There is a collectivist psyche in Asia, whereas there is an individualist psyche in the West. Here, it's an emphasis on the family and three generations living in a household. What flows from that is graciousness and courtesy and a suppression of the ego."

Consequently, MTV Asia tries to address multiple levels of affinity among Asian youth, tapping global techniques, strategies, and programming when appropriate, regional ones when necessary, and national ones as well. While trying to operate at all three levels, the network also seeks to leverage popular local musicians to regional and even global stardom. Coco Lee, the Taiwanese pop singer who performed the title track for *Crouching Tiger, Hidden Dragon*, became an MTV favorite around 2000. Likewise, Dadawa, a Chinese pop singer from Guangzhou, China, who in 1995 began to embrace Tibetan culture as her musical inspiration, was launched into global circulation as a world music act around the same time. MTV is furthermore distributing music from its Chinese and Indian channels to cable services in London, Sydney, and San Francisco. Brown concedes it's ironic that global MTV localized its operations in Asia and now, in turn, is globalizing that local product. Of course, MTV has refigured its strategy to benefit from both globalization and localization, but that's a far cry from its original strategy when it entered Asia in 1995. "The homogenization of culture has been demonstrated, I think, to be a myth," admits Brown. "When the international broadcasters came to Asia, in the back of their minds, all of them expected Western product to have immediate appeal and to influence the media culture in this part of the world. Of course, what happened was that, rather than Western broadcasters changing Asia, Asia changed Western broadcasters."

Brown's observation seems to be true regarding both the institutions and the personnel that represent global media conglomerates operating in Asia. Like many Western executives during the early 1990s, William Pfeiffer was captivated by the stratospheric discourse of satellite TV. Then the head of Disney's video distribution business in Japan, Pfeiffer tried repeatedly to convince his superiors in Los Angeles to let him put together a branded pan-Asian satellite service. Those attempts failed, however, largely because company brass were then preoccupied with problems at Euro Disney, which was both losing money and generating complaints about cultural imperialism. While fighting that battle in Europe, Disney executives didn't see the need to open another front in Asia. Nevertheless, Pfeiffer wasn't easily dissuaded, and he kept chatting up colleagues and business acquaintances about the potential of satellite TV. One of his interlocutors was Nobuyuki Idei, a junior board member at Sony who would later become CEO. "We would go out drinking sake and talk about satellite TV," recalls Pfeiffer, "and I could see that he was getting more and more interested in these ideas. I was talking about the value of having the Dalai Lama talking directly to people in the Middle East about world harmony, about the globalizing potential impact of satellite TV and simultaneous translation. He was fascinated by all this. His eyes sparkled, and he asked all the right questions. After a several meetings, he began to introduce me to a number of people at Sony Pictures, and they ended up inviting me into the company. The condition I set for joining them was that I be allowed to move to Hong Kong, because I felt that that was where the growth opportunities were."

Like Idei, Sony brass may have been interested in satellite TV, but just as likely they were interested in the young Disney executive who built from scratch a $300 million-a-year video business in Japan. When Pfeiffer arrived in Hong Kong in 1992, he confronted a similar challenge, since Sony Pictures' Asia division was then only a fledgling production and distribution operation. Pfeiffer spent the first few years traveling throughout the region selling Sony films and television programs to local and national broadcasters. Yet at the same time he was reflecting on his company's market position and scouting for fresh opportunities. Although Sony had a substantial motion picture library, it didn't have a brand identity like that of Disney, MTV, or CNN. Thus, it would be difficult to mount a niche satellite service that would draw premium audiences interested in a recognizable global brand. Instead, Pfeiffer felt that Sony would have to build its television brands from the ground up, and therefore it made sense to follow a different path, crafting mass-market satellite services featuring locally produced films and television programs. Pfeiffer took this proposal to the Sony board, and it sparked a spirited debate about the company's capacity to become a major producer in Asia. "I remember Jonathan Dolgen, who was head of Sony Pictures, saying, 'We don't even know how to make movies right in Hollywood. How are we going to go do it right in China or India?' The meeting lasted eight hours with a lot of people getting red in the face, but to their credit, they decided to go for it."

Sony's willingness to embark on this new venture may have been fueled by the initial forays that other global conglomerates, such as News Corporation, Pearson, and Time-Warner, were making in the region. Like the others, Pfeiffer focused his initial attention on China and especially on negotiating a deal with TVB, believing that it would play a pivotal role in the region. His negotiations with Run Run Shaw proceeded all the way to a handshake buy-out agreement that fell apart at the last minute, much to his dismay. Afterward he shifted his attention to Beijing, setting up an office to facilitate program sales and to coordinate a number of coproductions. Yet these were minor pieces of the puzzle. For although coproductions helped to build relationships with mainland stations and provided a learning experience on both sides, such projects had limited value, since PRC distribution rights would stay with the local partner and therefore did little to build a distinctive Sony brand. Likewise, syndication of Sony's existing library of Hollywood movies and television programs brought in new revenues but contributed little toward establishing a mass-market identity. Progress was steady but exceedingly slow. Then, in 1993, Rupert Murdoch posed his infamous challenge to authoritarian regimes, inviting a backlash from the Chinese leadership that suddenly made *all* foreign satellite services suspect, including Sony's prospective channels. "Rather than banging my head against the Great Wall trying to find a way back into China, I decided to refocus on growing our business in other parts of Asia," recalls Pfeiffer.

India was widely considered the next biggest prize, and Zee TV had already launched a mass-market, Hindi-language satellite service that was generating strong ratings and popular buzz. Although a joint venture between Star TV and Indian tycoon Subhash Chandra, the service had a relatively weak program schedule that left the door open to competitors. "I didn't know Hindi," recalls Pfeiffer, "but I knew we could make better shows than that. The question was, how?" Shifting his attention south, Pfeiffer started from scratch once again, since Sony had no office, no employees, and very little experience in the Indian market. He began by scouting for joint-venture partners and pulled together a group of seven investors, one of them a major entertainment star, another a Bollywood producer, giving Sony crucial entrée to the creative community. Just as important, these new partners had recently purchased four hundred popular Indian films and said they were willing to invest $11 million of their own money. Splitting the ownership as sixty-five and thirty-five, with Sony taking the larger share, the partnership struck a deal, and Sony staff went to work. In the year leading up to the launch of the Sony Entertainment Channel in October 1995, Pfeiffer spent less than a month in his Hong Kong home. Instead, he was in India most of the time, hiring staff members by day and screening prospective programming by night. From an initial investment of $50 million, the channel broke even within two years, becoming one of the leading Hindi-language satellite services in South Asia. By 2000, it was battling for the ratings lead among satellite providers, generating close to $30 million in prof-its on $125 million in revenues, quite favorable when compared, for ex-ample, with Phoenix TV. Like Liu Changle, Pfeiffer decided it was time to place an initial public offering, floating 8 percent of the company's stock for $200 million, which established the overall value of the company in the neighborhood of $2.5 billion. As with Phoenix, this fantastically high as-sessment was based on sheer growth potential. Although China has a larger population and is reputed to have a stronger economy and better infra-structure than India's, the Indian television market was considerably more open to foreign investment and foreign satellite operators, and at the time of the IPO, investors clearly anticipated explosive growth potential in South Asian TV and advertising.

Although Sony succeeded with a mass-market Indian channel, it was still making little headway in mainland China. With that avenue closed off, Pfeiffer decided in 1998 to escalate the company's investment in a Tai-wanese cable channel, Super TV, hoping that the challenge of running a suc-cessful Chinese channel in the competitive Taiwan market might provide useful experience for the future opening of the PRC market. It furthermore provided an opportunity for Sony to build a library of Mandarin-language TV series, part of its overall strategy to amplify program production in the world's major languages. Pfeiffer tapped Nicholas Wodtke, the head of Sony's Action Television Network, AXN, to head Super TV, and the com-pany invested more than $50 million dollars in the venture, following a business model quite similar to the Indian channel: strategic program ac-quisitions, local production, and sophisticated brand promotion. The results, however, were underwhelming. Local productions seemed to attract audi-ences initially, largely as a result of heavy promotion, but they failed to hold viewers for more than a couple of episodes. According to some industry practitioners, the Sony series were innovative and edgy, but they lacked star power, a crucial ingredient with audiences. And although Wodtke had the power of the Sony name behind him, he lacked a strong local partner who could negotiate with talent and advertisers. Success in Chinese television therefore continued to elude Sony, largely because the company found it difficult to generate compelling content.

Sony had more success, however with its Chinese film production unit, ratcheting up investment and putting together projects that mixed local and global resources, such as *Crouching Tiger, Hidden Dragon*. Helmed by vet-eran Hollywood director Ang Lee and budgeted at $15 million, the film was released in the summer of 2000, grossing $240 million at the international box office and drawing ten Academy Award nominations and four awards.

Similarly, *Lagaan*—an epic drama about cricket, India's national passion—scored a dramatic success at box offices across South Asia and the United Kingdom, garnering an Academy Award nomination in 2002 for best foreign picture, the first Indian film to be nominated since 1957. Both projects were green-lighted by Pfeiffer, but by the time *Lagaan*'s nomination was announced, Pfeiffer had already moved on to begin yet another Asian satellite service with some of the very same partners that had helped start the Sony Entertainment channel in India.

With primary backing from Ananda Krishnan, one of Malaysia's richest tycoons, Pfeiffer launched Celestial Pictures in 2001, aiming to create a vertically integrated studio to produce and distribute movies, TV shows, and animation for Chinese audiences around the globe. Krishnan, a reclusive entrepreneur of Indian descent, owns and operates Usaha Tegas, a vast conglomerate with extensive real estate, petroleum, and telecommunications interests. His MEASAT subsidiary, which grew rapidly during the 1990s, provides satellite infrastructure for his Malaysian mobile phone and cable television systems. By the end of the 1990s, however, Krishnan started shifting his attention to regional opportunities, looking for content partners for a satellite system that could reach audiences within a footprint that stretched from Pakistan to Korea to Indonesia. Like other tycoons in Asia, Krishnan was intrigued by the growth potential of the communications industry, but his first inclination was to invest in infrastructure rather than content. After successfully setting his satellite system in place, he then sensed the importance of content, aiming to attract Indian, Malay, and Chinese audiences. It's therefore not surprising that Krishnan was one of the lead investors in Sony's Indian satellite channel, nor was it remarkable that he became closely acquainted with Run Run Shaw when he negotiated with TVB executives regarding potential collaborations with its Galaxy platform. Although those talks eventually stalled, Krishnan emerged as the primary financial backer of William Pfeiffer's fledgling Celestial TV service, aimed at Chinese audiences worldwide.

The company's first objective was to develop a movie channel modeled after HBO, carrying feature films, upscale TV series, and special events. Like Ted Turner twenty years earlier, Pfeiffer reasoned that a collection of classic movies would be necessary to provide a core programming resource, but they needed to be movies that had not yet received broad exposure. Most of the popular Golden Harvest and Cinema City titles had already been cycled through video and cable release windows during the 1990s. Only Run Run Shaw had kept much of his studio's feature film output under lock and key, even resisting the temptation to screen his films on TVB for fear that video copies might fall into the hands of pirates. Despite numerous attempts to convince Shaw to open the vault, he demurred, with some observers speculating that piracy was his main concern and others suggesting that Shaw was simply waiting for the right offer. As the number of Chinese television channels proliferated and as the demand for Chinese-language content intensified, the value of Shaw Brothers' collection continued to appreciate. Finally, in 2000, Shaw's management team entered into protracted negotiations with Sony and Warner Bros., when all of the sudden Celestial swooped in and snatched up rights to the most valuable titles for $76.9 million. "Rather than bringing in a big team of lawyers like Warner," recalls Pfeiffer, "Krishnan got in there with his checkbook and, billionaire to billionaire, was able to close the deal."

Cherry-picking 760 films from Shaw Brothers' collection, Pfeiffer then developed an integrated marketing campaign to re-release the most famous titles to theaters first, where they would act as tent-pole features designed to draw attention to the collection as a whole. These films would subsequently move to video, in which they would be marketed individually and in boxed sets. The very same features would screen on the Celestial satellite channel and would be sold to theatrical distributors in markets outside East Asia. Pfeiffer spent three years and $15 million pouring over the initial batch of releases and working with technicians as they digitally remastered 120 gems from the collection. After theatrical screenings, Celestial began to market its first DVD products in November 2002, followed shortly thereafter by the rollout of the movie channel, which Pfeiffer describes as a quality service rather than a nostalgia channel. Following the HBO model, Celestial is also investing in original feature films, aiming ultimately to release ten to twelve movies each year with budgets ranging from $1 million to $8 million each. "We're negotiating with the biggest stars to create quality stuff that will not only generate theatrical profits but also serve as tent-pole pictures to drive the satellite channel." Likewise, Celestial is exploring television series production for its new channel, hoping to make it a destination for quality drama produced by Chinese talent from around the world.

It will, however, take some time for new productions to play a significant role in the Celestial schedule, so Pfeiffer anticipates that he will draw 30 percent of his programming from the Shaw library and another 50 percent from other leading movie studios, such as Shanghai Film Studio, Beijing Film Studio, Central Motion Pictures (Taiwan), and Golden Harvest. The remaining 20 percent of the schedule is to come from other Asian countries, especially Korea, Japan, and Thailand, all of which are producing films that play well throughout the region. Already the satellite channel is airing in such markets as Hong Kong, Malaysia, Indonesia, and Australia. Eventually, Celestial executives hope to take the service to audiences around the world, including cult film fans in North America and Europe.

Although the packaging and promotion of Shaw Brothers classics have proven to be a boon for Celestial and a mainstay of its satellite service, the ventures into local production have been less successful. Pfeiffer says his ambition is to "develop new businesses that will meld the best of Asian talent, culture, and content creation with the highest international standards of business practice, technology, and quality," but one Hong Kong movie producer confided that global business practices sometimes create tensions when dealing with local creative talent. For example, Pfeiffer hired Wong Jing as the first production chief at his Hong Kong studio, but the two had a falling out only months after Wong's arrival, largely regarding conflicting business practices. Wong's freewheeling style of deal making apparently didn't fit well with the meticulous contractual style favored by the Celestial CEO. Pfeiffer has also had troubles with his boss, Ananda Krishnan. "Poor William," chuckles a movie executive who has worked with the Malaysian tycoon. "Krishnan built this satellite TV platform, and he doesn't really know what to do with it. He has the infrastructure, but he needs something to pass through the pipelines. The Shaw library solves part of the problem, but only a small part. What he needs is original, compelling content. I know Krishnan doesn't have a formula for that, and Pfeiffer doesn't seem to have one either." Indeed, even though Celestial's marketing of the Shaw collection has proven largely successful, the company has yet to develop a capable strategy for content production. Initial plans for ten to twelve movies per year were dramatically scaled back, and by 2006 the company had little to show other than a handful of coproduction and distribution agreements. Although aspiring to build an integrated film studio, Celestial has so far been forced to content itself with successes in the film and television distribution businesses, largely repurposing product from the golden age of Shaw Brothers studio.

When satellite TV technology was first introduced in Asia, it seemed to surmount a number of obstacles that confronted media conglomerates with global aspirations. It could deliver signals across a vast continent without requiring the construction of terrestrial stations in each nation and locality, thereby annihilating spatial barriers that had previously seemed intractable. Satellite technology promised expansive and instantaneous diffusion of audiovisual products, thus fully and cheaply exploiting the centrifugal logic of distribution. It also seemed immune to government regulation, one of the most vexing sociocultural variables, because transmissions came from outer space and reception technology was radically decentralized. And it offered a new and exciting window of opportunity to advertisers, who imagined themselves hawking their products to the far ends of the earth.

Yet, as we've seen in this chapter, the forces of sociocultural variation continue to exert powerful constraints on media institutions with global or even regional ambitions. In large part these limitations have been bound up with the diverse and complex terrains of audience interpretation, requiring at each step that global satellite services balance the opportunities of productive and distributive efficiency against the necessity of adapting and positioning products with respect to audience tastes, market competition, and semiotic context. As Frank Brown of MTV observed, audiences have multiple loyalties, each of which is activated at particular moments in particular circumstances by particular artifacts. Although broadcasters may feel pressed to make maximum use of mass-appeal productions, they must also craft products for different scales of geographical affinity (local, regional, national, global) as well as different scales of sociocultural affinity (gender, generation, ethnicity, education, and class). Brown claims that many young viewers in Asia carry a dual passport (modern on the outside and traditional on the inside), but he could have just as likely referred to a multiple passport, since the scales of variation are far more complicated and broad ranging. Even in the satellite era, those providing television services must consider these variations when they scale programs to their audiences, and they must take account of competitors who are likewise fashioning services for particular segments of the audience.

Consequently, even though the arrival of a new global satellite service may evoke initial fascination among viewers, it must nevertheless compete on an ongoing basis against an array of global, national, and local services, each of them shifting its mix in response to market forces and cultural trends. Transnational brands must therefore adapt when other global competitors enter the market and when local broadcasters appropriate and adapt global styles, creating their own hybrid services. In most cases, the initial attractions of a global TV service will diminish under these pressures, unless the service localizes its offerings. As Russell Wolf of ESPN/Star puts it, establishing a panregional reach may be the opening gambit for a satellite service, but over time forces of gravity bring global services to earth, where they must compete under conditions that are not of their own making. By the end of the 1990s, many satellite executives had come to understand these hard-earned lessons, but as we shall see that did not prevent Richard Li from resurrecting the stratospheric rhetoric of satellite TV, marrying it to the irrational exuberance of the Internet economy, and offering it up to gullible investors across Asia.

11 The Promise of Broadband and the Problem of Content

In the years immediately following the sale of Star TV, Richard Li turned down an offer from his father to take charge of Hutchison Whampoa. Instead, he gathered up his share of the Star proceeds—an estimated $200 million—and used it to launch an enterprise that he boldly christened Pacific Century. Working with many of the same staffers who had helped him launch Star TV, Li established a venture capital firm focusing on the cutting-edge industries of Asia, especially communication. Despite Pacific Century's exuberant PR, its strategy seemed vague; the company dabbled mostly in real estate rather than media, in part because of a five-year noncompetition clause in the Star TV contract. As late as 1997, an article in the *South China Morning Post* summarized the accomplishments of the Pacific Century Group as all right but "not great."[1] Its property development division was underperforming the market, and its technology division was virtually dormant.[2]

In March 1999, however, the company suddenly burst into the headlines, having negotiated an unprecedented contract with the government of the Hong Kong Special Administrative Region (SAR) to develop a prime parcel of real estate along the relatively bucolic southwestern coast of Hong Kong Island. The $1.68 billion dollar deal entitled Pacific Century to build twenty-five hundred luxury apartments overlooking the South China Sea in exchange for developing Cyberport, a facility on the same site that would aim to lure leading Internet companies to Hong Kong with new high-tech facilities, which would be made available at below-market rents. The government characterized the project as an economic development initiative that would bolster a sector of the local economy that lagged behind other Asian counterparts, such as Singapore and Taiwan. Hong Kong property developers saw it differently, however, noting the close business ties between the

SAR's chief executive, Tung Chee-hwa, and Richard's father, Li Ka-shing.[3] Conventionally, government land sales in Hong Kong are subject to an open bidding process, but in this case the deal was sealed before competitors were even aware the land might be available.

Pacific Century was moving on another front as well, buying up a small electronics distributor in an apparent effort to secure a "backdoor listing" on the Hong Kong stock exchange. Securities regulations require that any company seeking a listing must first report two years of profits before applying for membership on the exchange. Lacking such a track record but urgently needing capital to feed its Internet aspirations, Pacific Century took over Tricom Holdings and renamed it Pacific Century Cyberworks. This new technology company would assume a leadership role in developing the Cyberport facility, but, even more ambitiously, Richard Li announced in August that PCCW would mark the arrival of the new millennium by launching a pan-Asian broadband Internet service. Claiming that it would "utilize the television structure world-wide to deliver new types of Internet services," Li envisioned a satellite-cable delivery system for text, sound, and imagery, operating five hundred times faster than the average household modem. Driven by advertising and subscriber fees, PCCW anticipated that the service would reach 110 million cable homes within two years, making Hong Kong a hub of e-commerce and digital content development. Backing the venture was the estimable Intel Corporation, investing $50 million in Cyberworks stock.[4] No doubt that endorsement, along with the Li family imprimatur and Richard's astounding success with Star TV, conspired to grab the attention of investors, causing PCCW stock to soar from $.06 per share to $.42. As it took off, Richard began to escalate the tempo of his deal making, announcing a series of Internet investments and joint ventures across the Asian continent at a rate of roughly one a week.

This flurry of activity received extensive press coverage, and by midfall several competing property firms in Hong Kong announced Internet ventures of their own. As one media executive gushed, "The reality is that the real estate world in Hong Kong is past."[5] With billions of dollars moving from bricks and mortar to clicks and portals, press coverage further fueled the flames of this new passion. Feature stories began to appear naming Richard Li—now attired in khaki slacks, a casual shirt, and a buzz haircut—as one of Asia's movers and shakers of the digital millennium. Having shrugged off conservative business suits and briefcases for geek couture and daypacks, Richard, a Stanford alum, assiduously stoked the presumption that he was linked to the soaring economy of Silicon Valley. Feature writers furthermore suggested that he, unlike his older brother, eschewed the gilded path laid out for him at Hutchison Whampoa and instead plunged back into the media world, again focusing his energy on the most speculative frontier in the field of communication. "There are some things that just put a smile on your face," Li told one reporter. "I like media. I like the people, I like their attitudes, I like the pace, I like what it can do, I like how it changes society."[6] Touting the prospect of digital convergence, Li sought to bring broadband technology to households across Asia. Again playing the visionary, Li exuded the confidence and daring of some of his California counterparts. "When people focus on only one piece of what we are, they just don't get it," he declared. "We're operators, but we're also a totally integrated Internet play, with an infrastructure side, a service platform and [a venture capital] incubator, all of which converge to make each other more valuable."[7]

By January 2000 the market capitalization of PCCW soared to $18.3 billion, an increase of 3,284 percent in only twelve months, making it even more valuable than Amazon.com, one of the darlings of the online economy in the United States.[8] In 1999, *Forbes* magazine ranked the Li family as the tenth richest in the world, and by January the following year the *Economist* estimated Richard's paper worth alone at some $12 billion.[9] Although estimates of Li Ka-shing's wealth varied little during this period, approximations of Richard's fortune fluctuated wildly with the most recent news of his venture capital investments in digital start-up companies. Likewise, the size and value of PCCW itself seemed difficult to gauge. The *Wall Street Journal* identified it as the seventh largest company in Hong Kong on the basis of market capitalization, but financial analysts were quick to note that virtually all of this worth was based on expectations of future performance.[10]

As Cyberwork's chief negotiator and CEO, Li kept making deals at a blistering pace, some of them concluded in a matter of minutes. Spurred on by the soaring expectations of investors, Richard seemed driven to live up to the expansive vision of the future that he deployed in PCCW's public relations puffery. Nevertheless, the pace of expansion, which was frenetic even by Hong Kong standards, did raise some concerns. "The challenge," observed Jay Chang, Internet analyst for Credit Suisse First Boston, "is to keep the ship in one piece as it goes 500 miles an hour. They will have to make sure there are no icebergs around."[11] With Richard moving ahead briskly into uncharted waters, one sensed an eerie similarity to his previous satellite TV venture, and although he repeatedly declared that PCCW was modeled on America's Excite@Home interactive service, one could just as easily see the venture as Star TV redux. Like Star, PCCW would use satellite distribution and local cable systems to reach most of its households, requiring expensive technology upgrades as well as the cooperation of some ten thousand cable operators and hundreds of government regulators, many of them wary of two-way broadband communication. Also like Star, PCCW would need to prove that its content could draw tens of millions of households to a service with a premium price tag. At the time, broadband services in the United States were having difficulties attracting American consumers, causing some critics to ask why Asian households with lower incomes would spring for the expensive new service. Moreover, PCCW's top managers, many of them veteran's of Richard's Star TV venture, were well aware that elite audiences dispersed across Asia were not large enough or cohesive enough to support an advertising-driven network. Eventually, Cyberworks would need to reach out to the masses if it was to become profitable. Furthermore, the service would have to charge subscriber fees, again requiring extensive marketing infrastructure on the ground and cooperation from local and national government officials. In the words of Simon Twiston Davies, CEO of the Cable and Satellite Broadcasters Association of Asia (CASBAA), "Network infrastructures are only as strong as their weakest link," and Richard's ambitious new media network clearly had more than a few weak links.

For example, PCCW would not be able to draw on existing content providers, such as BBC and MTV, since they already had developed their own Asian brands. It would instead need to develop its own programming, placing it in direct competition with companies such as News Corporation and TVB. Accordingly, PCCW amassed a war chest of more than $500 million in venture capital and by January 2000 had taken an equity interest in nearly thirty Internet start-up companies, most of them content producers. Moreover, Richard Li announced that his company would itself become a leading creative enterprise by establishing a production operation ambitiously titled Network of the World. Whether content-related or infrastructural, the complications outlined above would need to be addressed quickly, because competitors would inevitably crowd the marketplace, and investors would soon grow impatient waiting for PCCW to turn a profit.

Company executives nevertheless appeared both optimistic and unflappable, perhaps never more so than in February 2000, when PCCW announced a $28 billion takeover bid for Hong Kong Telecommunications (HKT). A cornerstone of the local economy since its founding in 1874, HKT enjoyed a 90 percent share of the local fixed-line phone market, with annual revenues of $3 billion. Specializing in what is referred to as POTS (plain old telephone service), the company was renowned for its "gentlemanly" corporate culture, which emphasized elegant system engineering as opposed to glitzy marketing or visionary experimentation. Owned by Cable & Wireless, the telecommunications monopoly that once stitched together the British Empire, HKT was more caustically characterized by financial analysts as a bloated, lumbering monopoly that was confronting the prospect of deregulation and rapid technological change. Most worrisome, it was now facing a host of low-cost competitors for its international calling services, which once represented some 70 percent of the company's total income, a figure that was expected over time to fall to as little as 40 percent.[12] Nevertheless, financial analysts agreed that the company had elements that Richard Li sorely needed: a network infrastructure with access to three million Hong Kong homes, an existing Web portal, and $4 billion of annual revenue. In other words, HKT had a *delivery network* and *paying customers* at a time when PCCW seemed to have little more than smoke and mirrors. Moreover, if PCCW could remake HKT in its own image, the operation might serve as a showcase for what Richard envisioned on a continental scale. "I want to create something like Sony," explained Richard, "not in terms of manufacturing products but creating something that is innovative, makes money, improves people's lives."[13]

First, however, Cyberworks needed to outmaneuver a rival suitor, Singapore Telecom, a company whose colonial pedigree and future prospects were very similar to those of HKT. In the face of government deregulation, both telephone monopolies were seeking to refashion their organizations with an eye toward value-added services and international ventures that would take up the slack of their diminishing returns as local POTS. SingTel executives, in presenting their bid, claimed that their ample size and cash flow could allow the merged companies to grow in new directions. Indeed, valued at $60 billion, the proposed merger would at a stroke create Asia's second-largest telecommunications firm and the world's sixth-largest carrier of international calls.[14] Talks between the two companies had been under way for several months when suddenly out of the blue PCCW intruded with its own offer in mid-February 2000.

Richard Li's seemingly brash maneuver, however, had a more complicated backstory relating to the apparent resentment that some members of Hong Kong's business elite felt about the incursion of a Singaporean interloper. For more than a decade, the two former British colonies competed fiercely in shipping, finance, and real estate. SingTel's bid for HKT reenergized these competitive anxieties, but, perhaps more specifically, it made some wonder if Singaporean executives might favor their homeland in the design and operation of a postmerger telecom network. Such preferences could prove influential, since the two cities were competing to become re-

Richard Li meets with reporters, extolling the virtues of PCCW's bid to take over Hong Kong Telecommunications in 2000. Courtesy South China Morning Post.

gional communication hubs. Although inchoate and difficult to gauge, these concerns were amplified by reports that Chinese government officials were quietly expressing reservations about SingTel, a company run by the son of President Lee Kuan Yew and 90 percent owned by the Singaporean government. Since HKT was already hatching plans for expansion into mainland China, some PRC officials took a strategic interest in the fortunes of the company. Moreover, with state-owned China Telecom holding 11 percent of HKT—which entitled it to a seat on the board of directors that would be evaluating the competing bids—government sentiment could not be ignored. It was therefore not surprising that the state-owned Bank of China and HSBC (Hong Kong's largest financial institution) cast their lot with Richard Li, putting together a consortium of banks to fund a $12 billion bridge loan that would form the cash component of the takeover offer. Within a matter of only two weeks, PCCW mounted a $38 billion bid, a feat that should have required months, even years, to assemble. This exceedingly nimble performance was perhaps as much attributable to the discreetly expressed concerns of Hong Kong's corporate and government elite as it was to the financial skills of Richard Li and his colleagues.[15]

At the last minute Rupert Murdoch threw a spanner into the works, however, offering to invest $1 billion in support of the SingTel offer, a move that some perceived as a personal swipe at Richard. More probably it was a defensive maneuver to protect the interests of Star TV, since the company was on the verge of rolling out high-speed Internet access, video-on-demand, and a fifty-channel pay-television service via the HKT network.[16] Star, which then enjoyed only limited access to households in the lucrative Hong Kong market, had formed a joint venture with HKT in 1999 to provide a set of services that were strikingly similar to those now being touted by PCCW. The HKT-Star venture was well under way when Li stepped into the picture, and Murdoch might justifiably have seen Richard's bid as a spoiler of his ambitions. Indeed, given the similarity between the two services, Murdoch had reason to believe that he would be elbowed aside should Li's bid for Hong Kong Telecommunications succeed.

When comparing the two offers, SingTel appeared to be a more reliable partner with an established customer base and a regular cash flow. PCCW, on the other hand, offered the glamour and seemingly limitless potential of the new digital economy. Furthermore, its bid appeared to be favored by the Chinese government, a factor that might prove influential during deliberations. While the Cable &Wireless board was reflecting on the merits of the merger proposals, market observers and social critics in Hong Kong began to reflect on the implications of a PCCW buyout. On the one hand, Li's company seemed to be a loopy Internet play based more on promise than on performance. "Richard's game is a confidence game," observed Stephen Brown, a financial analyst who knows Li Ka-shing personally. "He's had to sell his ideas, whereas his father sold property." Referring to the elder Li's up-by-the-bootstraps career, Brown continued, "K.S. Li knows what it's like to be making plastic flowers. I think that always stays with you, [but] I think it's impossible for the U.S.-educated second generation to feel that."[17] Indeed, to some critics, Richard seemed to be defying conventional wisdom, and they wondered if his aggressive entrepreneurship at PCCW was intended to send a message to his father and to the investment community that his success with Star TV was anything but a fluke. From Richard's perspective, he and his staff had *earned* their first fortune by building a satellite television service that was visionary for its time. And now, even though some might envy the doors that opened for him because of his famous family name, Richard insisted that his vision and energy were the foundational elements driving the astronomical growth of Pacific Century Cyberworks. So intent was he to step out of his father's shadow that Richard refused to speak about the elder Li in public forums or news interviews. Whenever the subject arose, he would brush the topic aside, declining to use the "f-word" (*father*, in this case) in public. On one occasion he half-jokingly told a reporter that other than the "chip on my shoulder the size of a railroad tie," he had no comment on his relationship with his father.[18] Yet, others had plenty of comments on the topic, and since so much of PCCW's value rested on the reputation of its CEO, speculation regarding the Oedipal dynamics of the Li family did not seem entirely out of place.

Still, it was difficult for many to imagine a decisive split within the clan, given the interlocking economic interests of the family. Pacific Century Group collaborated on numerous business ventures with Cheung Kong and Hutchison Whampoa throughout the 1990s, and Li Ka-shing even came to the aid of Richard's company when two of his ventures hit rocky shoals. Clearly, father and son communicated and cooperated, even if their personal relationship was strained at times. And although Richard may have wished to make his mark, it was difficult for him to chart an entirely independent course, given the elder Li's extensive holdings in shipping, real estate, utilities, energy, banking, retailing, and telecommunications. It was for precisely this reason that some critics viewed the PCCW-HKT merger with concern. As Hong Kong moved into the future, would the Lis control the digital economy as well? Critics estimated that after the HKT takeover the family's diverse enterprises would account for as much as one-third of the Hong Kong stock market's total capitalization of $600 billion.[19] Social commentators were further riled by the elder Li's 1999 complaint about politicians spoiling the investment climate by advocating democratization of local government.[20] Li Ka-shing clearly had the power to influence the SAR's economy with the wave of his hand, and he seemed willing to use that power in his own interests. Closely linked to the increasingly unpopular Tung Chee-hwa—Beijing's hand-picked chief executive of the SAR—Li Ka-shing was losing his luster as the Horatio Alger of Hong Kong capitalism and instead beginning to loom as a threat to free speech and free enterprise. The sweetheart deal that Richard negotiated for the $1.6 billion Cyberport only helped to fuel speculation that links between Li Ka-shing and Tung Chee-hwa were helping to pave Richard's way to a position of dominance in the digital economy.

Such criticisms failed to sway the C&W board, however, for it voted to accept the PCCW offer and notified a jubilant Richard Li that he now had bricks and mortar to serve as the foundation for his cyberaspirations. After a company celebration that lasted into the wee hours of the morning, Richard surprisingly appeared in the office at 7 A.M. and only three hours later announced yet another coup: a strategic alliance with Legend Holdings, the largest computer manufacturer in China. "We just have to keep going," Li told a *Newsweek* reporter. "I think we are at the very small beginning of a new revolution."[21] Such exuberance might in retrospect be forgiven, since many businesspeople around the world were at the time acting on comparable suppositions. Only two months earlier, Steve Case blazed a new path in the American media world with AOL's startling takeover of Time-Warner, a deal that was strikingly similar to the HKT buyout. With cyber-enterprises starting to colonize their larger, more conventional counterparts, financial analysts began to refer to the "weightless economy" of the digital era, suggesting that market behaviors now seemed to defy the laws of gravity.

Yet Internet stocks were already starting to feel pressure from fairly conventional forces. As with bubble economies that had accompanied earlier technological innovations, such as railroads and radio, the dotcom expansion of the 1990s was driven by investor expectations regarding future profitability and broad-ranging social change. Consequently, the adventures of Hotmail, Yahoo!, and eBay achieved legendary status, and the leaders of such firms became renowned visionaries who ruminated on a wide range of social issues while continually pointing toward a speculative future. Just as the railroads spurred the emergence of agribusiness and radio fostered the growth of mass advertising, so too would digital technologies create future opportunities that were difficult to anticipate. Investors seemed willing to dream along, while overlooking short-term concerns about customers, revenues, and price-to-earning ratios.

Exhibiting all the characteristics of a bubble economy, the dotcom era was nevertheless distinctive in that many companies had business plans that called for them to monopolize their respective sectors through "network effects," which refers to a service that becomes the standard in its market, much as DOS became the dominant software standard for PCs or Hotmail became the standard for free e-mail service. In such cases the value of one's service multiplies with the addition of each user, growing in geometric rather than arithmetic proportion. For example, each new seller that brings a product to eBay for auction enhances the value of the service both to buyers and to other sellers, creating a spiral of growth as eBay becomes an ever more robust and expansive marketplace. Moreover, references to a weightless economy made it appear as if the reputedly immaterial nature of the Internet were opening the door to new patterns of social and economic interaction. Embracing this philosophy, PCCW proclaimed that it would become *the* portal for a wide range of online interactions throughout Asia, from banking to shopping to entertainment. And, therefore, by servicing a substantial share of the Asian population, it could become the most valuable network in the world. Yet, like the business plans of its counterparts, PCCW's strategy suffered from numerous flaws.

First among them is that not all companies succeed at establishing themselves as the standard bearer within their markets. For every success like Hotmail's, dozens of other e-mail enterprises failed, and, even in the case of Hotmail, its success stemmed in part from the fact that the owners sold out to Microsoft at a propitious moment, thereby avoiding the fate suffered by Netscape, the Internet's first graphical browser, an innovation that seemed destined to dominate the World Wide Web until it ran into crushing competition from Microsoft Explorer. In other words, preexisting market leaders don't yield their advantage easily. Instead, they tend to adopt the innovations of emerging competitors and put them to use in their already existing networks. While Richard Li shuttled about Asia, stumping for his new broadband service, Star TV was quietly putting in place very similar technologies and working in collaboration with an already existing base of cable operators and satellite TV subscribers. And when, at the last minute, Rupert Murdoch cast his lot with the SingTel takeover bid, it was a not-so-subtle indication that he understood the competitive threat posed by PCCW and was willing to take action to defend his position in the Global China market.

Second, although the immateriality of the Internet was considered one of its most dynamic aspects, it is important to recall that tangible hardware and hard-earned institutional collaboration provided the foundation for the system itself. The U.S. government invested tens of billions of dollars developing the infrastructural backbone of the Internet as well as the software protocols that made "internetworking" possible. These investments were not value-neutral; indeed, the government first conceived of the Internet as a military necessity and later as an economic development tool. Contrary to the claims of the neoliberal digerati, the Internet was as much a product of social policy as it was a product of individual genius. By comparison, Richard Li lacked such a system to exploit. Instead, PCCW would need to mobilize thousands of cable operators and telephone companies and would have to comply with hundreds of different government technology standards and regulations if he were to succeed transnationally in Asia. It was a daunting challenge, very much unlike the comparatively coherent hardware network and software protocols that made internetworking viable in the United States.

Third, PCCW presumed that household media budgets were relatively elastic, when in fact many Asian consumers have been cautious about media expenditures, as is amply demonstrated by the experiences of i-Cable and Star TV, as well as by the pervasiveness of video and computer piracy. For example, consumers will generally opt for a cheap handful of VCDs rather than an expensive pay-TV movie channel. Moreover, PCCW's broadband service would prove to be especially difficult to market, because one of the big attractions of digital media was the diverse content the Internet provided at relatively low or no cost. A proprietary broadband service would therefore need to deliver *exceptional* content and services if it were to alter the consumption patterns of Asian Internet users.

This brings us to perhaps the most fatal flaw in PCCW's strategy: Li's failure to understand that although some Internet enterprises have succeeded as portals or conduits, most of them have done so because they deliver compelling content to their customers. Developing such content is a tremendous challenge for new media entrepreneurs. During the early years of any new medium, artists tend to experiment with innovative expressive forms while also drawing on successful styles and genres used in previously existing media. For example, the variety shows of early radio in the United States drew from the performance conventions of vaudeville, and situation comedies in early television were inspired by the domestic comedies of network radio. To be sure, "new" forms of information and entertainment, such as reality TV and the television news magazine, emerge from time to time, but they invariably draw on representational practices from existing genres. The key for any new medium is to appropriate popular conventionals from competitors while also exploring the distinctive opportunities offered by new technology.

Perhaps with this in mind, Li launched Network of the World (NOW) through PCCW in July 2000 from a west London studio, promising to spend $1.5 billion over five years in developing fully interactive entertainment and commerce over a broadband network. To blaze the trail, Li tapped Michael Johnson, the one-time Hollywood executive who played a central role in the development and launch of Star TV. Charged with creating "killer content" for PCCW, Johnson set up shop in London rather than Asia, explaining that he wanted to locate the NOW studio in a city that was perceived as a global trendsetter. London has "edge," he told one reporter, "young edge, fashion edge, young cutting edge. Hollywood comes here to get design ideas."[22] Tapping that pool of creative energy, NOW began to roll out a host of new services, including a channel devoted to unknown musical groups offering free downloads of their songs; a video gaming channel featuring tournaments among players from the universe of NOW subscribers; and an agricultural channel running infomercials about seeds and farming equipment aimed at rural audiences. Plans for a vaunted sports channel took longer to develop, having hit some snags in negotiations over sports rights, many of which were already sewn up by competitors such as ESPN and Star Sports. Undaunted, NOW executives declared they would develop distinctive content that would unlock the potential of broadband communication. NOW "has nothing to do with TV," explained Richard Li. "We think TV is so cheap. TV is such a commodity now, so easy to produce, so intellectually unchallenging."[23] Yet in the end, NOW proved to be little more than a TV service with an affiliated Web site, and given the lack of broadband customers in Asia, it was likely to stay that way for some time. Rather than offering an exciting new world of interactive online communication, NOW seemed like warmed-over Star without the content, prompting wags to refashion the basis of the network's acronym as "No One is Watching."

Richard Li nevertheless continued to cast about for other sources of programming, signing a joint venture with the ERA conglomerate of Taiwan and taking an equity interest in Star East, an upstart Hong Kong studio that lined up a stable of Chinese pop stars by offering each an equity interest in the company. Star East was launched by Charles Chan, a Hong Kong property developer who hoped to score exclusive contracts with leading pop stars so that he could cycle their talents through the company's Internet portal, providing audiences with access to film, television, and musical performances, as well as to online merchandise, concert bookings, and fan clubs. Furthermore, it was hoped that the star-studded Web site would promote Star East's restaurants and nightclubs, creating a synergistic package built on the appeal of pop icons such as Leon Lai and Anita Mui.[24] Widely perceived as an attempt to monopolize creative talent in Hong Kong, Star East began to have problems operationalizing its vision, which in turn undermined the enthusiasm of performers who had signed on with the service. Never quite off the ground, the service sputtered out before it could build a viable business, and its misfortunes became part of a larger trend.

Throughout 2000, dotcom stocks began to falter, and the NASDAQ exchange hit its peak in March before it began to spiral downward, picking up speed in 2001 and dropping to a low water mark in the wake of the attack on the World Trade Center in the fall. During that stretch, most new enterprises burned through their venture capital and ceased operation without ever posting a profit. Likewise, the telecommunications industry found itself in a sorry state, since the strategies of many leading companies had been predicated on the expanding demand for bandwidth. Leading telecom executives had used the surging digital economy as justification for massive investments in fiber optic cable. Indeed, it was commonly believed at the time that network traffic would rise exponentially, and one legendary CEO, Bernie Ebbers of WorldCom, flatly declared that network traffic would double every hundred days for the foreseeable future, a prediction that proved horribly mistaken. In the telecommunications industry, WorldCom not only led the way up, it also led the way down, collapsing in July 2002 from the weight of its overinvestment in network capacity.

Given the structure of the newly merged PCCW-HKT, the company suffered reversals in both the digital and telecom industries, amassing losses of $886 million in 2000 and resulting in the collapse of the PCCW share price, which fell to less than 10 percent of its peak value, making it the worst-performing stock on Hong Kong's Hang Seng index.[25] PCCW was not alone, however, for Internet stocks around the world suffered similar meltdowns. Yahoo! shares in the United States plummeted 88 percent, and Softbank shares in Japan dropped 90 percent.[26]

In the midst of this decline, a minor scandal erupted in March 2001, when it came to light that Richard Li had not in fact graduated from Stanford with a degree in computer engineering but instead had left at the end of his junior year. After a tumultuous few days, Li publicly admitted that PCCW's public relations staff had inadvertently spawned the error and that he had been remiss in not correcting it. "I was in a rush to go to work for an investment bank, so I didn't finish my course," he said.[27] Nevertheless, the brouhaha that surrounded the disclosure was perhaps less motivated by a concern about Li's education than by a larger concern with the excessive amounts of spin frequently deployed by his lieutenants. If Richard was not in fact a Stanford graduate, what other questions might be raised about his corporate biography or even about PCCW itself? The company had characterized Li as an independent young man during his Stanford years who preferred a part-time job as a golf caddie, McDonald's cashier, or Swenson's ice cream scoop (take your pick) to the dreaded thought of turning to his father for extra allowance. Li's vaunted independence was part of his entrepreneurial mystique and part of the reason that the HKT takeover was not perceived as a surreptitious maneuver by Li Ka-shing's corporate octopus.

According to PCCW spin, Richard Li, unlike his older brother, had been his own man since the day he left Stanford. He reportedly moved out of his father's house only months after returning to Hong Kong, seeking to make his way with Star TV rather than being sequestered at Hutchison Whampoa under the tutelage of the elder Li's management staff. As the fortunes of Star grew, so too did the legend of Richard Li. Lavish press coverage characterized the twenty-six-year-old as a seasoned executive who followed his Stanford career with additional training at Harvard University and the London School of Business before a four-year stint in the world of investment banking at Gordon Capital in Toronto. Press accounts at the time suggested that Li had crammed an exceptional number of professional achievements into a twenty-six-year lifespan, all topped off by colorful anecdotes about his expertise as a jet skier, scuba diver, and airplane pilot. Of course, résumé padding was perhaps the least of it. More significant was PCCW's effort to cultivate and promote Richard Li as a legendary figure of the next generation in Asian capitalism. At the time of the Star TV sale, for example, stories circulated that Richard, dressed in a dark suit and sincere tie, rode out to the Murdoch yacht in an inflatable dinghy and boarded the vessel with grim determination to exact a premium price for the enterprise. Five years later, however, the story had morphed into the tale of the debonair young CEO helicoptering in for a dramatic tête-à-tête with his Australian counterpart. As one former staffer commented, "He loves to play up the wonderboy image about how he was helicoptered on to Murdoch's yacht, blew smoke in his face and hammered out the Star deal in a couple of hours, but the fact is there'd been bankers and lawyers negotiating for months. He's got a very good PR machine, they're good at corporate myth-making."[28] Yet even the spinmasters were at a loss once Cyberworks began to unravel and the whole venture seemed instead to be a cautionary example of rampant greed and corporate sleight of hand. A survey of executive pay in Hong Kong showed that, in 2001, PCCW directors were rewarded with $100 million in salary and other benefits, despite two years of dramatic losses.[29] Even more galling, the report came to light when the company began to announce layoffs of HKT personnel, eventually shedding more than a fifth of its workforce.

Throughout 2002 it became clear that PCCW was quietly but dramatically changing course. NOW and Star East both fizzled, and most of the company's Internet executives departed. Instead, the firm's focus shifted to debt refinancing and to the core telecommunications business while Richard receded from a position of prominence to become "something of a misfit in his own company."[30] No longer the bold Internet visionary, Richard tried to find a place for himself, investing his energy in real estate and telecommunications ventures in the mainland and leaving operational management in the hands of executives from Hong Kong Telecommunications. Reflecting on this change of course, Li told a reporter that, although shareholders want vision, they also "want to see your earnings, they want to see your cash flow, they want to see that your debt is manageable." These things now became the focus of the company and of a more sober Richard

Li. "'It's interesting,' confided Li with a wry smile, 'I declined to work at a conglomerate and I ended up with something similar.'"[31] Of course, Li ended up with much more, including a fortune worth an estimated $741 million, while investors in PCCW racked up record losses.[32] Moreover, the company continued to falter when the core fixed-line telephone business stagnated and PCCW sold off many of the growth-oriented parts of the business in order to service the massive debt it had assumed during the merger. Rather than blazing a trail into the digital future, PCCW was now little more than a plain old telephone service, and not a very profitable one at that. Finally, in June 2003, Richard Li stepped down as CEO, handing the reins of the company over to Jack So, the highly regarded chief executive of Hong Kong's Mass Transit Railway Corporation.[33]

The parallels between Richard Li's storied careers at Star and PCCW are, with the exception of their final chapters, quite striking. In both cases, he seized a first-mover advantage and traded on his family name in order to bring together investors and suppliers for media plays that were long on ambition and rhetoric and short on tangible infrastructure and results. Unlike his father, who made his first fortune manufacturing plastic flowers, Richard was a pitchman riding the global wave of venture capital that engendered the last two speculative market bubbles of the twentieth century. Both Star and PCCW entered the market with great fanfare, targeting their products at high-end consumers. After failing to generate adequate revenues, they then turned their attention to mass audiences, who in the case of Star have so far responded lukewarmly and in the case of NOW did not respond at all. Like his counterparts in Taiwan, Richard discovered to his surprise that even in wealthy households, consumers are cautious with the resources they devote to media products and that compelling content and operable network systems must be put in place in order to attract paying customers. At the time that Richard began PCCW, Star was already in the early stages of building a satellite television system with viable programming and a technological infrastructure that could attract paying subscribers. The notion that PCCW could leapfrog this endeavor and put in place a transnational broadband, interactive network strained credulity. As with his success exploiting the stratospheric rhetoric of satellite TV, Richard shrewdly traded on the speculative fever then gripping the Western and Japanese economies, arguing that he would bring the wonders of the digital economy to Chinese markets. Systematically stoking his legendary status as a brash young product of Silicon Valley, Richard inspired investors and imitators as well as the wealthy real estate barons of Hong Kong who tried to reinvent their own enterprises in Pacific Century's likeness. As the competition intensified and the trading grew ever more frenzied, few seemed to be looking back at the constellation of deficiencies in Star TV at the time that Richard unloaded it on Rupert Murdoch: a lack of verifiable market data, a shortage of local and national advertisers, and a lack of technological infrastructure. Even fewer seemed to grasp that at the very center of that constellation was the absence of compelling content crafted with an awareness of the audiences who might actually make use of the service.

Richard also exploited the bias among Chinese entrepreneurs toward infrastructural investments that create high barriers to entry by competitors. PCCW portrayed itself as the first mover that would set the industry standard, creating a cash cow destined to dominate media markets throughout Asia. The company's frenzied deal making furthermore fostered the impression that a grand alliance was being assembled that would lock in a privileged group of suppliers and investors. Richard seemed to believe that PCCW was uniquely positioned to establish cartel arrangements that would shape and constrain the production and circulation of the next generation of media products. What he failed to grasp, however, was the importance of establishing a creative enclave in Asia in which screen stars and creative artists might flourish, further attracting like-minded souls and setting the stage for a revival of content production in commercial Chinese media. For without lively and imiginative content, even the most powerful media cartel seems destined to falter.

12　From Movies to Multimedia

Connecting Infrastructure and Content

Although this is an age of changing technologies and corporate conglomeration, it's fitting for us to return to where we began, the Chinese movie business, which, like its Western counterpart, is the locomotive for the commercial entertainment industry in Asia. Feature films deserve special attention because they are singular media events with a very narrow time frame in which to succeed. Movies are hailed as triumphs or failures within the first two weeks of release, requiring intensive promotional campaigns. Moreover, the distinctive artistic challenges posed by feature filmmaking and the concerted publicity efforts behind such projects are reasons why most actors and directors aspire to the big screen. Indeed, a successful feature film can turn an actor into a star and a director into an auteur, fully anointing them as marquee attractions that will draw the attention of even the most reluctant moviegoer. In the world of Chinese popular entertainment, singers, writers, and TV artistes often migrate to the medium, seeing it as an important career move that can elevate them into the pantheon of topflight talent, along with such megawatt stars as Stephen Chow, who started his career in television, and Sammi Cheng, who began as a singer.

Feature films furthermore shape perceptions of media industries as a whole, since good movies signal that a creative community is thriving, which in turn helps to attract audiences, investment, and new talent. The movie industry is therefore central to Hong Kong's pretension as the capital of the Chinese entertainment world and crucial to its ability to tap creative labor from such far-flung locales as London, Beijing, and Kuala Lumpur. Finally, Hong Kong movies represent a point of strategic convergence among the increasingly interconnected media industries. Feature films can drive TV syndication deals, provide core programming for video and cable services, attract Internet traffic to a Web portal, and bolster the careers of singers and other performers. Yet the patina of spectacle, quality, and distinction so necessary to the Chinese movie business had worn thin by the end of the 1990s, and a discourse of reform started to sweep the industry when executives and artistes began searching for ways to revive a storied cinema with an uncertain future.

In March 2000, such reflections permeated conversations in the lobby of the Harbour Front Hotel during the opening week of the annual Hong Kong International Film Festival. At first glance, one can't help but wonder why this particular site was chosen for a meeting of producers and directors from the exuberant and mercurial world of Asian filmmaking. The hotel's ornate lobby with its breathtaking view of the harbor seems more appropriate to a bankers' convention, which is perhaps what the organizers had in mind when they established the Hong Kong–Asia Film Financing Forum (HAF). The event brought together more than one hundred directors and producers to meet with financiers, lawyers, and completion bond agents for two days of intensive discussions about international funding prospects for the industry. With declining ticket sales and the collapse of overseas presales, Hong Kong filmmakers seemed anxious to learn more about new strategies for movie financing and production.

This sentiment was exemplified at a luncheon in the grand ballroom hosted by action star Jackie Chan and director Peter Chan—two of the leading lights of the industry but polar opposites in most every other respect. Jackie had just finished shooting *Shanghai Noon,* which—following successes with *Rush Hour* and *Rumble in the Bronx*—solidified his status as a Hollywood headliner. Peter arrived fresh from his directorial debut in the United States, helming Kate Capshaw's *Love Letter,* a 1999 melodrama that was smothered at the box office by *Star Wars: The Phantom Menace* but nevertheless established Chan's credentials as the first and only Hong Kong director to deliver a respectable Hollywood feature film in the romantic comedy genre. When their arrival was announced, the two Chans (no relation) appeared at the ballroom entrance, Jackie in wraparound, oversized shades, wearing a black Nehru suit set off by a brilliant pink T-shirt, and Peter attired in khaki bush pants and a rumpled military fatigue jacket, his shoulder-length hair and wire-rimmed glasses completing the contrast.

Working their way through the banquet hall, mingling with filmmakers and financiers, Jackie and Peter couldn't have appeared more different, yet the distinctions between them run deeper than appearances. Jackie was raised in a Chinese opera school, where he trained in a traditional art form whose days were clearly numbered. Like many of his counterparts in the 1970s and 1980s, he made the transition to film via the bone-crunching stunt work that eventually drew global attention to the Hong Kong cinema. Peter grew up in Bangkok and Hong Kong, attended film school at the University of Southern California, and, fluent in English, landed a job as an interpreter for a Chinese film crew that was shooting on location in Europe. While still in his twenties, Peter began directing for United Filmmakers Organization (UFO), a production house that during the 1990s turned out popular melodramas pitched at young urban audiences across East Asia. At a time when box office figures were starting to sag, UFO films were credited with bringing mature, cosmopolitan viewers back to the cinema with urbane and witty comedies. In the spring of 2000, Peter again seemed to be riding the crest of innovation in cofounding Applause Pictures, devoted to the production and distribution of pan-Asian films. Given their widely divergent styles, tastes, and backgrounds, the two Chans decided to host the opening luncheon because they believe that it's time for significant change in the Hong Kong movie business.

Throughout the HAF sessions, the message from international funding sources was fairly consistent: filmmakers need to secure insurance and completion bonds if they are to attract international investors. To do that they would have to jettison their seat-of-the-pants style for a more transparent and systematic approach to filmmaking. Whereas Hong Kong projects in the past had been launched before scriptwriting even began, now a completed script had to become the cornerstone to financing arrangements. Whereas presales had relied on informal agreements, films now had to be secured by completion bonds that ensured timely delivery in accordance with specific quality standards. Completion bonds require more meticulous accounting practices; therefore, casual bookkeeping had to give way to daily production reports.

The sessions were well-attended, and private conversations between creative talent and financiers were lively, yet probably more than a few smiles crept across the faces of filmmakers whenever they considered the distance between their local craft style and this dollar-denominated global movie business. As they mentioned in interviews with me, the most distinctive characteristic of Hong Kong cinema during its heyday was improvisation. In that era it was fairly common for cast and crew to assemble on location with little more than a story outline. While the scriptwriter was still scribbling away, actors rehearsed their lines and the director deliberated about camera angles. Advance planning was minimal at best, since the whole point was to make movies, not to *talk* about making movies. Whenever one asks a Hong Kong filmmaker with Hollywood experience to compare the industry in the two locales, the first thing he or she mentions about Hollywood is the meetings—the seemingly endless planning sessions that precede the initiation of a U.S. film, a sharp contrast to the Chinese counterpart. Indeed, during the golden age, Hong Kong films were to Hollywood films as jazz is to opera. Yet in this new era, the ensemble style would have to be refashioned into a more scripted, more "professional" mode of production if the industry was to attract international investment.

Besides informational sessions, HAF also provided an opportunity for producers and directors to talk among themselves about the problems that had beset the industry in recent years. Among the key themes: the Hong Kong film industry had lost touch with its audiences, overexposed its stars, failed to cultivate fresh talent, and succumbed to the temptations of overheated demand. The industry furthermore had grown solipsistic and sloppy at the very moment when the ground was shifting dramatically under its feet. New politics, new technologies, and new trade relations throughout Asia demanded institutional and creative reforms, yet the movie business resisted such pressures even in the face of accumulating evidence that globalization had fundamentally altered the calculus of distribution and exhibition. Although most agreed on the need for change, HAF participants expressed different opinions regarding the direction of change. "To go global, are we going to the West or going north to China?" pondered film critic Law Kar. "Do we go more international in style or more Chinese? Some companies are focusing on mainland China. Others are building alliances among [other] Asian filmmakers. And others are working with the U.S. and Japanese film industries. We are at a crossroads: Which way is global?"

This chapter examines the strategies and operations of three of the most prominent movie studios in Hong Kong, each of them transforming its operations in response to market conditions that are refiguring the spatial geography of Chinese commercial media as well as the linkages and synergies among media. As we shall see, Golden Harvest has stepped back from the movie production business in order to concentrate its resources on rebuilding and expanding its distribution and exhibition operations. Like Shaw Brothers during the first half of the twentieth century, Golden Harvest will expand its theater chains in Southeast Asia, but it will also complement this expansion with the acquisition of cinemas in Taiwan and the construction of multiplex theaters in Guangdong Province of the PRC. Believing that secure distribution and exhibition are the keys to a full-fledged studio production program, Golden Harvest is rebuilding its operations with the aim of becoming the biggest theater operator in East Asia. The China Star studio is likewise concentrating resources on distribution but focusing instead on video sales in the PRC. Although pirated VCDs and DVDs command more than 90 percent of the mainland market, China Star is developing strategies to compete head-on with pirates in hopes of taking away market share from unauthorized retailers and building a brand identity that could pave the way for theater investments in the future. Finally, Media Asia is also extending its distribution network, but, unlike Golden Harvest's emphasis on theatrical exhibition or China Star's focus on video distribution, Media Asia is pursuing a multimedia global strategy that is integrated with the larger ambitions of the eSun conglomerate. Still an active and highly successful producer of high-profile feature films, Media Asia is successful largely because it pays careful attention to promotion and marketing concerns from the very earliest planning stages of any given movie project. It furthermore aims to leverage resources of the complementary divisions in the eSun conglomerate, hoping to realize synergistic opportunities much like its global counterparts, such as Viacom or Time-Warner. All three companies direct our attention to the significant new strategies that Chinese movie studios are pursuing as they refigure the scope, scale, and strategic focus of their operations.

According to Phoon Chiong-kit, managing director of Golden Harvest Entertainment, mainland China is currently the most tantalizing opportunity for the Hong Kong movie industry. Phoon, an investment banker who specializes in corporate restructuring, arrived atGolden Harvest in 1998, shortly after the death of Leonard Ho. At the time, assessments of the overall health of the company varied widely, with rumors circulating that Golden Harvest was teetering on the brink of insolvency and one former employee confiding that the company's books "were a mess." Some speculated that Raymond Chow might sell the studio or at the very least restructure it. Indeed, Phoon was called in to build a firewall around profitable core assets while reorganizing and refinancing the debt-ridden ancillary enterprises. Taking stock of the declining fortunes of Chinese movies in markets such as Taiwan, Phoon decided Golden Harvest needed to cultivate new markets. Quietly shifting attention from production to distribution, Phoon expanded the company's theater operations in numerous countries, including mainland China. Although the PRC may in the long run prove to be an especially promising market, Phoon remains cautious for a number of reasons.

The PRC maintains tight restrictions on its domestic film industry, even though most government-owned studios are languishing as a result of censorship, piracy, low movie attendance, and the disappearance of state subsidies. Since mainland studios aren't producing many films and the number of imports is limited to fifty government-approved movies each year (twenty of them classified as big hits and the rest a mix of relatively obscure titles), one of the biggest problems PRC theater managers confront is the limited supply of new movies, which in turn forces them to run films for longer stretches. Since movies make most of their money in the first three weeks, these longer runs depress box office revenues, making it difficult for theaters to meet their overhead costs, let alone make a profit. As a result, many theaters have closed in a country that is already dramatically under-screened. It is estimated that the PRC has only twelve hundred theater screens nationwide, 80 percent of them in a state of disrepair.[1] As for the operators who remain in business, they do so by underreporting ticket sales so that they can pay lower revenue splits to distributors. Nevertheless, Phoon believes that improvement is possible over the next ten years. "Let's be realistic," he confides. "All the cinemas in China are stealing me blind on my films. But China is a big place. If we can find partners [to build and operate theaters of our own], we can change the situation."

The key, says Phoon, is to develop multiplexes in the major urban centers of eastern China, such as Shanghai, Beijing, and Guangzhou. "If you go to these cities, you will see that every time a modern multiplex cinema opens up, ticket sales go up. There is demand for good, modern facilities. The second thing that happens is that demand shifts from all the other cinemas in the city to the new multiplex, which takes in a disproportionate share of the box office." Phoon believes pent-up demand is substantial. In 2004 alone, mainland box office revenues rose by 60 percent (to $185 million), surpassing Hong Kong's total ($111.5 million) for the very first time. Analysts expect revenue to climb steeply for the foreseeable future, projecting annual ticket sales of more than $1 billion before the end of the decade.[2]

Such projections have encouraged Golden Harvest to focus its energy on building theaters in key locations, but this strategy is also influenced by the impact of piracy. "I can't compete with pirated DVDs," concedes Phoon, "so I'm going upmarket," a tactic that has worked well in Malaysia despite rampant video piracy in that country. "There will always be people who appreciate a big screen, big sound, and are prepared to pay for it," he declares. Phoon is furthermore optimistic about the likelihood of regulations in the mainland loosening over time, making it easier for Hong Kong investors to operate there. One indication of this is the 2004 Closer Economic Partnership Agreement (CEPA) between the PRC and the Hong Kong SAR, which among other things aims specifically to assist thecity's moribund film industry. In 2003 Hong Kong produced only seventy-seven films, compared with the more than two hundred films produced annually during its heyday, and its filmmaking workforce was down to four thousand, compared with more than ten thousand employed during its peak years. CEPA now allows the territory's film companies privileged access to mainland markets by removing import quotas and fostering coproduction opportunities. Similarly, Hong Kong investors can now take a 70 percent interest in PRC audiovisual companies and a 90 percent ownership share of mainland theaters.[3]

These reforms should have a significant impact on Hong Kong studios, especially since their Hollywood counterparts don't enjoy such access. When Golden Harvest first invested in a Shanghai multiplex in 1997, the arrangement went sour over differences with its local partner regarding box office reporting practices and film rental agreements. Other foreign investors, such as Warner Bros. and UA Theaters, experienced comparable problems, and as a result the emerging wave of joint-venture theater projects suddenly began to stall in the early 2000s. By 2003, Phoon was thoroughly frustrated with management at his Shanghai theaters and thinking of pulling out of the PRC entirely, but with the adoption of CEPA Golden Harvest did an about-face, since it now could take a controlling interest in mainland theater ventures, thereby ensuring transparent management practices. Shortly after CEPA was negotiated, Golden Harvest announced construction on a new twelve-screen, twenty-four-hundred-seat multiplex in Shenzhen and detailed plans for a chain of theaters in nearby Guangdong Province. Majority ownership and direct supervision will allow Golden Harvest to control release dates and orchestrate promotional campaigns for each movie. Computerized ticket sales will provide an accurate accounting of box office receipts, making it possible to gauge the popularity of particular films and to track the effectiveness of promotional campaigns. Moreover, unlike the circumstances of his company's earlier partnership in Shanghai, Phoon is determined to control the hiring and training of theater managers and employees.

Yet the PRC represents only one prong of Golden Harvest's exhibition strategy. It has also expanded its stake in Malaysia, where it now commands 85 percent of the total box office; Singapore, where it has a 50 percent market share; and in Taiwan, where, in autumn 2004, the company joined two Taiwanese partners to buy out Warner Village for $19.1 million, thereby securing a 45 percent market share.[4] With annual ticket sales in Singapore, Malaysia, Taiwan, and Hong Kong now totaling more than $350 million, Phoon expresses satisfaction that his company has become the leading exhibition chain in Chinese markets outside the mainland, with a total 318 screens. Golden Harvest is also a leading distributor in these markets, handling both Hollywood and Chinese movies. Phoon would like to complement this profile with significant growth in the PRC and is exploring the prospect of using new technologies to deliver films to Chinese audiences around the world. "Previously, we physically delivered [film] prints to theaters in neighborhoods with concentrations of Chinese-speaking people all over Asia. Now we've got the Net, which can show six Chinese cooks working in Johannesburg the same film on the same day as the guy in Singapore or Hong Kong watching on the big screen. Within ten years, when I have my big release at Chinese New Year, I could envision that in Singapore some people would be watching in the theater because they like the big screen, the comfy seats, and it's part of a social occasion, but there might be another family at home watching on a fifty-inch flat plasma screen and someone else pulling it off the Net."

All of this positions Golden Harvest for the anticipated revival of Chinese movies and a reentry into the field of film production after several years on hiatus. In 2002, Golden Harvest chose not to go forward with its typical slate of twelve to fifteen productions, preferring instead to scale back its movie-making ventures until exhibition issues could be resolved in the PRC and video piracy problems addressed by governments throughout the region. During the interim Golden Harvest has cautiously positioned itself as a lending institution, offering financing to film producers in exchange for "first money" returns and the right of first refusal on the film's distribution. Phoon says this allows him to keep track of the pulse of the creative community without risking capital. No doubt that strategy will ultimately change as a result of the company's substantial and growing stake in theater chains in Chinese markets. As Steve Kappen, general manager of Village Roadshow, pointed out in chapter 4, the Warner Village multiplex chain is persistently searching for alternative titles, both to show on its ninety-three screens and to use as leverage in its negotiations with Hollywood distributors. Put simply, the reality is that major theater chains in Asia require far more movies on an annual basis than Hollywood can provide. Golden Harvest executives are well aware of this problem, but the question is, when and how to jump back into production?

Phoon claims it doesn't make sense to produce a small handful of movies each year, dismissing that strategy as a casino player's fantasy. Instead, Phoon wants to be the house, spreading his bets and regularizing his return. Accordingly, Golden Harvest won't return to hands-on production until the time is right to launch an annual slate of movies, much as it did throughout the 1980s and 1990s. At that time, according to production chief David Chan, Golden Harvest would produce five to eight big-budget films specifically for the school holidays—Chinese New Year, Easter, summer, and Christmas—and another seven or eight medium-budget films for the rest of the year. Once the pipelines are in place and distribution is more secure from piracy, Golden Harvest executives say they will be back in the thick of Chinese filmmaking, based either in Hong Kong or abroad or both.

Although Phoon is resolutely keeping his focus on *Chinese* audiences, he's also aware that some filmmakers are playing to an emerging pan-Asian audience. For example, director Peter Chan joined forces with director Teddy Chen and producer Allan Fung to set up Applause Pictures, a company that specializes in financing and distributing films to "chopstick cultures," as they call them. Applause is trying to capitalize on a growing interregional flow of movies among such territories as Korea, Thailand, and Taiwan. In part, the venture is a response to the recent popularity, for example, of Korean films in Singapore and Thai films in Hong Kong. Yet it's also based on the presumption that a transnational youth culture is becoming a powerful factor in media markets throughout East and Southeast Asia. Phoon concedes the viability of such pan-Asian strategies, but he's more cautious. "Cultures are meshing, and it's happening at a tremendous rate," he observes, "so I agree with Peter and Allan, but remember, they are coming at it from the standpoint of the producer. On the other hand, I'm the company. I look at this situation and ask, what is my greatest strength? I look at it and I say that my greatest strength remains in Chinese film. I will distribute Korean films or Thai films or anything, but I need to keep a focus. In managing this reorganization for Golden Harvest, I need to define a very simple objective for my people, and that is to make us the leading player in Chinese-language multimedia entertainment. In five years' time or ten years' time, when I've built my network, I can pump other products through it, but I have to move in one direction first. I can't be everywhere at the same time."

Phoon acknowledges that overall his is a very conservative approach, but he believes that the Chinese movie industry has a long way to go before it can revive its fortunes. "The culture of the industry is such that change is very difficult. The entire industry is very localized, very family. You could compare it to the old days in Hollywood when the moguls ran the studios. You can change it when times are good, but when you are running into a storm, it's not easy to accomplish." On the one hand, Phoon believes the industry has to modernize and globalize its operations, while on the other he believes it must continue to nurture its distinctive connections to the storytelling conventions of the past and the cultural affinities of the audience. Golden Harvest's future therefore relies not on mimicking Hollywood or selling out to a global media conglomerate but rather on the extension of its leadership in Chinese theatrical markets, the revival of its film production business, and the development of a global distribution system for Chinese entertainment. Phoon perceives the company as a long-term institutional player that must embrace global practices while sustaining its distinctive identity as a leader in Chinese commercial cinema.

Since the 1990s, most small movie producers in Hong Kong closed up shop because of difficulties with financing and distribution, and once the easy money from overseas presales disappeared, so too did the triad producers, moving on to more lucrative scams. Those at the helm of the movie companies that remain see the industry as weathering a down cycle and are positioning their businesses for what they believe will be an inevitable reversal of market conditions. These companies also remain because they are managed by people who are passionate about movies. Interestingly, one of those passionate survivors is Charles Heung, the son of Heung Wah-yim, the head of Sun Yee On, perhaps the largest triad society in Hong Kong. Despite his familial ties, Charles vehemently denies that he or his company, China Star Entertainment, has a triad affiliation. Moreover, many of the filmmakers and actors who have worked for him claim that he has a genuine commitment to cinema, even if his family background associates him with troublesome aspects of the industry's history. When Charles and his brother Jimmy first set up an independent production company in 1984, they, like many triad producers, focused on securing contracts with some of the biggest stars of Chinese cinema, including Anita Mui, Jet Li, and Stephen Chow. Yet, unlike other producers with triad associations, Charles Heung developed a reputation for treating performers with respect and for sheltering them from pressures exerted by some of the shady characters in the industry. Indeed, Heung benefited from the widespread presumption that creative talent who worked for him would be duly protected. During the early 1990s, China Star provided top stars a haven that coincidentally helped to build the company into one of the leading studios, producing such major hits as *God of Gamblers* and *Fight Back to School*, which featured megawatt actors, such as Chow Yun-fat, Andy Lau, and Stephen Chow, and included bit parts for Charles himself.

Heung's reputation flourished throughout the 1990s while he set up a film distribution company, built a spacious studio in nearby Shenzhen, and expanded into television production, much of this financed through public stock offerings. Yet, by 2000, Heung realized that the Hong Kong movie business was deteriorating rapidly, and he therefore recruited Johnnie To, one of the territory's most prominent directors, to lead a new filmmaking unit dedicated to the revival of commercial Chinese cinema. Like Golden Harvest, China Star agrees that the mainland market holds tremendous promise, but the most immediate challenge is to restore the confidence of local moviegoers. "We have to win back the Hong Kong audience first," To says, "and that's why we began with local movies, especially comedies."

Like most industry players, To recalls the 1980s audience as primarily made up of multigenerational families who appreciated hybrid movies that mixed genres and cultural references freely. During the 1990s, when teens became the primary theatrical audience, filmmakers appealed to them with heroic action films about cops, gangsters, and warriors. By 2000, the theatrical audience took another turn as young women rose to prominence, filling a void left by teenage boys, who migrated to video games and pirated DVDs. According to industry executives, young women in their twenties attend films as part of a social occasion, either with friends or partners, and their tastes are decidedly different from their younger male counterparts. "I know that outside Hong Kong, people want our studios to make more actions movies," says Johnnie To, "but we know that in Hong Kong what works at the box office is comedy. Many of the most successful films have comic appeal: love stories, light comedies, that sort of thing. We're working on films like *Needing You* and *Love on a Diet*. We're also doing some dramas and action films, but for right now at least half of our theatrical releases are comedy." Comedy seems a safe bet, since the genre trades on star appeal and therefore generates a great deal of free publicity in the Chinese entertainment press. Indeed, both of the films mentioned above proved exceptionally popular, in large part because of the on-screen chemistry of pop singers Sammi Cheng and Andy Lau. Moreover, the films moved easily into the mainland video market, since light romantic comedies evoke few concerns among government censors. And they were relatively immune from Hollywood competition, because they rely heavily on the star appeal of two very popular singers, both of whom have toured extensively in core Chinese markets.

Although Johnnie To's strategy succeeded at bringing local audiences back to the theater, his larger ambition is to grow the company's presence in the mainland video market. "We cannot risk a lot of money promoting movies for theatrical release, because if people don't go to them, we lose money," he observes. "But if you take the same film and distribute it through various video outlets over the course of ten years, you might make a good return. Same movie! And often times these are quality movies. The fact is that [nowadays] people have a choice as to where they want to watch movies. When we interview audiences, we find that some people only go to the movies once a year or maybe not at all. How do they see movies? VCD!" He gasps in mock surprise, shakes his head, and knocks the ash off his cigarette. "It's okay," he smiles. "The important thing is to keep making movies. Who knows what will happen in ten years? Maybe then the big market for movies will be over the Internet."

Unlike Golden Harvest, China Star is focusing on video by crafting output deals with Star TV and by aggressively developing a video distribution infrastructure in the PRC, with offices in eighteen cities across the country. Ironically, company executives believe some of their most viable prospective retailers are video pirates, who are now faced with intense competition and diminishing profit margins. China Star made overtures to them, because, according to Charles Heung, "they have very good distribution networks in place, but it was all small shops. We are helping them to get into the supermarkets and the department stores. They like that, because it gives them big face. We just signed a deal with Carre Fore, the French department store chain. It used to be that you went into their stores and they had only that much," he says, pointing to the south wall of the conference room, which runs about twenty-five feet, "and it was all Hollywood movies. Now," he enthuses, waving his hand toward the four walls, "this much space is all video, and that much [an entire wall] is all ours." Heung says that, in addition to growing the size and location of its offerings, his staff trains local distributors how to develop in-store displays, how to organize the shelves, and how to promote the product. "It takes time," he says. "You have to build a network of distributors, and you have to win the confidence of the audience. So when they go shopping, maybe they buy some vegetables, or maybe they shop for clothes, but they also see the video display and say, 'That looks interesting.' No big deal. Almost every family that has a television also has a VCD. For us, the challenge is to create the buying habit, to put our videos in every home."

China Star has dropped the price of its authorized videos to twelve yuan, only a few yuan more than the pirated version and well within the reach of middle-class household budgets.[5] Heung explains that another big challenge is to time the release of a new video so that retail shelves are fully stocked on the very same day that each movie premieres in the theaters. "We know that the pirated copies will hit the market shortly after the premiere or even before. We have to beat the pirates to the customers, and we need to make sure there's plenty of product available to the retailers." Heung believes that staggered release windows simply don't work in the current market environment and that video audiences are usually different from those who go

China Star CEO Charles Heung is attempting to build a video distribution network in the People's Republic of China. Author photo.

to the theater as a part of night on the town. Moreover, with the current shortage of theaters, Heung contends that China Star must for the time being focus on building its brand identity in preparation for the day when theatrical exhibition becomes more viable. Although China Star was expanding into TV, music, and nightclubs during the boom years of the 1990s, Heung's current strategy is far more cautious and calculated. Producing six to ten medium-budget movies a year, he says he is ready to increase production as the distribution infrastructure matures, something he believes is inevitable, even though the timing is uncertain.

Executives at other studios express similarly guarded optimism about the future of the movie business in the PRC. One source explained that although some top-ranking Chinese officials continue to resist market liberalization, many film and TV personnel are doggedly pressing for reform. "The hardliners have been losing ground since the late 1990s," according to this source, "but they still have influence, especially over propaganda and culture. And right now, reformers within the government are busy with other things and don't want to fuss about media, leaving it to the hardliners." Nevertheless, outside the ruling cliques and outside Beijing, pressure is mounting, and it's coming from theater operators and movie distributors who believe their industry is jeopardized by current regulations. But change may take time, since the ministries that deal with media are some of the most conservative and bureaucratic. "You have to understand that within the civil service in China, the Ministry of Culture does not get the best of the crop," explains one movie executive. "The best and the brightest go to the ministries that are most progressive—the Ministry of Finance, the Ministry of Trade, the Ministry of Telecommunications—then heavy industries, and then you go down and finally you get to the Ministry of Culture. In the top ministries, the way that you advance is by coming up with a bright idea and pushing forward some sort of reform. You try to really change the world. You take over an ailing state industry and you turn it around. In the Ministry of Culture, the way that you advance is by keeping your head down. They got where they got by being survivors, by not taking risks. In [that ministry], there's a regular cleaning up. Whenever there's a backlash, the heads that stick up are the ones that get chopped off."

This institutional conservatism is compounded by the ideological caution of the very top Chinese leadership. Although somewhat cosmopolitan, top government officials express sincere concern about cultural pollution, especially from Hollywood, which they believe trades in sex, violence, and familial disarray. "That's one part of American life that they don't want," says one executive. "And they truly, truly believe that the American media machine is responsible for propagating this lifestyle. In that regard, they cite chapter and verse from a lot of prominent Americans. They say, 'Even thoughtful Americans don't want this, why should we?' Their idea of the perfect world is something like Singapore, where markets are liberal, but the social order is much tidier. Now of course Singapore is a much smaller place, and it would be hard to [achieve] in a vast country like China, but it's still something that they fervently hope for."

PRC censorship presents something of a quandary for Chinese film producers who are trying to appeal to audiences in cosmopolitan urban centers like Singapore, Taipei, and Shanghai, as well as Tokyo, Toronto, and London. For the very same textual qualities that tend to appeal to cosmopolitans tend to generate concern among mainland officials. Such conflicts are made ever more complicated by the lack of a film category system in the PRC, so all movies must be approved for a broadly defined general audience. By that standard more than 50 percent of the titles produced by Hong Kong and Hollywood fail to pass muster, which means the films must be edited if they are to have any chance of gaining approval. Targets for censorship include satire, social taboos, and violence as well as movies with ghosts or criminals as major characters, all of them elements for which Hong Kong movies are renowned. Although deliberations regarding the establishment of a movie rating system are currently under way, progress has been slow and uncertain. Accordingly, many movie executives argue that, despite the potential upside of the PRC market, one shouldn't grow too dependent on it. Far better, they say, is to nurture a transnational strategy that targets urban audiences in the mainland along with a mix of other territories worldwide.

Media Asia tends to follow this approach, focusing on event films that play well throughout Asia. In the late 1990s, it scored a number of hits with splashy action titles, some of them coproductions with U.S., Japanese, and Singaporean film companies. Founded in 1994, at the very moment that the Chinese movie business was beginning a downward spiral, Media Asia was first among the Hong Kong studios to set up a multipicture development fund that established a revolving pool of financing that could be deployed over a five-year period to launch the studio's core projects. This alone was something of a revolution, and soon Golden Harvest, China Star, and Meiah followed suit with their own funds. Moreover, Media Asia amplified the value of this strategy by tapping resources from coproduction partners and by altering the production planning process, giving less weight to input from overseas distributors who had previously provided crucial financing through presale agreements. "We wanted to go back to pleasing the audience before we pleased the dealer," says Wellington Fung, one of the founding partners, "because if the audience is happy, the dealer will be happy."

In 1997, Thomas Chung took charge as CEO, saying he was determined to change not only the company's films but also its promotion techniques. "In the old days, people would simply produce a film and let go of it to the presale market. From 1997 on, I wanted to produce a better-quality movie and take control of the destiny of our films in the Asian marketplace. I wanted to set up distribution offices so that we could take control of what the movie poster would look like, to determine which screens we would release to, and to decide when and how we would release it to video. We wanted to refine the process from the ground up." It was an ambitious agenda, given the industry's continuing decline and the fact that, like other independent producers, Media Asia did not operate its own chain of cinemas. It did, however, run a substantial distribution business, managing a library of film titles for Star TV.[6] Thus the company that Chung took charge of in 1997 had the essential components of a major studio, operating both production and distribution divisions. The challenge then was to develop creative projects that would complement the activities of the distribution division.

The film that established the company's brand identity was *Gen-X Cops*, a movie about a group of ne'er-do-well young officers that are recruited by a gruff and wily superior to take a dangerous undercover assignment against a gang of terrorists. As one producer put it, "It's a remake of *The Dirty Dozen* with teenage pop idols and lots of explosions." Chung acknowledges that the film used a proven generic formula, but he contends it was also a pathbreaking production in a number of respects. First of all, it incorporated high-quality special effects, which at the time were rarely used in Chinese movies. Unable to find what he wanted in Hong Kong, the Media Asia CEO flew to Hollywood and hired an effects house to craft the climax of the film: a showdown between the young cops and terrorists at the Hong Kong Convention Center, nestled on the harbor front in the heart of the financial district. Chung and other local filmmakers knew that it would be extremely difficult to get permission to shoot an elaborate action sequence there, but a special effects sequence might do the job, if it were high quality. Anything less would be derided as cheesy, especially since the convention center is a well-known landmark to audiences throughout East Asia. In fact, Chung grew so enthusiastic about the concluding sequence that shortly before he flew to Los Angeles in November 1998, he decided to double his order. "Joe Viscoza built a model of the convention center, and we blew it up one morning [for *Gen-X Cops*]," Chung recalls. "Then in the afternoon of the same day, we blew up a miniature of another building for another movie, *Purple Storm*, months before we even shot the movie. That's how determined I was to change the look of our films, to make them appear grander and—even though I don't want to say it—to make them look more like the Hollywood movies that our audiences have embraced."

Given this penchant for special effects, Chung could ill afford the salaries demanded by Hong Kong's leading actors, and so he decided instead to develop fresh talent, such as Nicholas Tse, Sam Lee, Stephen Fung, and Daniel Wu. Since the release of *Gen-X Cops*, all of them have gone on to become popular performers, but at the time, Media Asia was venturing into risky terrain. Chung's strategy developed partly in response to the flight of big name Chinese stars to Hollywood, such as Chow Yun-fat and Michelle Yeoh, but it was also a response to the escalating cost of marquee talent who remained in Hong Kong. During the early 1990s, as overseas presale revenues rapidly escalated and as the number of productions increased, topflight actors demanded higher fees, sometimes as much as half the cost of production. By the late 1990s, Chung had decided it was better to use the money for high-tech special effects and cultivate rising young actors instead.

Media Asia followed a similar strategy with its next major film, *Purple Storm*, casting Daniel Wu for a part that was originally slated for Tony Leung. "I simply did the arithmetic and realized [his salary] would take up too much of the budget," recalls Chung. "So I thought, rather than having Tony Leung, why don't I put the money into marketing Daniel Wu?" Furthermore, Wu's persona offered a distinctive angle, since he is a multilingual, multicultural overseas Chinese. As film critic Winnie Chung puts it, "Media Asia signed a whole bunch of young ABCs (American-born Chinese), BBCs (British-born Chinese), and CBCs (Canadian-born Chinese)—bilingual, young, cosmopolitan—and they are going for topics and stories that can travel. *Purple Storm* is the type of story that can happen anywhere, here, Japan, Europe. It's not especially local, nor especially Chinese." Indeed, Media Asia was aiming for action films that could travel across national boundaries and across media formats—from theatrical to video. "We have to consider long-term profit," explains Wellington Fung. "Even though we invest more money making action films, the market [for these films] is eventually bigger, and the life cycle of the action film is very long. So when we are talking about the subsequent asset value, these are films that can travel to Africa, to Chile, to somewhere in Iceland—we sold a film to Iceland! [By comparison], romantic films tend to be very domestic, where you have different cultures that have different values about emotions, relationships, and family."

Under Chung's leadership, Media Asia self-consciously positioned itself as a producer of movies that were no longer tied to the traditional Hong Kong audience. Fighting against declining theater revenues and increasing video piracy, the company decided that it needed to produce event films that would draw audiences to the theater, regardless of language or ethnicity. If the traditional markets like Taiwan no longer generated reliable revenue and if prospects in the mainland remained uncertain, company executives reasoned that Media Asia would have to present itself as a truly international studio that provided a low-cost alternative. "We deliver all the ingredients you expect from a Hollywood film," says Wellington Fung, "and we do it less expensively, which is what gives us a chance to compete with Hollywood. Before, Hong Kong films played to a niche market, and that's why you could see the local flavor, because it was purely for domestic viewers. But once it comes to the point that you need bigger revenue to compensate for bigger production values, then you need a bigger audience, and then it becomes less specific, less like a traditional Hong Kong movie." Indeed, the golden age of Hong Kong cinema that has been widely hailed by critics and fans was premised on a distinctive cultural moment in a particular locale.

When that moment passed and the production and distribution practices of that era began to erode, studios such as Media Asia began looking for new formulas for success.

Although the studio was modestly successful throughout the late 1990s, its original investors began to go their own ways, and in 2001, Peter Lam, the son of a wealthy real estate and apparel mogul in Hong Kong, offered to take a controlling share in the company and fold it into his emerging media empire, eSun Holdings, a venture that had been hatched in the midst of the dotcom fever. No stranger to the world of media, Lam and his father owned ATV in Hong Kong for over a decade, losing more than $100 million trying to turn it into a viable competitor with TVB. Toward the end of the 1990s, the Lam family sold its controlling interest in the station but maintained a minority stake while venturing into the world of digital media and multimedia promotion. At a moment when both the media and the real estate industries were under siege, Peter Lam assembled a company portfolio that included artist management, concert promotion, publishing, local television, and Internet services. eSun was also promoting East TV, a proposed satellite service and studio complex, the latter to be constructed as part of a casino resort and convention center that is slated to break ground in 2007 at an estimated cost of almost $2.6 billion.[7]

Widely known for his nocturnal adventures in the nightspots of Hong Kong and for his friendships with media celebrities, Lam is angling to build a multimedia enterprise that hinges on star promotion, a clear departure from Media Asia's previous emphasis on splashy special effects and low-budget young talent. The company's first project under Lam, *Infernal Affairs*, featured two of Hong Kong's most famous leading actors. "Peter thought that because Andy [Lau] and Tony Leung hadn't acted together since a TV series they did in 1989, it would be a good promotional angle," recounts Wellington Fung. "Then he thought, why not put four award-winning actors together? So Anthony Wong and Eric Tsang were added. Then the production team and the marketing team said, 'Well it's kind of old, how about some young faces?' And Peter said, 'Okay, how about Edison Chan and Shawn Yue?'"

Although the cast of *Infernal Affairs* seemed ambitious by the standards of a depressed film industry, slick production values and energetic promotion turned it into a major hit locally and then, surprisingly, in other territories as well. Centering on a complicated story about a triad infiltrator inside the Hong Kong police department and a police mole inside a triad gang, the script allowed the actors to develop complex characters and relationships on screen, an attribute that received heavy promotion in the local media, es-

Wellington Fung at Media Asia headquarters. Behind him is a poster featuring Andy Lau *(left)* and Tony Leung *(right)*, flanking their costars in the enormously popular *Infernal Affairs*. Author photo.

pecially in media that were part of the eSun family. Budgeted at $5 million, the movie furthermore made extensive use of promotional tie-ins and product placements, which amplified the production and marketing budgets considerably. With the film grossing more than $7 million at the Hong Kong box office and performing strongly in Singapore and Malaysia, the producers also were able to market a video version in mainland China by shooting a final scene in which the infiltrator inside the police department is uncovered and arrested, thereby pleasing government censors. The film furthermore performed well in Japan and South Korea, and, noting its popularity, Warner Bros. bought the remake rights for close to $2 million, recruiting director Martin Scorsese, Matt Damon, Jack Nicholson, and Leonardo DiCaprio to the project and retitling it *The Departed*. Media Asia then followed *Infernal Affairs* with a successful sequel and prequel and has consistently ratcheted up the budgets of subsequent tentpole projects. In the summer of 2005, for example, it released *Initial D*, a $12 million manga-inspired street racing drama starring Taiwanese singing sensation Jay Chou. Designed as a movie with regional appeal, *Initial D* raked in more than $16 million during its first three weeks, including a remarkable $7 million at mainland theaters. Media Asia then launched three more projects with even bigger budgets, lots of star power, and marquee directors Johnnie To, Andrew Mak, and Feng Xiaogang.

Still, Nansun Shi, who developed the business plan for Media Asia after the eSun takeover, says that despite the success of *Infernal Affairs* and *Initial D*, the company has no single filmmaking formula. Yes, it will use its artist management services and its worldwide concert promotion business to cultivate star power for its feature films, and yes, it will expand its distribution activities in the PRC, but it will also produce a diverse array of projects with an eye to exploiting a catalog of more than three hundred titles that are marketed through broadcast, cable, and video exhibition windows as well as theatrical venues. The winner of close to one hundred film awards since its founding in 1994, Media Asia is nevertheless a very commercially driven company that integrates market calculations into every project. Such was the case, for example, with *Naked Weapon*, an English-language action drama shot in the Philippines employing a multicultural cast. Conjured up by Media Asia distribution executives when they were trying to package a number of films for non-Chinese markets, the movie is premised on a simple concept, "very sexy girls kick ass," which they believed would dovetail with a particular batch of Hong Kong movie titles. Although never released theatrically, *Naked Weapon* still served its purpose as part of a video packaging strategy aimed at the international market. Such strategic flexibility is an important component of the company's attempt to manage the complexities of the Global China market.

"You can't say, 'I'm going to develop our [PRC] operations and forget everything else,'" declares Nansun Shi. "With *Infernal Affairs*, from day one we knew that it could not be a mainland coproduction, and we would not be able to get theatrical distribution in China, but still it made commercial sense for Hong Kong, Singapore, and some other places as well. The market is always changing, and with each project you have to take into consideration your organizational capacity, your staff, your production slate, your relationships with distributors, your position in all the different territories, and of course worldwide trends." The key for Media Asia, Shi explains, is to position its products in the transnational marketplace, carefully exploiting distinctive strengths while avoiding head-on competition with Hollywood. A far cry from the local Hong Kong movie business when Shi first started making films in the 1980s, Media Asia is globalizing its organizational structure and its strategic calculations, but it still has a ways to go.

"In the Chinese market," says Shi, "there are no entertainment companies that think of intellectual property as the core of the business. There's no corporate thinking, no thorough exploitation of themes or characters. Nothing like the way Disney treats *The Lion King*. And it's much more personal, too: Mr. Heung, Mr. Lam, Mr. Chow, the majority holder is one person. There's nothing wrong with that, but there's something wrong with not having a *corporation* that fully operates as a studio over the long term." Indeed, even though Golden Harvest, China Star, and Media Asia are crafting strategies that are increasingly similar to global Hollywood, they remain at their core family enterprises that are tied to the aspirations, status, and wealth of particular clans. Consequently, Golden Harvest confronts a succession crisis with no visible heir apparent, China Star cannot shake free from its triad associations, and Media Asia, though seemingly successful in developing a synergistic conglomerate, could just as easily disappear with the shifting fortunes, or even whims, of the Lam family, whose principal wealth relies on real estate and apparel enterprises.

The industry is furthermore burdened by piracy, which tends to affect B-grade movies far more than blockbusters or small independent films. A strategically distributed tentpole feature film that is simultaneously rolled out in theaters and video shops around the world will still return healthy revenues and oftentimes a profit to boot. Thus, piracy doesn't kill a successful film, and if studios can beat the pirates to the market shelf with superior-quality video copies that are competitively priced, many believe they can still realize a reasonable return. As for small independent films, video pirates generally pay little attention to them, since they don't sell quickly and therefore require complicated inventory management. Small-budget films continue to be made by passionate artists who occasionally break through the clutter to win prominent film awards or score an occasional box office success, but rarely do they face competition from the underground video economy. B-grade movies, however, are prime fodder for the pirates, because audiences now tend to purchase cheap video versions as opposed to seeing them in the theater or purchasing an authorized copy. Until the perception of such films changes and until these revenue streams become more secure, B-movies in the Chinese market will continue to suffer, and as a consequence, the movie industry as a whole will suffer. Piracy of these films will not only cut into urgently needed cash flow but also undermine the creative climate in Hong Kong. As one producer put it, "When Hong Kong was making three hundred films a year, even if most of them were bad films, you learn from them and you grow and you attract creative people to the industry. Now there are very few people working, and there aren't a whole lot of places for young people to break into the business." Thus, the interruption of cash flow from consumers to studios has undermined the reproduction of the movie industry's labor force and interrupted the migration of creative talent to Hong Kong.

On the other hand, the industry is also realizing some positive benefits from the emergence of new delivery technologies. Now that the Lis, the

Koos, the Lams, the Shaws, the Murdochs, and the Krishnans need movies to pump through their satellite and cable systems, satellite and cable rights have become an important component of film financing and marketing. Indeed, Celestial Pictures was founded as a movie channel designed to attract new subscribers to Ananda Krishnan's satellite ventures, and, likewise, Shaw Brothers returned to the movie production business in order to serve the expanding satellite and cable ventures of TVB. Although progress has been slow and sometimes erratic, improved distribution networks, more aggressive strategies for competing with pirates, and massive investments in cable, satellite, and broadband infrastructure are all contributing new revenue streams that may help to revive the industry.

Seasoned executives such as Nansun Shi and Wellington Fung believe the revival of the Chinese movie business depends on the development of organizational structures that strategically exploit the commercial value of a given piece of intellectual property across media platforms and in as many markets as possible. "Before 1992, nobody knew how to assess the value of film rights," recalls Fung. "You might own a lot of films, but back then the rights weren't worth anything. Then suddenly, when Star TV tried to acquire films from Cinema City and Golden Harvest, libraries became an asset." Managing those assets has now become one of the most important parts of the film business. At Media Asia this was the rationale for its original film distribution operation, and later it became the basis for establishing its film-financing fund. In many ways, the origins of Media Asia and the trajectory of its development provide an emblematic example of how the financial, institutional, and creative practices of the Chinese movie business are changing and how, in turn, that refigures the geography of media capital. During the studio era of Shaw Brothers and Cathay, vertically integrated movie companies presided over the technologies of production, reproduction, and exhibition. That is, because these companies controlled the cinema seats and the reproduction of movie prints, they could extend their reach transnationally but nevertheless ensure the return of revenues for reinvestment in further production. The independent era of the 1980s created a similar, though more informal, network of relations, with local theater chains providing seed funding that was complemented by overseas presales. Again, by controlling the reproduction of prints and limiting territorial rights to distribution, the creators were able to ensure a centripetal flow of revenue that could be reinvested in production. The new technologies of cable, satellite, and video initially brought new revenue streams, but in the end they also disrupted control over reproduction (leading to unauthorized duplication and transborder flows) and exhibition (making it possible for audiences to access content through multiple media in locations around the world). The spatial patterns of flow and consumption were therefore radically transformed, and the new Chinese commercial cinema must cope with these transformations by becoming an asset-building operation that aggregates and markets intellectual property through diverse channels to the increasingly content-hungry multimedia services in Asia and beyond.

During the late 1980s, the Hong Kong movie business was renowned for the dozens of small independent producers feeding local theater circuits and shipping products off to distributors in overseas markets. At the time, demand was so great that creative boutiques flourished, since one could focus on the business of making films while trusting others to deliver them to audiences. Pleasing the audience was relatively straightforward, since the viewers that mattered often attended the very same midnight previews in the very same cinemas as the filmmakers themselves. By the early 2000s, the market had grown far more complicated, however. The local mass audience had fragmented and the theatergoing audience was now largely made up of young people, many of them suspicious of the quality of Hong Kong movies and receptive to films from other parts of the world. With attendance declining, piracy growing, and stiff competition from other forms of entertainment, the movie industry confronted not only a creative crisis but also a distribution crisis. As many small production houses shuttered their operations, the survivors in the industry refocused their attention on reforming the distribution and exhibition businesses, believing that Chinese commercial cinema could be rescued only by reestablishing effective conduits of circulation for creative products, which could in turn generate dependable cash flow for reinvestment in production. With this in mind, Golden Harvest is building a prominent theater chain in core Chinese markets, a mode of "up market" delivery that it believes is relatively insulated from piracy and from competing entertainment. China Star is rolling out a video distribution network in mainland China in hopes of recruiting retailers who might capture a share of the burgeoning video market with authorized products made readily available at competitive prices. As for Media Asia, its new corporate owner is folding it into a multimedia conglomerate that seems increasingly aware that core creative content will drive the overall fortunes of its many divisions.

The geographical scope of their strategies varies as well. The PRC, of course, looms large in the calculations of all three studios, but censorship, piracy, and transparency are only three of the most obvious challenges that movie companies face in the mainland market. Therefore, Golden Harvest maintains its core strength in overseas markets while investing cautiously in new PRC theaters over which it can exercise majority ownership and managerial control. Likewise, Media Asia is expanding its distribution operations in the PRC while insisting that it nevertheless conceives of its movie projects on a case-by-case basis, assessing how each film fits within the broader marketing strategies of the company. For example, the *Infernal Affairs* trilogy was developed with an eye on the local market and then leveraged into broader orbits of circulation, whereas *Initial D* was a regional movie from the outset but nevertheless a breakout hit in mainland China. The key to success with both projects was to target specific audiences at the time of financing and conception and to ensure that the marketing and promotional infrastructure was in place to roll out the product in an orderly fashion.

Interestingly, no single narrative formula has been developed for the movies themselves. Comedies, gangster movies, and action films with special effects have all succeeded, but none has come to define the market niche of current Chinese commercial cinema. Instead, producers and directors seem to agree that the most important objective must be to develop movies with familiar faces, compelling narratives, and strong production values and, perhaps most important, to avoid head-on competition with Hollywood products. That means doing what Hollywood doesn't, with perhaps the most obvious example being the local comedies with popular Chinese singing stars. Martial arts movies with flamboyant physical stunts and special effects have now become part of global cinema, and Hollywood, having recruited some of Hong Kong's most talented stunt directors, now turns out movies that appear even more attractive to the action-film fan. Chinese versions today seem to succeed largely on the basis of their ability to tap recognizable stars, legends, and cultural symbols that are distinctively attractive to their audiences. The same can be said for the crime genre, as suggested by the fantastic popularity of *Infernal Affairs* and by Hollywood's choice to remake the movie as *The Departed,* a gangster saga featuring American stars as Irish characters set in Boston. On both sides of the Pacific, sociocultural variation distinguished the conception, execution, and circulation of a story idea that originated in Hong Kong.

Conclusion

Structural Adjustment and the Future of Chinese Media

One of the primary aims of this book is to encourage readers to think spatially about the history and performance of media industries. As mentioned at the outset, a prominent, though often unstated, preoccupation of international media studies is the question of location: Where in the world should we expect to find concentrations of media production? Where in the world do the products of these industries circulate? And what does that circulation tell us about relations of power among various cultures and societies? Initially, international media studies approached these questions through the prism of nationalism, exploring how particular states developed their respective screen industries, achieved positions of prominence in transborder media flows, and influenced the citizens of other states with their cultural output. The Chinese film industry complicated these questions, however, because it has operated transnationally for much of its history.[1] Television has likewise grown increasingly transnational under manifold pressures toward globalization. Yet rarely have scholars discussed Chinese screen industries within a single analytical framework, nor have they considered film and television through the same lens. Instead, separate studies of, for example, Hong Kong television and Taiwanese cinema have tended to prevail.[2] In this chapter, therefore, I will attempt the synthesize the insights gleaned from the various case studies discussed in this book within the broader framework of media capital. I will close with reflections on the concept itself and on the future of Chinese screen industries.

Much like their Hollywood counterparts, Chinese movie companies competed fiercely during the early part of the twentieth century with little government regulation or oversight, allowing the logic of accumulation to play a dominant role during the initial development of the industry. In Shanghai, the Shaw brothers experienced early success, but their Tian Yi studio soon found itself contending with companies that commanded more resources, political connections, and even ties to the underworld, thereby encouraging the Shaws to seek alternative markets in the relatively prosperous and stable territories of Southeast Asia. Like those at the helm of the major American movie companies, the Shaws established an extensive chain of cinemas and fed them feature films produced by their studios in Shanghai, Hong Kong, and Singapore, each of them releasing movies with different emphases and in different varieties of Chinese. Rapidly escalating audience demand encouraged them also to exhibit products by other producers, especially American studios, making the Shaws a significant force in distribution as well as exhibition. This strategy regularized cash flow, established a consistent source of film financing, and gave them competitive advantages over independent theaters and smaller cinema circuits. It also provided the Shaws with a significant amount of leverage when bidding for products from suppliers. Consequently, they enjoyed many of the same advantages as the fully integrated film studios of Hollywood.

The Shaws' enterprises prospered even though challenged by world war, civil war, and, in the 1950s, by the anticolonial independence movements that swept through their core markets in Southeast Asia. With nativist political rhetoric intensifying, however, the Shaws began to reassess their conception of the market, noting especially the swelling populations of Hong Kong and Taiwan, where many mainland refugees settled after the Maoist rise to power. As the topography of Chinese audiences began to change, the competing Cathay theater circuit established a sophisticated studio in Hong Kong and started turning out Mandarin musicals that proved surprisingly popular in diverse markets, suggesting the potential of a pan-Chinese Mandarin cinema.

Shaw Brothers responded by announcing plans for an even grander production facility, Movie Town, but such a substantial investment of resources demanded careful consideration about location. With its cinema circuit headquartered in Singapore, the company was no doubt disposed to expand in situ; however, pressures from national independence movements in Southeast Asia created market uncertainties at the very moment when new opportunities seemed to be arising in Hong Kong and Taiwan. Just as important, Hong Kong had taken in a substantial number of refugee artists from the mainland studios in Shanghai, Guangzhou, and Chongqing, swelling the size of the creative labor force. Furthermore, the city's relative political stability and the colonial government's benign neglect of Chinese media industries provided artistic freedom that seemed likely to endure for some time, unlike the prospects for Singapore or Taipei. Finally, the emergence of Hong Kong as the most important financial center of the Chinese diaspora provided ready access to capital and other commercial resources. This convergence of "chance occurrences"—most of them engendered by forces of sociocultural variation—provided the foundation on which Hong Kong would rise to become the Chinese media capital of the late twentieth century. Like Hollywood during the classical studio era, Movie Town's fully integrated operations represented a coherent managerial response to the centripetal tendencies of production and the centrifugal tendencies of distribution.

Yet, only a decade after Run Run Shaw had relocated to Hong Kong and asserted his desire to build a pan-Chinese Mandarin cinema, he began to shift his attention to television, declaring cinema a sunset industry. No doubt numerous factors influenced his decision, but perhaps most prominent was Shaw's view of television as offering a government-sanctioned domestic media market that was less subject to vicissitudes than the transnational movie business. Exploiting TVB's first-mover advantage, Shaw turned his considerable production resources to the new medium, thoroughly dominating the local advertising market and reaping the benefits of Hong Kong's growing prosperity. TVB's leading position resulted from both Shaw's aggressive marketing strategies and his ability to recruit, train, and manage creative labor. Attracting performers from an array of related cultural domains, TVB became a magnet for talent, fostering a golden age of television programming in the colony.

Interestingly, the Hong Kong movie industry soon recovered from its downturn during the early 1970s and ultimately flourished alongside TV and a growing popular music industry. In fact, the three industries appeared to complement one another. For example, new singing stars would launch their careers on TVB variety shows, grow to prominence in the local music industry, gravitate to starring roles in TV dramas, and then move into the world of cinema. Likewise, directors and writers often began their careers in television only to move to cinema once they had honed their craft and built their creative reputations. Hong Kong therefore flourished as a media capital by embracing television, adopting a mode of disintegrated film production, and agglomerating related industries that nurtured a sizable pool of talented labor, which in turn generated mutual learning effects. The city consequently persisted as an important node of centripetal and centrifugal media flows throughout the twentieth century.

Golden Harvest represented one model of disintegrated film production at the time, whereby independent producers and marquee stars were contracted to provide services on an as-needed basis. The company's prosperity was premised on a robust distribution operation and an increasingly prosperous exhibition business. Golden Harvest exercised creative and managerial control by monopolizing knowledge over the entire cinematic apparatus. Producers knew little about distribution, investors knew little about production, and exhibitors knew little more than the stars, genre, and price of the movies they rented. With Golden Harvest situated at the center, its executives managed the flow of information in order to sustain control and extract profit at each link in the commodity chain. Like its predecessors, the company also became a leading distributor of Hollywood products and, furthermore, established a production office in Los Angeles that allowed it to consolidate ties to the American industry and to overseas financial resources. Golden Harvest nevertheless targeted many of its productions at the local market, attracting talent from the local television and music industries and producing primarily in Cantonese (although subtitled and Mandarin versions were also available for export).

During the 1980s, Hong Kong's increasing wealth and prominence seemed to encourage this tendency toward localization of media products, but the trend was also stimulated by competition among local theater chains. These cinema circuits operated exclusively within the territory and developed a retinue of producers who fashioned films for their local audiences. Neither the theater chains nor the independent producers who served them had ambitions or resources to operate transnationally. Nevertheless, both relied on overseas presale agreements to complement local film financing. With production costs persistently rising, presales provided crucial resources and served the interests of overseas theaters in countries with more diminutive productive capacity. Such aftermarkets enhanced the budgets and the quality of Hong Kong movies, making them ever more attractive to Chinese audiences in Taiwan and Southeast Asia and accelerating the centripetal flow of movie revenues towards Hong Kong.

Although the local film industry flourished, the transnational distribution system never became fully integrated with the production system, allowing Taiwanese independent distributors to wield increasing influence as their contribution to presale revenues mounted. This disjuncture was exacerbated by the emergence of video, cable, and satellite technologies, providing new revenue streams that further swelled the value of territorial distribution rights in Taiwan. Competing fiercely for Hong Kong products, distributors bid up presale prices, making them the largest contributors to movie financing. As a result, the industry spiraled into a cycle of hyperproduction, aiming to please overseas distributors rather than local theater audiences.

The movie business in Taiwan began to experience problems, too, as a result of cartel behavior that discouraged distributors from adapting to changing market conditions. Preoccupied with milking cash cow revenues, distributors failed to adjust to the more diverse and competitive media economy that arose after the end of martial law. They also failed to take sufficient account of emerging gray and black market video sales, which undermined the value of authorized theater exhibition. Consequently, hyperproduction and cracks in the distribution infrastructure destabilized the centrifugal distribution of product and the centripetal flow of resources back to moviemakers in Hong Kong. When the quality of films began to decline, audience demand dropped off as well, and the film industry collapsed, even though audiences still expressed a preference for Chinese entertainment. Hollywood gladly filled the void, coming to dominate Taiwan and other overseas markets and pushing the Chinese movie business into a phase of structural adjustment.

During the twentieth century, the logic of accumulation and trajectories of creative migration influenced the Chinese film industry, fostering a spatial bias toward centralized production and transnational distribution. Hong Kong became to Chinese audiences what Hollywood was to Western audiences. On the other hand, forces of sociocultural variation asserted themselves most powerfully in the realm of broadcasting, in which government services in Taiwan, Singapore, and the People's Republic of China, as well as Indonesia, Thailand, Vietnam, and Malaysia, established tight control over the airwaves and sought to foster native talent as well as the distinctive cultural attributes of their respective societies. State-sanctioned broadcasting institutions clustered talent and resources in the political capital of each country, creating enclaves of national production and circulation.

Even under Hong Kong's comparatively liberal regulatory regime, the government closely monitored broadcasting with the intention of promoting local expression on the airwaves. Within this protected environment, TVB lavished resources and attention on the local market: broadcasting in Cantonese, nurturing local artistes, and following public service standards set by the government. But it also made full use of its resources to outmaneuver its few licensed competitors. Although at arm's length from the government, TVB exercised an effective monopoly over Hong Kong's airwaves, largely because of its sagacious programming and marketing strategies and its control of leading talent. Insulated from local competition, it was nevertheless constrained by regulations that discouraged cross-media ownership and by quotas in overseas markets that prevented it from exporting its programming abroad. Yet, even more tightly regulated systems arose in Taiwan, where the government held sway over a lucrative commercial oligopoly, and in Singapore, where state-run channels wielded monopoly power, providing ideological as well as commercial leadership.

In all three territories broadcasting changed profoundly beginning in the late 1980s. In Hong Kong the population continued to grow wealthier, but the once large and dominant middle class began to fragment, as did the television audience. New media technologies and new entertainment options lured youngsters and wealthier families away from TVB's mass programming. The government further contributed to the trend by embracing cable technology, hoping both to promote competition in the TV industry and to sustain Hong Kong's reputation as a prominent center of the global communication grid, a matter of prime importance to the financial industries.

Not only in Hong Kong but also in countries throughout the region a growing sense of geographical competitiveness became an important feature of media policy toward the end of the twentieth century, while the U.S. and British governments pressed persistently for trade liberalization and the end of the Cold War drew all nations more tightly into the orbit of transnational market forces. This liberalized commercial and media flows among Asian countries, and it also prodded India and the People's Republic of China to develop their television infrastructures and grow their consumer economies. These transformations of the geopolitical landscape, although clearly influenced by capitalist institutions, were also stimulated by expressions of popular will, with citizens seeking reform in societies around the world, beginning with the wave of popular uprisings in 1989. Governments that once emphasized trade protection and internal development now began to stress interconnection, communication, and comparative advantage as crucial factors in the increasingly integrated and re-regulated global economy. These sociocultural forces would ripple through the media economies of Asia, profoundly altering trajectories of flow, patterns of use, and infrastructures of distribution.

For its part TVB found itself responding not only to the above changes but also to a decline in profit growth during the late 1980s. With TVs in every household, a thoroughly saturated advertising market, and a highly rationalized production infrastructure, TVB's growth opportunities in the domestic market were limited. It needed what David Harvey has referred to as "a spatial fix." That is, Hong Kong's leading broadcaster needed to expand its distribution infrastructure and diversify its services if it was to revive profitability. Restricted from pursuing cross-media enterprises locally, the company looked to overseas markets, first with video rental, then cable, satellite, Internet, and a return to film production. From its previous iteration as a locally licensed broadcaster, it increasingly took on the appearance of a transnational multimedia conglomerate, producing and distributing content for both mass and niche audiences in far-flung locales. Executives believed that a geographical extension of the distribution system would make coping with the demise of mass-market local broadcasting possible by cobbling together new transnational niche audiences. This change would involve a respatialization of institutions and flows, a refiguring of boundaries between media, and a reordering of temporal patterns of media consumption. Moreover, it was commonly asserted that this new media universe would represent one of the most dynamic and promising investment sectors of the global economy.

Such media forecasting likewise animated the Hong Kong government's decision to solicit bids for an exclusive license to develop the territory's first broadband cable system. Although two of Hong Kong's leading shipping and real estate tycoons competed to secure the license, neither appeared interested in television per se, largely because of cultural biases against the entertainment industry among the city's elite. Instead they hoped to build a telecommunications network that would provide them with monopoly rents in the new informational economy. Almost reluctantly, the winning bidder—Wharf Holdings—slowly rolled out a cable TV service that grew in capacity and value throughout the 1990s, until at the height of the dotcom bubble it rebranded itself as i-Cable, a seemingly visionary moniker that obscured the company's profoundly conservative market strategy. Rather than seeking a leadership position in television or even telecommunications, i-Cable sought merely to survive long enough to cash in on the fiber optic network it built. The company emphasized infrastructure rather than content, believing that it could master the former but not the latter.

Similarly, Li Ka-shing focused his attention on building a pan-Asian satellite telecommunications infrastructure. Yet it was the company's fledgling content service, Star TV, that captured the imagination of audiences, investors, critics, and policy makers when the nascent platform showered MTV, the BBC, Chinese movies, and Western sports programming on countries across the continent. Seizing the opportunity, Richard Li, who headed the television service, assiduously stoked enthusiasm for Star with a stratospheric rhetoric of satellite TV, suggesting that pan-Asian services like his would have a transformative impact on countries across the region.

Yet Star lacked a government franchise that might protect it from competitors, and its infrastructural advantages were rapidly diminishing while other regional satellites came online. More worrisome, global media conglomerates began looking for gateways of opportunity in Asia, hoping to make use of their considerably greater productive resources and programming libraries. Lacking a creative staff and a substantial infrastructure for content production, Li's first-mover advantage seemed to be shriveling by the day, and he therefore sold Star TV to Rupert Murdoch in 1993, retreating to industries that were more in keeping with the Li family's mercantilist enterprises.

In nearby Taiwan, the cable industry also experienced a consolidation of technological infrastructure, with two leading industrial families, the Wangs and the Koos, grabbing at the potential of new media and using their political connections and financial resources to assert duopoly control over the sprawling and decentralized cable networks on the island. Despite the consolidation of cable infrastructure, content production proved to be fraught with uncertainty, primarily because of the rise of dozens of new cable channels. As TV ratings for each channel migrated into the single digits, production budgets diminished, forcing the former terrestrial oligopolists, such as CTV and TTV, to look to overseas markets and coproduction partnerships in order to sustain their productive capacity. Although they have tentatively extended their geographical reach, all three terrestrials still confront stiff challenges in the domestic market, which continues to diminish the resources available for transnational expansion.

As for the new cable competitors, they too are strapped for resources, given their diminutive audience shares and advertising revenues. By focusing initially on low-cost genres, such as news, talk, musical variety, game shows, and studio dramas, a few successful cable services succeeded by targeting niche audiences underserved by existing providers. Yet these very same genres have proven to be unlikely candidates for overseas distribution, putting limits on profitability and growth. Subject to fierce competition in the local market, most cable services are pressed to increase the size of their audiences by multiplying the number of channels they program and refiguring their target audiences. In some cases this means "putting away the local," as with FTV and Sanlih, so as to pursue larger islandwide ratings, whereas for others it has meant strategizing to refashion their operations as transnational services, as in the case of ERA. Nevertheless, these ambitions to expand have been circumscribed by recurring talent shortages because Taipei has failed to become a magnet for the migration of Chinese talent. Consequently, these shortages along with market fragmentation, limited resources, and political patronage have persistently undermined the accumulation of media capital in Taipei.

In Singapore, television emerged more tentatively from its government cocoon when policy makers prodded the industry toward privatization and overseas expansion during the 1990s. Anticipating the transition from an industrial to a service economy, government planners invested heavily in satellite and cable infrastructure, hoping to expand the country's prominence as a global financial center. This expansion of infrastructure and growing emphasis on a globally competitive service economy necessitated a more open attitude toward transnational communication flows, and the government was therefore pressed to reorganize media institutions, encouraging companies to become more creative and entrepreneurial, to explore new markets, and even to imagine themselves as regional, if not global, players. Yet, many in the media industry and in the population as a whole continue to embrace a more regulated and conservative perspective on the future. Indeed, sociocultural forces, such as institutional complacency and conformity, remain two of the key challenges facing media industries in Singapore. Consequently, coproductions by MediaCorp and Raintree aim to realize strategic market opportunities and furthermore they seek to enhance creative resources and to secure learning effects for a historically insulated industry.

Coproductions have indeed exerted a salutary effect on the Singaporean media, but, like similar endeavors in Taiwan, these in Singapore present their own challenges, since they involve not only a sharing of resources but also a complicated mix of talent and thematic content. Coproductions succeed when the mixture is right, but their attempt to manage sociocultural differences can prove unwieldy. The programs must present themselves to audiences as both local and somewhat exotic, mixing elements from, say, Singaporean and Taiwanese cultures in a single series. Ironically, series with contemporary settings invite closer scrutiny from viewers than programs featuring historical narratives based on Chinese legends or programs that incorporate elements from contemporary non-Chinese societies. In other words, temporal and spatial distance seems to provide an abstract diegetic setting that is acceptable to audiences, but programs fashioned around themes and characters set in contemporary Chinese societies tend to invite closer scrutiny. Therefore, scholarly presumptions regarding the comparative popularity of culturally proximate programming from overseas sources need to be recalibrated to take into account the relative comfort that many audiences seem to feel with exotic products—either spatially distant or temporally removed—compared with products from culturally similar societies. It appears, as Koichi Iwabuchi argues, that programs from abroad are perceived according to their location in the hierarchy of modernity, with audiences embracing shows from societies that represent progress or aspiration rather than those that seem out of step with contemporary trends and fashions.[3] For example, Taiwanese viewers contend that mainland culture seems more foreign to them than contemporary Japanese culture, and Singaporean audiences feel they have much in common with Hong Kong audiences, but Hong Kongers may not reciprocate. In other words, historical and culturally exotic programs appear to audiences as operating within relatively abstract tableaux, while contemporary and culturally proximate TV series exhibit subtle cues regarding the hierarchy of modernity.

Tain-dow Lee and Yingfen Huang have criticized the increasing scale of media institutions, arguing that the most commercially successful pan-Chinese cultural products tend to flatten out markers of local specificity, contributing to memory loss and the amplification of power by dominant commercial and political institutions.[4] On the other hand, one also needs to acknowledge that the rapid proliferation of media companies since the 1980s have, in turn, made it possible for niche products to flourish, since these new competitors must distinguish themselves from their mass media counterparts. While some creative work does indeed tend toward hegemonic abstraction, other products are characterized by their complex specificity aimed at niche consumers. The key challenge for Chinese media is to figure out ways to grow and consolidate institutions so that they can amplify their productive resources and secure their lines of distribution, allowing both transnational and local products to flourish. Companies that succeed transnationally (e.g., TVB), are quite likely to be viable local and niche producers as well (e.g., TVBS).

Of course, Chinese media companies were not the only ones maneuvering to extend their reach in Asia before the turn of the new century. During the 1990s, Western conglomerates also began to position themselves for new opportunities engendered by political transitions, market reregulation, and new technologies. Most attractive was the lure of mainland China, often breathlessly referred to in the 1990s as a nation of one billion consumers. Although still profoundly impoverished by global standards, China under Deng Xiao-ping underwent dramatic transformation as it sought to modernize its infrastructure and economy in the wake of the Cultural Revolution. By the late 1980s, the economy was expanding briskly, as was television ownership. Consequently, Richard Li's inflated promotion of Star TV in the early 1990s was in part stimulated by dramatic changes taking place on the ground. When Rupert Murdoch's News Corporation took over Star, it too had expansive ambitions for the service, but, as we have seen, numerous sociocultural forces—infrastructural, political, and textual—attenuated the centrifugal potential of satellite distribution.

Star TV wasn't the only company constrained by such limitations. Services such as MTV and ESPN also embraced the early promise of satellite technology, hoping to overcome spatial obstacles and achieve expansive distribution without the need to staff local stations or construct terrestrial transmitters. Seemingly immune from government regulation, Western satellite services could offer superior programming that, although foreign, would nevertheless trump the very best that local and national Asian broadcasters could provide. What global conglomerates didn't anticipate was the laborious effort it would require to establish marketing operations on the ground and to secure clearances from government authorities. Nor did they anticipate that local broadcasters would quickly emulate some of their programming and production strategies. Soon they found themselves battling hundreds of competitors in dozens of territories, requiring that they fashion their programs and advertising to meet evolving audience expectations in each particular market. In the end Western conglomerates realized that their Asian satellite services would need to balance production and distribution efficiencies against distinctive local circumstances, accounting for audience tastes, market competition, and stylistic variations. Moreover, they came to understand the multiple affinities of viewers, each of them activated by different temporalities and contexts of media use. In other words, transnational satellite television, unlike Hollywood movies, must insinuate itself into *domestic* settings, where the forces of sociocultural variation seem exert themselves more vigorously. One might occasionally attend a movie with the intention of sampling the exotic, but one lives with television as a part of everyday life at home. One Chinese media executive analogously observes, "I like to go out for a nice Italian meal, but that doesn't mean I want to eat Italian food every day."

Accordingly, global TV services have learned to respond to local tastes and circumstances, a response that in turn has sparked cycles of adaptation among local competitors. This interactive constitution of plural media markets revolves around the self-conscious mixing of global and local artifacts and of popular and traditional genres, with global services bringing superior productive resources to bear and local services tapping their superior cultural competencies. Consequently, panregional satellite TV proved to be only an opening gambit, and over time forces of sociocultural gravity have engendered multiple and prolific media cultures, which have proved to be far more competitive than initially envisioned.

Yet, the heady enthusiasm for new media technologies persisted throughout the 1990s, helping to revive Richard Li's expansive ambitions when he returned to the scene with the launch of Pacific Century Cyberworks in 1999, at the height of the global dotcom bubble. Li quickly cobbled together an ensemble of loosely related enterprises in hopes of establishing the first regional interactive broadband media service. Although Li openly disparaged TV as cheap and uninteresting, his new venture bore a striking resemblance to his previous Star TV service: PCCW traded on the connections of the Li family, asserted its first-mover advantage, and inflated its promotional rhetoric while coming up short on infrastructure and deliverables. With little cash flow or content, the company pitched its services at high-end users before it finally broadened its appeal. Like his counterparts in Taiwan who were also rolling out broadband services at this time, Li found consumers to be cautious with their household media budgets, attracted less by the glitz of the technology than by the functionality of the network and the utility of the content. Racing against rising expectations, PCCW executives were caught up in whirlwind of deal making, seemingly distracted from the mundane demands of core operations. Inspired by Richard Li, other Hong Kong capitalists started to invest in new media opportunities, but few seemed to take note that the lessons of Star TV were repeating themselves in Li's new enterprise: PCCW lacked verifiable market data, reliable advertising revenues, and compelling content. Moreover, Richard showed little inclination to nurture an enclave for creative talent in Asia, preferring instead to locate the production headquarters for his "Network of the World" in London.

In part, Li's failure is attributable to the discrepancy between his mercantilist proclivities and the operational realities of media industries. Although he mastered the art of tapping Chinese financial networks, orchestrating cartel alliances, and riding the bubble of investor enthusiasm, he failed to invest in core creative resources. Not unlike the movie industry bubble of the early 1990s, deal making got in the way of pleasing the audience, so it was no doubt appropriate that at the very moment when PCCW was on the precipice of disaster, the movie industry was struggling to recover the confidence of its audiences and, most centrally, to restore quality to its products.

If the importance of content has dawned on Chinese satellite, cable, and broadband companies, the importance of infrastructure seems to be a growing preoccupation of the movie industry. Golden Harvest, the largest studio, has temporarily withdrawn from production, choosing instead to restore and expand the spatial integrity of its distribution and exhibition chain. Meanwhile China Star is producing movies aimed specifically at Hong Kong audiences, believing that it can channel successful films through the video distribution network it is building in the PRC. Both companies are trying to secure the circulation of cultural products in response to the challenges posed by piracy and market uncertainties. Only Media Asia, which is now part of the growing eSun media conglomerate, seems to be finding success on the creative side, with the rollout of big-budget, star-studded tentpole films that are heavily promoted and channeled through its regional distribution operation. With its emphasis on high production values, sophisticated marketing, and asset management, Media Asia comes closest to embracing the techniques now employed by Hollywood studios. Whether its parent company, the eSun conglomerate, can likewise embrace the synergistic strategies and techniques of its global counterparts remains to be seen.

The most daunting challenge for commercial Chinese media companies, however, may be posed by the talent deficit in Hong Kong. Since the 1990s, Hong Kong's stock of screen employees has been significantly depleted, with the film industry now employing a third as many workers as in the 1980s.[5] Likewise, ATV has suffered significant cuts over the past decade, and TVB, though still the largest employer of screen talent, seems to have lost its creative edge. Cable TV has experienced some employment growth, but i-Cable has relatively modest programming ambitions. Overall, screen industry employment is languishing, and the future seems uncertain. According to one industry executive, "People want to return to the times when Hong Kong turned out two hundred films a year, but in my view, the industry will never come back. Once it has shrunk to a point where there is no longer a core of creative people producing a significant number of movies each year, then everything else starts to shrivel up—the support services, the financing, the training. Everything starts to disappear, and before long the core of the industry is gone, and it's very hard—even impossible—to rebuild it, unless you go the route of Germany or France and decide to subsidize the filmmakers. There will always be some dreamers who want to make films—people with tremendous passion for the art of cinema—and there will always be a few places for them to realize their dreams, but it doesn't have to be in Hong Kong."

While the Chinese screen industries move through this era of structural adjustment, many questions remain regarding institutional transformation and the geographical location of media capital. Hong Kong's creative resources have indeed diminished, but it still retains a relative wealth of creative talent in a variety of media and an experienced cohort of distribution and exhibition executives. Moreover, local capitalists are continuing to expand their investments in media enterprises, led by Li Ka-shing, the bell-wether of the Hong Kong stock market, who has quietly amassed a collection of enterprises under the Tom.com banner. Likewise, a TVB-led consortium of film and TV companies has built an expansive new state-of-the-art production center, and Peter Lam has unveiled ambitious plans for a studio city in nearby Macao. The Hong Kong government has also awakened to the significance of its media industries, seeing the film business as a defining feature of the city's glamour quotient with tourists and seeing electronic media as an important component of the growing service economy. The government is now actively investing in educational programs and financing initiatives aimed at propping up the screen industries, and it has actively advocated on behalf of local companies that wish to expand into the mainland. Having successfully negotiated the Closer Economic Partnership Agreement (CEPA) with the PRC, media enterprises now seem poised to expand ventures in the mainland, especially in neighboring Guangdong Province.

Meanwhile, in Taiwan, the industry remains under heavy competitive pressure. Eastern Multimedia and United Communications have emerged as the dominant cable system providers, and they eagerly anticipate the rollout of digital and tiered premium services, but neither has been able to parlay its infrastructural dominance into creative productivity. Nor have the once powerful terrestrial broadcasters figured out a way to hold on to audience share, and all four are now under government pressure to reorganize their operations and reduce their connections to political parties. Even the most successful new cable services have seen their initial burst of growth begin to taper off, encouraging cost efficiencies in program production. Fragmentation of the marketplace continues to disperse creative resources and undermine the qualitative improvement of programming, especially drama programming, which is the most likely candidate for transnational distribution.

In Singapore, the television market is likewise beginning to follow the tendency toward fragmentation, but the government closely monitors developments in the media industries and has recently intervened in an attempt to consolidate screen resources after a spurt of intense competition between MediaCorp and SPH. Although policy guidance has helped to spur institutional reform, the legacy of authoritarianism engenders a cautious approach to industry restructuring and complacency among audiences and the creative community. MediaCorp has the institutional capacity to pro-

The SAR government has finally awakened to the role that media enterprises play in drawing visitors to Hong Kong. Here, a tourist poses at the Walk of the Stars, Hong Kong's version of the Hollywood Boulevard Walk of Fame. Author photo.

duce prodigious amounts of programming, but whether it has the creative culture to make it a successful regional producer remains an open question.

In mainland China, the film industry is suffering from government censorship and a lack of investment capital. Successful films of recent years have tended to be blockbusters produced by a relatively small circle of directors with international investment partners. Movies with midsized budgets languish, and smaller films tend to play the international art circuit, gaining little exposure at home, since they are less successful at clearing government censorship.[6] The TV industry generates far more cash flow and programming, but among provincial and local stations, whose activities are circumscribed by the national government, ad revenues fail to provide enough income to fund high-quality programming. Consequently, talk, variety, and game shows, as well as other low-cost genres, tend to prevail. With dozens of competitors on any given cable system, success breeds endless imitation, engendering a cloning culture with diminishing returns as other stations follow the leader.[7] Although joint ventures and coproductions have provided some opportunities to break out of these constraints, in 2005 the government announced new restrictions on foreign media that are part of a cyclical pattern of liberalization and retrenchment that discourages innovation. Only the national CCTV networks appear flush with revenue and resources, but because of their headquarters' location in Beijing and their comprehensive national distribution system, their content is closely monitored by government officials. Although pockets of creativity exist and new opportunities for distribution are emerging, Michael Keane explains that CCTV and other big organizations, such as the Shanghai Media Group, remain conservative in their programming strategies.[8] This state-controlled institutional structure, along with the legacy of authoritarian leadership, makes it difficult for new cultural forms to percolate up from the grass roots. Meanwhile, consumers grow more discriminating via exposure to foreign media products through the Internet, unauthorized satellite channels, and black market video goods, all of which invite comparisons to the narrow range of programming available on mainland TV.

Finally, piracy casts an ominous shadow over the future of Chinese media worldwide. In order to build production capacity and attract talent, the industry must secure its lines of distribution in Asia as well as in markets around the world. Currently, Hollywood is the most vociferous advocate of strict piracy regulations, claiming that it loses billions of dollars each year to the black market. Yet Hollywood remains prosperous despite these losses, whereas Chinese media companies are navigating much more treacherous waters. The very same technologies that enable them to extend the reach of their distribution operations and carve out new market niches at the same time undermine their ability to control the exposure of talent and the exhibition of creative products. Without secure distribution and exhibition channels, companies find it difficult to sustain the artificial scarcity that is the basis for pricing media services and artifacts.

Chinese companies confront challenges in financing, production, distribution, and exhibition. Although the industry has gone through periods of structural adjustment before, the outcome of the current transition is in many respects uncertain. One can, however, posit some general tendencies on the basis of the foregoing analysis. As a result of increasing transnational trade flows and new technologies, Chinese media companies are likely to grow in size, multiply their services, and extend the scope of their distribution operations. Successful companies will seek to exploit global opportunities, even if they operate in more localized markets as well. At all levels, one of the keys to future success is creative capacity, and therefore Chinese screen industries must continue to cultivate a distinctive pantheon of stars and creative talent, and they must trade on cultural differences from the West, all the while putting in place expansive, secure, and durable distribution systems.

Government policy, although still influential, can no longer expect to exercise territorial sovereignty over media circulation and consumption. Restrictions on imports only encourage black market sales, with audiences under even the most restrictive regulatory regimes pursuing their interests through new technologies. Paradoxically, import regulations and censorship seem to diminish government influence over consumption practices in markets as diverse as mainland China, Taiwan, and Malaysia. The principles of media capital should therefore encourage governments to focus on supply, figuring out ways to nurture creative industries and encourage the growth and concentration of media resources in particular locales. But which cities seem especially promising sites for such attention? Where might we expect to find the media capitals of twenty-first-century Asia?

Elaborating on the concept of media capital, Michael Keane identifies four levels of media agglomeration.[9] The first tier belongs to Hollywood, a global media capital par excellence, followed by second-tier centers such as Hong Kong, Cairo, and Mumbai. The media industries of these cities are historically transnational and commercial, serving dispersed but loosely coherent cultural-linguistic formations. Third-tier centers, such as Seoul, Taipei, and Dubai, have historical legacies of state oversight and therefore are characterized by residual conservatism and national policy imperatives. Their prominence in international media markets is a relatively recent phenomenon, driven primarily by external demand for their products rather than by strategic expansion of their distribution capacity. Fourth-tier centers, such as Beijing and Shanghai, remain strongly influenced by national policy guidance, even though government officials openly express a desire to see their media industries extend their reach into international markets. Such aspirations are constrained, however, by content regulations and policy requirements that media first and foremost serve the interests of the state. Keane's template provides a useful set of distinctions among the various centers of media activity worldwide. One might ask then, what makes a city rise through these levels to become an ever more significant center of media flows?

As we have seen throughout this book, media capital is geographically relational. That is, one cannot imagine a capital without envisioning a terrain over which it holds sway and a constellation of related nodes of cultural endeavor. Hong Kong emerged as a media capital because movie companies were able to put in place a transnational distribution and exhibition network that allowed it to circulate and deploy products in cinemas that were either owned by the studios or aligned with them via territorial distribution deals. Taipei on the other hand arose as a center of media activity because the government established an integrated broadcasting system that regulated the flow of cultural products within the island. In other words, institutional, technological, political, and legal frameworks help to establish the spatial integrity of media circulation systems and to define the relations among locales and the directions of flow. Fourth-tier capitals tend to be articulated with national regulatory regimes and national economies but may nevertheless aspire to broader spheres of influence, as is the case with third-tier capitals that are self-consciously and actively extending their reach, in some cases as a matter of national policy. Second-tier capitals are home to media enterprises that have successfully situated their operations throughout a transnational sphere of economic and cultural-linguistic forces and flows. Finally, first-tier media capitals tend to be thoroughly globalized in their operations, even if some industry operations and practices are more narrowly focused or even parochial. Media centers grow more prominent to the extent that policy and institutional frameworks foster creative activity and extend the circuits of distribution so that revenues and talent flow centripetally through the system.

In addition to institutional determinants, cultural markers (language, myth, ethnicity) are used to fashion, differentiate, and deploy the products of media capitals. Hong Kong feature films must, for example, exhibit some distinctive characteristics even if at the same time they flatten other cultural markers while seeking the broadest audience. Thus, kung fu dramas may possess many of the same generic characteristics as American Westerns and may circulate widely among Chinese audiences worldwide, but they must ultimately distinguish themselves from their Hollywood counterparts so as to sustain their particular value in the marketplace. Even within more circumscribed, less global domains, cultural markers play an important role in fashioning products to attract local mass constituencies or to interpellate geographically dispersed niche constituencies who see themselves as part of a social, gendered, or generational formation or any combination of these. Formosa Television accordingly produces family dramas in Taiwanese primarily for audiences in the south of the island, while Media Asia creates action-romance films featuring Chinese pop music idols, such as *Initial D*, for young audiences throughout East Asia. Media capitals, therefore, constitute their relation to other media capitals culturally as well as institutionally. And the higher the tier, the more likely a media capital is to produce products with varying scales of cultural appeal—global, regional, national, and local.

To say that media capitals are relational is to acknowledge that they are constantly absorbing influences from near and far, distinguishing their productions from competitors, and extending the circulation of artifacts as far as possible within existing institutional and cultural spheres of possibility. Such tendencies help to explain why, during an era of technological, political, and trade liberalization, media institutions tend spatially to concentrate their managerial and productive operations at the very same time that their markets tend to expand and fragment and their cultural products diversify. Although commodification and globalization produce structural similarities in practices among media companies worldwide, market forces nevertheless encourage them to probe persistently for sociocultural variations that reveal new market opportunities and spur the production of cultural texts with distinctive, if hybrid, characteristics. Consequently, the most prosperous media enterprises tend to circulate products at multiple geographical scales through flexible and far-reaching distribution operations that interface effectively with local nodes of exhibition and marketing.

As we have seen, most of the companies discussed in this volume, such as TVB, MediaCorp, and ERA Communications, are in the process of spatially extending their distribution networks. To the extent that they succeed and demand grows, the issue of location reasserts itself, since these companies must be willing to reassess their current sites of production in light of changing markets. Certainly chance occurrences, institutional inertia, and cultural resources play important roles in such decision making, but another prominent determinant is the availability of talent.

Under what conditions do some locations nurture and attract creative labor? Employment and training opportunities are important factors, but another significant, though less tangible, variable is the chance to work with others whose creative endeavors inspire emulation and engagement. Geographer Allen J. Scott has shown that creative talent tends to migrate to locations where job opportunities are plentiful and where mutual learning, both formal and informal, can occur.[10] Richard Florida concurs, furthermore pointing out that members of the "creative class" tend to seek out locales that foster cultural diversity and tolerance.[11] Recall for example that the brightest moment for Hong Kong media was when migrations to the city and a growing cosmopolitanism among the population made it an attractive and relatively welcoming destination for talent from afar. Moreover, the city's openness encouraged many young residents to seek education and life experiences abroad, so that talented individuals were both reaching out and flowing in.

Although Florida, Scott, and others help to delineate some of the attractions of creative cities, they fail to comment on others that should not be taken for granted in the Asian context. For example, they make no specific mention of political stability or expressive freedom as baseline requirements for the emergence of a media capital. Run Run Shaw's migration from Shanghai to Singapore and then to Hong Kong was very much motivated by these concerns. And, indeed, it's also worth noting that Hong Kong's fortunes as a media capital began to wane at the very moment when the 1997 handover of sovereignty presented a host of uncertainties. Thus, since the early 1900s stability and liberty have been persistently attractive to creative labor in the Chinese screen industries. Popular culture in Hong Kong during its prime was renowned for its biting satires and self-reflexive parodies, with producers and talent playing (and preying) on a broad range of characters, topics, social mores, and stylistic conventions. Taipei likewise seemed to be a rising cultural force at the very moment when popular passions regarding the end of martial law spilled over into the rapidly proliferating media outlets of the 1990s, and even Singapore is now going through a political and generational transition, during which policy makers self-consciously aspire to promote liberty and creativity. Indeed, the principles of media capital seem to favor those times and places that genuinely nurture personal expression. Media capitals, therefore, seem to emerge where opportunity, prosperity, expressive freedom, and rich cultural resources converge.

Moreover, expressive freedom seems to flourish where a diversity of creative venues are available. Storper, Christopherson, and Scott pay only brief attention to this factor, focusing instead on the fact that disintegrated production in the poststudio era of Hollywood largely revolves around independent production houses that are connected to large media corporations.[12] They overlook talent who aren't networked with the major media companies, those who ply their craft in niche or even noncommercial creative venues. As we have seen, a diverse range of production houses operated during Hong Kong's boom years of the 1980s and 1990s, and many of them had only scant access to the largest distributors. Nevertheless, their creative experiments circulated throughout the production community, and their very existence swelled the overall ranks of experienced and available labor. Likewise, politically and artistically motivated talent in post–martial law Taiwan, many of them operating in noncommercial contexts, contributed to the surge in creative activity and the multiplication of media outputs during the 1990s. Consequently a city's ability to attract creative labor and make effective use of it seems to rely on not simply the number of creative venues but the diversity of them as well.

Taken together, government policies can influence the factors discussed above, but, just as important, they must be designed to cultivate and exploit the often serendipitous confluence of variables that seem to attract and sustain pools of creative labor. By encouraging the growth of media enterprises and the transnationalization of their operations while also fostering a secure and diverse creative community, governments can aspire to improve the chances that particular cities will emerge as media capitals. Hong Kong has enjoyed a preeminent status as the transnational capital of Chinese media for more that four decades, but as mentioned at the outset of this volume, media capitals can wax and wane, and a city's status as one can likewise be won or lost. Just as the conditions of the Chinese media industry are currently in flux, so too are the trajectories of creative migration.

The globalization of Chinese media has unleashed new forces, created new challenges, and provided new opportunities. Media products flow more freely across national borders as national policies and new technologies have loosened previous restrictions. Channels of distribution have multiplied, new enterprises have emerged, and competitors from afar have dramatically escalated their interest in Chinese audiences. These trends will no doubt continue as Chinese audiences grow larger and wealthier. Yet the analytical model that shaped this investigation does not suggest that raw commercial forces have achieved a stranglehold on the industry, nor does it suggest inevitable outcomes for Chinese media. Instead, it shows how the logic of accumulation unfolds in relation to flows of talent and forces of sociocultural variation. These very same principles will furthermore play a role in fostering one or more Chinese media capitals that could, within the next century, aspire to first-tier status and challenge Hollywood's current hegemony, not only among Chinese audiences, but also in other parts of Asia and beyond where Chinese geopolitical, economic, and cultural influence is growing by the day.[13] As distribution systems become more robust and secure, production budgets for film and TV are likely to rise, as are production values. Only by transcending the presumption that Hollywood hegemony is forever and by carefully attending to the complex forces at play can we begin to glimpse the growing significance of Chinese media in the global era.

Industry Interviews

Frank Brown, president, MTV Networks Asia and chair of CASBAA, June 14, 2000.

David Chan, chief operating officer, Golden Harvest Film Productions, April 18, 2000.

Michael Chan, deputy general manager, TVB International, April, 26, 2000.

Penny Chan, brand manager, Discovery Channel Asia, June 20, 2000.

Peter Chan, principal, Applause Pictures, April 11, 1997; April 19, 2000.

James Chang, executive vice-president, Tempo International Mass Media, December 27, 1999.

Yvonne Chang, media research team leader, Sanlih Entertainment Television, February 11, 2000.

Frank Chen, director, Motion Picture Affairs, Taiwan Government Information Office, December 22, 1999.

Sabrina Chen, marketing manager, CMC Movie Corporation, March 6, 2000.

Teddy Chen, principal, Applause Pictures, April 13, 2000.

Wolf Chen, vice-president of film distribution, ERA Communications, March 6, 2000.

Michael Cheng, general manager, MTV Taiwan, June 28, 2000.

Su Ming Cheng, CEO, China Television, March 13, 2000; March 22, 2000.

Peggy Chiao, producer, Taiwan Film Center, March 9, 2002.

Vivian Chien, international acquisitions and sales, Formosa TV, January 28, 2000.

Ko-lin Chin, professor of criminal justice, Rutgers University, November 15, 1999.

Ava Chiu, assistant commissioner, Television and Entertainment Licensing Authority, HK, April 16, 2000.

Peggy Chiao, independent producer, Taiwan, March 9, 2002.

Jessie Chou, senior manager of operations, Warner Village Cinemas, March 21, 2000.

Thomas Chung, managing director, Han Entertainment, March 2, 2002.

Winnie Chung, entertainment editor, *South China Morning Post,* April 12, 2000.

Vivek Couto, editor, *Asia Cable and Satellite World,* May 9, 2000.

Simon Twiston Davies, CEO, Cable and Satellite Broadcasting Association of Asia, May 12, 2000; March 21, 2003.

Allan Fung, principal, Applause Pictures, May 8, 2000.

Wellington Fung, executive director, Media Asia, April 12, 2000; March 18, 2003.

Ann Gavaghan, media critic, Taiwan News, January 15, 2000.

David Gibbons, head of telecommunications research, HSBC Securities Asia, May 9, 2000.

Stefan Hammond, associate editor, filmbazaar.com, April 25, 2000.

Charles Heung, chairman, China Star Entertainment, March 17, 2003.

Howard Ho, general manager of distribution and marketing, Phoenix TV, May 12, 2000.

Sam Ho, film critic and programmer, Hong Kong Film Festival, April 25, 2000; March 19, 2003.

Sun-sea Ho, editor-in-chief, CTN News, March 16, 2000.

Vivian Hsieh, supervisor, Dadi Channel, Chinese Television Network, December 14, 1999.

Hu Zhengrong, director, National Center for Radio & Television Studies, PRC, October 29, 2005.

Patrick Mao Huang, deputy managing director, New Action Entertainment, March 14, 2000.

Simon Huang, marketing manager, UIP, Taiwan, March 2, 2000.

Ann Hung, general manager of distribution, China Star Entertainment, March 17, 2003.

Jiang Weimin, president, Channel Young, Shanghai TV, Shanghai Media Group, October 29, 2005.

Steve Kappen, general manager, Warner Village, Taiwan, March 21, 2000.

Shu Kei, director and distributor, Shu Kei's Creative Workshop, March 1, 2001.

Clifton Ko, writer-director, April 4, 1997.

Jeff Ko, marketing manager, Spring International, February 24, 2000.

Cheung Chi Kwong, line producer, Golden Harvest, May 11, 2000.

Emma Lai, chief of program acquisitions, ERA TV, January 2, 2000.

Yiu-kuen Lau (Law Kar), programmer, Hong Kong International Film Festival, May 10, 2000.

Esmond Lee, assistant commissioner, Television and Entertainment Licensing Authority, HK, April 16, 2000.

Helena Lee, marketing communications manager, TVB International, June 26, 1997.

Kuang-hui Lee, general manager, Star TV, Taiwan, May 29, 2000.

Sherman Lee, assistant division manager, Telecast Licensing, March 20, 2003.

Tao Lee, general manager, TVBS, June 2, 2000.

Gigi Leung, assistant marketing manager, ATV Enterprises, June 21, 1997.

Kuo-ching Lin, general manager, Chinese Television Network, March 16, 2000.

Samuel Lui, assistant secretary, Information Technology and Broadcasting Bureau, HK, April 16, 2000.

Jingle Ma, director and producer, Golden Harvest Film, May 11, 2000.

James Marturano, senior vice-president, HBO Asia, June 23, 2000.

Todd Miller, vice-president of sales and marketing, Columbia Tri-Star TV Asia, June 22, 2000.

John O'Loan, director of network services, Star TV, July 8, 1997.

William Pfeiffer, CEO, Celestial Entertainment, May 12, 2000; March 2, 2002; March 18, 2003.

Phoon Chiong-kit, CEO, Golden Harvest Entertainment, May 12, 2000; March 19, 2003.

Garrie Roman, managing director, KPS Video, July 5, 1997.

Scott Rosenberg, Asian Movie Works, April 13, 2000.

Kai-Ming Shea, senior investment analyst, Tai Fook Securities, May 9, 2000.

Tiffany Sheu, director of program acquisitions, Sanlih Entertainment Television, January 2, 2000.

Nansun Shi, executive vice-president, Media Asia, June 1, 2000; March 17, 2003.

Eric Shih, general manager, Warner Bros. Film Distribution, Taiwan, December 22, 1999; January 27, 2000.

Ismail Sudderuddin, director, Singapore Film Commission, June 22, 2000.

Peter K. Tam, executive director, Astoria Films Limited, April 4, 2000; April 6, 2000.

Augustine Tan, manager, Network Programming 5, MediaCorp, June 22, 2000.

Tina Teng, senior research manager, AC Nielsen, Taiwan, February 21, 2000.

Johnnie To Kei-fung, chief operational officer, China Star Entertainment, May 10, 2000.

Kelvin Tong, film critic, Singapore Press Holdings, June 22, 2000.

Patrick Tong, managing director, Mei Ah Entertainment, April 13, 2000.

Peter Tsi, programming director, i-Cable, May 14, 1997; May 8, 2000, March 18, 2003.

Tom Wang, Marketing manager, Buena Vista Entertainment, Taiwan, February 25, 2000.

John Wigglesworth, creative director, MTV Asia, June 15, 2000.

Nicholas Wodtke, chief operating officer, Super TV, Sony Pictures, February 11, 2000; March 20, 2000.

Russell Wolf, senior vice-president of programming, ESPN-Star Asia, June 23, 2000.

Anthony Wong, vice-president of Asian productions, Sony Pictures, May 9, 2000.

Francis Wong, assistant general manager, TVB International, March 20, 2003.

Franklin Wong, CEO, MediaCorp Studios, June 13, 2000.

Michael Woo Her Yee, assistant vice-president of marketing and distribution, MediaCorp, June 13, 2000.

Nien-jen Wu, writer, director, actor, March 9, 2002.

Clark Xu, vice-president, Warner Cable, China, October 29, 2005.

Eric Yang, program planning manager, Taiwan Television, February 23, 2000; June 27, 2000.

Johnny Yang, manager, Long Shong Entertainment, December 17, 1999.

Michelle Yeoh, director, Han Entertainment, March 2, 2002.

Daniel Yun, CEO, Raintree Pictures, June 13, 2000.

Notes

INTRODUCTION

1. Toby Miller, Nitin Govil, John McMurria, and Richard Maxwell, *Global Hollywood* (London: BFI Publishing, 2001).

2. Most of the quotations in this volume are derived from interviews with industry practitioners, a list of which can be found in the appendix. Please note that most of these industry quotations are directly attributed to particular interviewees in the text. Some of the quotations, however, are generically attributed, for instance, to a "television executive" or "movie director." In those cases, either I am trying to protect the source, given the sensitive nature of certain topics, or I am restricting the number of names and characters in the text in order to sustain the flow of analysis and avoid confusion.

3. I use the term *Global China* instead of *Greater China*, because the latter has taken on connotations of cultural essentialism, suggesting that northern China, especially Beijing, is the political, cultural, and geographical center of Chinese civilization. Alternatively, *Global China* suggests a more dynamic and contested set of institutions, relationships, and interdependencies. My use of *global* and *globalization* does not imply an inevitable process of increasing uniformity and homogenization but rather implies a growing tendency for people and institutions to take into account forces from afar when imagining opportunities, responding to challenges, or hatching plans for action.

4. Robert McChesney, *The Problem of the Media: U.S. Communication Politics in the 21st Century* (New York: Monthly Review Press, 2004).

5. For example, John Sinclair, *Latin American Television: A Global View* (New York: Oxford University Press, 1999); Koichi Iwabuchi, *Recentering Globalization: Popular Culture and Japanese Transnationalism* (Durham, NC: Duke University Press, 2002); Mohammed el-Nawawy and Adel Iskandar, *Al-Jazeera: The Story of the Network That Is Rattling Governments and Redefining Modern Journalism* (Boulder, CO: Westview Press, 2003); Shanti Kumar, *Ghandi Meets Primetime* (Urbana: University of Illinois Press, 2005); Marwan Kraidy, *Hybridity, or the Cultural Logic of Globalization* (Philadelphia: Temple Uni-

versity Press, 2005); Terhi Rantanen, *The Media and Globalization* (London: Sage Publications, 2005); Serra Tinic, *On Location: Canada's Television Industry in a Global Market* (Toronto: University of Toronto Press, 2005); and Michael Keane, Anthony Fung, and Albert Moran, *New Television, Globalisation, and the East Asian Cultural Imagination* (Hong Kong: Hong Kong University Press, 2007).

6. Throughout this book I use the term *Chinese* to refer to social institutions and cultural formations that commonly invoke the term in a variety of ways, for a variety of purposes. As we shall we, Chinese and Chineseness are dynamic and contested concepts that refer to groups with diverse cultures, languages, cuisines, geographies, and histories. Despite such diversity, the term *Chinese* has been repeatedly employed by those who wish to use it as an instrument of hegemonic leadership, a practice that goes back at least as far as the Qin dynasty. I therefore use the term with this self-critical awareness in mind. For a critique of Chinese, Chineseness, and "Greater China," see Allen Chun, "Discourses of Identity in the Changing Spaces of Public Culture in Taiwan, Hong Kong, and Singapore," *Theory, Culture & Society* 13, no. 1 (1996): 51–75; Allen Chun, "Fuck Chineseness: On the Ambiguities of Ethnicity as Culture as Identity," *boundary 2* 23, no. 2 (1996): 111–38; Aihwa Ong and Donald Nonini, *Ungrounded Empires: The Cultural Politics of Modern Chinese Transnationalism* (New York: Routledge, 1997); Aihwa Ong, *Flexible Citizenship: The Cultural Logics of Transnationality* (Durham, NC: Duke University Press, 1999); and Ien Ang, *On Not Speaking Chinese: Living between Asia and the West* (London: Routledge, 2001).

7. Thomas H. Guback, *The International Film Industry: Western Europe and America since 1945* (Bloomington: Indiana University Press, 1969); Herbert I. Schiller, *Mass Communication and American Empire*, 2nd ed. (Boulder, CO: Westview Press, 1992).

8. Ariel Dorfman and Armand Mattelart, *How to Read Donald Duck: Imperialist Ideology in the Disney Comic* (New York: International General, 1975).

9. Kaarle Nordenstreng and Tapio Varis, *Television Traffic—a One-Way Street? A Survey and Analysis of the International Flow of Television Programme Material* (Paris: UNESCO, 1974).

10. Sean McBride, *Many Voices, One World: Communication and Society, Today and Tomorrow: Towards a New More Just and More Efficient World Information and Communication Order* (New York: Unipub, 1980).

11. Chin-Chuan Lee, *Media Imperialism Reconsidered: The Homogenizing of Television Culture* (Beverly Hills, CA: Sage Publications, 1979).

12. Fred Fejes, "Media Imperialism, an Assessment," *Media, Culture and Society* 3, no. 3 (1981): 281–89; Ien Ang, *Desperately Seeking the Audience* (New York: Routledge, 1981); Tamar Liebes and Elihu Katz, *The Export of Meaning: Cross-Cultural Readings of Dallas* (New York: Oxford University Press, 1990); James Lull, *China Turned On: Television, Reform, and Resistance* (New York: Routledge, 1991).

13. Sumita S. Chakravarty, *National Identity in Indian Popular Cinema, 1947–1987* (Austin: University of Texas Press, 1993); Ananda Mitra, *Television and Popular Culture in India: A Study of the Mahabharat* (Thousand Oaks, CA: Sage Publications, 1993).

14. Arjun Appadurai, *Modernity at Large: Cultural Dimensions of Globalization* (Minneapolis: University of Minnesota Press, 1996); James Clifford, *Routes: Travel and Translation in the Late Twentieth Century* (Cambridge, MA: Harvard University Press, 1997).

15. Michael Tracey, "Popular Culture and the Economics of Global Television," *Intermedia* 16, no. 2 (1988): 9–25; Joseph D. Straubhaar, "Beyond Media Imperialism: Asymmetrical Interdependence and Cultural Proximity," *Critical Studies in Mass Communication* 8 (March 1991): 39–59; Geoffrey Reeves, *Communication and the "Third World"* (London: Routledge, 1993); John Sinclair, Elizabeth Jacka, and Stuart Cunningham, eds., *New Patterns in Global Television* (New York: Oxford University Press, 1996); Sinclair, *Latin American Television.*

16. Lull, *China Turned On;* Michael O'Neill, *The Roar of the Crowd: How Television and People Power Are Changing the World* (New York: Times Books, 1993); McKenzie Wark, *Virtual Geography: Living with Global Media Events* (Bloomington: Indiana University Press, 1994).

17. Michael Curtin, "Feminine Desire in the Age of Satellite Television," *Journal of Communication* 49, no. 2 (1999): 55–70; Kumar, *Ghandi Meets Primetime.*

18. Michael Curtin, "Murdoch's Dilemma, or 'What's the Price of TV in China?'" *Media, Culture and Society* 27, no. 2 (2005): 155–75.

19. John Tomlinson, *Cultural Imperialism: A Critical Introduction* (Baltimore: Johns Hopkins University Press, 1991), 175.

20. Appadurai, *Modernity at Large;* Gilles Deleuze and Felix Guattari, *A Thousand Plateaus: Capitalism and Schizophrenia* (Minneapolis: University of Minnesota Press, 1987).

21. David Harvey, *Spaces of Capital: Towards a Critical Geography* (New York: Routledge, 2001), 237–66.

22. Karl Marx, *Grundrisse: Foundations of the Critique of Political Economy* (New York: Vintage, 1973), 539.

23. Monopoly rents are an exception, but as we'll see later these have proven less tenable in an era of changing technologies and increasing transborder flows.

24. Alfred D. Chandler, *The Visible Hand: The Managerial Revolution in American Business* (Cambridge, MA: Belknap Press, 1977).

25. Related arguments regarding the spatial tendencies of print media can be found in Harold Innis, *Empire and Communications* (Toronto: University of Toronto Press, 1972); and Benedict Anderson, *Imagined Communities: Reflections on the Origin and Spread of Nationalism* (New York: Verso, 1983).

26. David Bordwell, Janet Staiger, and Kristin Thompson, *The Classical Hollywood Cinema: Film Style and Mode of Production to 1960* (London: Rout-

ledge and Kegan Paul, 1985); Eileen Bowser, *The Transformation of Cinema: 1907–1915* (New York: Scribner's, 1990); Allen J. Scott, *On Hollywood: The Place, the Industry* (Princeton, NJ: Princeton University Press, 2005).

27. Bordwell et al., *The Classical Hollywood Cinema*, 123.

28. Ibid., 93.

29. Vance Kepley Jr., "From 'Frontal Lobes' to the 'Bob-and-Bob' Show: NBC Management and Programming Strategies, 1949–65," in *Hollywood in the Age of Television*, ed. Tino Balio (Boston: Unwin Hyman, 1990), 41–62; David Hesmondhalgh, *The Cultural Industries* (London: Sage Publications, 2002).

30. Douglas Gomery, *The Hollywood Studio System* (New York: St. Martin's Press, 1986); Tino Balio, *Hollywood as a Modern Business Enterprise, 1930–1939* (New York: Scribner's, 1993).

31. Kristin Thompson, *Exporting Entertainment: America in the World Film Market, 1907–34* (London: BFI Publishing, 1985).

32. Asu Aksoy and Kevin Robins, "Hollywood for the 21st Century: Global Competition for Critical Mass in Image Markets," *Cambridge Journal of Economics* 16 (1992): 12.

33. Although it does not deal with the media industries specifically, an extensive literature discusses the impact of human capital on the clustering of business firms in particular locations. Jane Jacobs, *Cities and the Wealth of Nations* (New York: Random House, 1984); Michael E. Porter, "Clusters and the New Economics of Competition," *Harvard Business Review* (November 1998): 77–90; and Richard Florida, *Cities and the Creative Class* (New York: Routledge, 2005).

34. Paul DiMaggio, *Non-profit Enterprise in the Arts: Studies in Mission and Constraint* (New York: Oxford University Press, 1986).

35. Douglas Gilbert, *American Vaudeville: Its Life and Times* (New York: McGraw-Hill, 1940); Albert F. McLean, *American Vaudeville as Ritual* (Lexington: University of Kentucky Press, 1965); Robert C. Allen, *Vaudeville and Film: 1895–1915: A Study in Media Interaction* (New York: Arno Press, 1980).

36. United Artists modeled many of the practices that would become associated with the rise of independent producers in Hollywood. Tino Balio, *United Artists: The Company That Changed the Film Industry* (Madison: University of Wisconsin Press, 1987).

37. Michael Storper and Susan Christopherson, "Flexible Specialization and Regional Industrial Agglomerations: The Case of the U.S. Motion Picture Industry," *Annals of the Association of American Geographers* 77, no. 1 (1987): 104–17; Susan Christopherson and Michael Storper, "The Effects of Flexible Specialization on Industrial Politics and the Labor Market: The Motion Picture Industry," *Industrial and Labor Relations Review* 42 (1989): 331–47; Miller et al., *Global Hollywood.*. Insightful critiques of "runaway production" can be found in Tinic, *On Location;* and Greg Elmer and Mike Gasher, eds., *Contracting Out Hollywood: Runaway Productions and Foreign Location Shooting* (Boulder, CO: Rowman and Littlefield, 2005).

38. Christopherson and Storper, "The Effects of Flexible Specialization," 113. Despite the development of new communication technologies that allow creative collaborations across vast expanses, creative labor also needs to congregate so as to build relationships of trust and familiarity that can enable and sustain long-distance collaborations. Giddens's discussion of facework and Bourdieu's notion of social capital both point to the importance of physical proximity. Anthony Giddens, *The Consequences of Modernity* (Stanford, CA: Stanford University Press, 1990); Pierre Bourdieu, "The Forms of Capital," in *Handbook of Theory and Research for the Sociology of Education*, ed. J. G. Richardson (Westport, CT: Greenwood, 1986), 241–58.

39. Allen J. Scott, *The Cultural Economy of Cities* (London: Sage Publications, 2000), 33.

40. The classic work on the Third Italy is Michael J. Piore and Charles F. Sabel, *The Second Industrial Divide: Possibilities for Prosperity* (New York: Basic Books, 1984).

41. Alfred D. Chandler, *Inventing the Electronic Century: The Epic Story of the Consumer Electronics and Computer Industries* (New York: Free Press, 2001).

42. Thompson, *Exporting Entertainment.*

43. Ian Jarvie, *Hollywood's Overseas Campaign: The North Atlantic Movie Trade, 1920–1950* (Cambridge: Cambridge University Press, 1992).

44. Paddy Scannell, *A Social History of British Broadcasting* (Cambridge: Blackwell, 1991); Michele Hilmes, "Who We Are, Who We Are Not: The Battle of Global Paradigms," in *Planet TV: A Global Television Reader,* ed. Lisa Parks and Shanti Kumar (New York: New York University Press, 2003), 53–73.

45. Anderson, *Imagined Communities.*

46. Scannell, *Social History of British Broadcasting;* and Michele Hilmes, *Radio Voices: American Broadcasting, 1922–1952* (Minneapolis: University of Minnesota Press, 1997). Similar arguments have been made about television. See Roger Silverstone, *Television and Everyday Life* (New York: Routledge, 1994); and David Morley, *Home Territories: Media, Mobility, and Identity* (New York: Routledge, 2000).

47. Interestingly, Hollywood also confronted political opposition on the home front from local and state censorship boards. The studios responded by formulating a collaborative production code as a mechanism intended to ameliorate the concerns of local groups and thereby ensure nationwide distribution. These struggles over the control of popular culture were also manifested in early regulation of radio when government officials wrote antimonopoly clauses into the 1927 Radio Act and furthermore established local trusteeship as the foundational, if anachronistic, principle of government licensing.

48. Bordwell et al., *Classical Hollywood Cinema.*

49. Thomas Streeter, *Selling the Air: A Critique of the Policy of Commercial Broadcasting in the United States* (Chicago: University of Chicago Press, 1996).

50. Christopher Anderson and Michael Curtin, "Mapping the Ethereal City:

Chicago Television, the FCC, and the Politics of Place," *Quarterly Review of Film and Video* 16, no. 3–4 (1999): 289–305.

51. My approach also aims to address supposed tensions between political economy and cultural studies scholarship by showing how insights from both schools can productively be brought to bear in the study of film and television.

52. The concept of "Greater China" gained currency in the 1990s in response to political, social, and economic transitions that encouraged transnational flows among Chinese societies and tighter connections between overseas Chinese and their counterparts in mainland China. Wei-ming Tu, ed., *The Living Tree: The Changing Meaning of Being Chinese Today* (Stanford, CA: Stanford University Press, 1994).

53. Of course, this perspective engenders its own limitations, because it tends to emphasize popular media (with their extensive production resources and expansive distribution infrastructures) over experimental art forms or alternative modes of expression. Dominant forms of media obviously engender alternative and oppositional forms with their own centers of production and patterns of flow. Exile media provide good examples of alternative cultural, political, and commercial practices with their own particular spatial logics. Hamid Naficy, *The Making of Exile Cultures: Iranian Television in Los Angeles* (Minneapolis: University of Minnesota Press, 1993), and Hamid Naficy, ed., *Home, Exile, Homeland: Film, Media, and the Politics of Place* (New York: Routledge, 1999).

54. Throughout the book, I use English-language titles of feature films and television series for the reader's convenience. In those instances where the English-language title may generate some confusion, I also provide the Chinese version, using the pinyin romanization system.

1. THE PAN-CHINESE STUDIO SYSTEM AND CAPITALIST PATERNALISM

1. Information regarding the history of Shaw Brothers is derived from Ian Jarvie, *Window on Hong Kong: A Sociological Study of the Hong Kong Film Industry and Its Audience* (Hong Kong: University of Hong Kong Press, 1977); Stephen Teo, *Hong Kong Cinema: The Extra Dimensions* (London: BFI Publishing, 1997); David Bordwell, *Planet Hong Kong: Popular Cinema and the Art of Entertainment* (Cambridge, MA: Harvard University Press, 2000); Jan Uhde and Yvonne Ng Uhde, *Latent Images: Film in Singapore* (Singapore: Oxford University Press, 2000); Stephanie Po-yin Chung, "The Industrial Evolution of a Fraternal Enterprise: The Shaw Brothers and the Shaw Organization," in *The Shaw Screen: A Preliminary Study*, ed. Ain-ling Wong (Hong Kong: Hong Kong Film Archive, 2003), 1–18; Cheng-ren Zhou, "Shanghai's Unique Film Productions and Hong Kong's Early Cinema," in *The Shaw Screen*, ed. Wong, 19–36; Poshek Fu, *Between Shanghai and Hong Kong: The Politics of Chinese Cinemas* (Stanford, CA: Stanford University Press, 2003); Sek Kei, "Shaw Movie Town's 'China Dream' and 'Hong Kong

Sentiments,'" in *The Shaw Screen*, ed. Wong, 37–50; and the Shaw Brothers Web site (www.shaw.com.sg/shawstory/shawstory.htm). I have also drawn on the vast resources generated by the annual publications of the Hong Kong International Film Festival, many of them published under the editorial guidance of Law Kar and Li Cheuk-to.

2. Sterling Seagrave, *Lords of the Rim: The Invisible Empire of the Overseas Chinese* (London: Corgi, 1996); and Claudia Cragg, *The New Taipans: A Vital Source Book on the People and Business of the Pacific Rim* (London: Arrow, 1996).

3. Gordon Redding, "What Is Chinese about Chinese Family Business?" in *Globalization of Chinese Business Firms*, ed. Henry Wai-chung Yeung and Kris Olds (New York: St. Martin's Press, 2000), 38.

4. Henry Wai-chung Yeung and Kris Olds, eds., *Globalization of Chinese Business Firms* (New York: St. Martin's Press, 2000).

5. Martin Booth, *The Dragon Syndicates: The Global Phenomenon of the Triads* (London: Bantam, 2000).

6. Uhde and Uhde, *Latent Images*; Ain-ling Wong, ed., *The Cathay Story* (Hong Kong: Hong Kong Film Archive, 2002).

7. Emilie Yueh-yu Yeh, "Taiwan: The Transnational Battlefield of Cathay and Shaws," in *The Cathay Story*, ed. Wong.

8. Uhde and Uhde, *Latent Images*; Poshek Fu, "Hong Kong and Singapore: A History of the Cathay Cinema," in *The Cathay Story*, ed. Wong.

9. Benjamin K. P. Leung, *Perspectives on Hong Kong Society* (Hong Kong: Oxford University Press, 1996); and Hoiman Chan, "Labyrinth of Hybridization: The Cultural Internationalization of Hong Kong," in *Hong Kong's Reunion with China: The Global Dimensions*, ed. Gerard A. Postiglione and James T. H. Tang (Armonk, NY: M. E. Sharpe, 1997), 169–99.

10. Jarvie, *Window on Hong Kong*; Paul Fonoroff, "A Brief History of Hong Kong Cinema," *Renditions* 29/30 (1988): 293–308; Po-King Choi, "From Dependence to Self-Sufficiency: Rise of the Indigenous Culture of Hong Kong, 1945–1989," *Asian Culture* 14, no. April (1990): 161–76; Teo, *Hong Kong Cinema*.

11. Poshek Fu, "Turbulent Sixties: Modernity, Youth Culture, and Cantonese Film in Hong Kong," in *Fifty Years of Electric Shadows: Hong Kong Cinema Retrospective*, ed. Kar Law (Hong Kong: Urban Council, 1997), 34–46.

12. Paul Siu-nam Lee, "The Absorption and Indigenization of Foreign Media Cultures: A Study on a Cultural Meeting Point of the East and West: Hong Kong," *Asian Journal of Communication* 1, no. 2 (1991): 52–72.

13. Pak-Tong Cheuk, "The Beginning of the Hong Kong New Wave: The Interactive Relationship between Television and the Film Industry," *Post Script* 19, no. 1 (1999): 10–27. Regarding the impact of television on popular culture and local identity, see Eric Kit-wai Ma, *Culture, Politics, and Television in Hong Kong* (London: Routledge, 1999); and Joseph Man Chan, "Mass Media and Socio-political Formation in Hong Kong, 1949–1992," *Journal of Communication* 2, no. 3 (1992): 106–29.

14. James Kung and Yueai Zhang, "Hong Kong Cinema and Television in the 1970s: A Perspective," in *A Study of Hong Kong Cinema in the Seventies,* ed. Cheuk-to Li (Hong Kong: Urban Council, 1984), 14–17; Choi, "From Dependence to Self-Sufficiency"; Terence Lo and Chung-bong Ng, "The Evolution of Prime-Time Television Scheduling in Hong Kong," in *Contemporary Television: Eastern Perspectives,* ed. David French and Michael Richards (New Delhi: Sage Publications, 1996), 200–220.

2. INDEPENDENT STUDIOS AND THE GOLDEN AGE OF HONG KONG CINEMA

1. The history of Golden Harvest and Cinema City is derived from interviews with interlocutors and from Jarvie, *Window on Hong Kong;* John A. Lent, *The Asian Film Industry* (Austin: University of Texas Press, 1990); Steve Fore, "Golden Harvest Films and the Hong Kong Movie Industry in the Realm of Globalization," *Velvet Light Trap* 34 (1994): 40–58; Teo, *Hong Kong Cinema;* and Bordwell, *Planet Hong Kong.*

2. Kar Law, "A Decade of Sword Grinding," in *A Study of Hong Kong Cinema in the Seventies,* ed. Cheuk-to Li (Hong Kong: Urban Council, 1984), 65.

3. Jenny Kwok Wah Lau, "Besides Fists and Blood: Hong Kong Comedy and Its Master of the Eighties," *Cinema Journal* 37, no. 2 (1998): 18–34.

4. Regarding the New Wave, see Esther C. M. Yau, ed., *At Full Speed: Hong Kong Cinema in a Borderless World* (Minneapolis: University of Minnesota Press, 2001).

5. Throughout the book, I have converted local currencies to U.S. dollar figures for ease of comparison.

6. This account from Wong Kar-wai, who lasted only a year at Cinema City before moving on, is quoted in Frederic Dannen, *Hong Kong Babylon: An Insider's Guide to the Hollywood of the East* (New York: Hyperion, 1997), 144. Now Hong Kong's most famous art-film director, Wong is notorious for scripting his movies on the fly and improvising on the set, a predilection that clearly did not mesh with the Cinema City style.

7. Bordwell, Planet Hong Kong.

8. Redding, "What Is Chinese?" 50–51.

3. HYPERPRODUCTION ERODES OVERSEAS CIRCULATION

1. In this chapter, I use the terms *Hong Kong movie* and *Chinese movie* interchangeably, because the Hong Kong product was the dominant commercial force in the island market after the demise of Taiwanese commercial cinema during the mid-1980s. A vibrant Taiwanese art cinema remains, but as we shall see, it is not a commercial force in the local market. Regarding Taiwanese cinema, see Emilie Yueh-yu Yeh and Darrell William Davis, *Taiwan Film Directors: A Treasure Island* (New York: Columbia University Press, 2005); and Alice Ou, ed., *Taiwan Films* (Taipei: Variety, 1993).

2. Most Hong Kong films are produced in six to eight weeks. The average Hollywood film takes at least one year.

3. See Dannen, *Hong Kong Babylon,* for a related account of triad involvement in the film industry.

4. Thompson, *Exporting Entertainment;* Colin Hoskins, Stuart McFadyen, and Adam Finn, *Global Television and Film: An Introduction to the Economics of the Business* (New York: Oxford University Press, 1997); Shujen Wang, *Framing Policy: Globalization and Film Distribution in Greater China* (Boulder: Rowman and Littlefield, 2003); Timothy Havens, *The Global Television Marketplace* (London: BFI Publishing, 2006).

5. Although problems with securing sufficient copies of popular videos very much contributed to the collapse of video rental outlets during the late 1990s, many distributors subsequently adjusted their practices, so that they now provide one master copy to retailers under a licensing agreement and allow the stores to make rental copies on an as-needed basis.

6. Booth, *The Dragon Syndicates.* Wang, *Framing Policy,* furthermore provides the most authoritative and broad-ranging account of video piracy in East Asia.

7. Wang, *Framing Policy.*

4. HOLLYWOOD TAKES CHARGE IN TAIWAN

1. Warner Bros. and Golden Harvest considered building multiplexes in Taiwan as early as 1988 but ran into problems securing real estate and government permits for construction in central-city locations. Local theater owners began to remodel their cinemas in the early 1990s by dividing existing theaters into smaller units, but few of them upgraded the quality of the screening experience. Shortly thereafter, United Artists opened a multiplex in Kao-hsiung and was soon followed by a Cinemark multiplex in Taoyuan, both of which preceded Warner Village but had less of an impact on the market.

2. Besides these theatrical revenues, Warner Bros. makes a comparable amount on cable, video, and broadcast sales of its films. This profit estimate and the ones that follow are based on documentation confidentially provided by a top executive in the film distribution business.

3. Box office and profit figures for 1998 were substantially higher than other years during this period, in part as a result of the "Titanic effect." *Titanic* made $12.1 million at the box office in Taipei; *Armageddon,* $5.1 million; *Tomorrow Never Dies,* $3.7 million; *Saving Private Ryan,* $3.5 million; and *Mulan,* $3.3 million. Islandwide, the box office revenues for these five films alone were well over $50 million. By comparison, the top ten Chinese films of 1998 brought in only $2.1 million in Taipei, among them, Taiwanese filmmaker Hou Hsiao-hsien's masterpiece, *The Flowers of Shanghai,* which grossed only $84,000. A useful discussion of the Taiwanese film market is Laurie Underwood, "The Tumultuous Tale of Taiwan Film," *Topics,* March 1999, 20–28.

4. In 1996, Hong Kong films took only 10 percent of ticket sales in a market

that overall was experiencing a significant downturn. Between 1992 and 1996, total ticket purchases in Taipei dropped from 16 million to 13.2 million, a decline of almost 20 percent. But Chinese films took an even more precipitous fall, from 8 million to a mere 1.3 million tickets, an 84 percent drop in movie admissions (ibid., 20).

5. THE GLOBALIZATION OF HONG KONG TELEVISION

1. Jon Vanden Heuvel and Everette E. Dennis, *The Unfolding Lotus: East Asia's Changing Media* (New York: Freedom Forum, 1993); Shelton A. Gunaratne, ed., *Handbook of the Media in Asia* (New Delhi: Sage Publications, 2000); David French and Michael Richards, eds., *Television in Contemporary Asia* (New Delhi: Sage Publications, 2000).

2. The declining profitability of TVB's domestic market is cited by To and Lau as the primary motivation for overseas expansion. Yiu-ming To and Tuen-yu Lau, "Global Export of Hong Kong Television: Television Broadcasts Limited," *Journal of Communication* 5, no. 2 (1995): 108–21.

3. In the television industry, "share" expresses the percentage of viewers then watching television who are tuned to a particular channel. "A seventy share" therefore indicates that, of the viewers watching television at that particular time, 70 percent were tuned to Chiu's imported Hong Kong drama.

4. A useful discussion of television use among TVB's diasporic audiences in Australia can be found in John Sinclair, Audrey Yue, Gay Hawkins, Kee Pookong, and Josephine Fox, "Chinese Cosmopolitanism and Media Use," in *Floating Lives: The Media and Asian Diasporas,* ed. Stuart Cunningham and John Sinclair (Boulder: Rowman and Littlefield, 2001), 35–90.

5. Regarding the popularity of Hong Kong TV in Guangdong Province, see Thomas Gold, "Go with Your Feelings: Hong Kong and Taiwan Popular Culture in Greater China," *China Quarterly* 136 (1993): 907–25; Joseph Man Chan, "When Capitalist and Socialist Television Clash: The Impact of Hong Kong TV on Guangzhou Residents," in *Power, Money, and Media: Communication Patterns and Bureaucratic Control in Cultural China,* ed. Chin-Chuan Lee (Evanston, IL: Northwestern University Press, 2000), 245–70; Anthony Fung and Eric Kit-wai Ma, "'Satellite Modernity': Four Modes of Televisual Imagination in the Disjunctive Socio-mediascape of Guangzhou," in *Media in China: Consumption, Content, and Crisis,* ed. Stephanie H. Donald, Michael Keane and Yin Hong (London: RoutledgeCurzon, 2002), 67–79; and Eric Kit-wai Ma, "Mapping Transborder Imaginations," in *In Search of Boundaries: Communication, Nation-States, and Cultural Identities,* ed. Joseph Man Chan and Bryce T. McIntyre (Westport, CT: Ablex, 2002), 249–63.

6. A detailed account of Li's enterprises and corporate strategy up to the mid-1990s can be found in Anthony B. Chan, *Li Ka-shing: Hong Kong's Elusive Billionaire* (Hong Kong: Oxford University Press, 1996).

7. Frank J. Prial, "Pao Yue-kong," *New York Times,* September 4, 1991, D31.

8. Much of the historical background regarding Pao, Woo, and Wharf is de-

rived primarily from news coverage in the *South China Morning Post* and the *Singapore Straits Times*. Especially extensive accounts were provided by Owen Hughes, "Who's Woo?" *South China Morning Post Sunday Magazine*, November 27, 1994, 21+; Gren Manuel, "Tuned In for Telly Channel Take-Off," *South China Morning Post*, September 6, 1998; and William Earl, "'Freedom' No Help for Broadcasters," *South China Morning Post*, August 30, 1998, M4.

9. Chan, *Li Ka-shing*, 164.

10. Ibid., 167–70.

11. Ibid., 170.

6. STRANGE BEDFELLOWS IN CROSS-STRAIT DRAMA PRODUCTION

1. John F. Copper, *Taiwan: Nation-State or Province?* (Boulder, CO: Westview Press, 1999), provides an overview of Taiwanese history and society, and accounts in Murray A. Rubenstein, ed., *The Other Taiwan: 1945 to the Present* (Armonk, NY: M. E. Sharpe, 1994), offer background on a range of social issues. Useful explanations of the general structure and philosophy of Taiwanese media can be found in Georgette Wang and Wen-Hwei Lo, "Taiwan," in *Handbook of the Media in Asia*, ed. Guneratne, 660–81; Flora Chin-Hwa Chang, "Multiculturalism and Television in Taiwan," in *Television in Contemporary Asia*, ed. David French and Michael Richards (New Delhi: Sage Publications, 2000), 405–19; and Yu-li Liu, "Restructuring the Television Industry in Taiwan," May 11, 2002, www.tukkk.fi/mediagroup/5WMEC%20PAPERS/Liu.pdf. Data and trends in Taiwanese media are published in Adam Thomas, Chris Groner, and Simon Dyson, *Asia Pacific TV: Incorporating CASBAA Asia Cable and Satellite Guide*, 7th ed. (London: Informa Media Group, 2003); Adam Thomas and Simon Dyson, *Asia Pacific TV: Incorporating CASBAA Asia Cable and Satellite Guide*, 8th ed. (London: Informa Media Group, 2004); and Adam Thomas, Simon Dyson, Alexandra Wales, and Xenobia Talati, *Asia Pacific TV: Management Report*, 9th ed. (London: Informa Media Group, 2005).

2. Thomas et al., *Asia Pacific TV*, 7th ed., 249.

3. Note the comparison to European soap operas as well in Tamar Liebes and Sonia Livingston, "European Soap Operas: The Diversification of a Genre," *European Journal of Communication* 13, no. 2 (1998): 147–80.

4. Bordwell, *Planet Hong Kong*, 150.

5. John Cawelti, *The Six-Gun Mystique* (Bowling Green, OH: Bowling Green State University Press, 1970), 71.

6. A useful discussion of generic adaptation and *wushu* production strategies in Hong Kong can be found in Wei Ling Lim, "Formatting and Change in East Asian Television Industries," PhD dissertation, Queensland University of Technology, Brisbane, 2006.

7. MARKET NICHES AND EXPANDING
ASPIRATIONS IN TAIWAN

1. Professor Yu-li Liu was most helpful in providing the historical background of the development of cable MSOs in Taiwan. This is complemented with information from interviews, the *Taipei Times,* and Asian news sources available through Lexis-Nexis. Especially useful were "Local Heroes," *Cable & Satellite Asia,* November 1996, 41–42; and Jesse Wong and Jason Dean, "Taiwan Heir Builds Media Empire, but at Heavy Cost," *Asian Wall Street Journal,* August 23, 2001.

2. Geoff Hiscock, *Asia's New Wealth Club* (London: Nicholas Brearly Publishing, 2000), 254–56.

3. Kevin Sinclair, "So Tell Me, James, Why I'm Tuned into a Falling Star," *South China Morning Post,* November 28, 2001, 13.

4. Ming-yeh T. Rawnsley, "Communications of Identities in Taiwan: From the 2–28 Incident to FTV," in *Political Communications in Greater China: Construction and Reflection of Identity,* ed. Gary D. Rawnsley and Ming-yeh Rawnsley (London: RoutledgeCurzon, 2003), 147–66.

5. An excellent analysis of family dramas in Taiwan during the 1990s is Szu-Ping Lin, "Prime Time Television Drama and Taiwanese Women," PhD dissertation, University of Wisconsin–Madison, 2000.

6. Regarding the circulation of television formats in Asia, see Albert Moran and Michael Keane, eds., *Television across Asia: Television Industries, Programme Formats and Globalization* (London: RoutledgeCurzon, 2004).

8. SINGAPORE: FROM STATE PATERNALISM
TO REGIONAL MEDIA HUB

1. In the movie *2000 AD*—a joint production between Hong Kong's Media Asia and Singapore's Raintree Pictures—the lead character is comically taken aback by the very same treatment on arrival at the Changi International Airport.

2. Informative assessments of Singapore's emergence as a global city are provided by Henry Wai-chung Yeung and Kris Olds, "Singapore's Global Reach: Situating the City-State in the Global Economy," *International Journal of Urban Sciences* 2, no. 1 (1999): 24–47; and Kris Olds and Henry Wai-chung Yueng, "Pathways to Global City Formation: A View from the Developmental City-State of Singapore," *Review of International Political Economy* 11, no. 3 (2004): 489–521. Background information on media institutions and policies can be found in Vanden Heuvel and Dennis, *The Unfolding Lotus;* David Birch, "Film and Cinema in Singapore: Cultural Policy as Control," in *Film Policy: International, National, and Regional Perspectives,* ed. Albert Moran (New York: Routledge, 1996), 185–211; Mark A. Hukill, "The Politics of Television Programming in Singapore," in *Television in Contemporary Asia,* ed. French and Richards, 179–96; Eddie Kuo and Peng Hwa Ang, "Singapore," in *Handbook of the Media in Asia,* ed. Gunaratne, 402–28; Petrina Leo and Terence Lee, "The

'New' Singapore: Mediating Culture and Creativity," *Continuum: Journal of Media and Cultural Studies* 18, no. 2 (2004): 205–18; Thomas et al., *Asia Pacific TV*, 7th ed.; Thomas and Dyson, *Asia Pacific TV*, 8th ed.; and Thomas et al., *Asia Pacific TV*, 9th ed.

3. Alastair Pennycook, *The Cultural Politics of English as an International Language* (London: Longman, 1994), 183–255.

4. Straubhaar, "Beyond Media Imperialism"; Hoskins et al., *Global Television and Film.*

9. RETERRITORIALIZING STAR TV IN THE PRC

1. Lull, *China Turned On;* Paul Siu-nam Lee, "Mass Communication and National Development in China: Media Roles Reconsidered," *Journal of Communication* 44, no. 3 (1994): 22–36.

2. Ben Bagdikian, "Lords of the Global Village," *Nation*, June 12, 1989, 805–20.

3. Rupert Murdoch, "Dawn of the Convergent, Interactive Era," *Business Times*, September 17, 1993, 24.

4. PRC policies were part of a larger pattern of government responses in Asia. Amos Owen Thomas, "Regulating Access to Transnational Satellite Television," *Gazette* 61, no. 3–4 (1999): 243–54; and Joseph Man Chan, "National Responses and Accessibility to Star TV in Asia," *Journal of Communication* 44, no. 3 (1994): 112–31.

5. Iwabuchi, *Recentering Globalization.*

6. Chan, *Li Ka-shing*, 175–81.

7. Michael Keane, "Broadcasting Policy, Creative Compliance and the Myth of Civil Society in China," *Media, Culture and Society* 23, no. 6 (2001): 783–98.

8. These data are derived from Phoenix Satellite Television Holdings, *Annual Report 1999–2000* (Hong Kong, 2000); Phoenix Satellite Television Holdings, *Annual Report 2001–2002* (Hong Kong, 2002); and Phoenix Satellite Television Holdings, *Annual Report 2002–2003* (Hong Kong, 2003).

9. Alex Cheng, "Ex-PLA Man's Long March to the Top of the Media World," *South China Morning Post*, March 20, 2003, A8.

10. Ibid.

11. By making reference to the Republic of China, Phoenix would have loaned legitimacy to Taiwanese assertions of political independence.

12. Cheng, "Ex-PLA Man's Long March."

13. See http://phoenixtv.startv.com/mainpage.htm.

10. GLOBAL SATELLITES PURSUING LOCAL
AUDIENCES AND PANREGIONAL EFFICIENCIES

1. For example, a studio might have sold the Asian territorial rights to another distributor who helped to finance the project initially. Often this is the case when Warner Bros. coproduces a film with Australia's Village Roadshow.

2. Keith Negus, *Music Genres and Corporate Cultures* (New York: Routledge, 1999), 157.

11. THE PROMISE OF BROADBAND
AND THE PROBLEM OF CONTENT

1. David Ibison, "A Rising Star in the Corporate World," *South China Morning Post*, September 29, 1997, B12.

2. At the time I was conducting my field research, it was nearly impossible to secure an interview with anyone in Li's organization. This was not only my experience but that of other researchers and journalists as well. As will become apparent, the offshoot company Pacific Century Cyberworks was preoccupied with a blistering round of deal making in 1999 and 2000, so the few interviews it granted were usually aimed at influencing the perception of investors. Consequently, information for this chapter is derived from press accounts and interviews with industry observers.

3. Most prominently, the two partnered in the development of Oriental Plaza in Beijing, one of the most lavish commercial spaces in the downtown area.

4. Erik Guyot and Michelle Lavender, "Cyberworks Plans Asian Internet Service," *Asian Wall Street Journal*, August 5, 1999, 1.

5. Eric Lai, "Property Barons Lured into Net," *South China Morning Post*, October 15, 1999, 16.

6. Katherine Bruce, "The High-Tech Son," *Forbes*, July 15, 1999, 156.

7. Thomas Beal, "Richard Li Bets Big on Internet Project," *Wall Street Journal*, February 2, 2000, 1.

8. Ho Swee Lin, "Mr. Internet Sets His Sights on Pan-Asian Network," *Financial Times*, January 18, 2000, 28.

9. See "The Messiah of Cyberasia," *Economist*, January 8, 2000. A more conservative estimate set Richard's net worth at $3.4 billion and his father's at $11 billion (Hiscock, *Asia's New Wealth Club*, 13).

10. Beal, "Richard Li Bets Big," 1.

11. Lin, "Mr. Internet Sets His Sights," 28.

12. Simon Pritchard, "Changes to Ring for HKT," *South China Morning Post*, February 16, 2000, B12.

13. Anthony Spaeth, "The Son Also Surprises," *Time*, March 13, 2000.

14. Tammy Tan, "Singtel's Offer Runs Smack into the Great Wall of China," *Straits Times*, February 28, 2000, 56–57.

15. Rahul Jacob and James Kynge, "China on the Line," *Financial Times*, February 29, 2000, 22.

16. Ibid.; and Jon E. Hilsenrath and Michael Flagg, "Star TV Tunes in Potential Internet Battle," *Asian Wall Street Journal*, March 1, 2000, 1.

17. Spaeth, "The Son Also Surprises."

18. Bruce, "The High-Tech Son."

19. Peter Wonacott, "Lis' Dominance in Hong Kong Seems Limitless," *Asian Wall Street Journal*, February 21, 2000, 1.

20. Joyce Barnathan, "How the Tycoons Are Hobbling Hong Kong," *Business Week*, January 18, 1999, 58.

21. Mahlon Meyer, "Generation Next," *Newsweek*, March 13, 2000, 48.

22. Peter Stein and Michelle Levander, "Richard Li Makes a Bet on Future of Entertainment," *Asian Wall Street Journal*, June 29, 2000, 1.

23. Stein and Levander, "Richard Li Makes a Bet on Future."

24. Michelle Levander, "Hong Kong Entertains Role for Web," *Asian Wall Street Journal*, July 6, 2000, 1.

25. Mark Landler, "Troubles Are Piling Up at Pacific Century," *New York Times*, March 29, 2001, 1.

26. Joe Leahy and Richard Waters, "Tech Stocks in Turmoil," *Financial Times*, December 23, 2000, 13.

27. Gren Manuel, "Richard Li Didn't Graduate, Cyberworks Says," *Asian Wall Street Journal*, March 23, 2001, 4.

28. Jason Gagliardi, "Empire of the Sons," *South China Morning Post*, July 5, 2000, 1.

29. Matthew Brooker and Stephen Seawright, "PCCW Directors' Pay Dwarfs Rivals," *South China Morning Post*, January 4, 2002, 1.

30. Matt Pottinger, "PCCW's Richard Li Seems out of Place at His Firm Today," *Asian Wall Street Journal*, March 20, 2002, A1.

31. Mark Landler, "Second Act for Hong Kong Billionaire," *New York Times*, March 21, 2002, W1.

32. Kelvin Chan, "Richard Li Still Tops HK Young Rich List," *South China Morning Post*, September 3, 2003, 6.

33. Angela McKay, "So to Replace Li as PCCW Chief," *Financial Times*, June 18, 2003, 31.

12. FROM MOVIES TO MULTIMEDIA

1. By comparison, the United States has more than thirty-five thousand theater screens.

2. Winnie Chung, "CEPA Promises to Be a Major Boost," *Hollywood Reporter*, May 2004; and Kirsten Tatlow, "Build It and They Will Come," *South China Morning Post*, April 7, 2005.

3. Chung, "CEPA Promises to Be a Major Boost"; May Chan, "Film Industry Seeks Extra Training Cash," *South China Morning Post*, August 4, 2004.

4. Anthony Tran, "Golden Harvest Expands in Singapore, Taiwan," *Financial Times*, July 21, 2004.

5. In January 2006, ten yuan equaled $1.23.

6. Shortly after Star TV launched, it became evident that the satellite service would need to enhance the quality of its programming in order to make it more attractive to advertisers and investors. As a result, Richard Li purchased

several hundred library titles from Golden Harvest and Cinema City in 1992, setting up Media Assets to manage the films both for Star's programming and for video distribution. But it's also quite likely that the distribution company was established as part of an asset-building strategy designed to make the company more attractive to prospective buyers. That is, it is common for Chinese mercantilist entrepreneurs to jump into a new market and rapidly cobble together a company that has the appearance of profitability, only to sell it off for a quick return before the market or the company matures, leaving the new owner to confront the challenges of actually running the business. Although this strategy is not uncommon in the West either, family ownership structures of Chinese enterprises can make it difficult for the purchaser to get a clear picture of what exactly he or she is buying, and, indeed, Rupert Murdoch apparently had little interest in operating a movie distribution company. As Star's John O'Loan observes, "Richard Li was building up assets in order to sell the company and had no intention of running these businesses well into the future. It's a classic Chinese investment style. My guess is that's why it was called Media Assets." Consequently, many believe Murdoch paid far too much for the ungainly enterprise that lurked beneath the shiny image of Star TV. In an attempt to trim costs and gain focus, the new managers decided to shut down Media Assets and lay off the staff. On hearing the news, a number of employees banded together and proposed that they run the unit as an independent company that would manage the film library in exchange for allowing Star TV unlimited and exclusive access to titles for satellite transmission. The new company, named Media Asia, therefore would have responsibility for film conservation as well as distribution of titles from the film library in any format except satellite TV. Media Asia also agreed to start producing movies of its own, with Star agreeing to provide partial funding in exchange for satellite rights.

7. Vicki Rothrock, "eSun Raises Coin for Macau Complex," *Variety*, March 15, 2006, www.variety.com/article/VR1117939794.html?categoryid=18&cs=1&query=esun+raises+coin.

CONCLUSION

1. Sheldon Hsiao-peng Lu, *Transnational Chinese Cinemas: Identity, Nationhood, Gender* (Honolulu: University of Hawai'i Press, 1997).

2. Although he does not deal with television, Yingjin Zhang's study of Chinese cinema provides a rare example of a text that integrates the various Chinese cinemas into a single analytical framework. See Zhang, *Chinese National Cinema* (New York: Routledge, 2004).

3. Iwabuchi, *Recentering Globalization*.

4. Tain-dow Lee and Yingfen Huang, "'We Are Chinese'—Music and Identity in 'Cultural China,'" in *Media in China*, ed. Donald et al., 105–15.

5. Chan, "Film Industry Seeks Extra Training Cash." This decline in the workforce has also been exacerbated by the migration of topflight talent to Hollywood. See Steve Fore, "Home, Migration, Identity: Hong Kong Film Workers

Join the Chinese Diaspora," in *Fifty Years of Electric Shadows: Hong Kong Cinema Retrospective*, ed. Kar Law (Hong Kong: Hong Kong Urban Council, 1997), 126–35.

6. Anna-Lucille Montgomery, "Between Scylla and Charybdis: Troubled Waters for the Development of China's Film Industry," paper presented at the Media Technology, Creative Industries, and Culture Significance Conference, Taipei, 2004; and Emilie Yueh-yu Yeh and Darrell William Davis, *East Asian Media Industries* (London: BFI Publishing, 2007).

7. Yin Hong, "Meaning, Production, Consumption: The History and Reality of Television in China," in *Media in China*, ed. Donald et al., 28–40; Michael Keane, "Send in the Clones: Television Formats and Content Creation in the People's Republic of China," in *Media in China*, ed. Donald et al., 80–90; Michael Keane, "A Revolution in Television and a Great Leap Forward for Innovation? China in the Global Television Format Business," in *Television across Asia*, ed. Moran and Keane, 88–104.

8. Michael Keane, "Brave New World: China's Creative Vision," *International Journal of Cultural Policy* 10, no. 3 (2004): 265–79.

9. Michael Keane, "Once Were Peripheral: Creating Media Capacity in East Asia," *Media, Culture and Society* 28, no. 6 (2006): 835–55.

10. Scott, *The Cultural Economy of Cities*, 1–39.

11. Florida, *Cities and the Creative Class*.

12. Storper and Christopherson, "Flexible Specialization and Regional Industrial Agglomerations"; and Scott, *The Cultural Economy of Cities*.

13. Tied to China's rise as a regional economic force is its growing cultural and linguistic influence. Indeed, the Chinese language is now even more commonly studied than English in countries such as South Korea and Vietnam. Howard W. French, "Another Chinese Export Is All the Rage: China's Language," *New York Times*, January 1, 2006, 3.

Bibliography

Aksoy, Asu, and Kevin Robins. "Hollywood for the 21st Century: Global Competition for Critical Mass in Image Markets." *Cambridge Journal of Economics* 16 (1992): 1–22.

Allen, Robert C. *Vaudeville and Film: 1895–1915: A Study in Media Interaction.* New York: Arno Press, 1980.

Anderson, Benedict. *Imagined Communities: Reflections on the Origin and Spread of Nationalism.* New York: Verso, 1983.

Anderson, Christopher, and Michael Curtin. "Mapping the Ethereal City: Chicago Television, the FCC, and the Politics of Place." *Quarterly Review of Film and Video* 16, no. 3–4 (1999): 289–305.

Ang, Ien. *Desperately Seeking the Audience.* New York: Routledge, 1981.

———. *On Not Speaking Chinese: Living between Asia and the West.* London: Routledge, 2001.

Appadurai, Arjun. *Modernity at Large: Cultural Dimensions of Globalization.* Minneapolis: University of Minnesota Press, 1996.

Bagdikian, Ben. "Lords of the Global Village." *Nation,* June 12, 1989, 805–20.

Balio, Tino. *Hollywood as a Modern Business Enterprise, 1930–1939.* New York: Scribner's, 1993.

———. *United Artists: The Company That Changed the Film Industry.* Madison: University of Wisconsin Press, 1987.

Barnathan, Joyce. "How the Tycoons Are Hobbling Hong Kong." *Business Week,* January 18, 1999, 58.

Beal, Thomas. "Richard Li Bets Big on Internet Project." *Wall Street Journal,* February 2, 2000, 1.

Birch, David. "Film and Cinema in Singapore: Cultural Policy as Control." In *Film Policy: International, National, and Regional Perspectives,* ed. Albert Moran, 185–211. New York: Routledge, 1996.

Booth, Martin. *The Dragon Syndicates: The Global Phenomenon of the Triads.* London: Bantam, 2000.

Bordwell, David. *Planet Hong Kong: Popular Cinema and the Art of Entertainment.* Cambridge, MA: Harvard University Press, 2000.

Bordwell, David, Janet Staiger, and Kristin Thompson. *The Classical Hollywood Cinema: Film Style and Mode of Production to 1960*. London: Routledge and Kegan Paul, 1985.

Bourdieu, Pierre. "The Forms of Capital." In *Handbook of Theory and Research for the Sociology of Education*, ed. J. G. Richardson, 241–58. Westport, CT: Greenwood, 1986.

Bowser, Eileen. *The Transformation of Cinema: 1907–1915*. New York: Scribner's, 1990.

Brooker, Matthew, and Stephen Seawright. "PCCW Directors' Pay Dwarfs Rivals." *South China Morning Post*, January 4, 2002, 1.

Bruce, Katherine. "The High-Tech Son." *Forbes*, July 15, 1999, 156.

Cawelti, John. *The Six-Gun Mystique*. Bowling Green, OH: Bowling Green State University Press, 1970.

Chakravarty, Sumita S. *National Identity in Indian Popular Cinema, 1947–1987*. Austin: University of Texas Press, 1993.

Chan, Anthony B. *Li Ka-shing: Hong Kong's Elusive Billionaire*. Hong Kong: Oxford University Press, 1996.

Chan, Hoiman. "Labyrinth of Hybridization: The Cultural Internationalization of Hong Kong." In *Hong Kong's Reunion with China: The Global Dimensions*, ed. Gerard A. Postiglione and James T. H. Tang, 169–99. Armonk, NY: M. E. Sharpe, 1997.

Chan, Joseph Man. "Mass Media and Socio-political Formation in Hong Kong, 1949–1992." *Journal of Communication* 2, no. 3 (1992): 106–29.

———. "National Responses and Accessibility to Star TV in Asia." *Journal of Communication* 44, no. 3 (1994): 112–31.

———. "When Capitalist and Socialist Television Clash: The Impact of Hong Kong TV on Guangzhou Residents." In *Power, Money, and Media: Communication Patterns and Bureaucratic Control in Cultural China*, ed. Chin-Chuan Lee, 245–70. Evanston, IL: Northwestern University Press, 2000.

Chan, Kelvin. "Richard Li Still Tops HK Young Rich List." *South China Morning Post*, September 3, 2003, 6.

Chan, May. "Film Industry Seeks Extra Training Cash." *South China Morning Post*, August 4, 2004.

Chandler, Alfred D. *Inventing the Electronic Century: The Epic Story of the Consumer Electronics and Computer Industries*. New York: Free Press, 2001.

———. *The Visible Hand: The Managerial Revolution in American Business*. Cambridge, MA: Belknap Press, 1977.

Chang, Flora Chin-Hwa. "Multiculturalism and Television in Taiwan." In *Television in Contemporary Asia*, ed. David French and Michael Richards, 405–19. New Delhi: Sage Publications, 2000.

Cheng, Alex. "Ex-PLA Man's Long March to the Top of the Media World." *South China Morning Post*, March 20, 2003, A8.

Cheuk, Pak-Tong. "The Beginning of the Hong Kong New Wave: The Interactive Relationship between Television and the Film Industry." *Post Script* 19, no. 1 (1999): 10–27.

Choi, Po-King. "From Dependence to Self-Sufficiency: Rise of the Indigenous Culture of Hong Kong, 1945–1989." *Asian Culture* 14, no. April (1990): 161–76.

Christopherson, Susan, and Michael Storper. "The Effects of Flexible Specialization on Industrial Politics and the Labor Market: The Motion Picture Industry." *Industrial and Labor Relations Review* 42 (1989): 331–47.

Chun, Allen. "Discourses of Identity in the Changing Spaces of Public Culture in Taiwan, Hong Kong, and Singapore." *Theory, Culture & Society* 13, no. 1 (1996): 51–75.

———. "Fuck Chineseness: On the Ambiguities of Ethnicity as Culture as Identity." *boundary 2* 23, no. 2 (1996): 111–38.

Chung, Alex. "Ex-PLA Man's Long March to the Top of the Media World." *South China Morning Post*, March 20, 2003.

Chung, Stephanie Po-yin. "The Industrial Evolution of a Fraternal Enterprise: The Shaw Brothers and the Shaw Organization." In *The Shaw Screen: A Preliminary Study*, ed. Ain-ling Wong, 1–18. Hong Kong: Hong Kong Film Archive, 2003.

Chung, Winnie. "CEPA Promises to Be a Major Boost." *Hollywood Reporter*, May 2004.

Clifford, James. *Routes: Travel and Translation in the Late Twentieth Century.* Cambridge, MA: Harvard University Press, 1997.

Copper, John F. *Taiwan: Nation-State or Province?* Boulder, CO: Westview Press, 1999.

Cragg, Claudia. *The New Taipans: A Vital Source Book on the People and Business of the Pacific Rim.* London: Arrow, 1996.

Curtin, Michael. "Feminine Desire in the Age of Satellite Television." *Journal of Communication* 49, no. 2 (1999): 55–70.

———. "Murdoch's Dilemma, or 'What's the Price of TV in China?'" *Media, Culture and Society* 27, no. 2 (2005): 155–75.

Dannen, Frederic. *Hong Kong Babylon: An Insider's Guide to the Hollywood of the East.* New York: Hyperion, 1997.

Deleuze, Gilles, and Felix Guattari. *A Thousand Plateaus: Capitalism and Schizophrenia.* Minneapolis: University of Minnesota Press, 1987.

DiMaggio, Paul. *Non-profit Enterprise in the Arts: Studies in Mission and Constraint.* New York: Oxford University Press, 1986.

Donald, Stephanie H., Michael Keane, and Yin Hong, eds. *Media in China: Consumption, Content, and Crisis.* London: RoutledgeCurzon, 2002.

Dorfman, Ariel, and Armand Mattelart. *How to Read Donald Duck: Imperialist Ideology in the Disney Comic.* New York: International General, 1975.

Earl, William. "'Freedom' No Help for Broadcasters." *South China Morning Post*, August 30, 1998, M4.

Elmer, Greg, and Mike Gasher, eds. *Contracting Out Hollywood: Runaway Productions and Foreign Location Shooting.* Boulder, CO: Rowman and Littlefield, 2005.

Fejes, Fred. "Media Imperialism, an Assessment." *Media, Culture and Society* 3, no. 3 (1981): 281–89.

Florida, Richard. *Cities and the Creative Class.* New York: Routledge, 2005.

Fonoroff, Paul. "A Brief History of Hong Kong Cinema." *Renditions* 29/30 (1988): 293–308.

Fore, Steve. "Golden Harvest Films and the Hong Kong Movie Industry in the Realm of Globalization." *Velvet Light Trap* 34 (1994): 40–58.

———. "Home, Migration, Identity: Hong Kong Film Workers Join the Chinese Diaspora." In *Fifty Years of Electric Shadows: Hong Kong Cinema Retrospective,* ed. Kar Law, 126–35. Hong Kong: Hong Kong Urban Council, 1997.

French, David, and Michael Richards, eds. *Television in Contemporary Asia.* New Delhi: Sage Publications, 2000.

French, Howard W. "Another Chinese Export Is All the Rage: China's Language." *New York Times,* January 1, 2006, 3.

Fu, Poshek. *Between Shanghai and Hong Kong: The Politics of Chinese Cinemas.* Stanford, CA: Stanford University Press, 2003.

———. "Hong Kong and Singapore: A History of the Cathay Cinema." In *The Cathay Story,* ed. Ain-ling Wong. Hong Kong: Hong Kong Film Archive, 2002.

———. "Turbulent Sixties: Modernity, Youth Culture, and Cantonese Film in Hong Kong." In *Fifty Years of Electric Shadows: Hong Kong Cinema Retrospective,* ed. Kar Law, 34–46. Hong Kong: Urban Council, 1997.

Fung, Anthony, and Eric Kit-wai Ma. "'Satellite Modernity': Four Modes of Televisual Imagination in the Disjunctive Socio-mediascape of Guangzhou." In *Media in China: Consumption, Content, and Crisis,* ed. Stephanie H. Donald, Michael Keane, and Yin Hong, 67–79. London: RoutledgeCurzon, 2002.

Gagliardi, Jason. "Empire of the Sons." *South China Morning Post,* July 5, 2000, 1.

Giddens, Anthony. *The Consequences of Modernity.* Stanford, CA: Stanford University Press, 1990.

Gilbert, Douglas. *American Vaudeville: Its Life and Times.* New York: McGraw-Hill, 1940.

Gold, Thomas. "Go with Your Feelings: Hong Kong and Taiwan Popular Culture in Greater China." *China Quarterly* 136 (1993): 907–25.

Gomery, Douglas. *The Hollywood Studio System.* New York: St. Martin's Press, 1986.

Guback, Thomas H. *The International Film Industry: Western Europe and America since 1945.* Bloomington: Indiana University Press, 1969.

Gunaratne, Shelton A., ed. *Handbook of the Media in Asia.* New Delhi: Sage Publications, 2000.

Guyot, Erik, and Michelle Lavender. "Cyberworks Plans Asian Internet Service." *Asian Wall Street Journal,* August 5, 1999, 1.

Harvey, David. *Spaces of Capital: Towards a Critical Geography.* New York: Routledge, 2001.

Havens, Timothy. *The Global Television Marketplace*. London: BFI Publishing, 2006.

Hesmondhalgh, David. *The Cultural Industries*. London: Sage Publications, 2002.

Hilmes, Michele. *Radio Voices: American Broadcasting, 1922–1952*. Minneapolis: University of Minnesota Press, 1997.

———. "Who We Are, Who We Are Not: The Battle of Global Paradigms." In *Planet TV: A Global Television Reader*, ed. Lisa Parks and Shanti Kumar, 53–73. New York: New York University Press, 2003.

Hilsenrath, Jon E., and Michael Flagg. "Star TV Tunes in Potential Internet Battle." *Asian Wall Street Journal*, March 1, 2000, 1.

Hiscock, Geoff. *Asia's New Wealth Club*. London: Nicholas Brearly Publishing, 2000.

Hong, Yin. "Meaning, Production, Consumption: The History and Reality of Television in China." In *Media in China: Consumption, Content, and Crisis*, ed. Stephanie H. Donald, Michael Keane, and Yin Hong, 28–40. London: RoutledgeCurzon, 2003.

Hoskins, Colin, Stuart McFadyen, and Adam Finn. *Global Television and Film: An Introduction to the Economics of the Business*. New York: Oxford University Press, 1997.

Hughes, Owen. "Who's Woo?" *South China Morning Post Sunday Magazine*, November 27, 1994, 21+.

Hukill, Mark A. "The Politics of Television Programming in Singapore." In *Television in Contemporary Asia*, ed. David French and Michael Richards, 179–96. New Delhi: Sage Publications, 2000.

Ibison, David. "A Rising Star in the Corporate World." *South China Morning Post*, September 29, 1997, B12.

Innis, Harold. *Empire and Communications*. Toronto: University of Toronto Press, 1972.

Iwabuchi, Koichi. *Recentering Globalization: Popular Culture and Japanese Transnationalism*. Durham, NC: Duke University Press, 2002.

Jacob, Rahul, and James Kynge. "China on the Line." *Financial Times*, February 29, 2000, 22.

Jacobs, Jane. *Cities and the Wealth of Nations*. New York: Random House, 1984.

Jarvie, Ian. *Hollywood's Overseas Campaign: The North Atlantic Movie Trade, 1920–1950*. Cambridge: Cambridge University Press, 1992.

———. *Window on Hong Kong: A Sociological Study of the Hong Kong Film Industry and Its Audience*. Hong Kong: University of Hong Kong Press, 1977.

Keane, Michael. "Brave New World: China's Creative Vision." *International Journal of Cultural Policy* 10, no. 3 (2004): 265–79.

———. "Broadcasting Policy, Creative Compliance and the Myth of Civil Society in China." *Media, Culture and Society* 23, no. 6 (2001): 783–98.

———. "Once Were Peripheral: Creating Media Capacity in East Asia." *Media, Culture and Society* 28, no. 6 (2006): 835–55.

———. "A Revolution in Television and a Great Leap Forward for Innovation? China in the Global Television Format Business." In *Television across Asia: Television Industries, Programme Formats, and Globalization,* ed. Albert Moran and Michael Keane, 88–104. London: RoutledgeCurzon, 2004.

———. "Send in the Clones: Television Formats and Content Creation in the People's Republic of China." In *Media in China: Consumption, Content, and Crisis,* ed. Stephanie H. Donald, Michael Keane, and Yin Hong, 80–90. London: RoutledgeCurzon, 2003.

Keane, Michael, Anthony Fung, and Albert Moran. *New Television, Globalisation, and the East Asian Cultural Imagination.* Hong Kong: Hong Kong University Press, 2007.

Kepley, Vance. "From 'Frontal Lobes' to the 'Bob-and-Bob' Show: NBC Management and Programming Strategies, 1949–65." In *Hollywood in the Age of Television,* ed. Tino Balio, 41–62. Boston: Unwin Hyman, 1990.

Kraidy, Marwan. *Hybridity, or the Cultural Logic of Globalization.* Philadelphia: Temple University Press, 2005.

Kumar, Shanti. *Ghandi Meets Primetime.* Urbana: University of Illinois Press, 2005.

Kung, James, and Yueai Zhang. "Hong Kong Cinema and Television in the 1970s: A Perspective." In *A Study of Hong Kong Cinema in the Seventies,* ed. Cheuk-to Li, 14–17. Hong Kong: Urban Council, 1984.

Kuo, Eddie, and Peng Hwa Ang. "Singapore." In *Handbook of the Media in Asia,* ed. Shelton A. Gunaratne, 402–28. New Delhi: Sage Publications, 2000.

Lai, Eric. "Property Barons Lured into Net." *South China Morning Post,* October 15, 1999, 16.

Landler, Mark. "Second Act for Hong Kong Billionaire." *New York Times,* March 21, 2002, W1.

———. "Troubles Are Piling Up at Pacific Century." *New York Times,* March 29, 2001, 1.

Lau, Jenny Kwok Wah. "Besides Fists and Blood: Hong Kong Comedy and Its Master of the Eighties." *Cinema Journal* 37, no. 2 (1998): 18–34.

Law, Kar. "A Decade of Sword Grinding." In *A Study of Hong Kong Cinema in the Seventies,* ed. Cheuk-to Li, 65–70. Hong Kong: Urban Council, 1984.

Leahy, Joe, and Richard Waters. "Tech Stocks in Turmoil." *Financial Times,* December 23, 2000, 13.

Lee, Chin-Chuan. *Media Imperialism Reconsidered: The Homogenizing of Television Culture.* Beverly Hills, CA: Sage Publications, 1979.

Lee, Paul Siu-nam. "The Absorption and Indigenization of Foreign Media Cultures: A Study on a Cultural Meeting Point of the East and West: Hong Kong." *Asian Journal of Communication* 1, no. 2 (1991): 52–72.

———. "Mass Communication and National Development in China: Media Roles Reconsidered." *Journal of Communication* 44, no. 3 (1994): 22–36.

Lee, Tain-dow, and Yingfen Huang. "'We Are Chinese'—Music and Identity in 'Cultural China.'" In *Media in China: Consumption, Content, and Crisis,* ed.

Stephanie H. Donald, Michael Keane, and Yin Hong, 105–15. London: RoutledgeCurzon, 2003.

Lent, John A. *The Asian Film Industry*. Texas Film Series, edited by Thomas Schatz. Austin: University of Texas Press, 1990.

Leo, Petrina, and Terrence Lee. "The 'New' Singapore: Mediating Culture and Creativity." *Continuum: Journal of Media and Cultural Studies* 18, no. 2 (2004): 205–18.

Leung, Benjamin K. P. *Perspectives on Hong Kong Society*. Hong Kong: Oxford University Press, 1996.

Levander, Michelle. "Hong Kong Entertains Role for Web." *Asian Wall Street Journal*, July 6, 2000, 1.

Liebes, Tamar, and Elihu Katz. *The Export of Meaning: Cross-Cultural Readings of Dallas*. New York: Oxford University Press, 1990.

Liebes, Tamar, and Sonia Livingston. "European Soap Operas: The Diversification of a Genre." *European Journal of Communication* 13, no. 2 (1998): 147–80.

Lim, Wei Ling. "Formatting and Change in East Asian Television Industries." PhD dissertation, Queensland University of Technology, Brisbane, 2006.

Lin, Ho Swee. "Mr. Internet Sets His Sights on Pan-Asian Network." *Financial Times*, January 18, 2000, 28.

Lin, Szu-Ping. "Prime Time Television Drama and Taiwanese Women." PhD dissertation, University of Wisconsin–Madison, 2000.

Liu, Yu-li. "Restructuring the Television Industry in Taiwan." www.tukkk.fi/mediagroup/5WMEC%20PAPERS/Liu.pdf. May 11, 2002.

Lo, Terence, and Chung-bong Ng. "The Evolution of Prime-Time Television Scheduling in Hong Kong." In *Contemporary Television: Eastern Perspectives*, ed. David French and Michael Richards, 200–20. New Delhi: Sage Publications, 1996.

"Local Heroes." *Cable & Satellite Asia*, November 1996, 41–42.

Lu, Sheldon Hsiao-peng, ed. *Transnational Chinese Cinemas: Identity, Nationhood, Gender*. Honolulu: University of Hawai'i Press, 1997.

Lull, James. *China Turned On: Television, Reform, and Resistance*. New York: Routledge, 1991.

Ma, Eric Kit-wai. *Culture, Politics, and Television in Hong Kong*. London: Routledge, 1999.

———. "Mapping Transborder Imaginations." In *In Search of Boundaries: Communication, Nation-States, and Cultural Identities*, ed. Joseph Man Chan and Bryce T. McIntyre, 249–63. Westport, CT: Ablex, 2002.

Manuel, Gren. "Richard Li Didn't Graduate, Cyberworks Says." *Asian Wall Street Journal*, March 23, 2001, 4.

———. "Tuned In for Telly Channel Take-Off." *South China Morning Post*, September 6, 1998, 1+.

Marx, Karl. *Grundrisse: Foundations of the Critique of Political Economy*. New York: Vintage, 1973.

McBride, Sean. *Many Voices, One World: Communication and Society, Today and Tomorrow: Towards a New More Just and More Efficient World Information and Communication Order.* New York: Unipub, 1980.

McChesney, Robert. *The Problem of the Media: U.S. Communication Politics in the 21st Century.* New York: Monthly Review Press, 2004.

McKay, Angela. "So to Replace Li as PCCW Chief." *Financial Times,* June 18, 2003, 31.

McLean, Albert F. *American Vaudeville as Ritual.* Lexington: University of Kentucky Press, 1965.

"The Messiah of Cyberasia." *Economist,* January 8, 2000.

Meyer, Mahlon. "Generation Next." *Newsweek,* March 13, 2000, 48.

Miller, Toby, Nitin Govil, John McMurria, and Richard Maxwell. *Global Hollywood.* London: BFI Publishing, 2001.

Mitra, Ananda. *Television and Popular Culture in India: A Study of the Mahabharat.* Thousand Oaks, CA: Sage Publications, 1993.

Montgomery, Anna-Lucille. "Between Scylla and Charybdis: Troubled Waters for the Development of China's Film Industry." Paper presented at the Media Technology, Creative Industries, and Culture Significance Conference, Taipei, 2004.

Moran, Albert, and Michael Keane, eds. *Television across Asia: Television Industries, Programme Formats and Globalization.* London: RoutledgeCurzon, 2004.

Morley, David. *Home Territories: Media, Mobility, and Identity.* New York: Routledge, 2000.

Murdoch, Rupert. "Dawn of the Convergent, Interactive Era." *Business Times,* September 17, 1993.

Naficy, Hamid. *The Making of Exile Cultures: Iranian Television in Los Angeles.* Minneapolis: University of Minnesota Press, 1993.

———, ed. *Home, Exile, Homeland: Film, Media, and the Politics of Place.* New York: Routledge, 1999.

Nawawy, Mohammed el-, and Adel Iskandar. *Al-Jazeera: The Story of the Network That Is Rattling Governments and Redefining Modern Journalism.* Boulder, CO: Westview Press, 2003.

Negus, Keith. *Music Genres and Corporate Cultures.* New York: Routledge, 1999.

Nordenstreng, Kaarle, and Tapio Varis. *Television Traffic—a One-Way Street? A Survey and Analysis of the International Flow of Television Programme Material.* Paris: UNESCO, 1974.

Olds, Kris, and Henry Wai-chung Yueng. "Pathways to Global City Formation: A View from the Developmental City-State of Singapore." *Review of International Political Economy* 11, no. 3 (2004): 489–521.

O'Neill, Michael. *The Roar of the Crowd: How Television and People Power Are Changing the World.* New York: Times Books, 1993.

Ong, Aihwa. *Flexible Citizenship: The Cultural Logics of Transnationality.* Durham, NC: Duke University Press, 1999.

Ong, Aihwa, and Donald Nonini. *Ungrounded Empires: The Cultural Politics of Modern Chinese Transnationalism.* New York: Routledge, 1997.

Ou, Alice, ed. *Taiwan Films.* Taipei: Variety, 1993.

Pennycook, Alastair. *The Cultural Politics of English as an International Language.* London: Longman, 1994.

Phoenix Satellite Television Holdings. *Annual Report 1999–2000.* Hong Kong, 2000.

———. *Annual Report 2001–2002.* Hong Kong, 2002.

———. *Annual Report 2002–2003.* Hong Kong, 2003.

Piore, Michael J., and Charles F. Sabel. *The Second Industrial Divide: Possibilities for Prosperity.* New York: Basic Books, 1984.

Porter, Michael E. "Clusters and the New Economics of Competition." *Harvard Business Review* (November 1998): 77–90.

Pottinger, Matt. "PCCW's Richard Li Seems out of Place at His Firm Today." *Asian Wall Street Journal,* March 20, 2002, A1.

Prial, Frank J. "Pao Yue-kong." *New York Times,* September 24, 1991, D31.

Pritchard, Simon. "Changes to Ring for HKT." *South China Morning Post,* February 16, 2000, B12.

Rantanen, Terhi. *The Media and Globalization.* London: Sage Publications, 2005.

Rawnsley, Ming-yeh T. "Communications of Identities in Taiwan: From the 2–28 Incident to FTV." In *Political Communications in Greater China: Construction and Reflection of Identity,* ed. Gary D. Rawnsley and Ming-yeh Rawnsley, 147–66. London: RoutledgeCurzon, 2003.

Redding, Gordon. "What Is Chinese about Chinese Family Business?" In *Globalization of Chinese Business Firms,* ed. Henry Wai-chung Yeung and Kris Olds. New York: St. Martin's Press, 2000.

Reeves, Geoffrey. *Communication and the "Third World."* London: Routledge, 1993.

Rothrock, Vicki. "eSun Raises Coin for Macau Complex." *Variety,* March 15, 2006, www.variety.com/article/VR1117939794.html?categoryid=18&cs=1&query=esun+raises+coin.

Rubenstein, Murray A., ed. *The Other Taiwan: 1945 to the Present.* Armonk, NY: M. E. Sharpe, 1994.

Scannell, Paddy. *A Social History of British Broadcasting.* Cambridge: Blackwell, 1991.

Schiller, Herbert I. *Mass Communication and American Empire.* 2nd ed. Boulder, CO: Westview Press, 1992.

Scott, Allen J. *The Cultural Economy of Cities.* London: Sage Publications, 2000.

———. *On Hollywood: The Place, the Industry.* Princeton, NJ: Princeton University Press, 2005.

Seagrave, Sterling. *Lords of the Rim: The Invisible Empire of the Overseas Chinese.* London: Corgi, 1996.

Sek Kei. "Shaw Movie Town's 'China Dream' and 'Hong Kong Sentiments.'" In *The Shaw Screen: A Preliminary Study,* ed. Ain-ling Wong, 37–50. Hong Kong: Hong Kong Film Archive, 2003.

Silverstone, Roger. *Television and Everyday Life.* New York: Routledge, 1994.

Sinclair, John. *Latin American Television: A Global View.* New York: Oxford University Press, 1999.

Sinclair, John, Elizabeth Jacka, and Stuart Cunningham, eds. *New Patterns in Global Television.* New York: Oxford University Press, 1996.

Sinclair, John, Audrey Yue, Gay Hawkins, Kee Pookong, and Josephine Fox. "Chinese Cosmopolitanism and Media Use." In *Floating Lives: The Media and Asian Diasporas,* ed. Stuart Cunningham and John Sinclair, 35–90. Boulder, CO: Rowman and Littlefield, 2001.

Sinclair, Kevin. "So Tell Me, James, Why I'm Tuned into a Falling Star." *South China Morning Post,* November 28, 2001.

Spaeth, Anthony. "The Son Also Surprises." *Time,* March 13, 2000.

Stein, Peter, and Michelle Levander. "Richard Li Makes a Bet on Future of Entertainment." *Asian Wall Street Journal,* June 29, 2000, 1.

Storper, Michael, and Susan Christopherson. "Flexible Specialization and Regional Industrial Agglomerations: The Case of the U.S. Motion Picture Industry." *Annals of the Association of American Geographers* 77, no. 1 (1987): 104–17.

Straubhaar, Joseph D. "Beyond Media Imperialism: Asymmetrical Interdependence and Cultural Proximity." *Critical Studies in Mass Communication* 8 (March 1991): 39–59.

Streeter, Thomas. *Selling the Air: A Critique of the Policy of Commercial Broadcasting in the United States.* Chicago: University of Chicago Press, 1996.

Tan, Tammy. "Singtel's Offer Runs Smack into the Great Wall of China." *Straits Times,* February 28, 2000, 56–57.

Tatlow, Kirsten. "Build It and They Will Come." *South China Morning Post,* April 7, 2005.

Teo, Stephen. *Hong Kong Cinema: The Extra Dimensions.* London: BFI Publishing, 1997.

Thomas, Adam, and Simon Dyson. *Asia Pacific TV: Incorporating CASBAA Asia Cable and Satellite Guide.* 8th ed. London: Informa Media Group, 2004.

Thomas, Adam, Chris Groner, and Simon Dyson. *Asia Pacific TV: Incorporating CASBAA Asia Cable and Satellite Guide.* 7th ed. London: Informa Media Group, 2003.

Thomas, Adam, Simon Dyson, Alexandra Wales, and Xenobia Talati. *Asia Pacific TV: Management Report.* 9th ed. London: Informa Media Group, 2005.

Thomas, Amos Owen. "Regulating Access to Transnational Satellite Television." *Gazette* 61, no. 3–4 (1999): 243–54.

Thompson, Kristin. *Exporting Entertainment: America in the World Film Market, 1907–34.* London: BFI Publishing, 1985.

Tinic, Serra. *On Location: Canada's Television Industry in a Global Market.* Toronto: University of Toronto Press, 2005.

To, Yiu-ming, and Tuen-yu Lau. "Global Export of Hong Kong Television: Television Broadcasts Limited." *Journal of Communication* 5, no. 2 (1995): 108–21.

Tomlinson, John. *Cultural Imperialism: A Critical Introduction.* Baltimore: Johns Hopkins University Press, 1991.

Tracey, Michael. "Popular Culture and the Economics of Global Television." *Intermedia* 16, no. 2 (1988): 9–25.

Tran, Anthony. "Golden Harvest Expands in Singapore, Taiwan." *Financial Times,* July 21, 2004.

Tu, Wei-ming. *The Living Tree: The Changing Meaning of Being Chinese Today.* Stanford, CA: Stanford University Press, 1994.

Uhde, Jan, and Yvonne Ng Uhde. *Latent Images: Film in Singapore.* Singapore: Oxford University Press, 2000.

Underwood, Laurie. "The Tumultuous Tale of Taiwan Film." *Topics,* March 1999, 20–28.

Vanden Heuvel, Jon, and Everette E. Dennis. *The Unfolding Lotus: East Asia's Changing Media.* New York: Freedom Forum, 1993.

Wang, Georgette, and Wen-Hwei Lo. "Taiwan." In *Handbook of the Media in Asia,* ed. Shelton A. Guneratne, 660–81. New Delhi: Sage Publications, 2000.

Wang, Shujen. *Framing Policy: Globalization and Film Distribution in Greater China.* Boulder, CO: Rowman and Littlefield, 2003.

Wark, McKenzie. *Virtual Geography: Living with Global Media Events.* Bloomington: Indiana University Press, 1994.

Wonacott, Peter. "Lis' Dominance in Hong Kong Seems Limitless." *Asian Wall Street Journal,* February 21, 2000, 1.

Wong Ain-ling, ed. *The Cathay Story.* Hong Kong: Hong Kong Film Archive, 2002.

Wong, Jesse, and Jason Dean. "Taiwan Heir Builds Media Empire, but at Heavy Cost." *Asian Wall Street Journal,* August 23, 2001.

Yau, Esther C. M., ed. *At Full Speed: Hong Kong Cinema in a Borderless World.* Minneapolis: University of Minnesota Press, 2001.

Yeh, Emily Yueh-yu. "Taiwan: The Transnational Battlefield of Cathay and Shaws." In *The Cathay Story,* ed. Ain-ling Wong. Hong Kong: Hong Kong Film Archive, 2002.

Yeh, Emilie Yueh-yu, and Darrell William Davis. *East Asian Media Industries.* London: BFI Publishing, 2007.

———. *Taiwan Film Directors: A Treasure Island.* New York: Columbia University Press, 2005.

Yeung, Henry Wai-chung, and Kris Olds. "Singapore's Global Reach: Situating the City-State in the Global Economy." *International Journal of Urban Sciences* 2, no. 1 (1999): 24–47.

———, eds. *Globalization of Chinese Business Firms.* New York: St. Martin's Press, 2000.

Zhang, Yingjin. *Chinese National Cinema.* New York: Routledge, 2004.

Zhou, Cheng-ren. "Shanghai's Unique Film Productions and Hong Kong's Early Cinema." In *The Shaw Screen: A Preliminary Study,* ed. Ain-ling Wong, 19–36. Hong Kong: Hong Kong Film Archive, 2003.

Index

Academy Awards, 223, 224

accumulation, logic of, 10–11, 19, 26, 269; cable TV and, 174; Hong Kong cinema and, 67, 273; sociocultural forces and, 22; Star/Phoenix TV and, 210; television and, 109, 131, 150; transnational expansion and, 41, 133

Aces Go Places (film), 24, 59, 60

action movies, 89, 99, 255, 268

Action Television Network (AXN), 223

actors, 51, 254; consumer lifestyles and, 146; higher fees demanded by, 260; Hollywood, 76; hyperproduction and, 70, 74; Japanese, 183

advertising and promotion, 90, 93, 98; "ad masking," 154; cable TV, 160; Hong Kong television, 130; news programs and, 172–73; in PRC, 197, 201, 204–5; prime-time television, 148; radio and, 237; sales reporting system and, 104; in satellite media, 129; in South Asia, 223; sports programming and, 214; television and, 109, 116, 136; tie-in campaigns, 94–96

Aksoy, Asu, 14

American Beauty (film), 91

AOL (America On Line), 237

Applause Pictures, 188, 247, 253

Asian Film Awards, 40

AT&T Corporation, 18

ATV (Asia Television), 110, 122, 128, 182, 196

audiences, Chinese, 1, 163, 272; cable TV, 161; Celestial Pictures and, 224; cinema attendance, 68, 103, 249, 256; consumer lifestyles and, 146; decline of Chinese film and, 106, 107; distribution/exhibition chains and, 24; East-West cultural divide and, 23; fragmentation of, 267; gender of, 255; generations of, 146–47, 166, 168–69, 174; in Hong Kong, 51, 60–61, 68, 261; language and, 165, 178, 180; on mainland, 116; in Malaysia, 32, 33; market research and, 172; martial-law era in Taiwan, 149; nationalist sentiments of, 210; new media technologies and, 285; New Wave cinema and, 60; satellite channels and, 2; shift from live performance to cinema, 31–32; in Singapore, 26, 182–83; size of markets, 116; social/political changes and, 38; sociocultural variation and, 277–78; in Taiwan, 89; Taiwan–PRC coproductions and, 139–40; television and, 26, 111–12, 143–44; translated film titles and, 91–92. *See also* Global China market

Text: 10/13 Aldus
Display: Aldus
Compositor: Binghamton Valley Composition, LLC
Indexer: Alexander Trotter
Printer and binder: Maple-Vail Manufacturing Group